Parables Unplugged

Parables Unplugged

Reading the Lukan Parables in Their Rhetorical Context

Lauri Thurén

Fortress Press
Minneapolis

PARABLES UNPLUGGED

Reading the Lukan Parables in Their Rhetorical Context

Copyright © 2014 Fortress Press. All rights reserved. Except for brief quotations in critical articles or reviews, no part of this book may be reproduced in any manner without prior written permission from the publisher. Visit http://www.augsburgfortress.org/copyrights/ or write to Permissions, Augsburg Fortress, Box 1209, Minneapolis, MN 55440.

Cover image: Romare Bearden (1911-1988). *Return of the Prodigal Son*, 1967. Photo: Albright-Knox Art Gallery / Art Resource, NY. Art © Romare Bearden Foundation/Licensed by VAGA, New York, NY.

Cover design: Ivy Palmer Skrade

Library of Congress Cataloging-in-Publication Data

Print ISBN: 978-0-8006-9979-6

eBook ISBN: 978-1-4514-6526-6

The paper used in this publication meets the minimum requirements of American National Standard for Information Sciences — Permanence of Paper for Printed Library Materials, ANSI Z329.48-1984.

Manufactured in the U.S.A.

This book was produced using PressBooks.com, and PDF rendering was done by PrinceXML.

Contents

Preface — vii

Part I.

1. Introduction — 3

Part II.

2. The Bad Samaritan (10:25-37) — 53
3. Persuading the Pharisees (15:1-32) — 77
4. The Unjust Steward (16:1-9) — 107
5. The Wicked Tenants (20:9-19) — 149

Part III.

6. The Overall Mapping of the Parables — 181
7. The Parables as Persuasion — 249
8. Re-Plugging the Parables — 345

Bibliography — 375

Index of Names	*391*
Index of Subjects	*397*
Index of Ancient Sources	*411*

Preface

As a young student, I was bewildered to see how both pastors and scholars adapted Jesus' parables to accommodate many different purposes. For the sake of hermeneutics or historical research, almost anything could be found in, added to, or removed from these simple stories. However, each parable must have meant something specific in its earliest known context, as presented in the synoptic gospels. Yet, few seem to read the parables as they stand, with their original context in mind.

After decades of applying novel, text-centered methods on the "Catholic" epistles and the Pauline literature, I ventured to turn to the fascinating world of the parables. I chose to focus on Luke, since he is, in my mind, the best storyteller among the evangelists, and his book offers the largest collection of parables. It turned out that there is so much to be found, if we respect the author's own version. This is not an easy task, as we now live in a world unfamiliar to Luke's putative audience. But I am convinced that this endeavor is worth the effort.

This book does not want to be the last word in parable research, but hopefully it will be a source of inspiration that provides a transparent and realistic approach to reading these stories. It consists of three parts, each of which can be read independently. Together, they aim to create a comprehensive view of Luke's parables and the original theology reflected in them.

First, I will present a novel approach that assesses the parables as rhetorical tools (chapter 1). I will ask, why and how should they be read as pieces of argumentation, detached from traditional questions. This method suits other biblical parables, as well. Second, some of the most captivating parables in Luke will be studied in depth (chapters 2–5). Third, I will provide a comprehensive, unplugged analysis of all the parables in Luke and briefly illuminate their function as persuasive writings (chapters 6–7). This inclusive study seeks to avoid unwarranted hypotheses based upon selective reading of the parables. It will lead to fresh insights into Luke's parable telling and provide material to traditional theological and historical perspectives. Moreover, it will shed light on the theological self-understanding of the Lukan Jesus (chapter 8).

I am grateful to my students at the University of Eastern Finland, and all the domestic and international colleagues for inspiration, constructive criticism, and new insights that have helped me to shape the ideas presented in this book. A very special thanks goes to Ruben Zimmermann and Gert J. Steyn for their hospitality and stimulating discussions in Mainz and Pretoria. My deepest gratitude extends to my incomparable wife Tiia and the rest of my wonderful family. I dedicate this book to my two ingenious Doktorvaters, Wilhelm Wuellner (†) and Lars Hartman.

PART I

1

Introduction

The parables told by Jesus are among the most fascinating and beloved of all tales, and the most studied as well. Values and ideas attributed to these short stories have inspired later cultures in many ways, and the teaching of the Christian churches constantly refers to them. Surprisingly, there is no unanimity about their meaning or purpose. Instead, a single parable can be interpreted in innumerable different ways.[1]

Perhaps the main reason for the diversity of interpretations is that the parables are used for a wide range of purposes. Spiritual readings have been mainly interested in the parables' christological[2] or ethical[3] content, whereas academic scholarship has traditionally pursued their original versions.[4] People ask what the parables mean to us, what the

---

1. *The Unjust Steward* (Luke 16:1-9) offers a good example of the bewildering diversity of interpretations (Ireland, "History," 293–94), while none of them has become obviously more popular than the others.
2. For example, the parable of the *Samaritan* (10:30-37) is understood in christological terms by both ancient and modern readers (Snodgrass, *Stories*, 347–48).
3. *The Samaritan* has also resulted in a great number of ethical interpretations, as reported by Zimmermann, "Liebe," 548–53.

historical Jesus sought to express thereby, or what they say about the context of the evangelist.

However, in the original documents the parables are not "boxes full of theology" or history.[5] Instead, they are devices whereby Jesus the Narrator persuades his audience, and the evangelist (the Author) convinces the recipients.[6] In this book I shall argue that detaching the parables from all other perspectives opens new possibilities for understanding their meaning and specific persuasive function, and that Jesus seldom teaches his audience anything new by his parables. Instead, they mainly enhance the recipients' adherence to already known facts, attitudes, or modes of behavior. This, in turn, is supposed to be applied to a new context. In some cases the result of this process may be a novel theological insight.

Toward a Natural Listening

Notwithstanding all this, the great fame of Jesus' parables is due to their applicability to various religious exigencies. Likewise, they offer invaluable material for studying the historical Jesus or "Jesus remembered."[7] Thus both perspectives are significant. However, the parables' high status as defining "the essence of Christianity" or as touching "the human condition like no other stories" may prevent us from hearing them properly.[8] Hence it is high time to focus on the text again and ask what the Luke the Author and his hero, Jesus the Narrator, wanted to achieve with these stories. In other words,

---

4. This is the goal of, e. g., Jeremias, *Gleichnisse*, 5–15.
5. Cf. Hartman's criticism of overtheologizing biblical texts ("Galatians," 127).
6. For the sake of clarity I shall refer to Jesus the *Narrator* telling the *parable*, and to Luke the *Author* telling the embedding *framework story*.
7. Zimmermann, "Parables," 162–64, discusses the theoretical problems involved when using the parables in the search for the historical Jesus, and prefers the paradigm of *memory* in Jesus research instead (cf. Dunn, *Jesus*).
8. Via, *Parables*, 163; Bovon, *Lukas*, 41, thus characterize the parable of the *Prodigal Son* (15:11-32).

how is the audience expected to be affected by them according to the documents as they stand? I am convinced that ultimately even other goals for studying the parables will benefit from answers to such questions. Since my goal is to read the final product, a comparison between the evangelists is not necessary.[9]

Avoiding Harmful Modifications

The passion for earlier versions or later applications of the parables typically involves two problems. First, one is easily tempted to alter the material; second, the function of the parable in its actual literary context is not fully taken into account. Both phenomena easily distort the natural sound audible in the source material.[10]

As the parables presented by the evangelist can seldom provide satisfactory answers to later religious or historical questions, most interpreters tend to adjust them to some extent. Each goal requires different changes. For example, when searching for the voice of the historical Jesus one can hardly abide by the Lukan wording but must make one's own reconstructions. Deep spiritual truths must be sought somewhere between the lines as well, since the plain stories often remain on the immanent level.[11] Consequently they are seldom read exactly as they stand. Some expressions are assigned astonishing content while others are disregarded. No wonder different religious interpretations abound! Academic explanations, too, show insufficient respect for the actual text. We are so accustomed to

---

9. Merz, "Einleitung," 513. Furthermore, it would be too complex a task to study each evangelist's versions simultaneously, as they all have their specific contextual functions as well as stylistic, ideological, and historical characteristics. "Luke" is simply a traditional name for the author of the Third Gospel.
10. The concept of *natural reading* of narratives is developed by Fludernik, *Narratology*. She emphasizes the narratives' universally valid cognitive components and the audience's experience.
11. To this end an allegorical reading is often preferred. See Snodgrass, *Stories*, 4–5.

traditional interpretations, spiritual or exegetical, and to a certain image of their narrator, Jesus of Nazareth, that those interpretations tend to remain unaffected, even when the actual text has a different bearing. Two examples may illuminate the situation.

> In one of his most adored parables (Luke 15:4-7, the *Lost Sheep*), Jesus presents himself, according to the traditional religious interpretation, as the Good Shepherd. Scholars may add that since a *shepherd* in the Old Testament often depicts the Deity, the parable simultaneously portrays an image of God. However, according to 15:4 the individual seeking the lost sheep is "one of you," that is, a member of Jesus' audience (τίς ἄνθρωπος ἐξ ὑμῶν), namely, the Pharisees and scribes. In fact, the text does not mention any shepherd, let alone the Good Shepherd, who appears in John 10. Even the traditional views of the main message of the parable are at odds with the narrative.[12]

> In another parable, belonging to his most bizarre, Jesus bids his disciples take a dishonest manager as their role model (Luke 16:1-9). They, too, should make friends by abusing stolen property and thereby secure their own future. Hence it is no wonder that attempts to exonerate the manager abound.[13] However, this occurs at the expense of the existing text. Central elements in the story are curtailed, tacitly omitted, or interpreted in ways that would never have crossed the original hearers' minds.[14]

The *literary* perspective involves a significant step toward focusing on the text of the parables, providing an alternative to the religious and historical readings.[15] It has a major advantage over the traditional approaches, as it meets one of the original main criteria of critical biblical exegesis. One of its founding fathers, Jean Alphonse Turrettini, argued that biblical texts should be studied with the same

---

12. See further chap. 3 below.
13. See chap. 4 below.
14. When hearing the story of the *Unjust Steward* (16:1-9) for the first time, who would think, for example, that it advocates another world based on "new coordinates for power, justice and vulnerability," as argued by Scott, *Parable*, 66.
15. An illustrative collection of such approaches to the *Samaritan* (10:30-37) is provided in *Semeia* 2: *The Good Samaritan* (1974): 1–131.

methods as any other literature.[16] This means that one should ask how stories are usually analyzed in Academia. Perhaps most problems with parables research are related to our failure to comply with this principle.

The integrity of the text was required particularly by the American New Criticism in the mid-twentieth century. It rejected external factors such as the role of the reader, the author, and their contexts while concentrating exclusively on the study of the text.[17] What matters are the words on the page, whereas biographical information about the author or context may be irrelevant and distracting.[18] When one is reading any document, be it a poem, a novel, or a detective story, its meaning and function are easily lost if anything is added to it. However, abstinence from all additional data and the historical context easily makes a text solely an aesthetic object. Its meaning is then in practice determined by the interpreter's own world, and thereby is rendered uncontrollable indeed.[19] This was a major problem with New Criticism, as it knew no limits for interpretation. Yet no author meant his or her text to be so ambiguous.[20] To be sure, all communication depends on its interpretation by the recipient, who in turn automatically

16. Turrettini, *De Sacrae Scripturae* (1728).
17. For an introduction and critical discussion see Searle, "New Criticism"; Jancovich, *Politics*.
18. Wimsatt and Beardsley, "Intentional Fallacy." Another eminent proponent of this train of thought is Barthes, "Death," who ends by exaggerating the freedom of the reader. Despite the absence of the historical author there is always an implied one.
19. New Criticism has not only been criticized for separating the text from its context but for seeing the text and the reader as absolute and stable entities. See Hawkes, *Structuralism*, 155–57. Moreover, in the late 1960s New Criticism was labeled politically conservative, as it isolated the text from contemporary problems. However, for a biblical scholar opposing unduly hasty hermeneutical applications this should not be a problem.
20. Already Richards, *Philosophy*, 39, claimed that a text never can have a single meaning. In the same manner Zimmermann, "Parables," 173–76, without referring to New Criticism, suggests that the parables automatically generate an "abundance of interpretations." They challenge any reader to search for a meaning. Yet the dynamics of interpretation are guided by the storyteller, who is conveying a message. Modern studies of literature have discarded the idea of the reader's total freedom. Although in principle every student attributes a meaning to its signs, a text is usually written in order to convey a specific message and has a "model reader." Not all

complements the data.²¹ However, the explanation should never contradict the information expressed or clearly implied in the text.

Honoring the integrity of the author's work of art means that the author's Jesus is assessed as a literary character. The same applies to the author, too, since he or she appears both explicitly and implicitly in the text. Just as it is important to observe the difference between the actual parable in the text and all hypothetical reconstructions of its original version, one should correspondingly separate the author and his or her recipients as explicit and implied in the text and in any hypothetical reconstructions of their historical equivalents. Their eventual identification with the historical Jesus of Nazareth and the historical author should not be axiomatically confused with the study of the literary document. The *implied audience*²² is not necessarily identical with the text's historical readers. After its publication, a text has a life of its own, yet this basic idea need not lead to "anti-originalism" whereby all references to the historical author and situation are rejected.²³

Despite the inherent problems of New Criticism, its basic idea of a careful scrutiny of a text as self-contained, without confusing the artist's work with too much extraneous information, is fascinating. Thus it has left some traces in various forms of contemporary literary analysis. Scholars typically still concentrate on the work of art as it is published, even though nowadays they seldom promote the

interpretations do justice to the original text, as they can be attained by questionable methods or are prompted by factors alien to the aims of the document.
21. See, e. g., Jakobson's classic model for communication ("Statements"). Thus a parable story invites each reader or listener to envisage the persons and action described, imagine their feelings, etc. Probably the parables' persuasive impact depends largely on such interaction with the recipient. However, for an intersubjective analysis such information may be misleading, as it depends on each recipient and is difficult to control. The perception of the central message and function of the parable cannot derive from such additional data.
22. The text indicates in many ways what knowledge its audience was expected to have. For the literary concept of the *implied audience* see Iser, *Leser*. The term was first introduced in 1961 by Booth, *Rhetoric*.
23. Here I refer to Gadamer's thinking. See Hoy, "Hermeneutics," 111–35.

interpreter's full autonomy.[24] Would this general paradigm apply to the parables of Jesus, too? Hitherto there have been few serious attempts to do so.[25]

Avoiding Distorting Questions

A greater challenge than avoiding harmful additions to the parables is to refrain from immediately inferring problems that require such external information. This is important for penetrating the message and function of a parable, as any questions extending beyond its immediate context tend to obscure the narrator's and the author's particular goal in the framework story. The postponement of later historical and religious interests helps us to recognize the text's own agenda. This will shift the perspective from the content of a parable to its function. At least as important as to know what Jesus said is to ask why he said it. As most parables were aimed at specific people in a specific situation, it is essential to focus on their actual purpose in their context(s). This is revealed only by the implied interaction between the author or narrator and their audiences. Hence we need to know what Jesus is doing with his hearers, and the evangelist with the recipients.

With a parable Jesus seldom simply teaches proper behavior or theology, nor is his immediate aim to describe his christological status. More often he attempts to influence his hearers in some way. The parables aim to persuade, not to inform. They typically meet some exigency. Jesus is provoked by some situation or some individuals; he responds to a person who is testing him, he answers his critics or otherwise reacts to a challenge. He aims at modifying the hearers' point of view and altering their values and behavior. Such

---

24. For example, Eco et al., *Interpretation*, 45–66.
25. Good exceptions are, e.g., Via, *Parables*, 77; and Hedrick, *Many Things*, 50–54.

goals shape the parable into a tool with a specific purpose. It becomes a persuasive device.[26] Moreover, the embedding framework story rarely depicts a one-way communication but shows the interaction between the partners in a dialogue. The way the audience is expected to react to the parable also impinges on the narrator. This is evident, for example, in Luke 10:30-37, the *Samaritan*, but can be found elsewhere as well.

Correspondingly, the evangelist has his own purpose in writing the text; he too addresses certain recipients who thereby play a crucial role for the way the text is formulated. Although little of them is explicitly presented, it is vital to ask how they are supposed to understand the text. Moreover, it is important to bear in mind that they know only what the author tells them or clearly presupposes. How is the text designed to affect this audience?[27] When answering these questions it is essential to realize that the audience is not historical but *implied*, an image in the mind of the author, and is reflected by the text.

To sum up: in addition to reconstructing historical backgrounds or spiritual truths behind the parables, it is interesting to attempt to listen to them as they are reported by the narrator or to hearken to them with the ears of the audience to whom they were told. What if one merely asked how Jesus wished to involve his hearers within the framework story and how the evangelist wanted his recipients to react to this narrative about Jesus and his audience? This leads to the aim of this book: to read the parables of Jesus "naked" or "unplugged," without any presuppositions, alterations, or later problems.[28]

---

26. Cf. Snodgrass, *Stories*, 8–9. Moreover, the heavy *pathos* element in many parables indicates that the ultimate goal is persuasion, not merely the sharing of information.
27. Such an endeavor would benefit other purposes too. The evangelist's view has undeniable historical value for the interpretation of the parable, and since the church has canonized the final text instead of its hypothetical predecessors its religious message should not be overlooked.

It may be surprising that this simple perspective is seldom applied to these parables. A glimpse at almost any commentary demonstrates how theological and historical issues are added to the story. The context presented by the evangelist is complemented or replaced by general extraneous historical information. Likewise, the parable's function in its context may be amended by some general theological exigency. These processes demonstrate the parable's ability to inspire new ideas and its applicability to new situations. Unfortunately, the interpretation thereby becomes shattered and arbitrary, as it is based on a poor contact with the actual text. The goal of my program is different: back to the text, back to the message and function of the parables in their real context. For this reason the integrity of the parables must be honored as regards their content and function.

Inquiring about the Persuasive Function

In Luke, Jesus (or in one case the Sadducees) attempt(s) to influence the hearers by telling stories. In order to discover the function of a particular story it is interesting to know whether the *parable* as a genre typically plays a specific role in persuading the audience. How does a parable influence its recipients? What is its benefit compared to straightforward speech?

Retelling the situation at hand with cover names, that is, using allegory, would hardly add anything to the persuasion. Claims about God or the audience would not benefit from barely presenting them in cameo roles. If a parable has any role in convincing the hearers, it must have another function.

---

28. To be sure, an *objective* interpretation is never possible. The theological importance of these texts and the intriguing possibility of reaching the words of the historical Jesus can hardly be completely disregarded by any scholar. Nevertheless, one should not make necessity a virtue.

I will argue that Jesus seldom teaches his audience anything new by his parables. Instead, most parables build on something the audience already knows and accepts or would assess as reasonable. A typical parable illustrates how this idea works well in a case that clearly *differs* from the question discussed, thereby excluding all distorting factors, exclusions, and explanations. After thereby enhancing the audience's awareness of or attention to this idea or principle,[29] the parable challenges them to employ the same principle in the case discussed. The parable's persuasive strategy is thus not to proclaim something but to suggest that, in order to be consistent, the audience ought to follow its own principles.

In Luke many parables refer to a known rule or custom followed in certain professions or roles. They present reasonable guidelines for or credible stories of typical behavior. Such characters are a healer (4:23; 5:31), a tailor (5:36), a winemaker (5:37-39), a debtor (7:41-43), a sower (8:5-8), a guard (11:21), a servant (12:36-48; 17:7-10), a guest (14:8-14), a king (14:31-32), and a judge (18:2-6).

Alternatively, Jesus refers to the addressees' own sense of normal behavior (τίς ἐξ ὑμῶν in 11:5-8; 11-13; 14:28-30; 15:4-7; 17:7) or own estimation (τίς . . . δοκεῖ σοι in 10:36; οἴδατε δοκιμάζειν in 12:54-56).

These known principles should then be applied to a different context. Typically it is the topic discussed in the framework story, often dealing with some theological or ethical question. Whereas the parable illustrates a normal procedure or attitude, Jesus then claims that God acts or the addressees should act like any reasonable individual (οὕτως . . . ἐν τῷ οὐρανῷ / ἐνώπιον τῶν ἀγγέλων τοῦ θεοῦ in 15:7, 10); not even the worst person would act otherwise (πόσῳ μᾶλλον ὁ πατὴρ ὁ ἐξ οὐρανοῦ in 11:13; cf. 18:6-7).

---

29. In terms of classical rhetoric this is an *epideictic* function; see Kennedy, *New Testament*, 19.

INTRODUCTION

Whereas in most of the cases mentioned above the parable's role as illustrating a principle is self-evident, the longer parables are more complicated. The basic story may be conventional and people may act normally, but the story ends with a surprise. Such parables include 8:5-8, the *Sower*; 12:16-21, the *Rich Fool*; 16:19-31, the *Rich Man and Lazarus*; 16:1-9, the *Unjust Steward*; 18:10-14, the *Pharisee and Tax Collector*; 19:12-27, the *Minas*; 20:9-16, the *Wicked Tenants*; perhaps even 15:11-32, the *Prodigal Son*.[30] However, I will suggest that even these cases do not merely proclaim new theological or ethical principles or theses. They, too, function as persuasive tools; instead of referring only to what is rational or customary, however, Jesus attempts to affect especially the audience's emotions. This indicates that his message is more difficult to accept.

This hypothesis about the parables' persuasive function means that much of the traditional interpretation, focusing on new ethical or theological messages found in the parables, is misleading. This idea will be substantiated by the particular analyses in this book. To this end I will turn to modern argumentation analysis.[31] This is a vast field offering excellent tools that are rarely applied to biblical studies.[32] Below I will present one of the best-known and most flexible methods, that of Stephen Toulmin. It will then be used to clarify the precise persuasive function of each parable in Luke.

---

30. The limits of the parables are discussed in more detail in chap. 6 below.
31. For a thorough introduction to and critical presentation of different approaches to argumentation see van Eemeren, *Fundamentals*.
32. Biblical scholars studying the patterns of argumentation have traditionally referred to Aristotle and other ancient texts. This is due to a one-sided preoccupation with historical research (see further Thurén, "Argumentation"). Siegert's *Argumentation* (1984) was the first major application of Perelman's already classic model. Thurén, *Argument and Theology* (1995) was the first full-scale study of a New Testament document using another classical method by Toulmin, and Hietanen, *Argumentation* (2005) was the first application to the New Testament of the most sophisticated approach to argumentation today, the Dutch pragma-dialectical method (van Eemeren el al., *Fundamentals*; eidem, *Maneuvering*).

The idea of the specific persuasive role of the parables in illustrating a known principle will be further applied and tested below, first when discussing the Sadducees' parable (20:29-32) and then when analyzing Jesus' particular parables. If the hypothesis holds true, it enables us to define more precisely the meaning and purpose of the specific parables, or at least many of them, provided that essential information about the situation and the recipients is at hand. Simultaneously it discourages interpretations claiming that Jesus in his parables provides new theological information. Allegorical readings are typical of such interpretations.

To sum up, for understanding a parable it is essential to define its function in the actual argumentation situation as precisely as possible. Different misleading interpretations will thereby be avoided. Current theories of argumentation analysis offer good tools to this end. Since the parables are presented as fictional, the persons or events therein, their actions, attitudes, or beliefs are not regarded as real or historical. As such they cannot persuade anybody. Instead, they illustrate models that should be recognized by the addressees as possible, typical, or ideal modes of behavior. Their argumentative force derives from their ability to resound in the minds of the recipients. Only in this way can they serve as backing for some general rule that should lead to acceptance of the goal put forward.

Functional Perspectives in Parable Research

Certainly the idea of focusing on the text and seeking its function rather than a timeless message is nothing new in parables research. Almost every commentary attempts to explain the story line, even if this task is typically compromised by other issues. To see the climax of the parable as key to its understanding and to interpret the message as a general principle or rule resembles Adolf Jülicher's classic thesis stipulating a single crux. Indeed, his theory had some major advantages. His critics typically looked for several messages in one story, thereby overlooking its narrative and persuasive characteristics. Although Jülicher based his suggestion on formal features and ended with too-noble theological statements in his search for such points, the main idea of one point only seems plausible from the viewpoint of narratology.

Klyne Snodgrass summarizes the critique of Jülicher's thesis in the following arguments:[33]

1. It is based on reference to Greek, not Jewish stories.
2. Parables are not straightforward and no literature is self-interpreting.
3. In opposing allegorizing, Jülicher rejected allegory as well.
4. Hardly anyone believes that parables lay down general religious maxims.

In defense of Jülicher it can be stated that:
1. The basic character of an anecdote is not determined solely by the culture. Several types of stories aim at one conclusion, irrespective of their cultural background. An American stand-up comedian ends his story with a punch line as did the prophet Nathan in telling his parable to King David (2 Sam. 12:1b-4). Thus it is not implausible that Jesus followed this universal principle when attempting to make an impact on his audience.
2. According to the evangelists most parables are told to a specific audience in a certain situation. In order to function they had to be easy to understand. Other ancient tales from the Near East are usually comprehensible to modern readers.

---

33. Snodgrass, *Stories*, 6–7.

3. Although a categorical rejection from the outset of any allegory would be unwise, the plausibility of allegory must be assessed based on the communicative situation. Did the author take it for granted that his audience would understand a certain image in the story in such a way? Does it send a message to the hearers in the text? I presume that in most cases the answer is "no."

4. Whereas some *religious* maxims suggested by Jülicher hardly fit the situation described by the narrator, the basic idea of a *general* maxim or rule is of value. Such a rule expresses a principle whereby the audience should assess the current situation.

Toulmin's model for argumentation offers a fresh way of developing Jülicher's thesis, enabling us to apply the principle emphasized by the parable to the actual discussion in the context. More recently many general literary perspectives have been applied to the New Testament and to the parables, especially under the heading "narrative criticism."[34] Scholars using narrative criticism first focus on formal features such as the unity and structure of the text[35] or on its aesthetic values and symbolic functions. The parables have been scrutinized in order to recover their semantic, narrative, rhetorical, ideological, or other structures. It is then customary to emphasize the text-internal and -external transfer signals.[36]

A deeper level of scrutiny of the text is demonstrated by several excellent studies applying the principles of contemporary literary criticism to the New Testament.[37] The parables are typically seen as fictional narratives, which are to be separated from factual accounts.[38]

---

34. Gowler (*Parables*, 16–40) describes "The American School," including several literary approaches. Funk, *Poetics,* and Hedrick, *Parables,* offer some interesting perspectives. See also Brown, "Parable," 392 n. 3 and Rau, *Auseinandersetzung*, 5.
35. E. g., Tannehill, *Unity*.
36. E. g., Zymner, *Uneigentlichkeit*.
37. Culpepper, *Anatomy*; Bar-Efrat, *Narrative*; Scott, *Parable*; Blomberg, *Interpreting*; Powell, *Narrative*; Rhoads, Dewey, and Michie, *Mark*; Rhoads and Syreeni, *Characterization*; and Hedrick, *Parables*.

Paul Ricoeur's interaction theory of metaphor has been applied to them,[39] as well as the idea of the "appellative structure" of the parables used in reader-response criticism,[40] influenced by New Criticism. Then scholars no longer focus on the intention of the historical gospel writer or the imaginary historical Jesus. Even if such questions are still posed, the main interest is to see how the stories function in their immediate textual framework.

Newer German parables research has made great progress by concentrating on the interaction between the characters (typically Jesus and the Pharisees or scribes) in the framework of the parables as well as the parable story itself.[41] The argumentative structure of the parable, the audience's perspective, and the aim of the author are taken into account. The parable appeals to its audience, whether that audience be text-internal, the implied audience of the gospel writer, or any reader studying the text.[42]

Some modern scholars thus offer interesting and eye-opening insights into these old stories. Application of contemporary literary theories has proved useful indeed. Yet the idea of the parables as functional narratives has not been adequately employed; even the best scholars fail to follow through. Despite numerous methodological approaches and good observations, the application has remained wanting. Several reasons can be identified.

One source of problems is preoccupation with old exegetical practices. Despite the influence of New Criticism, abstaining from adding external information may still prove difficult.[43] Alternatively,

---

38. For the difference, see Genette, *Fiction*, 78–88.
39. Merenlahti, *Poetics*.
40. Zymner, *Uneigentlichkeit*.
41. E.g., Wolter, "Streitgespräch."
42. The reader's perspective is emphasized, e. g., by Zimmermann, "Parables," 173–76.
43. Unfortunately, even the most promising attempt adds external data to the parables. Thus the founding father, Wilder, can argue that "in the parable of the Lost Sheep the shepherd is an actual shepherd" (*Language*, 81), although no shepherd appears in the text. A corresponding

the traditional historical perspective may compromise the new approach. Thus it is telling that the whole of Luke 15 has been characterized as a conflict story (*Streitgespräch*), reflecting a typical dispute between Jesus and his Jewish "adversaries."[44] A third example of an older preoccupation is the use of literary approaches in addition to redaction criticism in an exclusive search for the unity of the text, whereby other possibilities of the new perspective remain unexploited.

The opposite problem is exclusive concentration on a new method without inquiry as to its contribution to essential traditional questions. Thus some "literary" analyses of the New Testament are chiefly interested in aesthetic or structural features in isolation.[45] Moreover, the application of high-level theoretical systems to the stories risks making their interpretation too complicated for any first-time hearer and thereby unlikely as the primary reading of the text.[46] In the worst case, applying a modern pattern to a parable may reveal more about the creative power of the interpreter than about the qualities of the text.

Furthermore, a literary perspective on the parables easily becomes misleading when they are seen as ambiguous stories that expect each reader to construct her or his own meaning.[47] The text offers numerous possibilities for interpretation, but I argue that the most important one pertains to the explicit audience of the parable, which is typically presented in the framework story. Thus a reader is not

---

addition is made by Hedrick (*Parables*, 104 n. 49), despite the effort to cleave to the text (*Parables*, 93–116). Other literary perspectives typically return to allegory; see Snodgrass, "Allegorizing," 19–22, 56.

44. Harnisch, *Gleichniserzählungen,* 201–31 and Wolter, "Streitgespräch,", 25–56. For discussion see chap. 3 below.
45. This may occur as a reaction to redaction criticism, or in order to praise the skills of the evangelists (e. g., Stibbe, *John*).
46. Cf. Mark Bailey's criticism of literary approaches to the parables of Jesus ("Guidelines," 29–30).
47. Cf. Zimmermann, ibid., 173–76.

free to interpret the chapter in any direction. In the text both Luke the Author and Jesus the Narrator want to convey a message and thereby provoke a specific reaction. Several elements in the text, such as rhetorical questions, serve this purpose. Thus a postmodern polyvalent interpretation suits us, but not the framework narrative. When Jesus responds to his critics with a story he is hardly sending numerous messages. In other words, every parable has one function per storyteller and audience.

In summary, we may say that contemporary general literary theories have in some measure inspired research into the parables of Jesus for some decades. For several reasons their contribution to our understanding has, however, remained wanting. They offer some valuable insights but do not suffice for an unplugged reading. Hence a fresh attempt is called for, one that focuses on the integrity of the story and its interactive function in its actual context.

Second Thoughts:
Is Allegory a Solution?

Despite focusing on the parable's narrative climax and its persuasive function as a whole, one cannot wholly escape the attraction of an allegorical reading. Academic parable research has generally had an ambivalent relationship to the allegorical perspective, and for a reason. Neglecting obvious signals in the text produces one-sided solutions.

At times, the framework story explicitly encourages an allegorical interpretation.[48] Moreover, If one sets aside wild allegories, which are anachronistic or otherwise irrelevant to the framework, it is often obvious that the characters and events—not just the climax—have

---

48. The most famous example is 8:11-15, where Jesus explains the parable of the Sower allegorically.

clear connections to the topic discussed in the framework.[49] If these signals are overlooked, the parable is artificially cut off from its context. This in turn enables noble theological or ethical interpretations that, however, may not be observed by any other reader of the parable. But is allegory the best way to interpret the direct resemblances between the parable and the "reality" of the story's framework? Several problems arise:

First, an allegorical reading means that the parable no longer functions as argumentation and becomes only a claim with no foundation. For example, 15:11-32, the *Prodigal Son*, is easily interpreted as follows: The father accepts his repentant son. The father is God, and the son means the repentant people. Thus God accepts repentant people. However, since the story is fictive, and since nothing proves the allegorical connection, the parable by no means guarantees that God will follow the father's pattern. Since this parable is generally felt to be persuasive there must be some way in which it affects its audience other than allegory.

Second, there is no limit to allegorizing the details in the story, and the gates are opened for importing extraneous material. Most allegories are based on information not available in the text. At some point the interpretation becomes too imaginative, especially when later theological concepts are brought to bear. Typically, discovering intertextual or theological allusions presupposes that the parable is already included among the canonical writings.

Third, a hunt for allegories neglects the narrative dimension of the story, as it diminishes the role of a possible punch line at the end. Thus allegorical explanations may satisfy later theologians but hardly fit the first listeners to the story.

---

49. Drury, *Parables*, 116–17, argues that although allegory is not needed, several allegorical images are used. For example, according to him, in 15:11-32, the *Prodigal Son*, the characters refer to God, "unreconstructed orthodox Judaism," and its non-orthodox counterparts. However, such an interpretation requires information not available in the text.

It is no wonder that several scholars feel that instead of allegories one should focus on the narrative and its *scopus* or punch line, since this approach blows fresh air into the interpretation. The story is read in its own right; the message of the whole story is more important than the details. This appears more natural in relation to the original situation and audience. These benefits explain the success of Jülicher's approach, but this manner of reading fits modern narrative theories as well.

In fact, there are better ways of interpretation that are analogous to the reality in the context. One of them is the Jewish *qal wahomer* reasoning. The (unjust) *Judge* (18:2-6) is not to be identified as God; an allegorical understanding would be not only misleading but too difficult and even blasphemous in the ears of the audience. Instead, Jesus argues that if such a judge will help the widow, *how much more* will God help you.

Some particular details should be assessed analogously as well, but only those relevant to the framework story. Together with the relevant punch line, these "allegories" combine the principle illuminated by the parable with the situation or question discussed in the framework story. But one should not axiomatically and exclusively identify any character in the parable with some person in the framework story, let alone with a theological concept, as flexibility is one of the chief virtues of the parables. The characters in a parable *are* not anybody in reality but illustrate different thoughts, models of behavior, and so on. The reference of the details in parables can oscillate. The characters, the plot, and other details may create among the recipients various connotations that are not necessarily mutually exclusive.

We can suggest in preliminary fashion how a parable functions as persuasion in its context. Instead of resembling the context situation as much as possible, its power lies in the differences: A parable presents another situation or story that, however, illustrates the same principle or rule to be applied, according to the speaker. By separating the principle or rule from the actual situation the parable enables the addressees to see it more clearly without bogging down in irrelevant details that may blur their mind's focus. When they accept the rule, it can then be applied to the original situation by pointing to the resemblances. Thus, for example, the parable told to David (2 Sam. 12:1-4) emphasizes a principle that is then applied to the situation (vv. 7-9).

Conclusion: the necessary analogy between the story and the "reality" displayed in the framework is found primarily when looking at the punch line and the principle highlighted by it. However, focusing solely on the obvious climax easily leads to neglect of its equally obvious resemblances to the framework story. Both dimensions, the dissociating narrative and the associating analogy, must be taken into account. But instead of allegories, more relevant methods for integrating the details and the story line with its punch line ought to be considered.

Guidelines for an Unplugged Session

The preceding discussion yields five basic principles of interpretation. Their purpose is to focus on the text and thereby lessen the influence on the interpretation of scholarly imagination and religious intentions. These guidelines are to a certain degree included in many modern analyses of the parables, but they are seldom followed systematically and without compromising the reading with historical and theological issues. In what follows I will discuss the practical guidelines and their application especially to Lukan parables.

Respect the Author's Cut: Add Nothing

The material is the parable and its embedding framework story in their actual form. These are considered as a solid work of art, produced by "Luke," irrespective of our knowledge of the sources on which he drew. No previous versions or historical circumstances are discussed.

Since Luke is responsible for everything he writes, everything can be treated as a "Lukan addition."[50] His literary consciousness and determination are thus respected. Redaction criticism has demonstrated that a romantic view of the evangelists as innocent collectors of historical data about Jesus of Nazareth cannot be defended. Despite common material and similar vocabulary, every gospel text is an independent product with its own strategy and ideology. With his text each author is conveying his own message to his audience. Although Luke refers (1:1) to his predecessors, he scarcely expects his audience to be making a synoptic comparison. Every story and feature addresses the audience in the same way.

In the scholarly discussion no decisive argument has been presented for or against the traditional identification of the author as Luke, the companion of Paul.[51] This, however, is not problematic for reading the text. When using the traditional name Luke, I am referring to the author appearing in the text, either explicitly or implicitly, not to any historical individual or group.

It would be more important to know the audience. Theophilus may be a general pseudonym for a larger group or anybody interested in Jesus or Judaism.[52] In any case, the document is too massive

---

50. For example, 18:14b is usually called a Lukan addition (Hultgren, *Parables*, 125 n. 36). However, regardless of the historical origin of the verse, one should not assume that the author less consciously chose the rest of the text. Accentuating typical Lukan features, e. g., those found in the so-called L-parables, easily leads to overemphasis on these (see, e. g., Forbes, *God*).
51. For attempts to identify the author see Nolland, *Luke*, xxxiv–xxxvii. Robbins, "Social Location," shows how much we can know about the implied author's social world.

to have been produced for one individual only. In order to avoid circular reasoning, the unwarranted hypotheses about a "Lukan congregation" with its specific needs, theology, or purposes should not be confused with the examination of the text.

It is safe to join a general scholarly opinion according to which the audience has a non-Jewish Hellenistic background but is interested in Judaism and Jesus. Luke's relationship to early Judaism has been extensively discussed, but his allegedly antagonistic attitude toward the Jews may be due to a biased reading of the parables.[53] Therefore it is unreasonable to take any stand on this question before scrutinizing the actual document. For interpreting the parables it would be important to assess how much knowledge about life in first-century Palestine they reflect. Apparently the author assessed his audience's awareness of such sociocultural data as limited.[54] This, however, did not prohibit him from telling the parables to them, since they were meant to be less historical than the whole Lukan two-volume document.

The incorporation into a parable of any external information not provided or implied by the author easily compromises its function. Introducing information not known to the implied audience, or reconstructing any earlier versions of the narrative or the characters mentioned therein, not only renders the interpretation arbitrary and hypothetical but easily distorts the way it is designed to affect the audience.[55] The exclusion of additional knowledge may create a problem for a modern reader, as the time of writing was long ago. However, the need for external cultural or historical information should not be exaggerated. The parables typically highlight a general

---

52. For discussion see Forbes, *God*, 311–27.
53. For discussion about the audience see Nolland, *Luke*, xxxii.
54. See further detail later in this chapter.
55. For example, a parable is typically designed to abstract from known role models and show people reality from different angles. Manipulating the text may paralyze such dynamics.

principle, not some specific information about the case discussed. Like any good story, they generate a world of their own.[56]

The need for external information is minimized by two factors. First, in his parables Jesus seldom refers to any actual historical situation or local conventions, but to knowledge on a general level. He can speak of a king planning to go to the war (14:31-32) although there were few such local kings in the neighborhood.[57] In any case, the audience lacked access to any warlord's cabinet where military plans were made. Second, Luke the Author writes in Greek, to an audience who hardly possessed specific information about the life and customs of Galilean peasants in the first century.[58] When he thinks the audience needs such information, he does not hesitate to provide it.[59]

Luke originally designed the parables to be understood by his putative audience. This idea is based on the assumption that the author is responsible for what he writes. As he has certain recipients in mind, he probably assumes that they are capable of comprehending the story and being affected by it, based on his information. The same applies to the narrator as well: his hearers are expected to understand him without external support. The implied addressees' knowledge of social, historical, theological, linguistic, and other issues can be at least partly assessed based on the text. Three criteria are important:

1. What is explicitly stated in the text;
2. What is clearly implied by the author, for example, the audience's knowledge of Greek;

---

56. Powell, *Chasing*, 108.
57. To be sure, the impending war between Herod Antipas and Aretas IV in 36 CE (Jos. *Ant.* xviii, 5) may have influenced this parable, but it is not mentioned in the text.
58. Thus, for example, it can be shown that Luke assumes recipients who are not well aware of the circumstances in first-century Palestine.
59. See Luke 20:27; thus also Powell, *Narrative*, 20.

3. What is based on the author's previous communication with the addressees, especially in the preceding chapters.

Narratology emphasizes that the audience is expected to see a story "in its own spacetime." The story has a world of its own that is not identical to the real world, and these two should not be confused.[60] Information provided by the author suffices for understanding. Examples of culturally distant yet wholly understandable and self-supportive stories abound in literature. Fairytales about kings, queens, and princesses, not to speak of dragons and other monsters, are fully comprehensible in countries without such real characters. Fairytales by the Brothers Grimm, the stories of the Thousand and One Nights, or the parable told by Nathan to King David (2 Sam. 12:1b-4) represent different cultures, religious backgrounds, and historical periods, yet for the most part they are comprehensible without excessive historical and cultural commentary. Little external information is needed for someone to be affected by them. Why would the parables of Jesus be any different?

Let the Audience Decide the Message

Understanding a parable as designed allows no open horizon for diverse interpretations. The parables are never absolute, but are told to an audience. The message of the parable must make sense. "It matters who tells them to whom and when."[61] Relevance is the crucial criterion for determining what the parable means and what it hopes to achieve. Any message that does not pertain to Jesus' hearers within the embedding story, or to Luke's audience, remains secondary at best.

---

60. See Segal, "Fictional Narrative," 64–66, 70–72.
61. Drury, *Parables*, 1.

When hearing a parable for the first time both the Lukan audience and that of his narrator, Jesus, were expected to grasp it and assess its significance. The characters in the embedding story are important for understanding Jesus.[62] On the second level, Luke the Author is addressing his contemporary audience. Our knowledge about them remains vague, though some information can be gathered. This, however, is by no means fatal, as "a text must reveal its context."[63] This context consists of the partners in communication, their discussion, and their behavior. The parable must express a reasonable statement in the context; no meaning that is apparently irrelevant there can be trusted.

Look for Narrative Conventions

For a narrative analysis the classical model of Wayne Booth, developed further by Seymour Chatman, provides a point of departure.[64] These authors focus on the narration rather than the history, the ideology, or even the story line. They acknowledge that outside the text there was a real author conveying a message to a real audience, yet we only have access to the author and the audience presented or implied in the text.[65] Whereas biblical analyses are often based on the intention of the historical author, general literary criticism long ago realized that such knowledge might be

---

62. This means that when, for example, Jesus responds to his critics with a parable it must convey a reasonable answer to them, despite any deeper or higher-level ideological messages. It is sensible to prioritize this textual function, as Luke uses it when addressing his audience. In other words, the framework story is not presented in vain but serves to affect the Lukan audience by guiding its understanding of the parable.
63. Sloane, "Rhetoric," 798–803.
64. Booth, *Rhetoric*; Chatman, *Story*, esp. 148–51; 253–54; 267; Genette, *Narrative*. In New Testament scholarship this theory has been applied, e. g., by Rhoads (see Rhoads, Dewey, and Michie, *Mark*) and Culpepper, *Anatomy*. Finnern, *Narratologie*, 1–246, provides a detailed presentation of more recent trends in narrative analysis.
65. For the concept of the "implied reader" see Iser, *Leser*.

not only questionable but misleading for understanding the existing text.⁶⁶ Still, the function of the text can be observed.⁶⁷ The primary aim of interpretation is thus to demonstrate how the implied audience is expected to perceive the story. In other words, Booth and Chatman study what the text-internal author is saying through the narrative to his text-internal audience.⁶⁸ Chatman's theoretical work combines aspects of modern rhetoric and narrative studies. Modern narratological scholars, especially Monika Fludernik, offer refined and valuable tools for analyzing the parables.⁶⁹ Knowledge of several narrative techniques illustrates how the narration is aimed at affecting the audience.⁷⁰ Thus delineating the stereotypical "round" and "flat" characters in the parables may help us understand the story,⁷¹ and the popular "rule of three" shows that after two incidents the audience expects the climax.⁷²

Perhaps the most important of the narrative conventions is that a parable typically follows the form of a joke. The opening includes an interesting hook, the audience's expectations increase during the telling, and finally the punch line (which the audience automatically recognizes) carries home the point of the story. In a joke this makes people laugh, whereas in a parable it affects the audience's thoughts, values, and behavior. Converting interpretations into allegories is tantamount to laughing at the wrong moment during the telling of a joke; it compromises the success of the storyteller. I argue that

---

66. Wimsatt and Beardsley, "Intentional Fallacy," 468–88. Finnern, *Narratologie*, 50–56, however, defends the uncritical idea of revealing the author's intention.
67. According to Sloane, "Rhetoric," 803–8.
68. Cf. Powell, *Narrative*, 19–23.
69. Fludernik's "natural narratology" emphasizes the importance of human experience in narrative. See Fludernik, *Narratology* and *Introduction*. Cf. also Bruner, *Acts*, and Prince, "Narratology." Others, e. g., Cortazzi, *Narrative*, remain too practical.
70. See, e. g., Bar-Efrat, "Narrative"; Berlin, *Poetics*; Malbon, "Narrative"; Rhoads, Dewey, and Michie, *Mark*.
71. Foster, *Aspects*; see also Booth, *Rhetoric*, 3–20; Bar-Efrat, "Narrative," 64; Berlin, *Poetics*, 33–42.
72. Jeremias, *Gleichnisse*, 202, refers to this rule in popular stories and in the parables.

when telling a parable in a specific situation the Lukan Jesus has a corresponding goal. He hopes to provoke a specific reaction.

Look for the Purpose

The identification of the meaning or message of the parable does not suffice, as neither the narrator nor the author is only sharing information. They are attempting to affect their audiences. Although modern users typically read the parables for other reasons, such tasks must be preceded by clarification of the parable's function within its textual frame of reference. Traditional classifications may often be misleading, as if the purpose of a parable could be perceived on the basis of formal observations.[73] For example, the old idea of "conflict stories" hardly fits the actual text.

As with the content and message, any suggested function of the parable must be meaningful to its audiences. It is crucial to determine how they are expected to modify their thoughts, values, and behavior after hearing the parable. Since this goal largely defines what is said and how, no general theological message or historical information can be derived from the parable without identifying that goal.

Since the parables are stories seeking to touch their audiences, both the narrative and the persuasive perspective imply certain conventions. These are virtually universal and are studied by experts in narratology and rhetoric. Such aspects are extremely helpful for understanding the parables of Jesus.

Modern rhetorical criticism and argumentation analysis scrutinize texts not merely as linguistic, aesthetic, or communicative objects, but as means for affecting their audience.[74] They help us to focus on general conventions of rhetoric and argumentation such as the

---

73. For the discussion and some sensible, yet formal classifications see Snodgrass, *Stories*, 9–15.
74. Thurén, "Rhetoric."

persuasive devices and strategy described in ancient and modern rhetorical handbooks. These may promote recognition of how the parable is designed to affect its audience.

Contemporary argumentation analysis offers a great number of sophisticated ways to illustrate and criticize any type of argumentation.[75] While the Dutch pragma-dialectical method may offer the most profound overall tool for analyzing argumentation, the Lukan parables can be more conveniently approached by using the basic model developed by one of the founding fathers of this discipline, the British philosopher Stephen Toulmin. In the late 1950s he discovered that human argumentation does not follow the rules of formal logic. Instead, it typically consists of certain persuasive elements, the role and characteristics of which can be defined more or less precisely.[76] This is important in a practical discussion, where many concepts tend to be implicit. Toulmin's model offers tools for explicating these elements in a comprehensible procedure. In what follows I will present a simplified version of his model, focusing on the specific argumentative functions of the different elements.

First there is a *claim*, that is, the opinion put forward. The audience is not expected to share this opinion, at least not wholly.[77] In the case of the parables the *claim* is the message, idea, mode of behavior, or the like that Jesus wants his hearers to adopt. The history of parables research illustrates the difficulty of identifying the *claim*.

---

75. For an extensive presentation of the development and current stage of argumentation analysis see van Eemeren et al., *Fundamentals*. This perspective is not to be mixed with an anachronistic use of the thoughts of Aristotle or other ancient scholars in order to find historical resemblances between them and the New Testament. For comparisons and discussion see Thurén, "Argumentation."
76. Toulmin, *Uses*; Toulmin, et al., *Introduction*, 29–77. For a brief introduction and critical discussion see van Eemeren et al., *Fundamentals*, 129–60; Thurén, *Argument and Theology*, 41–46.
77. Toulmin et al., *Introduction*, 6–7, 25, 29–32.

Second, the *claim* is supported by the *data*,[78] by which Toulmin means the facts on which the *claim* is based. This information is typically not general but case-specific. The audience is expected to accept the *data*. Otherwise, preliminary argumentation is required. Sometimes it is necessary to start from a distance in order to find a common point of departure.

Third, the *data* alone seldom suffice. Although the audience accepts the *data* they may ask whether they have any bearing on the case discussed. What is needed is a rule, or *warrant* in Toulmin's terminology, that shows how the *data* support the *claim*.[79] The *warrant* guarantees that it is possible to draw the conclusion from the *data* to the *claim*. In contrast to the *claim* or the *data*, the *warrant* must remain on a general level. The *warrant* often remains implicit, but it is easily identifiable.

These three factors are necessary for any reliable argumentation. The general *warrant*, in particular, plays so crucial a role that in the event of the audience's rejection of it the *claim* would fail. Therefore an additional factor, *backing*, is often needed. This consists of general information or experience the audience is assumed to possess. According to Toulmin the *backing* typically relies on historical examples, universal human needs, expert opinions, statistics, and so on.[80] The structure of argumentation is open-ended: every element can be disputed and supplemented by additional information.[81] Toulmin presents the example in Figure I.1, to which I have added the *rebuttal*.[82]

---

78. Ibid., 26, 37–44.
79. Ibid., 26, 45–56.
80. Ibid., 26, 61–69.
81. Ibid., 73–77; Thurén, *Argument and Theology*, 44. For example, one could doubt the *data* and argue that Petersen is a typical Danish name, whereas a Swede would be called Pettersson.

Figure I.1

Backing: The Proportion of Roman Catholic Swedes is less than 2%[83]

▼

Warrant: A Swede is not a Roman Catholic

▼

Data: Petersen is a Swede ▶ *Claim*: Petersen is not a Roman Catholic

▲

Rebuttal: Unless a Swede belongs to a small minority

In practical argumentation several factors may remain implicit, but they can be made explicit on the basis of other factors and knowledge of the function of the missing element. Moreover, the factors must often be slightly modified in order to fit the presentation.[84]

When applying Toulmin's model it is essential to focus on the grade of generality and acceptability of the factors of argumentation. Otherwise the reconstruction of the elements becomes unreliable:

	Accepted	Disputable
Specific	Data	Claim
General	Backing	Warrant

---

82. According to Toulmin, *Uses*, 81–101, the *rebuttal* expresses the circumstances under which the *claim* is valid [here: "Unless Petersen belongs to a small minority"]. Moreover, a *qualifier* presents how probable the conclusion is.
83. Modern statistics confirm Toulmin's *backing*: http://www.nationmaster.com/country/sw-sweden/rel-religion.
84. Van Eemeren et al., *Fundamentals*, 288–98, presents a sophisticated system for such modifications.

Now this model can be applied to the parables in Luke. According to my hypothesis above, a parable typically illustrates a common rule that Jesus then applies to the topic discussed. In Toulmin's scheme this means that a parable typically functions as the *backing*. It thereby supports a general rule, a *warrant* that should be accepted by the recipients. This rule, in turn, is expected to persuade them that because of what they already think (the *data*) about a certain issue they ought to accept something new (the *claim*) suggested by Jesus. Thus, for example, the brief parable "It is not the healthy who need a doctor, but the sick" (5:31) illustrates a rule: "one should not help those who are not in need," which leads to the explicit theological principle "[one should not] call the righteous, but sinners to repentance" (5:32), which in turn explains Jesus' table fellowship with tax collectors and sinners.

Figure I.2

Backing: It is not the healthy who need a doctor, but the sick (v. 31)

▼

Backing: One should not help those who are not in need

▼

Warrant: One should not call the righteous, but sinners to repentance (v. 32)

▼

$Data^1$: Jesus is eating with tax collectors and sinners (v. 30)
$Data^2$: Jesus' eating with them means calling them to repentance (v. 32) ▶ *Claim*: Jesus' behavior is reasonable

In this case the *backing* represents accepted general information and the *data* accepted specific information. The acceptability of the *warrant* is not so self-evident, thus it needs support provided by the accepted *backing*. Moreover, Data[1] may or may not be accepted by the audience; this makes it another vulnerable point of this reasoning.

A practical complementary tool for identifying the function of a particular parable is a set of questions modified from the classical "Five Ws,"[85] which resemble Paul Ricoeur's way of determining a narrative. These questions help to avoid naïve misunderstandings as well as too hasty theologizing of the text.

- Who? The author and the narrator are identified. They may be at least partially implicit.
- To Whom? The audience is recognized. It may be multifaceted. The main divisions include main hearer/by-hearers; primary audience (of the parable as told by the narrator)/secondary audience (of the story as told by the author); implied/explicit/ideal audiences.
- What? The data offered in the text are carefully recognized and separated from traditional information axiomatically attached to the story.
- When? The situation(s) and the exigency of the parable and its embedding story are identified. They are seen in their wider context.
- Why? The function of the parable in the given situation for the partners in discussion is recognized: what do the narrator and the author want to achieve among their recipients by telling the parable and its embedding story?

Conclusion: when identifying the function of the parable in its context it should first be disconnected from the framework situation and studied in its own right so that the punch line and the principle exemplified by it can be identified. Second, one can ask the relevance

---

85. The general concept of a set of five or more questions in research or journalism derives from ancient rhetoric, asking for circumstances: Robertson, "Note"; see also http://en.wikipedia.org/wiki/Five_Ws. Ricoeur, *Time*, 55, correspondingly uses the questions "what," "why," "who," "how," and "with whom," or "against whom."

of this principle to the topic discussed in the framework. To this end it may be good to look for signals connecting the parable's individual characters and themes to the framework story as well. However, such an "allegorical" reading should not strive for any perfect matches since the power of the parable often lies in the flexibility and oscillation of the characters: The same figure may represent different people in the framework. For example, the father of the Prodigal Son may simultaneously resemble the Pharisees, scribes, God, or even Jesus. Thus any fixed identifications should be avoided.

Ask the Evangelist for the Theological Level

Recognizing the parable's function for Jesus' hearers within the framework story is hardly enough for modern readers, nor did it suffice for the evangelist, who apparently found in the parable a more general message, as he wanted to convey it to his own hearers. From his way of using the parable the step to a general theological message is not too great.

Comparison with the surrounding document is especially important in order to avoid the risk of importing one's own thoughts into the story. To cross-check any hypothesis about the meaning and function of the parable one can look for resemblances to other parables and teachings of Jesus within Luke's writings. It is likely that corresponding ideas will recur; a unique topic or an exclusive message is less probable. However, the evident function of a particular parable should never be overruled by any construction of "Lukan theology." Furthermore, references to the hero portrayed by other evangelists may be disturbing, as Luke was not necessarily aware of them or supposed his audience to be. Again, the subject of study is the theology of Luke's Jesus, not the historical one.

Essential Questions

The guidelines for an unplugged reading are compatible with other good principles for interpreting the parables, but on certain conditions. Moreover, their relationship to traditional approaches may raise many justified questions.

Relating to Other Principles

There is no shortage of good directions for reading the parables, and most of them are helpful. However, even the best of them seldom focus on the function of the parables in the text. Instead, they mingle historical and theological perspectives in their search for the message displayed in the text. The guidelines above do not repeat these directions but hope to improve some aspects in order to enhance the accuracy of the interpretation. Changes to two such good sets of rules may illustrate the difference between the unplugged reading and these more traditional approaches.

Mark L. Bailey recommends a five-step procedure:[86]

1. understand the setting of the parable;
2. uncover the need that prompted the parable;
3. analyze the structure and details of the parable;
4. state the central truth of the parable and its relationship to the Kingdom;
5. respond to the intended appeal of the parable.

Bailey's steps are sensible and help the interpreter to concentrate on the message of the text, albeit with some precautions. All the steps are inherent in the reconstruction of the message of the historical Jesus.

---

86. Mark Bailey, "Guidelines," 30–38.

However, as he remains a hypothetical character his incorporation into the text impairs the controllability of the interpretation. Even other steps that require material not included in the parables may distort the interpretation. Fortunately, Bailey's rules can be modified so that no harmful additions are needed. Thus in step 4 the "central truth" can be seen as referring to the point of the parable without taking a stand on its accuracy, and there is no need to infer "the Kingdom" or any other all-encompassing factor in the teaching of Jesus; a reference to other corresponding ideas by Jesus within the same gospel suffices. Likewise, step 5 is viable only insofar as it seeks to identify the persuasive appeal or function of the parable, without any hermeneutical aspect.

Klyne R. Snodgrass argues that the text should be analyzed according to eleven "rules of interpretation:"[87]

1. thoroughly;
2. without presuppositions;
3. recognizing its oral characteristics;
4. asking the intention of Jesus and the perspective of the Palestinian hearers;
5. identifying the redactional elements and asking how they fit the evangelist's plan;
6. asking how it functions in the story of Jesus;
7. basing the interpretation on what is given, not on what is omitted;
8. not imposing real time on the story;
9. focusing on the end stress;
10. comparing the message to Jesus' teaching elsewhere;
11. asking its theological intent.

---

87. Snodgrass, *Stories*, 24–31.

Again, most of the rules are reasonable; however, in order to avoid disturbing the historical imagination or contemporary religious emphasis, some restrictions are necessary. Point 4 should not be taken historically, as the intention of the historical Jesus remains hypothetical. Moreover, since Luke did not write for a Palestinian audience, their perspective is not to be preferred. Instead, the readers implied by the evangelist take precedence. In point 5, comparison with the evangelist's general ideas is indeed useful, but for this reason focusing exclusively on redactional elements is too narrow a method. Not merely the details changed by the evangelist but also those preserved by him carry similar weight. Point 10 pertains to the Jesus within the same document, as the evangelist's audience could hardly have been expected to be familiar with other New Testament texts. Moreover, references to the corresponding character in other documents are of minor importance as the author, in this case Luke, is not responsible for them.

Ruben Zimmermann has developed "an integrative and open model of analysis of parables" to be used as a general structure for studying any parable.[88]

1. Linguistic-narrative analysis

    Semantic, syntactical, and pragmatic elements in the text, as well as narrative conventions, are described and understood.

2. Socio-historical analysis

---

88. Zimmermann, *Understand*. Most parables researchers in Germany have agreed to use this model. Different applications can be seen in Zimmermann, ed., *Kompendium*.

The reality envisaged in the stories, individual concepts, and processes is illustrated.

3. Analysis of the background meaning

The traditional symbolic references of individual motifs are identified.

4. Summarizing analysis

Instead of considering merely at the historical meaning, multiple meanings for any reader are recognized.

5. Aspects of reception history

Different ways of understanding the parable are surveyed.

The first step covers most questions relevant to my approach, provided that one distinguishes between the different levels of narration. The meaning and function of the parable necessarily vary if the reader looks at the historical Jesus and his audience,[89] the historical author and his audience, the implied author and his audience, or at Jesus in the framework narrative and his audience.

The second step involves a major problem discussed above: knowledge of issues not presupposed by Luke may distort the interpretation. To a great extent the Lukan work provides his audience with all the necessary information, even if additional data may be needed in some cases. Only when seeking the level of the historical Jesus is a thorough search for Palestinian sociohistorical data relevant.

---

89. Zimmermann, *Understand*, assesses the reconstruction of the historical meaning of a parable as not merely impossible but also as too limited.

The third step involves in large measure a return to the allegorical interpretation, which excludes any historical or text-internal audience, as the original audience hardly knew that the parable would form part of the Holy Scriptures.[90] Thereby it paves the way for steps 4 and 5, which go beyond the text level and clearly belong to the hermeneutical sphere. In general, Zimmermann's emphasis on the parables' wide polyvalence[91] does not suit their actual context, as each parable must be a relevant statement within the discussion reported by the author. At times the parables are unnecessarily mysterious, as if they were intentionally made difficult to understand. While this may be true in some cases, several stories, such as the parable in the Sadducees' question to Jesus in Luke 20, carry a simple and unambiguous message. To be sure, a broad openness to multiple readings is reasonable if the goal is to create a "theological meaning for current life questions." Whether such an objective befits an exegetical analysis depends on the scholarly tradition.

In contrast to Zimmermann's broad hermeneutical approach, my goal is narrower: to shed light on the parable within its actual context(s). Additional steps pave the way for using the parable in modern religious contexts, but as these may involve interacting with the analysis of the existing text, I prefer to focus exclusively on the latter.

---

90. As stated above, not every "king" or "shepherd" in early Jewish discussions represented the Deity.
91. To be sure, Zimmermann, *Understand*, admits that there are clear limits to the interpretation, set by "philological unambiguity or historical plausibility."

INTRODUCTION

Mission Impossible?
Questions and Answers

Q: Can the text ever be fully unplugged? There is always a reader, who eventually determines the interpretation.

A: The principal reader is the one implied in the text. One should try to read the texts through his or her eyes.[92] To be sure, everyone reads the parable in his or her own way, and there is no "objective" interpretation. However, the attitude of the modern reader is not a virtue; it should be recognized and minimized.

Q: If the parables are unplugged from their context, from Luke and his readers, is not the result anachronistic and arbitrary?

A: They should never be unplugged from either Luke or his audience, but only from the questions of modern readers and the information added by them.

Q: Is not interpreting an ancient text while disregarding essential sociohistorical factors doomed to fail? There is an enormous cultural gap between modern readers and the evangelist. "Any interpretation that does not breathe the air of the first century cannot be correct."[93]

A: One should not overestimate the need for cultural information Luke presupposes but with which modern readers are unfamiliar. Most good stories or fairytales provide any audience with all the necessary information. The Lukan recipients did not consist of Palestinian peasants, and yet he assumed that they would understand him. Thus, unless proven otherwise, the information with which he provides his recipients in the narrative and in its wider context, or that he assumes they already possess, suffices. In practice, assessing the implied information may be difficult.

---

92. See more detail in Powell, *Chasing*, 76.
93. Snodgrass, *Stories*, 25. However, he simultaneously states that the pursuit of an original version of a parable is misguided, as they were told several times on various occasions.

However, whenever external data are imported the interpreter runs the risk of transgressing the limit at some point.

Q: *Why prefer the message of Luke to that of the historical Jesus? Most people want to "hear a parable as Jesus' Palestinian hearers would have heard it"[94] rather than Luke's historical addressees, not to speak of some literary audience. Should we not strive to cleanse the text of Luke's revisions in order better to perceive what Jesus wants to say?*

A: As Luke writes the text, it conveys his message. Studying a reconstructed reality instead of the printed story is rare in the general academic scrutiny of literature.[95] While the historical Jesus and his message to his historical audience are certainly of interest, reconstructing them should not axiomatically replace the endeavor to understand the text *per se*. At the end of the day this may have some implications for the historical Jesus as well.

Q: *Is it enough to understand the discussions between Jesus and the ancient Pharisees? Considering the reasons why the parables are currently read in modern religious communities, should one not rather look for general theological messages and principles, even if such are not immediately apparent in the text?*

A: Recognizing the parable's meaning and function on the text level by no means excludes its use for hermeneutical purposes. Indeed, it may yield new possibilities. Yet one should bear in mind that for the first readers the parable was not a hypertext in which clicking a word opened an endless chain of new pages, even if the text has later proven to have such qualities.

Q: *If each parable carries a simple message, why are there so many interpretations? Why do so many students experience a need for supplementary information?*

---

94. Ibid.
95. See, e. g., Jefferson and Robey, eds., *Theory*; Prince, *Narratology*.

A: An essential reason for the multiplicity of interpretations is that no reader is a *tabula rasa*. Everyone has heard interpretations and explanations that inevitably influence the way she or he understands a parable. As the plain story rarely fits these interpretations, additions are required—but they run the risk of alienating us from the story in the text. Instead, we should attempt to forget all the previous explanations and listen to the story as it stands.

Q: *What guarantee is there that interpretation according to the suggested method provides the final explanation of the parables?*

A: The method does not provide any answers, but it does furnish essential criteria for reading the parables. The results depend on how well those criteria are applied to the text.

Q: *How can external information about the context be harmful, if it is correct?*

A: The crucial criterion is the implied audience. Information not known to them may distort the story, even if correct. For example, if they were not expected to be familiar with the holiness codes of Jewish priests serving in the temple, such data, reliable in itself, may distort our interpretation of the parable of the *Samaritan* (10:30-37).

Q: *How can a modern method for analyzing argumentation illuminate ancient parables? Shouldn't we use Aristotle instead?*

A: Human reasoning and persuasion are less bound to time and culture than one might think. With certain reservations, modern methods for argumentation analysis apply even to ancient documents in an excellent way.[96] We do not use ancient grammars for studying ancient Greek, either.

---

96. For discussion and several examples see Thurén, *Argumentation*, 77–92.

An Alternative Parable:
The Wife with Seven Husbands

A neglected parable,[97] the Sadducees' story of a woman with seven husbands in 20:29-32, demonstrates how the unplugged reading described above is a natural way of perceiving the parables. The Sadducees' parable does not share the problems inherent in studying stories told by Jesus. Its integrity is well respected, since it deals not with Jesus' theology or words but with those of his adversaries. Exegetes commonly see no need to reconstruct the words of the historical Sadducees or to use their story for other purposes than those obvious in the immediate context, 20:27-28, 33-40.

> *Some Sadducees, those who say there is no resurrection, came to him and asked him a question, "Teacher, Moses wrote for us that if a man's brother dies, leaving a wife but no children, the man shall marry the widow and raise up children for his brother. Now there were seven brothers; the first married, and died childless; then the second and the third married her, and so in the same way all seven died childless. Finally the woman also died.*

> In the resurrection, therefore, whose wife will the woman be? For the seven had married her."

Most interpretations of this parable focus on the text-internal function between the characters in the framework story, following the principles presented above. In other words, it is easy to see what the Sadducees would say to Jesus. For most readers the Sadducees are using the story to illustrate a known problem with resurrection in order to prove the impossibility of the concept. The content and function of the parable are lucid and easily recognizable. If a woman can legally have one husband after another, due to the death of each predecessor, canceling their deaths by resurrection would lead to an illegal and ridiculous situation. "Granted your belief in resurrection,

---

97. Cf. Beavis, "Reflections," 603–17.

does not the given scenario produce for you a knot that cannot be untangled?"⁹⁸ The Sadducees are ridiculing Jesus and attempting to diminish his authority.⁹⁹

The scholarly interpretation of the parable proper has not been subject to substantial traditional theological, historical, or literary modification because the parable is not attributed to Jesus but to his opponents. The framework setting (vv. 27-28, 34-40), where Jesus appears, has proved far more interesting. Thus scholars or even religious interpreters rarely feel the need to assume further details about the woman's or her husbands' personal history. To be sure, references to historical data not explicit in the story have been retrieved.¹⁰⁰ For example, it can be shown that Luke has obviously modified the Markan material.¹⁰¹ Yet the story is clear enough without reconstructions, and additional information is not necessary for understanding the point the Sadducees are making. In principle their story could inspire the reader to numerous additions or hermeneutical reflections, but those would be superfluous. The parable functions well within the embedding story; it makes sense as a statement in the discourse between the two partners. For the purpose of the argument the story suffices as it stands.

What about the cultural gap? Is not some contextual information necessary? Indeed so, but this was already perceived by Luke and his predecessors. Following Mark 12:18,¹⁰² Luke provides his addressees with background information about the historical context, which he adjudged necessary: the Sadducees "say that there is no resurrection." This is because the addressees Luke has in mind do not share

---

98. Nolland, *Luke*, 965.
99. Marshall, *Luke*, 737; Klein, *Lukasevangelium*, 633.
100. Gerwing, *Konfliktverhalten*, 36–37; Maier, *Mensch*, 116–26.
101. For the details see Nolland, *Luke*, 963.
102. Another source has been suggested as well, but without essential substantiation. See Nolland, *Luke*, 963.

information about the basic theological differences among Jewish groups. This allows one to assume that other sociohistorical information is also missing. When Luke does not provide such knowledge he obviously does not regard it as necessary.[103] The relationship of the passage to the historical Jesus has been discussed,[104] but this has no major relevance to the interpretation of the Sadducees' story. The scholars' main interest has been on Jesus' answer to them.

An argumentation analysis of this parable illustrates its precise function. The *claim* put forward is that the idea of resurrection is impossible, unacceptable, or ridiculous (20:27). Jesus is not expected to agree; thus argumentation is required. The *claim* requires two or three supporting factors, but only one of them is explicitly presented: the parable in 20:28-32, including an abbreviated version in 20:33b, "the seven had married her," and a question based on it, 20:33a, "it the resurrection, whose wife will she be?"

What role does this parable play? The story is fictitious. Jesus is not expected to know the woman or even believe that she exists. Thus the story hardly presents facts that state the point of departure for the argumentation, that is, *data*, nor does it provide a general rule, a *warrant*. However, it offers an example from which such a rule can be formulated: "The idea of resurrection may result in an impossible (unacceptable, ridiculous) situation."[105] It presents a theoretical example, a case story, the feasibility of which must be accepted by the recipient. Thus the story serves as a *backing* for this *warrant*, which in turn leads from *data* to *claim*. What remains is to identify the *data*, the assumed point of departure. This can be derived

---

103. An alternative explanation would be to assess as Luke a less capable author who combines traditional elements without considering his audience.
104. Ibid.
105. This formulation can be replaced by more specific rules that carry the same basic idea, such as "marital relationships may vary through life to the degree that a particular situation cannot be restored in the afterlife."

either by studying the factors already recognized or by looking at Jesus' answer to the argumentation. The whole argumentation is based on an implicit belief, which the Sadducees assume Jesus shares with them: "marital status remains the same in resurrection," or more generally, "life after resurrection closely resembles life on earth."

Figure I.3

Backing: The example of a woman with seven husbands

▼

Warrant: The idea of resurrection may result in an impossible situation
Or: Some changes in life on earth are irrevocable

▼

Data: Life after resurrection resembles life on earth ▶ *Claim*: The idea of resurrection is impossible

In his answer in 20:34-36 Jesus does not dismiss the internal logic of the argumentation. Instead, he attacks the assumed point of departure, the *data*, which are expected to support the *claim*. According to him the afterlife is so different that the example, though valid in itself, does not apply.

For a first-time hearer the Sadducees' parable is easy to understand. Everyone can focus on its function within the discussion presented in the framework story and grasp the point the Sadducees are trying to make. No allegorical or christological explanations are needed, and the historical information provided by Luke suffices. My question is: What if the parables of Jesus were studied in the same way?

Replugging the Parables

Finally, the impact of the unplugged reading on the traditional historical and theological questions is interesting. Can the results of this approach influence these questions as well?

As the unplugged perspective is influenced by modern literary and rhetorical approaches, it may and will be criticized for being a-historical. I shall emphatically reject such a claim. Unlike the approach of extreme New Criticism, respect for the existing text does not imply that its historical circumstances are refuted, only that their influence on the interpretation process should be limited. In fact, historical questions are extremely interesting and important. Moreover, the difference between modern conventions and ancient culture may require additional information that can be provided by careful historical studies. However, the historical tasks must not precede the study of the text or we risk losing its message. On the contrary, recognition of the message and function of the text may serve the historical task. That, however, is not possible if such perspectives are present from the outset.

Not only can the parables be used as a source for studying the sociohistorical circumstances of ancient Palestine; more importantly, the results can profit the search for the historical Jesus as well. For example, an unplugged reading of Luke 15 will provide material for assessing his attitude to the Pharisees. However, such an investigation should not be undertaken before understanding the text as such. It is my thesis that as the text provides us with more reliable "hard" data for assessing its message than any historical assumptions, the message in turn yields dependable information for historical research.

Correspondingly, focusing on the narrator as portrayed and implied in the text and seeking his message and purpose only within the particular literary context may yield interesting theological insights. The evangelist has already begun the hermeneutical process by assessing the message of the parable as applicable to another situation as he conveys them to his own audience. For him they obviously contain weighty theological meaning. This provides a good starting point for any hermeneutical application of the parable.

In what follows in chapters 2 through 5 the best contemporary principles of parable research, combined with the five guidelines for unplugged reading, are borne in mind when analyzing some of the most crucial and interesting parables in Luke. The practical procedure will depend on the individual story, as each poses different challenges. First I will provide an overview of previous research, focusing on central problem areas. Then I will define the message and function of the parable in its embedding framework story by focusing on the text-internal interaction between the key characters in both narratives. To this end perspectives from modern rhetoric, narrative criticism, and argumentation analysis will be applied. The text is studied only from the point of view of its implied audience. In other words, I attempt to disconnect the parables from axiomatic traditional interpretations, especially from disturbing historical questions, superfluous historical information, and later theological applications.

After these particular analyses I will provide a comprehensive "unplugged" analysis of all the Lukan parables of Jesus in chapters 6 and 7 to test how the method applies to several types of parables and whether the observations about the particular cases are relevant to other Lukan parables.

I will first provide a general overview of the parables in chapter 6. The actual texts will be identified and several technical features will be mapped. The particular parables are not discussed at length. Second, an argumentation analysis of each parable in chapter 7 will illuminate their persuasive functions. Their setting, way of affecting the audience, and grade of credibility will be discussed. Finally, chapter 8 will summarize the messages of the Lukan parables and focus on their general function. I shall argue that releasing the parables from unnecessary theological and historical burdens permits us a better view of their actual theological message.

This discussion, together with Spreadsheets 1 and 2^{106}, which combine all the information in a useful way, will provide a convenient tool for a deeper study of each parable. Such an analysis would involve broader discussion with previous research as well as studying the narrative and rhetorical features evoking emotions, that is, the *pathos* effect, which ultimately creates the power of a parable to move the audience. The study seeks to reveal interesting technical, rhetorical, and theological features of the Lukan way of telling parables. Perhaps it may emerge that some of this applies to all parable-telling in the gospels.

---

106. Visit fortresspress.com/thuren and click on the "Additional Supporting Resources" tab to view and download the spreadsheets.

PART II

2

The Bad Samaritan (10:25-37)

Introduction

The touching story of a lonely man traveling from Jerusalem to Jericho has become an invaluable source for christological[1] and ethical[2] interpretations. Historical reconstructions abound.[3] The parable has served as a test case for modern and postmodern readings as well.[4] However, its meaning and function in the existing text should not be neglected. An unplugged reading offers a fresh perspective.

---

1. See Gerhardsson, *Samaritan*, 3; Snodgrass, *Stories*, 347–48. These readings have some modern support, too. See Nolland, *Luke*, 590.
2. Zimmermann offers an overview in "Liebe," 548–53.
3. Thus Mattill, "Samaritan," 359–76, reconstructs an original version in which the Samaritan is replaced by a Jewish layman. For more on this phenomenon see Sellin, "Gleichniserzähler," 27–28. A typical reconstruction of the parable is presented by Crossan, "Parable," 285–307.
4. Such fascinating structures are presented, e.g., in *Semeia* 2: *The Good Samaritan*, 1–131; Hedrick, *Parables*, 100–2.

Various Interpretations

The parable in 10:30b-35 is often used for purposes that have little relevance to the situation described in the framework narrative (10:25-30a, 36-37). When it is exploited as a source of information about the historical Jesus and his sociohistorical environment, or as a basis for theological and ethical systems, the original problem "*Who is my neighbor?*" is converted into such questions as "*How should I behave?*" "*Where in the story is Christ?*" or "*What is the order of precedence between different commandments?*" As the parable is unable to provide adequate answers, interpreters rewrite it to some extent. They tend to reconstruct "original" versions or add historical information, ideological details, and new questions. Such approaches are well suited to their specific purposes, but when the goal of the interpretation is to grasp the message of Luke and his Jesus they can be superfluous, if not misleading.

To be sure, some external data are needed for understanding Luke as well, since modern readers are not familiar with the background known to the audience for which the text was written. Yet any material added to this parable may obscure its meaning and function.[5] The knowledge attributed to the putative audience can be estimated on the basis of different signals in the narrative and the previous communication, in Luke 1–9. Only the details of which Luke thinks his recipients are aware can be included, if one is interested in the message he is sending by the story. Thus although the discovery of ancient information related to the parable is interesting, it is not certain that the expert in law (νομικός) to whom it was told, or the

---

5. Hedrick correctly attempts to read the story from the auditor's or reader's perspective, and emphasizes that "the story is silent on a whole range of questions" (*Parables*, 93–116). Unfortunately, he nevertheless adds intrusive traditional information to the text, for example, by claiming that the man was robbed of "what goods and money he may have had" (ibid., 104 n. 49). This small detail obscures the lucid setting of the story; see below.

audience of the Lukan work for whom it was written, ever shared such knowledge.[6]

Guidelines for Perceiving the Lukan Message

Some guidelines presented in the Introduction (chap. 1) are especially important here.

First, the parable must make sense to its audience within the framework story. Jesus is replying to the expert in law; thus the parable should answer his question in terms he can comprehend. Moreover, the audience of the Lukan narrative must be capable of understanding the answer even when hearing it for the first time. This excludes sophisticated theological explanations or multiple main messages.[7] To be sure, the practical function of the parable in the text may be irrelevant to modern readers who are not early Jewish experts in law. It must somehow be conveyed to different audiences. But even this process starts within the text itself, since Luke has found it worthwhile to tell his audience the parable. Empirical evidence from early recipients, the Fathers, indicates that the parable contains seeds for christological interpretation, and later readings show its potential as an ethical example. The fame of the parable may to a great extent be attributed to such contexts. This, however, does not mean that the expert mentioned in the framework or the audience implied in the Lukan account are supposed to read it in such a way. Their opinion is crucial for understanding the parable.

---

6. For Luke and his audience, see above, chap. 1. Suggesting an unplugged reading of the parable by no means denies the value of the traditional theological and historical interpretations. However, when the goal is to understand the message and function of the parable and its framework narrative in the Lukan text, a different approach is necessary.
7. Blomberg, *Interpreting*, 233, learns from the parable three "lessons" that were hardly accessible for the Lukan audience.

Second, we should look for the function of the parable. Jesus is teaching neither proper behavior nor theology, nor is he describing his christological status. He responds to a person who is testing him. The heavy *pathos* element indicates that the ultimate goal is persuasion. Thus Jesus is trying to influence the expert, to change or modify his point of view, and more: to transform his values and behavior (v. 37b). Such goals make the parable a tool with a specific purpose, a persuasive device. This dynamic is not properly observed in a narrative analysis.

Third, we should focus on the narration in the text. There are several levels of communication, as Luke tells the *narrative* (10:25-37) and Jesus the *parable* (10:30b-35).[8]

Fourth, in order to crosscheck any hypothesis about the meaning and function of the parable it is important to look for resemblances to other parables and teachings of Jesus within Luke's writings.

In what follows I shall read the whole narrative from these viewpoints. I shall argue *inter alia* that the classical title "Good Samaritan" and its slightly better German counterpart "barmherzige Samariter" are misleading.

Defining the Question

The setting is described in a framework narrative (10:25-30a, 36-37) consisting of a dialogue. The introduction is lengthy in comparison, for example, to 15:1-3, which indicates its importance for interpretation. The framework enables the Lukan audience to understand why the definition of the concept of πλησίον is relevant. Simultaneously it shows the theological dimension of the immanent narrative.[9]

---

8. One could further differentiate between "Luke" and the implied author as well. See Powell, *Narrative*, 27. A simpler model is provided by Crespy, "Parable," 31.
9. The secularity of the parable is discussed by Braun, *Jesus*, 179–89.

THE BAD SAMARITAN (10:25-37)

Who is My Neighbor?

The audience's curiosity is aroused when an expert on the Torah asks Jesus too simple a question (v. 25).[10] That question is expressed in several ways: What shall I do in order to inherit eternal life (v. 25, ζωὴν αἰώνιον κληρονομήσω), to live in the life to come (v. 28 ζήσῃ), or to be justified (v. 29 δικαιῶσαι)?[11] The logic is simple: right behavior makes one righteous, which in turn guarantees inheritance of eternal life.[12] Both men agree on the answer, which is confirmed in the framework: loving one's neighbor is crucial (vv. 27-28, 37).

According to Toulmin's model of persuasion the basic setting is obvious. There is a common point of departure (*data*): Loving one's neighbor guarantees inheritance of life (vv. 25-29). The opinion proposed (*claim*) seems clear as well: The Samaritan represents correct neighborly love, which thus ought to be practiced (v. 37). However, what the Samaritan models must be expressed more precisely to allow formulation of the exact *claim*. What is the major characteristic of his behavior that needs to be emulated? Then a general rule (*warrant*) must be identified. It will combine the *data* and the *claim*. Another criterion for the *warrant* is that, if my hypothesis is correct, the parable presents an example (*backing*) supporting this *warrant*.

---

10. Jeremias, *Gleichnisse*, 201, observes the abnormality of the professional theologian asking a layman such a question, but explains that he was "in seinem Gewissen aufgeschreckt." Luke has a better explanation: He was an examiner (ἐκπειράζων in 10:25). The word does not in itself imply bad intentions (*contra* Forbes, *God*, 59).
11. Contra Nolland, *Luke*, 591, according to whom δικαιῶσαι means "to appear in a good light." Correctly interpreted by, e. g., Kenneth E. Bailey, *Eyes*, 39, and Keesmaat, "Neighbors," 277.
12. To earn an inheritance by behavior may sound odd to us, but was a commonplace for the audience; see Kenneth Bailey, *Eyes*, 35–36.

Figure II.1

Backing: The parable (how?)

▼

Warrant: ?

▼

Data: Neighborly love is a condition for inheriting life ▶ *Claim*: One has to adopt the Samaritan's practice of neighborly love (how?)

A hint at the actual *claim* is contained in the expert's follow-up question. He is not content, as he is actually interested in a detail: How should one delimit the concept of one's *neighbor* (v. 29)? He seeks to define the command to love one's neighbor so that it can be fulfilled. The end of the framework (v. 37b) indicates that the parable presumably provides the solution (vv. 29, 36) and thereby answers the original question.

The expert did not invent the dilemma *ad hoc*; it was a known topic in early Judaism: Should one love Samaritans and even Gentiles like fellow Jews?[13] The Torah and the tradition are not unequivocal on this question: both positions are supported. Several scholars have observed that this ethnic definition is essential for the parable.[14] But am I now incorporating correct, yet intrusive data into the storyline? The dilemma was certainly known to the expert, but are the Lukan recipients assumed to be familiar with it as well? Several details in the narrative suggest that they are. The explicit question deals with the identity of the neighbor, and the designation of the main character

---

13. Keesmaat, "Neighbors," 277. Corresponding test questions are found in Matt. 22:15-22, 23-33; John 8:3-11.
14. Esler, "Jesus," 335–37.

as a Samaritan, combined with the victim's deliberate lack of identity markers, shows that—from the audience's point of view—the question of ethnicity is involved.[15] In the same way, the final Toulminian *claim* can be restated: One must adopt the Samaritan's definition of neighborly love and act accordingly.

The omniscient author reveals the expert's primary intention (v. 10:25, ἐκπειράζων): he is testing Jesus, trying to discover to which side he belongs. Thus the interrogation is not necessarily hostile,[16] and neither is Luke or his Jesus. An antagonistic discussion is evident only if they seek to denigrate the expert or if he disparages Jesus. Yet no external audience who would testify to such a confrontation is presented. If the parable is aimed at persuading the partner in communication, his vilification is not an effective means. To be sure, Luke turns toward his own audience by revealing the thoughts of the expert (vv. 25a, 29a), but even these comments are not unsympathetic. Jesus' final exhortation to the expert is probably meant for Luke's recipients as well.

The Unknown Patient

The setting is reminiscent of that in the Sadducees' parable of the wife with seven husbands (20:29-32), which also presents a theoretical problem in the form of fiction.[17] That parable displays a scenario that effectively illustrates the difficulty of comprehending resurrection.

---

15. To be sure, the early Fathers' and later scholars' inability to assess the main question as ethnic proves that the parable does not function in the way I am describing for all audiences. But they are not its "ideal audience," and we must not presume the omniscience of the real author.
16. *Contra* Esler's unwarranted claim: "The lawyer hopes that Jesus will give an unsatisfactory answer" (ibid., 333). The verb as such does not indicate hostility. For further discussion see Snodgrass, *Stories*, 353.
17. The parable also indicates Luke's awareness of his audience's ability to comprehend the stories he presents. The introductory verse (20:27) and the whole framework (20:27-28, 33-38) provide the non-Jewish audience with the cultural background information necessary for understanding the parable.

There are no unnecessary details, and the point of the story is easy to perceive. The parable shows how a clear-cut story and a fictional character, ἡ γυνή, were created in order to resolve a theological dilemma.[18]

An analogous figure, illustrating another theological dilemma, is depicted here by Jesus the Narrator. When ἄνθρωπός τις is traveling toward Jericho his outstanding feature is that, in contrast to the other three wayfarers, his nationality is unknown. The axiomatic interpretation of him as a Jew is a fatal, misleading addition to the theme and ruins the dynamics of the whole parable.[19]

In the text the man is unrecognizable from the outset for the audiences of Luke and Jesus. The subsequent course of events obscures his background even for the passers-by. Robbers attack him and take his clothes. About his other possessions nothing is said.[20] Furthermore, he is badly beaten. For the newcomers this means that he (a) obviously needs immediate help and (b) is naked and unable to speak. These details are not reported in order to make the story more vivid but belong to the core of the setting, in accordance with the conventions of early Jewish storytelling.[21] The lack of clothes and the inability to speak indicate that the evidence of the wayfarer's national identity is absent.[22] Speculation about whether or not the passers-by

---

18. See above, chap. 1. This technique has its root already in the Scriptures. The book of Job deals in a corresponding way with another theological dilemma, unjust suffering. If suffering is a result of sin, why do righteous people have to suffer, too? See further Clines, *Job*, xxxviii. The question is approached by telling a story, for which a stark theoretical figure is designed: Job is "perfect (תָּם), upright, fearing God, and turning away from evil" (Job 1:1, 8), yet he has to suffer greatly. He serves as a personification of the theological question.
19. An unwarranted identification is provided by, for example, Adolf Jülicher, who argues that only Jews traveled from Jerusalem to Jericho (*Gleichnisreden*, 2: 586). The text indicates otherwise! Funk's ("Samaritan," 77) and Kenneth Bailey's (*Eyes*, 42) "proof" is even more telling: "Naturally." Forbes (*God*, 62) simply adds the information to the parable.
20. So also Nolland, *Luke*, 593, but *contra* p. 597. Hedrick (*Parables*, 104 n. 49) attempts in vain to explain why the goods were stolen as well.
21. In a corresponding way the attributes of Job are fundamental for understanding his story; see above. This does not mean that the audience must be familiar with the story of Job.

could determine whether the victim was circumcised or not has no support in the text.[23]

The victim has no other characteristics than those reported by the narrator. By creating this figure Jesus is exhorting the expert to envisage a theoretical situation in which the nationality of a person in urgent need of help cannot be determined.[24] The man thereby personifies the expert's question in a specific fashion: What if we do not know whether the victim is a Jew or a Samaritan? Is he a neighbor or not? In order to inherit eternal life, should such a person be loved or not?

Where Is the Camera?

The correct viewpoint is essential for understanding the parable. The primary perspective on 10:30b-35 is not behind the eyes of the victim, the Samaritan, the reader, or the narrator, but through the eyes of the two audiences envisaged by Jesus the Narrator and Luke the Author. In contrast to several other parables (for example, 11:5; 15:4), the audience is not explicitly placed inside the story.

However, as the core of all argumentation and persuasion is identification,[25] it is important to know the onlookers' target of identification. Robert Funk's idea that their perspective is that of the man "in the ditch" has become a commonplace.[26] Indeed, Jesus' last

---

22. Thus correctly Kenneth Bailey, *Eyes*, 42–43. Following him, Esler points out that failure to recognize the victim's ethnicity is "absolutely essential" ("Jesus," 337–39).
23. Although the man lacked clothing, the parable does not describe the position of his body or otherwise indicate whether the priest could examine his genitals.
24. *Pace* Nolland, according to whom "for the dynamics of the story we need to know nothing of the man except that he has been reduced to a state of desperate need" (*Luke*, 592). Hedrick rightly argues that the man's anonymity is important but does not see the connection to the expert's question (*Parables*, 103–4).
25. Burke, *Rhetoric*, 55.
26. Funk, "Metaphor," 77–78; followed by several scholars, e. g., McDonald, "Grace," 43–44, Hedrick, *Parables*, 111–13; Nolland, *Luke*, 591.

question invites the expert to suggest the identity of the neighbor from the victim's viewpoint: "Which of these three do you think proved to be a neighbor?" (10:36). Moreover, the parable begins by introducing an ἄνθρωπός τις, just as in 15:11 where ἄνθρωπός τις is a counterpart to "one of you [the Pharisees and the scribes]" who lost a sheep, and the woman who lost her coin.

However, several additions to the existing text are required before Funk's arguments become plausible,[27] not to mention that the story does not refer to any ditches.[28] Unlike the audience of Luke 15, they are not "forced" or even implicitly told to identify with the ἄνθρωπός in the parable.[29] Most importantly, the framework does not support this perspective. It displays the audience's basic question: "Whom should I regard as my neighbor?" or "Whom should I love in order to inherit eternal life?" (vv. 25, 29). When the parable begins by presenting a victim needing love, the expert and the Lukan audience are thought to view him from the perspective of the passers-by: Is he a neighbor? Would I help him or not? The other three characters represent two different solutions to this question.[30] Jesus does not urge the expert to imagine himself in the place of the John Doe until the very end, and even then only for a second. Jesus' next words return to the basic setting, as he tells the expert to see one of the passers-by, the Samaritan, as his role model: "Go and do likewise!" (10:37).

---

27. Snodgrass shows that many of Funk's arguments require the invention of new information for the story. The victim is not present in v. 35; he is not necessarily conscious, and he does not wonder whether to accept help from an enemy (*Stories*, 354).
28. Although this by no means suffices to refute Funk's hypothesis, it shows how interpreters unconsciously tend to add material to the parable. Actually, for geomorphological and meteorological reasons the ancient Roman road to Jericho did not have any ditches; the soil consists of nearly watertight cenomanian limestone. See Aharoni, *Land*, and David Burton, "Groundwater."
29. Contra Hedrick, *Parables*, 112 n. 90.
30. Their odd number is due to a general narrative convention known in Luke 15 as well as in old fairytales or our contemporary jokes. Jeremias, *Gleichnisse*, 202, refers to a "regel-de-tri" of popular narratives and gives several examples in the New Testament.

It is remarkable that the question about the *victim's* neighbor, formally reversing the original question, by no means surprises the expert. The very image of πλησίον is obviously reciprocal, as it indicates that two persons are close to each other.[31] The question is reformulated for the sake of persuasion.[32]

To claim that the audience would from the outset view the parable from the suggested victim's viewpoint requires that the last question be anticipated beforehand. This is possible only when re-hearing the parable. Another option is that the framework setting is cut off. This, in turn, would mean rejecting the existing text and reconstructing a new hypothetical setting for the parable.

The Passers-By

Stereotypical literary classification of the characters as the chief figure, the hero, or the villain of the story is too crude a method for assessing how the audiences—the expert and the Lukan recipients—are expected to be affected by the parable. For the study of persuasion it is more important to discover how the different characters are intended to affect the audience. I shall first sketch their attributes and then examine how they combine to serve the persuasion in the parable.

The Priest and the Levite

The priest and the Levite are traditionally characterized in a way incompatible with the text. This is achieved by adding external material to the parable. As a result, the characters' function in the

---

31. The only extra emphasis is in the word γεγονέναι. No other deep philosophical message is proposed (Contra Esler, "Jesus," 344–45; Snodgrass, *Stories*, 357–59).
32. It would be meaningless to ask "who, in your opinion, considered the victim a neighbor?" The actual text is but a stark version of the question "was the Samaritan, in your opinion, right when considering the man a neighbor?"

persuasion is lost. A classic explanation of the priest's and the Levite's behavior is their fear of the robbers.[33] However, their first reaction when catching sight of the victim, to pass by on the other side of the road (ἀντιπαρῆλθεν in 10:31, 32) would hardly have increased their physical security. More probably the lateral movement indicates the opposite reaction to that of the Samaritan (ἐσπλαγχνίσθη in 10:33)—they did not feel any compassion for the victim; quite the contrary.

According to another common explanation the priest simply obeyed the purity laws when avoiding contact with the victim, who could be dead. Richard Bauckham makes this the main theme of the whole narrative.[34] This interpretation is a mutually exclusive alternative to the setting described above: is a person who obviously needs help, but whose national identity cannot be determined, a neighbor?

However, the priest and the Levite are designed to attract little interest from the implied audience. They serve as forerunners of the third figure, the Samaritan. Jesus the Narrator speaks of the Samaritan's feelings and describes his action in detail, whereas there are no explicit words that reveal why the priest and his lighter version, the Levite, did not stop to help.[35] If these reasons were crucial to the parable one would expect at least some signal for the audience.

The interest in the purity laws is based on a single reference in the text: ἡμιθανής. But this word emphasizes the victim's need for first aid, not burial.[36] Moreover, regardless of our knowledge of early Jewish halakhic discussions, Luke's audience hardly consisted of

---

33. E.g., Scott, *Parable*, 195; Snodgrass, *Stories*, 344.
34. Bauckham, "Priest," 457–89.
35. *Pace* Zimmermann: "Nichts erfahren wir über die Motive, Argumente oder gar Seelenzustände von Priester und Levit" ("Liebe," 540). In the explicit text this is true, yet the framework lets the audience guess at their motivation.
36. Cf. Nolland, *Luke*, 592. He rightly argues that the question of the purity law is "a misplaced interest."

scholars (whether early Jewish or modern), and yet he did not add even a hint to help them with this issue.[37] Thus for them the parable does not deal with such questions. The audience of the framework narrative, the expert, wanted to define the concept of *neighbor* in order to inherit eternal life. As he was not a priest, their purity practices were hardly relevant to that end.[38]

Halakhic discussions are not only incompatible with the storyline, in which the victim does not appear to be dead, but ruin the argumentation by giving the priest a valid excuse for failing to help. If the audience regards his reaction as legitimate, so that only the Samaritan, a person not bound by Jewish law, was allowed to help the victim, the argumentative force of the parable collapses. Thus the incorporation of such information and questions is not only superfluous or unsatisfactory but devastating for the persuasion.[39]

Despite many commentators' reports, the priest in the parable does not think or feel anything save what is mentioned or alluded to in the text. The reason is simple: he does not exist in the real world. The commentators too easily make him a historical person whose motives can be reconstructed. But as the information given to the audience is limited to the text, the priest does and thinks only what the narrator says concerning him—or lets the audience assume. Such assumptions, if not directly suggested by the text, must be based on a general stereotypical level that even Luke's audience was able to share. Any conjecture about the persons may obscure the narrative and its function.[40] Thus the priest's motive must be found in the text.

---

37. Therefore Bauckham's claim ("Priest," 477) that "any first-century Jew alert to halakhic issues would readily have recognized" the halakhic problem a half-dead man creates is irrelevant, even if it were correct.
38. Becoming impure was not a sin and could be remedied by performing acts of purification (see Klawans, "Purity," 267), whereas not helping a person was a sin. Moreover, the priest was off duty when coming from Jerusalem. These factors attract no interest from the author.
39. So Snodgrass, *Stories*, 354–55.
40. Thus Kenneth Bailey knows many details about the characters' status, plans, values, hopes, and fears that are not mentioned or hinted at in the text (*Eyes*, 41–54). Similarly, one can invent

The Samaritan

The common attribute *good* is not imputed to the Samaritan in the text. For a modern reader, *Samaritan* denotes an unselfish individual who is devoted to helping others.[41] For the expert or any other Jew almost the opposite is true: Samaritans were stereotypical villains.[42] The goal of the narrative is not to prove the opposite. In the end neither Jesus nor Luke claims that Samaritans are actually good, or that the behavior of this particular character in the parable applies to all Samaritans.[43] Even if such a claim was part of Jesus' or Luke's implicit agenda, the argumentation would be weak indeed. The expert or any recipient could argue that the fictional story does not accord with reality.[44]

Despite his sudden *ad hoc* compassion (σπλαγχνίζομαι in the aorist), the Samaritan remains a member of a hostile nation. But were the Lukan recipients aware of this? They needed no additional sociohistorical information about the Samaritans. A brief narrative in 9:51-56, where Jesus is rejected by the Samaritans, provides them with the conventional view of these people. Thus the Samaritan in this narrative is not an underdog who automatically attracts sympathy from the audience.[45] He becomes exemplary not because of what he

---

twists of the plot or characters in a film or novel, or imagine details in their background. This actually happened with Jesus, too, when stories about his childhood were invented in the second century CE. But one should not mix these ideas with data explicitly present or strongly implied in the source document.

41. According to the *Oxford Dictionaries* a Samaritan is "a charitable or helpful person" (http://www.oxforddictionaries.com/view/entry/m_en_gb0731110#m_en_gb0731110); according to the *Longman Dictionary*, 984, "a person who gives kind and unselfish help to someone in need"; according to the *Merriam-Webster Dictionary* "a person who is generous in helping those in distress." See http://www.merriam-webster.com/dictionary/samaritan?show=0&t=1286446993.
42. The relationship between Jews and Samaritans is illustrated by Esler, "Jesus," 329–32; see also Snodgrass, *Stories*, 345–47.
43. Contra Esler, according to whom the parable aims at "reducing divisions between Judeans and Samaritans" as well as other intergroup tensions ("Jesus," 351).
44. Nolland, *Luke*, 594: ". . . it is not there to prove anything about the Samaritan."

is but because of what he does. This is emphasized by both Jesus and the expert: the one who did the right thing (ὁ ποιήσας τὸ ἔλεος in 10:37) became (γεγονέναι in 10:36) a neighbor.

John Nolland makes an important observation: "In the parable itself the Samaritan's compassion functions on something of the same level as the giving of good gifts to one's children in 11:11-13 . . ."[46] Indeed, not only "you bad people" giving gifts, but even more the wicked judge in 18:1-8 are the closest counterparts to the Samaritan in Luke. To a certain extent several other examples, such as the assumed behavior of Jesus' critics in 15:4-6 or the disciples' irritated friend in 11:5-8 fit the same train of thought. In principle they *are* bad (or unsympathetic), but nevertheless *do* good on a specific occasion. Whereas "you" are explicitly called bad (11:13), the judge is defined by his general attitude and the Samaritan by his nationality. The members of the audience are not guided to think that their wickedness is a misconception or that it changed because of their action. In each case the wickedness has a function, providing a dark background to the good deed.[47] The *qal wahomer* argumentation reads: if a bad person on some occasion does good, how much more a good one. In the other cases this emphasizes the naturalness of God's goodness. In the "secular" case of the Samaritan, the exhortation to the expert to do good is thereby enhanced: If a wicked Samaritan helped the victim, how much more should you do likewise.

All these examples lose significance if their unpleasant characters are domesticated. Thus even if the parable succeeds, the expert is hardly converted to admire Samaritans. Whereas the common title

---

45. Correspondingly, in 18:9-14 *Pharisee and Tax Collector*, the roles are misleadingly reversed by traditional interpreters, who from the outset describe the former as an ugly person whereas the latter evokes pity. For the correct interpretation, see Nolland, ibid., 877.
46. Nolland, *Luke*, 594.
47. McDonald rightly stresses that the Samaritan represents the "other," the enemy. What matters is what he does ("Grace," 50).

for 18:2-6, "The Unjust Judge," is slightly misleading,[48] our parable can well be called "The Bad Samaritan."

The Persuasive Function of the Passers-By

For persuasion, the interplay between the three figures is essential. We should ask how they are together intended to affect the audience.

For the audience the priest and the Levite represent stereotypical decent Jews. Criticism of the temple is not indicated. When the Levite emulates the priest's reaction, the audience is well informed about the upcoming third person. The narrative structure lets them expect a final character who will solve the problem with the victim in one way or another. In the corresponding structure of Luke 15 the sheep owner is followed by a poor woman, and the third, final character is a wealthy farmer. In Luke 10 the third passer-by should thus be more than the priest—perhaps another expert in law?[49] The anticlimax is obvious when a wicked Samaritan appears on the scene. The assumed good reputation of the two passers-by, combined with the bad image of the Samaritan, enhances the surprise evoked by the latter's reaction.

For the Lukan audience the Samaritan hardly represents an alternative option in the Jews' internal discussion of the priority of purity laws versus ethical principles. Whereas all three travelers are said to (a) come, (b) see the victim, and (c) react, the Samaritan represents a different first reaction to the encounter with the unidentified victim: compassion. This is followed by action left

---

48. Nolland claims: "He is exactly how a judge should not be" (ibid., 580). However, in the story the judge's professional skills are not questioned; on the contrary. The problem is his unwillingness and self-centeredness.
49. Keesmaat claims that the "rhetorical context" implies that the expected hero is a poor Jewish peasant ("Neighbors," 279). However, it would be more natural for the third person to be the most prestigious one (cf. Luke 15).

THE BAD SAMARITAN (10:25-37)

undone by the forerunners. Yet the parable is not just about compassion. After all, based on the framework story, something can be said about the priest's and the Levite's motives. The question of the national limits of the concept of a neighbor and the victim's tailor-made lack of means of identification must be related to the different reactions of the passers-by when catching sight of the victim.

When the expert is invited to follow the three persons' reactions in the challenging situation he is induced to imagine himself in the place of each: How would I react in a corresponding case? All were obliged to love their kinsmen; they were undoubtedly "neighbors." Perhaps this does not apply to foreigners. But what if the nationality of the victim is unknown? In that case there were two options for any Jew: (a) I must help the victim in case he happens to be a Jew—even if I run the risk of helping the enemy; (b) I must not help him, in order to avoid helping a Samaritan or a Gentile—even if I run the risk of letting a kinsman die. If the Samaritan was unwilling to help foreigners he had corresponding options.

On the basis of the parable we do not know whether the Samaritan chose his version of alternative (a) or if he merely disregarded all national boundaries and was guided by his compassion. The latter sounds radical, but as it is supported by the only hint (ἐσπλαγχνίσθη) given to the audience, its members are probably intended to understand the parable in this light. The deep feeling overruled a strict national principle. However, it was not *against* any principle, as the victim's identity was, after all, unknown. In 15:20 ἐσπλαγχνίσθη is used to explain the father's reaction to the return of his son. In that case, too, the father had several options. The one he chose was somewhat radical, but not impossible or contrary to proper behavior. In both cases Jesus expects the audience to prefer compassion to conventional conduct or their theological presuppositions.

Compassion may be a good *pathos* effect in Jesus' argumentation, but the parable lays heavier emphasis on the deeds of the Samaritan (twice in 10:37). Thus the issue is not only following compassion rather than convention but its result, that doing the right thing is what justifies and gives eternal life. The lengthy, detailed description of how the Samaritan helped the victim is intended to attract the audience's interest. It corresponds to the extravagant reception of the Prodigal Son in 15:20-25. Although the difference from the plain beginning of the parable is striking, no additional messages or allegories should be invented. The description of what the compassion of the Samaritan meant in practice seeks to augment the *pathos* effect of the parable. After all, it is this effect, not the juridical situation, that Jesus uses for his persuasion. One could think that this ending to the parable resembles Middle Eastern narrative customs, for there lavishness is a virtue. However, the Samaritan only acts according to the commandment to love his neighbor as himself.

The argumentative strategy of the parable is somewhat unfair. Not only the deep emotion and first-aid given by the Samaritan but especially the following verses make him a hero and thereby support the theoretical solution behind his course of action.[50] The opposite view, whereby one should so hate an enemy that one cannot show any mercy to a John Doe, even if a kinsman may die as a result—is reserved for the villains of the parable, the priest and the Levite. As the storyline makes it impossible for the audience to identify with these characters, their theoretical solution is thereby rejected. This application of the narrative may be inappropriate argumentation but, given the expert's answer, it seems to work well. Luke and Jesus use a

---

50. That solution remains obscure. Probably a maxim "everybody in need must be helped" is meant, but logically another principle is even better: "It is not wrong to help the enemy if he is not recognized."

corresponding technique in 15:28-30, where unacceptable thoughts are attributed to the elder brother.[51]

A simplified Toulminian structure, in which *data* expresses the specific common ground, *claim* the thesis of the speaker, *warrant* the general rule, and *backing* the material supporting the rule, could read as shown in figure II.2.

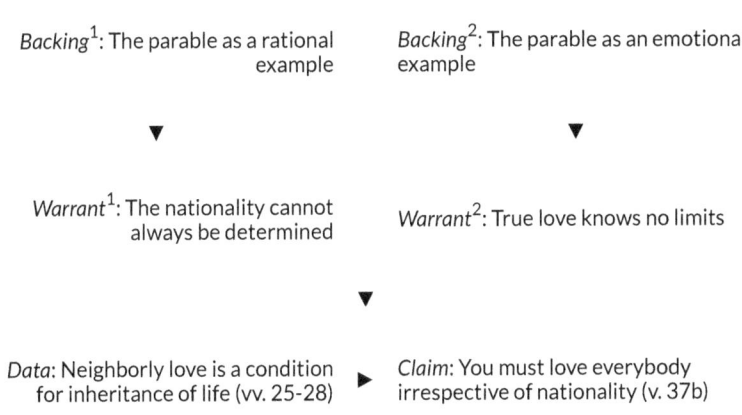

Figure II.2

The Aim of the Parable and the Narrative

At the outset I suggested that, besides all the religious and historical readings, the parable should be studied in its Lukan context, as a piece of persuasion aimed at modifying the recipients' attitudes, values, and behavior. When aiming at such a goal it is crucial to determine how the parable is designed to be received by the audiences in the text, those of the narrator and of the author. Jesus' utterances must make sense to his partner in discussion, and Luke must have something in mind regarding his readers.

---

51. See further in chap. 3.

Reaching a Theological Level

The subject of the discussion, what to do in order to inherit eternal life or to be justified, is repeated so that it cannot be missed by the audience. Thus the parable combined with the following discussion must answer this question. All other messages, be they ethical, christological, or theological, are secondary. As both partners agree that obedience to the commandment to love is the basic answer, the problem is reduced to the limits of the target of love, and further to the question of nationality as a possible excuse for not loving. The parable and the following discussion seek to convince the audience that neither national affiliation nor enmity suffices to modify the commandment if one wants to inherit life.

Still, not everybody is adjudged equal; national borders are still valid. Luke does not here claim that the Jewish view of Samaritans as enemies was misleading.[52] On the contrary, the theoretical content of the parable is annulled if an axiomatic admiration of Samaritans is introduced and the *qal wahomer* reasoning is obscured. If the Samaritan ceases to represent the enemy, the parable no longer promotes the unwonted concept of loving an enemy.[53] Similarly, if the judge in 18:2-6 is considered good, that parable loses its point.

Since the discussion takes place on a theological *cum* theoretical level its message and purpose for the expert are applicable to the Lukan audience without extensive modification or generalization. As the parable aims at enhancing a *warrant*, "True love knows no limits" or the like, corresponding statements are not difficult to find. In 6:27-36 hatred, cursing, indignation, violence, and failure to pay

---

52. Luke's general view of the Samaritans would require a wider discussion. For example, Acts 8:14-25 reflects a positive attitude. However, this knowledge has only secondary importance for seeking the thrust of this parable, as it runs the risk of introducing "authorial intent," as discussed above.

53. Piper, *Enemies*, considers loving one's enemy to be the only original commandment in Christian ethics.

THE BAD SAMARITAN (10:25-37)

debts are rejected as factors limiting the love command. By likewise rejecting these the audience is said in 6:35 to gain a "great reward" and become "children of the Most High" (ὁ μισθὸς ὑμῶν πολύς, καὶ ἔσεσθε υἱοὶ ὑψίστου), which resembles the goals mentioned in 10:25-37.[54] Together these texts argue that, for salvation, no restrictions of the love command are acceptable.

The ultimate persuasive goal of the parable is more difficult to discover. Both audiences should begin to act as enjoined and thereby deserve justification, (eternal) life, or divine sonship. But the relationship between this objective and other means of salvation in Luke requires further discussion.[55] Nor can traditional christological and ethical readings be wholly excluded. This is true not only because the history of exegesis shows that the text allows such interpretations. More importantly, since Luke uses the same aorist form (ἐσπλαγχνίσθη) of Jesus in 7:13,[56] a careful reader may observe that he is said to follow the example of the Samaritan (10:33) and the father (15:20). The latter's action resembles Jesus' behavior in the corresponding framework narrative (15:2). Thus a certain connection between the behavior of the Samaritan in Luke 10 and of Jesus elsewhere in the Lukan text can be assumed.

More significant is a theological message beyond the secular story. Jesus' recurrent emphasis in Luke is that human love is reciprocated by God's love. The examples of the reluctant friend, the sheep owner, the woman, and the wicked judge are said to have a heavenly counterpart (11:9-10, 13; 15:7, 10; 18:7-8). The father (15:11-32), by implication, belongs to the group as well. Thus even the Samaritan's behavior may well indicate a similar attitude on the part of God,

---

54. To claim that 6:35 does not refer to "future judgment" but to a "present manifestation" is problematic, as the verbs are in the future tense (Nolland, *Luke*, 300).
55. This seems to be a sore point for many commentators; see, e. g., Kenneth Bailey, *Eyes*, 55; Snodgrass, *Stories*, 358–59.
56. Zimmermann sees this a signal for the christological interpretation ("Liebe," 548).

although both parables are in themselves earthly. Moreover, God is presented as the ultimate cause and example (καθώς)[57] of unlimited love in 6:36. In reverse, when the disciples forgive debts (11:4) this serves as ground for God's forgiveness. Thus the parable describes God in terms similar to those in the parables in Luke 11 and 15. Although, following such a theological trajectory, the message of the parable of the Samaritan transcends its primary function, it is not feasible to confine its aim to the ethical level.

Figure II.3

Warrant: God follows God's own rules

▼

Claim/Data[1]: Unconditional neighbor love is, according to God, a condition for inheritance of life ▶ *Claim*[1]: God loves everybody unconditionally

Concluding Remarks

Reading the parable as a piece of persuasion and limiting its study to the existing text and its implied audiences have served as a test case for how our approaches to the parables must be reconsidered.

First, viewing the story from the implied audiences' perspective means that any data unknown to them may obscure its meaning and function. This also applies to much of the reliable information about the early Jewish context and to novel readings envisaged in the church or in the academic world. The priest is not excused for his behavior, the course of events is not to be watched from the ditch, and the Samaritan is not good.

---

57. For the logical relation indicated by the comparative dependent conjunction see Thurén, *Argument and Theology*, 74–76.

Second, focusing on persuasion enables a critical assessment of the author's and narrator's strategy. The persuasion in the parable may be successful, but it is not wholly fair.

Third, and most important, the parable's persuasive function becomes more visible. The expert is not vilified, but is convinced by *qal wahomer* reasoning that, if one is to be justified, the love command cannot be restricted in any way.[58] For the Lukan audience the parable is just another illustration of this principle, which has a theological dimension as well.

---

58. To differentiate between *help* and *love* is here irrelevant. Cf. Zimmermann ("Liebe," 546–47).

3

Persuading the Pharisees (15:1-32)

Introduction

The story of a man with two sons (Luke 15:11-32) would certainly benefit from an unplugged reading, as its later high status appears to have resulted in suffocation of the narrative and its main figures. The same applies to the preceding parables in 15:4-10.

Great Themes of Christian Doctrine?

The *Prodigal Son* is typically assessed as touching "the human condition like no other story."[1] It has been "the most influential on the mind of the church and of Western man as a whole," as it deals with "the great themes of the Christian Doctrine," and the most profound human questions.[2] Its influence on art and literature, too, has been immense.[3] Moreover, the parable has served as a shortcut to

---

1. Brown, "Parable," 391.
2. Via, *Parables,* 163; Bovon, *Lukas,* 41.

the historical Jesus and his context, or to a later Lukan setting.[4] Such enormous expectations have resulted in skewed perspectives on the narrative. Insofar as it provides a foundation for different dogmatic structures, religious messages, and historical reconstructions, its internal dynamics, narrative functions, and rhetorical strategy are easily obscured.[5]

In the early church the parable was used for both dogmatic and ideological purposes.[6] Dogmatic and allegorical approaches have continued to some extent in modern exegetical research.[7] All such interpretations require vivid hermeneutical imagination and run the risk of uncontrollable allegorizing, as they are hardly reflected in the parable or its framework. To be sure, an underlying theological message is obviously one of the reasons why the parable has so firm a foothold. But when, for example, the alleged conversion of the younger brother comes into focus the result resembles the old allegorical interpretation.

The principal academic concern has been historical. Besides reconstructing the parable's original form and different historical settings, scholars have sought out the judicial and sociological information reflected therein. Yet in order to reach its audience a story must be intelligible despite ignorance of technical details. For example, specific information on the juridical character of the contract between the prodigal and his foreign employer is hardly

---

3. Drury, *Parables*, 139, refers to "ballet, opera and numerous pictures and sculptures." See also Ostmeyer, "Dabeisein," 631–32; Bovon, *Lukas*, 60–65.
4. Niebuhr, "Kommunikationsebenen," 481–94; Ollilainen, *Jesus*; Räisänen, "Gentile," 1617–36.
5. For an overview see Nolland, *Luke*, 777–89; Brown, "Parable; Bovon, *Lukas,* 39–66. For example, a third son has been introduced; see Bovon, *Lukas*, 63.
6. Patristic interpretations can be divided into ethical, soteriological, ethnic, and sacramental types. Numerous later theological discussions cited this story (Bovon, *Lukas*, 53–60).
7. Most commentators engage in sophisticated theological discussions. See, for example, Hultgren, *Parables*, 86–87. Some have returned to allegorical readings: see Snodgrass, "Allegorizing," 20. Blomberg, *Interpreting*, 166, speaks of a "controlled use of allegory." Psychological, sociological, and other creative readings are presented by Snodgrass, *Stories*, 126–28.

necessary.⁸ Correspondingly, extrinsic details at the outset would make it difficult for the audience to follow the storyline.⁹

The Focus on Persuasion

An unplugged reading studies Luke 15 as a piece of persuasion in its actual context. Instead of searching for its origin and historical circumstances, or reconstructing ideological or semantic features, the main interest lies in how the three parables are designed to function in the setting provided by the immediate textual framework.

This principal shift of focus is challenging indeed. Even progressive scholars resort to allegorical explanations about who the characters in the story are, what is the symbolic meaning of the father's house or of being with the father.¹⁰ However, since the parable actually responds to criticism by the Pharisees and scribes its function as a whole is to be preferred. Jesus the Narrator does not present his theology to his audience, let alone to later Christianity. Nor is he reporting the situation with cover names. The three parables in Luke 15 function together as a single device used to exert an effect on its audience. Before reconciling the stories with any historical or theological conceptions, the analysis should start by determining the narrator's aim.¹¹ This can only be achieved by focusing on the text.¹²

---

8. Hoppe, "Gleichnis," 3, wonders whether the younger son really could demand his share of the father's property according to Jewish law, and Harrill, "Labor," studies the terms of the Prodigal's agreement with his foreign employer. If these details absorb the audience's interest, the focus of the parable is lost.
9. Wondering if ninety-nine sheep could be left in the desert, or whether a son could ask to receive his inheritance in advance, is thus irrelevant. The audience is assumed not to be offended by these details. *Contra* Kenneth Bailey, *Poet*, 161–65, who favors modern evidence against ancient documents. Cf. Nolland, *Luke*, 782.
10. For example, Ostmeyer, "Dabeisein," 629–31. Blomberg, *Parables*, 174–75, argues for "the impossibility of avoiding an allegorical interpretation" and that "Each character clearly stands for someone other than himself."

In the effort to understand the function of the chapter as a whole, old form-critical assessment of Luke 15 as a conflict discussion has attracted renewed interest.[13] Wolfgang Harnisch and Michael Wolter in particular regard it as reflecting a typical conflict between Jesus and his adversaries.[14] Although even their analyses are compromised by historical and dogmatic preoccupations, they emphasize the rhetorical and persuasive function of the text and use perspectives from modern rhetorical and literary studies, such as persuasive strategy, literary function, and rhetorical situation.[15]

According to Wolter a conflict story, a *Streitgespräch*,[16] presents antagonists who criticize the protagonist and distance themselves from him; the protagonist replies with an objection.[17] Consequently, in Luke 15 the author wants his "intended readers" to identify the Pharisees and the scribes as antagonists and Jesus as the protagonist.[18] Whereas the antagonists are the protagonist's primary audience, there may be a second level: the sinners and tax collectors mentioned in the framework, and perhaps also some disciples.[19] Jesus is thus primarily

---

11. Once again it must be emphasized that reading a parable as a means of persuasion need not imply that theological or historical questions are neglected. Yet no assessment of the underlying ideas or historical setting is possible until the persuasive nature of the story is scrutinized.
12. After all, whereas the "historical Jesus," the historical "Luke," or any "original" version of the narrative derives to a certain degree from scholarly imagination, and inherent theological principles found in the story tend to reflect the reader's own convictions, the explicit framework story and the parable provide hard data for the exegesis.
13. Albertz, *Streitgespräche*; Bultmann, *Geschichte*, 39–56; Hultgren, *Jesus*, 52–53.
14. Harnisch, *Gleichniserzählungen*, 201–31. The idea is developed further by Wolter, "Streitgespräch," 25–56.
15. Harnisch, *Gleichniserzählungen*, 230–31; Wolter, "Streitgespräch," 49, 56. In terms of understanding the function of the parable this is a major step forward compared to Berger's historically bounded rhetorical analysis ("Gattungen," 1110–24). However, Wolter, "Streitgespräch," 49–50, also uses problematic concepts such as the "intended readers" or the "intention of the author." See Wimsatt and Beardsley, "Intentional Fallacy."
16. Actually Wolter, "Streitgespräch," 26–27, dislikes *conflict story* because the reference is not to verbal activity only.
17. Bultmann, *Geschichte*, 40, 51, uses the words "Gegner," "Angriff," and "Kampf." Correspondingly, Hultgren, *Jesus*, 54–56, speaks of "attack" and "necessary polarity."
18. Wolter, "Streitgespräch," 26–27.
19. Cf. Merz, "Last und Freude," 610.

defending himself against his critics' accusations. He seeks to protect himself, at least in order to save his reputation. Perhaps he speaks for his life, wanting to avoid being stoned. Simultaneously, the story is a verbal counterattack. By demeaning the Pharisees and scribes in the eyes of the audience Jesus (and Luke) seek to dissociate the audience from persons who are labeled as villains.

Reading Luke 15 as a description of a conflict has resulted in various historical and dogmatic interpretations, mainly depending on whether the Pharisees here denote contemporary or later Pharisees, Jews in general, Jewish Christians, or some form of undeveloped or corrupted theology.[20] These interpretations lose credibility if the axiom of the hostile encounter is misleading. In fact, two observations are called for.

First, in Luke 15 the stories are explicitly addressed to the Pharisees and the scribes, not to the sinners and tax collectors, who remain in the background. The multiple rhetorical questions in the first two stories require consistent interaction by the audience, which is not allowed to disappear from the scene. To be sure, the Pharisees' and scribes' reaction is not recorded at the end of the third parable, yet even this story is aimed at the same audience. The imagined interpretation of any other group remains secondary and may obscure the existing narrative. Thus Jesus is not describing to the sinners, the tax collectors, the implied audience, let alone us, what the Pharisees and the scribes are like. Instead, he responds to what they have just said, seeking to provoke a reaction.

Second, the tone of the narrative is difficult to combine with a hostile encounter. Unlike some other stories in which Jesus faces the Pharisees, Luke 15 is astonishingly mild and positive.[21] The first

---

20. For discussion see Rau, "Auseinandersetzung," 19–28; Nolland, *Luke,* 788–89. Beavis, "Power," 3–30, also criticizes the hostile interpretations of the parables of Jesus and seeks alternative functions. Her perspective is, however, historical.

stories are full of joy, and even in the third the criticism by the elder brother is met with a gentle invitation. All this indicates that the chapter aims at something other than victory or vilification.[22]

An alternative to the traditional hostile setting is that Jesus the Narrator has an optimistic vision of the Pharisees here. I shall argue that he is honestly trying to make the Pharisees and scribes understand his own position, or even change their point of view and behavior. In order to discern his purpose, the internal structure and functions of the chapter as a whole, and all the three stories within it, must be scrutinized. Verses 11-32 will be read as an integral part of the chapter, and as a third evolutionary version of the first (vv. 4-6) and the second (vv. 8-9) parable. They follow good narratological conventions resembling a triple jump:[23] after the hop comes a step, which prepares for the jump, the aim of which is to bring home the eventual result of the action.

The Preparatory Stories

Creating a Meeting of Minds

In argumentation, the discovery of common ground (the "meeting of minds") allows the persuader to move toward more difficult, hazardous claims that, however, better suit the case at hand.[24] This is precisely what happens in Luke 15. The chapter consists of a unilateral, incomplete framework (vv. 1-3) and three subsequent

---

21. Usually the situation is tense, but Jesus says nothing offensive (5:27-32; 6:1-11; 14:1-24). In 10:25-37 the tone is polite. Thus these passages do not indicate to the Lukan audience that Jesus' attitude toward the Pharisees or scribes was negative.
22. Nolland, ibid., 788–89. Correspondingly, Räisänen, "Gentile," 1622–27, observes the mild tone, but simply states that this "causes difficulties" concerning Luke's view of the Pharisees and the scribes.
23. Jeremias, *Gleichnisse,* 202, gives several examples of this narrative technique in the New Testament, but does not mention Luke 15.
24. Perelman, *New Rhetoric,* 14–17.

stories. The three parables form an integral, sophisticated system. They are designed to work as coordinates in the given situation, where Jesus is criticized by the Pharisees and scribes. The combination of the stories is designed for persuasion.[25] The first and second parables modify the rhetorical situation and prepare the audience for the third. To this end the minor stories need to be examined first. Only then can we consider the story of the Prodigal from the point of view of the parties to the communication.

Several features concerning the structure, details, and persuasive techniques of the three stories make their differences particularly interesting. The contrast to the minor stories as regards applicability and affect is crucial for understanding the third parable. In each story the main character loses something and, after its retrieval, celebrates with friends. God is supposed to act likewise.[26] But there is a remarkable shift: in the first parables the property involved and the emotional impact connected to the lost object is rather small, but the main character's course of action is presented as self-evident.[27] In the third parable it is the opposite. There are major property and deep feelings involved, but the main character's reaction to regaining the lost one is placed in doubt. This change serves the narrator's persuasive strategy.

The two opening parables serve to effect a *meeting of minds*. The first begins with a rhetorical question referring to the audience's own attitude. This indicates the storyteller's expectation that the listeners, the Pharisees and the scribes, agree with him on this point.[28] However, their relevance in the framework situation is

---

25. Snodgrass, *Stories*, 93–94, correctly states that the whole chapter is designed for a rhetorical function.
26. For the audience, "heaven" in v. 7 and the parallel expression "God's angels" in v. 10 refer to the Deity even without prior knowledge of Jewish ways of circumventing God's name.
27. To be sure, there is a hint of *hyperbole* in the first parables as well. Calling friends together to celebrate may not be the most natural reaction to finding a sheep or a coin.
28. Tannehill, "Varieties," 109–10, discusses the function of rhetorical questions in parables.

questionable,[29] as there is a moral difference between the sheep, the coin, and the sinners. We are not told why and how the sheep was lost. We do not know if it strayed because it was stupid or whether the shepherd was careless. The question of guilt is absent. But the "sinners" in the framework are responsible and stray deliberately.

Although the third story better suits the framework, it does not display a self-evident model of behavior either. However, in light of the structure of the whole chapter the audience seems to perceive an implicit rhetorical question, corresponding to that posed to the Pharisees and the scribes in 15:4, as if Jesus had asked: "which of you would not act as the father did?" I maintain that instead of merely praising the father's action and attitude, or blaming the elder brother, or using them as pseudonyms for God and a Pharisee, Jesus the Narrator is telling the story in order to challenge his audience with this very question.

Avoiding Allegorical Identifications

The lost sheep is axiomatically interpreted as the sinners in the framework.[30] Such a trend is due to a traditional, misleading allegorical style. Due to the crucial difference concerning guilt, we cannot take for granted that the Lukan audience, let alone the audience in the framework story, is expected to associate the lost sheep with the sinners and tax collectors. Instead of finding allegories, Jülicher's principle of seeking a single point should be observed here: of course, everybody would act just as did the owner of the sheep.

The second parable not only reiterates but also crystallizes the main ideas of the first by omitting unnecessary details.[31] It lacks comment

---

29. Nolland, *Luke*, 769, acknowledges a tension between the two stories and the opening setting, since they do not actually justify Jesus' behavior.
30. For example, Nolland, *Luke*, 780.

on the reference group—coins not lost—which indicates that they are not very relevant. Moreover, the coin cannot be held responsible for its fate any more than the sheep. The idea of repentance is even less important, as a coin cannot repent.[32] The different pathos-aspect and the different proportion of the lost in the story compared with the framework also discourage any direct identification. The coin is not a sinner. However, the main idea remains: of course, everybody would act just as did the woman.

Similarly, the persons searching for the sheep or the coin have little to do with Jesus. Although even academic commentators usually regard the shepherd without hesitation as an alias of God or Jesus,[33] resembling the Good Shepherd of John 10 and his OT predecessors, we should bear in mind that there is no shepherd in the story, just an owner of the sheep.[34] Moreover, τίς ἄνθρωπος ἐξ ὑμῶν refers to the audience, namely, the Pharisees and scribes, hardly to the narrator himself. The audience in the text, let alone any original hearers of the parable, could hardly see an intertextual connection to the OT, not only because there is no shepherd in Luke 15 but because they did not know that this story would be included in the Holy Scriptures. It is highly improbable that people in ancient Palestine thought about Israel and God every time someone mentioned sheep and their owner! The distance between the main figure and God

---

31. Repetition is one of the most effective devices in persuasion, for example, in commercials. See also Lausberg, *Handbook*, §434 and Thurén, "Argumentation," 91.
32. Merz, "Last und Freude," 615–16. Since the opening word ἤ signifies that both parables share the same goal, this applies to the first one, too. Reference to μετάνοια in the explanation in v. 10 highlights the difference between the parable and the actual situation.
33. Nolland, *Luke*, 771–74; Hultgren, *Parables*, 54, 58–59.
34. *Contra* Hultgren, *Parables*, 49; Snodgrass, *Stories*, 102–9. Forbes (*God*, 122) knows that the *shepherd* is God, and Jesus "acts as the *shepherd king*," thereby introducing two new figures into the parable (my emphasis). The difference is essential: an owner is more easily identified and less likely to evoke theological connotations. Moreover, even if a shepherd would not abandon ninety-nine sheep in the desert, an owner might abandon them to the shepherds. Nolland sometimes speaks correctly about the "owner of the sheep," (*Luke*, 769, 773).

is even more obvious in the second story, in which the actor is a woman, a less typical picture of the Deity in the Jewish milieu.

The references to similar joy in heaven in v. 7 or among God's angels in v. 10 are often seen as precisely connecting the parables with the situation.[35] Nevertheless, since the innocent animal and coin are essentially different from tax collectors and sinners, the connection between vv. 7, 10 and the given situation remains obscure because the audience has not yet heard the upcoming third parable.

The Message of the Opening Stories: No Extraordinary Love

Instead of referring directly to Jesus, verses 7 and 10 suggest a striking connection with God between "one of you [Pharisees and scribes]" having sheep or the woman having a coin. A corresponding, even starker picture appears in the parable in 18:1-8, which builds on the resemblance between an unpleasant, selfish judge and the Deity. Claiming that the judge *is* God would create a blasphemous image hardly possible in early Judaism.

Luke 18:1-8 discourages any allegorical reading. Instead, one should seek its persuasive function. The reasoning resembles that of Luke 15. If so wicked a person acts appropriately when importuned, why not God? The message is not based on the judge's goodness. The train of thought goes in the opposite direction. Anyone who believes that God does *not* help those who ask implies that God is worse than a selfish judge.[36] Moreover, the parables in 11:5-13 closely resemble this *qal wahomer* reasoning: an irritated person wakened in the middle of the night, or "you evil people," are not the most virtuous individuals.

---

35. For example, Nolland, *Luke,* 776.
36. This view, of course, differs radically from that of Job or Ecclesiastes.

If even they do good, how much more certainly does God?[37] The natural aspect of God's love is stressed. Whoever claims that God does not help has the burden of proof.

According to convention the main message of 15:3-7 is the overwhelming or divine joy that results from finding the lost object.[38] I disagree. The rhetorical question implies that the abandonment of the remaining property, the search for what was lost, and the summoning of friends and neighbors to be happy are but natural reactions to what has happened. Jesus the Narrator must count on a positive answer to his rhetorical question; otherwise the stories do not work.[39] We need little information about life in ancient Palestine in order to understand that the loss and finding of a sheep or a coin were not unique events. Correspondingly, there was nothing extraordinary or divine in the man's or woman's call for joy.

The implicit alternative to their behavior is absurd. Calling friends to rejoice since no more than one percent or ten percent of the property is lost would be ridiculous or impossible. However, if vv. 7, 10 suggested that there were great joy in heaven over the righteous, this would correspond to an imaginary, foolish behavior on the part of the woman or the owner of the sheep. Thus, based on the stories, it would be blasphemous to argue that God ought to be especially joyful because of the righteous ones. The implicit rhetorical question reads: why should God act in a stupid, unnatural way if the man who lost his sheep, the woman who lost her coin, and you Pharisees and scribes act naturally?

According to a less edifying interpretation, the parables reveal "the value [God] places on *even* the least deserving."[40] On the contrary,

---

37. *Pace* Nolland, *Luke,* 870, 632.
38. For example, Jeremias, *Gleichnisse,* 135.
39. Wolter, "Streitgespräch," 35–36, 39; Snodgrass, *Stories,* 104–5; *contra* Hultgren, *Parables,* 53. Thus abandonment of the ninety-nine sheep in the desert cannot be a problem for the audience.

they refer to a general principle that nobody can deny: lost property attracts the most interest. Finding it causes greater joy than possessing even much more. By referring to the audience's own experience the parables lay the burden of proof on those who claim the opposite. They do not argue for God's overwhelming love toward sinners. They do not simply proclaim that finding them causes great joy in Heaven. Instead, they emphasize that when there is great joy in Heaven it is for the same reason that there is joy on earth: it is natural to rejoice when something lost is found, not when something is not lost.

According to Toulmin's scheme:[41]

Figure III.1

Backing: Two parables, referring to one's own attitude (vv. 4-6, 8-9) and that in heaven (vv. 7, 10)

▼

Warrant: Finding something lost causes great joy

▼

Data: The tax collectors and sinners are lost and found ▶ *Claim*: It is natural to rejoice

When verses 7 and 10 are seen as *claims*, an additional *theological* scheme can be found, as shown in figure III.2.

---

40. Emphasis supplied. Snodgrass, *Stories*, 109, continues: ". . . the God revealed by Jesus is a caring God who values even those without value and seeks them."
41. For the model see chap. 1. In brief, *data* presents the indisputable specific grounds, *warrant* the general rule whereby one moves from *data* to *claim*, *backing* displays general examples or information in order to support the *warrant*, and *rebuttal* shows when the *warrant* is invalid.

Figure III.2

Backing: General conception of God

▼

Warrant: God cannot be worse than you

▼

Data: You rejoice when the lost is found ▶ *Claim*^{1}: God too will rejoice when the lost is found

When connected to the situation at hand, this *claim* yields to additional results.

▶ *Claim*^{2}: Jesus' feasting with sinners is accepted by God

▶ *Claim*^{3}: The audience ought to join the feast

Claim¹ and Claim² are connected with an implicit warrant such as "joy implies acceptance" and "what suits God must suit the Pharisees."

Redefining the Case

When the third parable, vv. 11b-32, begins, the implied audience is led in a specific direction by the two previous stories. The rhetorical situation is thereby modified. Rather than facing criticism head-on, Jesus the Narrator has modified the subject in order to mitigate the critical atmosphere and invite the audience to a positive interaction. Members of the audience are expected to agree on what causes communal joy on earth as in heaven. Remembering this principle may help to overcome the obvious shortcoming of the third parable:

unlike the case with the woman or the owner of the sheep, the father's behavior is not his only option.

Although the characters in the parable are not identical with the individuals depicted in the framework story, the success of the story as a whole derives from certain connotations. On some level the audience ought to identify Jesus' fellow guests and the lost sheep or coin. Their miserable status is by no means questioned or their morals defended. On the contrary, they are labeled with the word ἀπολωλός/ἀπόλλυμι, like the sheep (vv. 4, 6), the coin (vv. 8-9), and the son (v. 17). This is a cunningly persuasive move on two grounds. First, Jesus indicates that he does not accept the sinners' morals, but shares the view of his critics. Such solidarity with the audience is important for persuasion. However, there is a catch: he hints that the sinners had lost their former high status. Thus Jesus is not only eating with some immoral individuals but celebrating their return.

In rhetoric this move is used in *status definitionis*.[42] By making use of the audience's zeal for moral condemnation it subtly entices the audience members to modify their view of the sinners. This shift is exploited in the third story. After the preceding parables it is easy for the audience to accept that the Prodigal, representing the sinners, is not only another wrongdoer but also a son of his father even when absent.[43]

The Third Story: Applying the Principle

As the applicability of the principle presented in the two stories is unclear, the main persuasive burden lies on the third. An expanded

---

42. Lausberg, *Handbook*, §232.
43. This is typical of Luke: similarly, in 19:9-10, Jesus describes Zacchaeus as "a son of Abraham" who was lost.

version (vv. 11b-24) of the first two stories is not, of itself, sufficient for the purpose. In the climax (vv. 25-32) the narrator faces the problem crucial in the framework: the responsibility and guilt of the lost. Not until then does the parable meet the criticism of the Pharisees and scribes.

As regards persuadability, the close connection to the problematic situation constitutes an obstacle. Unlike the sheep and the coin, the younger brother is himself guilty of becoming lost. This makes the father's behavior less acceptable. In order to meet the challenge, the parable builds on the pattern of the previous stories, which is already assumed to be accepted by the audience. However, it has to excel the preceding stories in every other respect. Thus the text is longer with more details; more property and emotion are involved. Both the absolute and the relative value of the lost is greater. Yet even in the introduction (vv. 11b-24) the narrator does not provide an explanation of why an individual who chose to be lost ought to be accepted. The reference to *two* sons in the beginning, however, requires consequences that lack parallels in the previous stories, and it is here that the issue is eventually discussed explicitly.

For the function of the story as a whole it is crucial to determine what manner of impressions the characters are designed to arouse among the audience. Both the elder brother and the father are exceptional: the former lacks a counterpart in the previous stories and is therefore a key figure in the applicability of all the stories to the framework situation. The father, in turn, is a more complex figure than his predecessors, the man and the woman.

The Father as a Pharisee

Scholars disagree about whether or not the father refers to God.[44] There are several factors that discourage the implied audience from making such an identification.

First, the story explicitly dissociates the father from God.[45] The preliminary stories have already presented aliases for God: heaven (v. 7) and angels of God (v. 10). In the third story the transcendence of God vis-à-vis the father on the farm is repeatedly emphasized: "I have sinned against heaven and before you" (vv. 18, 21).

Second, although God is often personified as "father" by Luke and in the Holy Scriptures, the text-internal recipients, the Pharisees and scribes, are not aware of the future canonical status of this story. Therefore an automatic connection between the man who is called "father" by his sons and God is unlikely. As was the case with the sheep, it cannot be proven that every time an ἄνθρωπος with sons was mentioned in early Jewish texts, reference was to the Deity.

The third argument carries the most weight. In the structure of Luke 15 the role of ἄνθρωπός τις in the third story corresponds to that of τίς ἄνθρωπος in the first and even τίς γυνή in the second. As the recipients are explicitly invited to see themselves in the place of the man who lost a sheep, and almost as clearly to identify with the woman who misplaced a drachma, their most natural approach to the third story is to identify with the man who lost a son.[46] Indeed, the honorable farmer was an even better target for identification

---

44. For example, Hultgren, *Parables*, 86: ". . . the father clearly represents God"; Wolter, "Streitgespräch," 38–39: ". . . jeder Hörer sofort wusste, dass mit ihr von Gott die Rede ist." But Nolland, *Luke*, 784, correctly notices: "The presence of God in the story line is a reminder that we must let the parable have its own integrity as story and not to simply identify the father with God."

45. *Pace* Harnisch, *Gleichniserzählungen*, 205.

46. *Contra* Kenneth Bailey, *Peasant*, 154, according to whom "the Pharisaic audience is led to identify with the older son, not the father."

for the Pharisees and scribes than a woman or an owner of sheep. Each parable shares the same situation, structure, and mode of appeal: would you not act as did the person in the story?[47]

The most obvious reason for leaving the plea implicit in the third story is that it contains one weakness lacking in the earlier parables. The father's reaction is not as obvious as the owner's or the woman's. Actually, one may assume that the man had several options. In other words, the audience could have answered the question "Who of you would not act like the ἄνθρωπος?" in several ways, varying from total rejection to quiet acceptance of the Prodigal. Nor was his actual choice as impossible as is sometimes claimed.[48] Corresponding behavior is mentioned even in the Scriptures (Isa. 49:15).[49] A parallel section earlier in Luke 11:11-13 also refers to the parent's unfailing love. In both cases such an attitude and behavior are so natural that a rhetorical question ensues.

Surprisingly, the narrator increases the difficulty of accepting the father's attitude by reporting his hyperbolic behavior. He not only accepts the son back but also runs to meet him and organizes an extravagant feast.[50] This immoderate idea may provoke a reaction among the audience: neither we nor God would ever go so far. Nevertheless, from the point of view of the narrator any strong reaction by the audience may serve his strategy. When they move according to his stimuli he thereby induces them to follow his lead. He emulates a good tennis-player, obliging his audience to run from one corner to another.

---

47. If, however, the father is axiomatically seen as representing God, the parable merely postulates that God acts in the way depicted. This radically diminishes its persuasive force and the direction of the earlier parables is lost. Only by continuing the "logic" inherent in the previous stories can the audience be persuaded to think likewise even in the third.
48. See Nolland, *Luke*, 784–85.
49. "Can a woman forget her nursing child and have no compassion on the son of her womb? Even these may forget, but I will not forget you."
50. Many commentators observe that running is inappropriate behavior in an old man; see Hultgren, *Parables*, 78 n. 37. Yet the father was probably in his forties and thus not very old.

The reference to a feast serves the *pathos* as well, but it is hazardous, as it closely resembles the annoying situation in the framework. Yet this is necessary in order to indicate the relevance of the story—and thereby of the preceding accounts as well—to the situation. Several other details also link this parable to the framework. Like the sinners and the tax collectors, the Prodigal is unequivocally deserving of his fate: he, too, acted of his own volition, and finally, yet significantly, in both cases there is no proof of any real repentance.[51] Yet both sets of sinners are rewarded with a banquet. The size of the feast may be another overstatement if it is thought to resemble the annoying situation in the framework.

To conclude: although the narrator has paved the way for persuasion with the preceding stories and now presents a final version with many further advantages, he cannot count on the audience's positive reaction. In the first part of the third parable the persuasion depends on the listeners' identification with the father. He is depicted as an honorable and sympathetic figure. Although his generosity toward the Prodigal is by no means obligatory, the narrator challenges the audience to approve it and to recognize that the father acted rightly. In any case he followed the principle emphasized in the previous stories. Moreover, the son had already been punished abroad. As a third aspect, the father has *patria potestas*. The story makes an implicit plea to the listener: would you not act as he did? Thereby, if the persuasion succeeds, the father "is" the listener, in this case a Pharisee or a scribe.

---

51. For discussion see Ollilainen, *Jesus*, 103. Despite the later interpreters' dogmatic needs, in the parable the action of the son is prompted by hunger, not repentance, and the sincerity of his speech is not attested.

The Father as God

Although the farmer in the story explicitly stays on the immanent level, an implicit theological interpretation by the addressees may be postulated.[52] Following the explanations of the shorter stories (vv. 7, 10), the narrator implies that heaven/God's angels/God acts like the father in the story. Although this is not the primary leitmotif, the earlier explanations lead the audience to expect that even here a similar course of events would ensue in heaven or among God's angels, both circumlocutions for God. Thus the third story, too, not only describes what is thought to be good human behavior but also claims that God cannot be worse than the ordinary people referred to in the chapter. If the listeners as fathers would act like the farmer in the story, so too does God. He accepts a returning sinner without hesitation or demanding proof of repentance. Instead, he is filled with joy. Yet the reference to God remains implicit and vague.

The Father as Jesus

It is often observed that the father emulates Jesus in the framework.[53] If this is how the audience should hear the parable, it points toward high Christology. Jesus thereby adopts the role of God, who alone has authority to forgive sinners. According to this interpretation the role of the elder brother is reserved for Jesus' critics. However, associating the narrator with the Deity involves heavy dogmatizing of the story. This hardly represents the primary mode of understanding the story within its textual framework, where it is told orally.

Instead of far-fetched theology, we need an alternative interpretation that is less dogmatic and makes more sense in the

---

52. *Contra* Harnisch, *Gleichniserzählungen,* 205.
53. E. g., Noyen, "Freude," 394, argues that Jesus identifies himself with the father.

context. A brief version of the chapter could read as follows: Jesus feasts with sinners. When criticized, he replies: "You would act likewise on similar occasions, after retrieving a lost sheep, a lost coin, or a lost son. Attitudes to returning sinners cannot be worse in heaven. Therefore we should feast with them, too." Thus understood, the parable functions as Jesus' answer to his critics instead of making daring theological statements. References to heaven need be no more than additional arguments to explain Jesus' behavior and invite the audience to join the feast.

Who Is the Elder Brother?

The tension created by the father's identity, role, and behavior requires an explanation. Something different, a surprise, is needed. This exigency is met by introducing a new character, only hinted at in the exordium of the third story. In order to understand the culmination of the story it is crucial to specify the function of the elder brother. The connotations of his character are closely related to the main thrust of the persuasion in the chapter as a whole.

The elder brother is traditionally identified with the Pharisees and scribes, since he complains about feasting with sinners as do these groups in the framework.[54] However, recent scholarship has indicated a weakness in this standard interpretation: the father does not address his elder son as hostile. Indeed, his statement, "all that is mine is yours" (v. 31), is difficult to relate to Jesus' adversaries.[55] It has

---

54. For example, Hultgren, *Parables,* 82. Lüdemann, *Jesus,* 365, has a slight modification: "The older brother represents a Jewish person who objects to God's compassion."
55. Wolter, "Streitgespräch," 50–53, recognizes the problems, but refers to ancient rhetorical categories in order to prove that the elder brother nevertheless stands for the Pharisees. However, the reference builds on a typical misconception of all rhetoric as *judicial,* seeking to judge past events. For the correct use of rhetorical genera see Kennedy, *New Testament,* 19.

been argued that his attitude is far too mild to be attributed to the historical Pharisees or to those discussed by Luke.[56]

Moreover, the persuasive dynamic of the story itself dissociates the elder brother from the Pharisees and scribes of the framework. If Jesus is appealing to them to modify their attitudes and behavior—precisely as does the father to his son in the story—simply blaming or mocking them hardly leads to the desired result. Although later Christian readers tend to label these Pharisees and scribes as the elder brother, they themselves would hardly identify with him. Who, indeed, would wish to be designated as the villain of the piece? If the elder brother is directly connected to the given audience, this means that they are abandoned as the target of the discourse and the story is aimed exclusively at its Lukan readers. Then it simply proclaims the inferiority of the Pharisees and scribes and the superiority of Jesus. This suits later interpretations and allegories in which the story describes the unacceptable attitudes of the Jews or the Jewish Christians to Gentile Christians. However, such an allegory does not fit the text as it stands. There we have a text-internal audience, which must be preferred to any hypothetical, reconstructed one. Thus it is crucial to understand how the Pharisees and scribes in the framework are thought to understand the story.

The setting of the story is ambiguous, as the elder brother is depicted with unusual attributes. He is not a stereotypical villain. Instead, he is presented as a morally exemplary individual. He did not abandon his father, he did not squander his fortune, and he did not follow a morally or religiously unacceptable way of life. Thus he, too, attracts the audience's sympathy to some extent, just as does the father. Structurally, the elder brother is on a par with the ninety-nine sheep and the nine coins. Those are not denigrated in the earlier

---

56. Räisänen, "Gentile," tries to solve the problem by suggesting that the figure refers to later Jewish Christians. However, this explanation wrongly imports external data into the storyline.

stories, and they are compared in the interpretations (vv. 7, 10) with the *righteous* people.

What, then, is wrong with the elder brother? He does not seem to share the belief emphasized in the previous stories: discovery of the lost causes more joy than knowledge that the rest are safe. In those stories a different point of view was regarded as unnatural. However, in the third story the situation is less straightforward. In terms of rhetoric, the first part of the parable, like its two predecessors, functions as *argumentatio*, providing positive persuasion for the *propositio*. The latter remains somewhat obscure, but vv. 7, 10 include a suggestion. The extra section (vv. 25-32), which lacks correspondence in the earlier parables, serves as a classical *refutatio*, where the possible criticism or objections of the audience to the *argumentatio* are treated.[57] Correspondingly, in the classical Toulminian argumentation scheme the elder brother represents *rebuttal*, which adds a critical viewpoint:

---

57. For the terminology, see Lausberg, *Handbook,* §§289, 346, 348, 430.

Figure III.3

Backing: General rules for behavior (ἔδει, v. 32a)

▼

Warrant: Finding something lost causes great joy

▼

Data: Your lost brother is found (v. 32b) ▶ *Claim*: You should join the feast (v. 32a)

▲

Rebuttal: Unless the Lost is guilty of getting lost (v. 30)

The elder brother thereby expresses a reasonable second opinion, which possesses validity. To make him play the part of such a critic does not automatically make him the villain of the piece. In this sense he offers Jesus' critics a good target for identification.

The audience (both that in the framework and the Lukan recipients) faces an ambiguous situation. Its members are expected to sympathize with both the father and the elder brother. This dilemma ultimately reflects the actual situation in the framework. By enticing his addressees to this point the narrator may well have undermined their fixed opinions and so prepared them for a change of view. The elements that make the elder brother an unwanted role model refer rather to *pathos* and *ethos* than *logos*: first to social perspective, and second to his personal character.

First, the elder brother is a killjoy, as he refuses to share in the great rejoicing of the father and the servants. The contrast is sharp when the joy is compared with the previous calls to rejoicing by the owner of the sheep and the woman. However, even more than the negative attitude, its practical outcome hardly finds favor with any listener. Irrespective of whether the audience fully accepts the father's solution of arranging a feast, the fact remains that a feast is held, and the elder brother intends to stand aloof. Luke uses a negative answer to an invitation as an example for discourteous and bad behavior.[58] Exclusion from a party is presented as the worst fate imaginable, often combined with "gnashing of teeth."[59] Refusing to attend the banquet is a stereotypical image of a gloomy destiny in a society where such festivities were of great importance. This renders such an individual an unlikely target of identification.

Second, even the bitter solution of separating from the social group was defensible if one was in the right morally or spiritually.[60] Why could not the elder brother be a martyr who rejects so much for the sake of honor? There seems to be another element in his character that finally makes him unacceptable as a hero. The problem lies in his *ethos*, namely, his personal credibility. The elder brother not only opposes his father and wants to spoil his pleasure. He is angry and refuses to enter. The language he uses is telling: "*So many years* I have been slaving away [δουλεύω][61] for you, I have *never* disobeyed your command, but *never* have you given me *even a young goat*." One can almost see the grown man stamp his feet in anger, and the tears in his eyes as he speaks to his father. The hyperbolic language, with the repetition of the word *never*, emphasizing both his merits and how little he has gained, all point in the same direction: this response is childish.[62]

---

58. Luke 14:15-23. In Matt. 22:1-6 both the refusal and the host's reaction are fiercer, but this may be due to Matthew's theology.
59. See Luke 13:28. Matthew specializes on this image: Matt. 8:12; 13:42, 50; 22:13; 24:51; 25:30. As with all parables, the exclusion from the banquet must function in itself as a harsh punishment even without regard for its theological or eschatological interpretations.
60. Cf. Ps. 1:1; Heb. 13:12-13.
61. Translation by Hultgren, *Parables*, 70–71, who argues that this colloquial translation reflects an angry son's outburst to his father.

This whining boy is not an adult man. The elder brother assumes the role of a small child before his father. The father's response, referring to the son's role as a sovereign, responsible landowner, an adult Jew, merely highlights the son's pitiable, if not ridiculous character. By his action and his words the elder brother loses face in front of his father, the servants, and the two audiences of the story. One can hardly overestimate the effect of such a humiliation in the cultural context.

The story does not allow the elder brother a more mature censure of the father's solution. Thus any criticism is condemned not only as leading to a socially undesirable result but also as puerile. By having this unacceptable character represent a critical attitude toward the father's behavior, the narrator makes it difficult for anybody to think likewise. When assessing his behavior in a negative light they simultaneously reject the opinions he represents. From the point of view of persuasion this is an unfair but effective move, recommended by classical rhetoricians.[63]

Thus the persuasion in the story is built on the *impossibility* of identifying the elder brother with the Pharisees and scribes.[64] In the first parable the audience is invited to be sympathetic to the owner of the sheep, whose attitude is the only acceptable one. This invitation is reiterated in the second parable. In the third the most natural target for identification continues to be the father who suffers a loss but is joyful in the end. This positive *argumentatio* is completed with a *refutatio*: having an opposite opinion would involve resemblance

---

62. Such absolute language is typical for children. "I'll leave home for*ever* and will *never ever* come back! And don't you forget to videotape *Batman*."
63. Above I have assessed vv. 25-32 as *refutatio*. Lausberg, *Handbook*, §902.4, argues: "...conceptual irony is a *sermocinatio*... from the thought-world of the opposing party.... Ultimately, its technically appropriate place is in *refutatio*... where it serves to represent the opponent's point of view." See also Thurén, "Argumentation," 90–92.
64. Harnisch, *Gleichniserzählungen*, 216–17, also wonders why anybody would identify with the elder brother.

to the pathetic elder brother deserving only pity. Since he alone condemns the father, his opinions too are to be rejected.

The persuasive strategy in Luke 15 is gentler and simultaneously more subtle than if the narrator merely sought to win over an enemy. Unlike the sharper images of Jesus in the other gospels, the Jesus of our Lukan framework story has not abandoned his hope concerning the Pharisees (at least for now); he is eager to convince them. His critics are not humiliated, since they are not obliged to "be" the elder brother but are invited to choose another role model. Either they can accept the role of the father, who is presented as the "hero" of the story, or they are led to believe that in a corresponding situation they would not act as did the wretched elder brother. Thus a modern interpreter must accept certain dynamics of the characters in the parable. The father is not Jesus, or God, or a Pharisee, yet in some respects there is hope they may share the father's role. The elder brother is not a Pharisee, yet in some respects they hold common opinions. This is because the goal of the parable is not description but persuasion.

The Punch Line as the Key to Persuasion

The story and thereby the whole chapter does not conclude with the elder brother's reaction but with the father's second answer. Its position at the end signals that it is the weightiest statement in the chapter, drawing conclusions from everything that has been said. Especially in this final plea the audience can hear the appeal by Jesus the Narrator to his critics. Just as the father seeks to persuade his son, so the narrator seeks to persuade his critics.

The father does not criticize the excellent record adduced by the elder brother, yet there is covert criticism in the expression "all that is mine is yours."[65] The answer refers to the son's hyperbolic statement in v. 29. Although the son has fulfilled perfectly the requirements set for a slave, as presented in 17:7-10, he has thereby rejected his proper role as the heir of the estate. This means that he has assumed too low a social status. He has not realized his opportunities of feasting and enjoying the property.[66] Thus the father's answer contains a critical tone aimed at his way of life: the elder brother has no wish to enjoy life!

The father does not ask the elder brother to join in any supernatural, unearthly love for the Prodigal but refers to what is a normal, appropriate, and suitable course of action in the situation. The household should (ἔδει) celebrate since the lost family member is found. In light of the framework story the verb suggests that feasting with the tax collectors and sinners was in Jesus' own eyes only natural behavior: they too are sons of Abraham (cf. 19:9). He invites the Pharisees and scribes not only to accept this but to do likewise, to participate in the feast.

Yet the structure of the chapter indicates that the audience is, by implication, hard to persuade. Whereas the two introductory stories refer to what is self-evident, the third parable needs to postulate the same principle explicitly. In addition, Jesus must appeal to the *pathos*-effect and ridicule the only individual who stands aloof, thereby making him an impossible target of identification. Although the third story meets the criticism in the framework far better than the first two, the questionable persuasive devices used therein reveal the weakness of the case. However, problematic argumentation may well produce successful theology.

---

65. Historical studies of the contingency of the son's ownership of the house during the father's lifetime are perhaps not the best means of discerning how the Narrator's and the Author's audiences are expected to perceive his message to his son. For discussion see Nolland, *Luke*, 782–83.
66. His legal rights to the property are referred to as self-evident by the father in v. 31.

The persuasion in vv. 11–32 can be presented according to Toulmin's system. See figure III.4:

Figure III.4

Backing: The parable in vv. 11-32, referring to emotions and general rules of behavior, and implying God's attitude

▼

Warrant: The return of a lost relative causes great joy, irrespective of his guilt [or: "Love covers all transgressions" (Prov. 10:12; 1 Pet. 4:8; Jas. 5:20)]

▼

Data: The sinners and tax collectors are lost and found ▶ *Claim*: You should join the feast

If all the three persuasive structures in chapter 15 are combined (Figures III. 2, III. 3, and III. 4), we can display the total argumentation as shown in figure III.5.

Figure III.5

Backing: Two parables in vv. 4-10

▼

Warrant: Finding something lost causes great joy

▼

Data: The sinners and tax collectors are lost and found ▶ *Claim*: You should join the feast

▲ ◀ *Counter-Rebuttal*: (Prov. 10:12) & *Backing*: The parable in vv. 11-32

Rebuttal: Unless the lost people are guilty (v. 30)

Figure III.6

Claim[1]: (above)/*Data*: It is natural for compassionate people to celebrate returning sinners

▼ ◀ *Warrant*: God cannot be worse than compensae people

Claim[2]: God celebrates returning sinners

▼ ◀ *Warrant*: God's example is important to you (Lev. 11:44)

Claim[3]: You should join the celebration

The fame of the parable of the *Prodigal Son* is based on its trajectories in religion and art. I hope that reading it as persuasion in its immediate context will give fresh air to the farmer and his sons. The story and even its predecessors are less theological than usually thought. But any good story is worth telling again, and I hope new options have emerged. No matter how the parable is recycled in search of the historical Jesus or Lukan theology, in Christian doctrine, literature, and art, the results should not contradict its primary function in the text. Luke 15 is not, however, a self-contained discourse. The theme will be continued in Luke 16, as will be seen.

4

The Unjust Steward (16:1-9)

The simple, vivid story of the *Unjust Steward* in Luke 16:1-9 is generally, albeit surprisingly, assessed as "the most difficult of the parables."[1] Its original meaning is either considered to be completely lost,[2] so that Luke too was perplexed,[3] or the parable is thought to convey a complex message that is hard to perceive at first reading. The reason for the bafflement is obvious: by presenting his hearers with a deceitful man as a role model Jesus appears to commend immoral behavior. For most religious and academic readers this is unacceptable. Moreover, it is difficult to combine the unethical parable with its extension in 16:10-13, which represents high morality. Thus "a bewildering number of explanations exist,"[4] most of which attempt to save the steward's or at least Jesus' reputation.

Typically the solutions are created by omitting material from the text, by modifying its expressions, or by adding to it novel

---

1. Landry and May, "Honor," 287; Ireland, "History," 293–94, referring to several commentators.
2. Bultmann, *Geschichte*, 199.
3. For discussion see Schellenberg, "Master," 264 n. 1.
4. Snodgrass, *Stories*, 401.

information of which the Lukan audience could scarcely have been aware. Thus it would be interesting to hear the parable as it stands, without alterations, with the ears of the audience implied by the text.

In what follows I shall first discuss the most typical explanations and then suggest an unplugged reading of the parable, following the guidelines presented in chapter 1. The story will be scrutinized from the implied recipients' viewpoint, without incorporating material unknown to them. I hope thereby to reach a simple, accurate meaning and function of the parable and its embedding narrative.

In Defense of Jesus

One can hardly deny that for any first-time reader it appears that the steward deceived his master. He used his master's property without permission, for his own benefit. This criminal action is not a detail that could be overlooked in pursuit of the point of the story, as the narrator devotes most of the parable to a careful documentation of the details of the fraud. The steward's guilt appears to be confirmed by the explicit definition of him as ὁ οἰκονόμος τῆς ἀδικίας (v. 8a). It must come as a surprise that the steward's behavior is then praised, either by his master or by Jesus. Moreover, Jesus tells the audience to do likewise: to use μαμωνᾶς τῆς ἀδικίας in a crisis situation in order to win necessary friends (v. 9). Does Jesus not thereby become the steward's accomplice?

The existing parable is only intelligible if one accepts the idea that Jesus actually incites his disciples to fraudulent behavior, but only a few commentators do so. First, the idea seems incompatible with the general picture of Jesus in Luke, let alone his public image in Christianity. Second, the following verses, 16:10-13, emphasize a diametrically opposite attitude to one's master and his property. Third, even if theft was recommended in vv. 1-9, the parable and its framework hint at a more theological version with reference to sons of light (v. 8), eternal tents (v. 9), and God (v. 13). But the recommendation of a deceitful attitude in theological matters would be equally unacceptable.

Thus most scholars attempt to exonerate the steward and/or Jesus. Several ingenious alternative solutions have been devised. Unfortunately, most of them would be incomprehensible at least for the Lukan audience, perhaps also for the hearers of his Jesus, as they are based either on information not provided by the Lukan text (in chapter 16 or earlier) or they are derived from a curtailed narrative. Efforts to save the reputation of Jesus and his suspect hero can also be based on some rare, artificial explanation of the central concepts that hardly represents a straightforward understanding of the text.

Although the exegetical explanations of the parable of the steward have been called a "jungle,"[5] most of them neatly follow the classification of *status* in Roman court rhetoric.[6] The steward, and his inventor, Jesus, appear to be accused of committing or recommending illegal acts, and the commentators serve as their attorneys. Their different strategies for exonerating the clients follow the classical scheme.

Status Coniecturae:
The Crime is not Factual—Non fecit.[7]

According to the classical explanation Jesus did not advocate the fraudulent use of others' property.[8] The steward may have been a rogue, but this lacks significance since the story focuses narrowly

---

5. Krämer, *Rätsel*, 27.
6. See Lausberg, *Handbook*, §§91, 85–90.
7. Lausberg, *Handbook*, §85.
8. For discussion see Ireland, "History," 295–305; Landry and May, "Honor," 292–93; Snodgrass, *Stories*, 407.

on how quick and determined he was. A similar attitude is then recommended for the audience, either in financial contexts or in the imminent eschatological crisis. Nothing else in the parable matters.⁹ This interpretation is to be commended for its avoidance of allegory. Indeed, not all the details in a parable will correspond to reality. Instead one must seek a single principle or a crucial message. This interpretation cannot be rejected because immorality is involved, for several other characters in Jesus' parables should be censured on similar grounds. For example, the judge in 18:1-8 is not a moral hero, yet he may reflect God in a particular light.¹⁰ This classic explanation is typically built on three suspicious operations:

1. The text is modified by the excision of v. 8 onward, since dishonest behavior is there praised.¹¹ Verse 9 is even more fatal for this interpretation, since there Jesus shows how the audience should apply the parable.¹² He urges his hearers to make friends with μαμωνᾶς τῆς ἀδικίας. Irrespective of how this expression is explained, it diverges from the classic interpretation. Since the steward tried to win friends by the illegal use of his master's property it is most natural to understand the commandment in v. 9 as referring to a similar course of action. The means whereby the friends are won over is in focus, not the speed—although no hesitation is allowed in v. 9 either. As any imitation of the steward's crime is inconceivable for later interpreters with high ethical standards, they must censor the verse. Thus this classic interpretation is based not on the Lukan text but on the scholars' own reconstruction of the parable.

---

9. Jülicher, *Gleichnisreden*, 2: 510–11; Jeremias, *Gleichnisse*, 30–33 represent this interpretation with different nuances.
10. *Contra* Kloppenborg, "Master," esp. p. 478. Schellenberg, "Master," 266–67, refers to 18:1-8 *Judge*, 11:5-8 *Friend at Midnight*, and 10:25-37 *Samaritan* as morally problematic parables.
11. E. g., Jeremias, *Gleichnisse*, 30–33.
12. For discussion see Snodgrass, *Stories*, 411.

THE UNJUST STEWARD (16:1-9)

2. The heart of the parable, the meticulous description of the steward's plan to survive and its execution, is disregarded. Instead, the implicit idea of his rapidity is lifted as the main issue.[13]

3. Central terminology is given a surprising interpretation. If v. 8 is accepted, (a) κύριος changes its meaning from the rich man (16:3, 5a, 5b) to Jesus, and (b) ἀδικία, referring to the steward, does not involve a negative epithet. Are these semantic solutions plausible?

a. κύριος

Does κύριος refer to the rich man of v. 1, or is he Jesus the Narrator? Theoretically both options are plausible, as in Luke the word can refer to human beings as well as to Jesus or God. However, there are no clear parallels indicating reference to Jesus at the end of the parable.[14] Thus almost all modern scholars favor the reference to the rich man within the story. Ryan Schellenberg, however, recently attempted to show that the other option is still feasible, and claims that the audience could not know for sure.[15]

For identifying the κύριος, and for interpreting the parables in general, the implied audience's understanding is decisive. Which meaning is more convincing? If the word is ambiguous for them, this must be deliberate, as Schellenberg argues. In antiquity such a deliberate ambiguity was rare, but it cannot be ruled out.[16] Alternatively, the meaning of κύριος is so obvious that Luke did not

---

13. Donahue, *Gospel*, 164, rightly rejects this reading as far too imaginative.
14. Contra Jeremias, *Gleichnisse,* 45, who refers to Luke 18:6. That verse contains a direct quotation from Jesus, indicating how to understand the parable. In 16:8 there is no quotation in any case, just a narrative voice. For further discussion see Snodgrass, *Stories*, 412–13; Landry and May, "Honor," 288–89; Nolland, *Luke,* 800.
15. Schellenberg, "Master," 265–68.
16. I have argued that in 1 Peter ambiguity functions as a rhetorical device (Thurén, *Strategy*, 164–76).

consider a further explanation necessary, as he was certain of a correct understanding.

The rich man, ἄνθρωπός τις, is called κύριος throughout the parable both by the steward and by Jesus the Narrator; he has no other titles. When the word occurs for the fourth time in v. 8 the audience is given no reason to think that its meaning has suddenly changed to alternative 2.[17]

Verse	Speaker	κύριος
3	steward	rich man
5a	Jesus	rich man
5b	steward	rich man
8 alt 1 / 2	Jesus / Luke	rich man / Jesus

There is no sign that Jesus' parable ends without a solution or punch line. On the contrary, the opening setting—the κύριος's dismissal of the steward when informed of his actions (vv. 2-3)—and the steward's exceptional operation (vv. 5-7) create high expectations for the conclusion. What will happen to him? Does he succeed? How does the κύριος react when he is informed about the steward's further crime?

As a part of Jesus' parable, v. 8 serves as typical surprising climax, or punch line, as required by the narrative conventions. This time, instead of the expected response, the master starts to praise (ἐπῄνεσεν, aorist) the steward. While this is indeed a surprising reaction, it should not therefore be rejected; on the contrary.[18] Most good stories

---

17. Verse 8b does not befit the master. However, it serves well as the opening of Jesus' explanation of the parable, even better than Luke's editorial comment, as suggested by Nolland, *Luke*, 800.
18. *Contra* Jeremias, *Gleichnisse,* 45; Kenneth Bailey, *Poet*, 86–110; Kloppenborg, "Master"; Landry and May, "Honor." The explanations are even harder to accept than the commendation. *Pace* Schellenberg, "Master," 266, who rightly rejects attempts to make the master's commendation easier to understand.

and anecdotes end with a surprise. If the surprises are censored, little is left of the parables of Jesus. However, from the audience's point of view, after this surprise an explanation by Jesus[19] (8b onward) is more than welcome.

To sum up: like most parables and anecdotes, this story requires a conclusion, which includes a surprise. This unexpected turn is probably the key to the message of the parable. Since v. 8a meets these requirements, and there is no reason for the audience abruptly to change their understanding of κύριος in this context, the word must refer to the rich man, as in the preceding verses.

b. ἀδικία

To what does the Semitic genitive construction in v. 8 (ὁ οἰκονόμος τῆς ἀδικίας) and in v. 9 (μαμωνᾶς τῆς ἀδικίας) refer? How should the adjective ἄδικος in vv. 10, 11 be understood? Does the κύριος explicitly state that the steward did wrong, and does Jesus urge his readers to act likewise?

John Nolland suggests that on the basis of vv. 8b-9 ἀδικία already means *worldly* in v. 8a.[20] However, for the audience this is an impossible interpretation; τῆς ἀδικίας of itself means *of unrighteousness*. The narrator has just described an unrighteous act by his protagonist. When he then calls him a "steward of unrighteousness" it is natural to understand the word as referring to his action. Even if in the following verses the word had another meaning, the audience could not know it at this point.

---

19. Nolland argues that the historical Jesus would never contrast a son of this age and sons of light (*Luke*, 801), but the comparison was not typical of early Christianity either (Snodgrass, *Stories*, 723 n. 119).
20. Nolland, *Luke*, 801.

Klyne Snodgrass presents a modified version of the classic interpretation by adding the reference to money. He admits that the steward is guilty in v. 8.[21] Thereby he rightly regards vv. 8b-9 as an integral part of the story and acknowledges that the parable deals with property, not simply quick action.[22] Then, however, Snodgrass denies that Jesus recommends a similarly problematic behavior to his audience. This he does by claiming that ἀδικία in the following verse abruptly changes its meaning to "something that tends to corrupt," so that μαμωνᾶς τῆς ἀδικίας means "money which so easily leads you astray."[23] An even more bizarre suggestion regards ὁ οἰκονόμος τῆς ἀδικίας as a reference to an "'eschatological realm' characterized by ἀδικία."[24] How would the audience, listening to the detailed financial procedure, suddenly arrive at this translation?

To understand ἀδικία in very different ways in vv. 8 and 9—first referring to money gained by corrupt means, then to money that tends to corrupt—is difficult to swallow. It yields an illogical message: the parable describes how the steward used his *master's* money for his own benefit; likewise the hearers should use their *own* money (which can be dangerous) for their own benefit.

It is most natural for the hearers to understand the same word in two consecutive sentences in the same way. The meaning can hardly vary widely without any signal. "Deceitful" or "unrighteous" fits all the four cases: the steward was deceitful, he made friends by means of deception, and so should the audience. This corresponds to the basic meaning of the word. In the parallel verses 16:11-12 μαμωνᾶς τῆς ἀδικίαςhas as an alternative meaning, "other people's property," which emphasizes a specific nuance in the deception—the very same nuance displayed in the parable: the steward won friends

---

21. Snodgrass, *Stories*, 721 n. 96.
22. Ibid., 414.
23. Ibid., 415.
24. Schellenberg, "Master," 279 n. 35, refers to several scholars who favor such an interpretation.

via abuse of other people's property, and this tactic is recommended for the audience, too, according to v. 9. No other meanings need be inferred. They are only artificial attempts to solve the major problem inherent in the story: How on earth can Jesus urge his followers to be deceitful?

Several other explanations seek to exonerate Jesus by neglecting essential features of the parable. For example, one can claim that the text is corrupt and then change the story line in order to modify the interpretation. Thus Douglas Parrott argues that originally the master would *not* commend the steward.[25] Another option is to resort to an imaginary Aramaic original in order to change the story.[26] Thereby Luke would be a simple copyist without editorial control of his material. N. T. Wright reads the story as an eschatological warning to Israel, represented by the steward. This interpretation excludes most of the parable, only the beginning being preserved.[27]

All these readings reflect one of the most effective persuasive devices in Roman court rhetoric, *narratio*. There the course of action was presented in terms of manipulation.[28] Correspondingly, it is easy to explain a difficult parable if one is allowed to alter the story line and modify the text. However, such an interpretation has no value for understanding the actual parable.

Status Definitionis:
The Name of the Deed is Misleading—Fecit, sed aliud.[29]

Another option for exonerating Jesus is to admit that he seems to have recommended bad behavior, but that he did not mean what he said.[30]

---

25. Parrott, "Steward," 513.
26. Ireland, "History," 308–9; see also Beavis, "Slavery," 52.
27. N. T. Wright, *Jesus*, 332, 638.
28. O'Banion, "Narration."
29. Lausberg, *Handbook*, §89a

In this option the story line is preserved but its general character is questioned. Thus Stanley Porter has revitalized an old claim whereby the whole parable is based on *irony*.[31] Dan Otto Via sees the text as a *comedy*, celebrating a "moral holiday."[32] For Paul Trudinger the parable is an example of *sarcasm*; Jesus tells it with a twinkle in the eye, or in anger.[33] Perhaps the readers are expected to have "fun at the master's expense"?[34]

The problem with these explanations is that neither the framework story nor the parable contains any hints at these styles.[35] Such an understanding was impossible for the recipients. On the contrary, the phrase ἐγὼ ὑμῖν λέγω (v. 9) is a typical assertion, emphasizing that Jesus is wholly serious.[36]

Status Qualitatis:
The Deed Was not Unlawful —*Fecit, sed iure*.[37]

Several scholars suggest that the steward actually did nothing wrong; hence Jesus cannot be recommending unethical behavior.[38] The steward only canceled illegal interest,[39] or he cut his own profits,[40] or at least he trusted that his master would approve his action.[41] Perhaps

30. Ireland, "History," 305–7, presents several options.
31. Porter, "Parable," cf. Fletcher, "Riddle," 23.
32. Via, *Parables*, 155–62.
33. Trudinger, "Depth," 121–37, 133.
34. For more detailed presentation and criticism of various literary solutions see Landry and May, "Honor," 290–92.
35. Snodgrass, *Stories*, 409, aptly calls reference to comedy "an act of despair." To be sure, referring to "eternal tents" seems an *oxymoron*, which could suggest irony, but this was a standard Septuagintal term (Nolland, *Luke*, 805).
36. This device is not used elsewhere in Luke but can be found six times in Matthew: 5:22, 28, 32, 34, 39, 44; in John 8:58; 10:7; and in Gal. 5:2.
37. Lausberg, *Handbook*, §89b.
38. For different explanations and their criticism see Ireland, "History," 309–15; Landry and May, "Honor," 289–90.
39. Derrett, *Law*, 48–77.
40. Fitzmyer, "Story," 161–84.

such squandering of his master's wealth made him a "skilled public-relations man," which pleased his employer.[42]

Some details in the story do not fit these suggestions. They exclude crucial information: in v. 8a the κύριος praises the *dishonest* steward (τὸν οἰκονόμον τῆς ἀδικίας). Moreover, the reduced amount is too large as the steward's salary, even if it referred to a fifty percent interest,[43] or if not, a man with so high a salary hardly ran the risk of becoming a beggar. Indeed, v. 5 explicitly says that the amount was owed to the master.

But even if the word ἀδικίας is assigned another meaning, that is, if the *alpha privativum* is omitted, this interpretation is unlikely as regards the audience. At the end of the day they set the chief criterion. Would they regard the steward's action as legal? Or would they assume that when implementing his plan the steward counted on his master's forbearance?

Before reporting the master's surprising reaction, and Jesus' even stranger commandment, the story as such contains no suggestions that the master was a kind, gentle, or broad-minded individual.[44] Explanations based on such a belief insert information into the text that at least the Lukan audience did not share. The opening of the story carries great weight in assessing the character of the κύριος. He dismisses his steward on the grounds of hearsay, without first giving him an opportunity to defend himself.[45] We can never know whether

---

41. Kenneth Bailey, *Poet*, 98.
42. Stephen I. Wright, "Parables," 226. He has a double strategy as an attorney: he first tries to show that the steward did nothing wrong, but in case this proves unconvincing he adds (p. 230) that the steward's action was "something that an ordinary person under pressure can do here and now."
43. Kloppenborg, "Master," 483–84; Snodgrass, *Stories*, 410. Nolland, *Luke*, 798, discusses the possibility that the amount reduced was a typical interest or rent, but states that in any case the master was simply losing more property and has no means of recovering it. Verse 5 does not suggest that the steward here wasted his own portion of the profits.
44. Contra Kenneth Bailey, *Poet*, 98, according to whom the master "shows unusual mercy and generosity" by not jailing the steward.

the steward was guilty or not, as the narrator does not tell us.[46] For this reason, and based on what they have heard earlier, the audience cannot expect the κύριος to have mercy on the steward, nor are they led to believe that the steward based his plan on such expectations. On the contrary, the steward explicitly puts his trust in the debtors (v. 4), not in the master. And with good reason: masters in Luke are generally harsh, austere individuals.[47]

To sum up: Luke and his Jesus devote much of the parable to a detailed explanation of the steward's deceit. Moreover, they cunningly create a major surprise at the end of the story by letting the master praise such a stratagem. Thereby good narrative conventions are followed. The depreciation of these essential features would ruin the whole parable, as would attempts to exonerate the priest and Levite in 10:25-37.

Status Translationis:
The Process is not Correct—Fecit/non fecit, sed actio non iure intenditur.[48]

Finally, some scholars suggest that the whole process against the steward or Jesus is misplaced, since the parable deals with the master and his conversion,[49] or with a foolish master.[50] Alternatively, Jesus is mocking the Essenes, the sons of light.[51] The master's honor is

---

45. Bailey, ibid., 97, convincingly argues that ἀπόδος τὸν λόγον τῆς οἰκονομίας σου (16:2) means "Turn in the books!" instead of balancing the accounts. In any case the operation will take place after the decision to dismiss the steward.
46. Scholars have discussed this question, but to no avail. E. g., Snodgrass, *Stories*, 413 n. 115, believes in the steward's innocence because he does not protest, whereas Beavis, "Slavery," 48, holds the opposite opinion. But as Luke was not interested in this detail we can never know. After all, as the characters in the story are fictional there is no historical *truth* behind the text level concerning them.
47. Cf. Luke 12:42-48; 19:11-27; 20:9-16. See below chap. 6.
48. Lausberg, *Handbook*, §90.
49. Kloppenborg, "Master," 474–95.
50. Donahue, *Gospel*, 162–69.

THE UNJUST STEWARD (16:1-9)

at stake, and the steward is attempting to save his reputation, and thereby regain his favor.[52]

Unfortunately, as with the previous explanation, the text postulates the opposite: the steward hopes that the debtors, not the master, will take care of him in the future (16:4). Moreover, it is difficult to believe that when a deceitful steward has put his master to shame and now succeeds in buying back some honor at a high price, involuntarily paid by the master, the master then swells with praise. The story and its context contain no indication that the audience(s) should perceive the parable according to the suggested readings. They are more likely to identify with the needy steward than the rich master. This perspective is enjoined by Jesus in v. 9, where they are told to learn from the steward's, not the master's behavior. Even other theories based on *status translationis* lack evidence from the text. According to many medieval interpretations the parable simply advocates almsgiving, or some deep spiritual truths.[53] Thereby the moral problems in the story are neatly disregarded.

Since the parable of Jesus (or at least Luke's framework story) in vv. 8-9 explicitly states that the steward was dishonest, and that the disciples ought to follow his example, we must consider that all the ingenious suggestions of the scholarly or spiritual attorneys are futile. They become valid only if the story line is altered, but then we are discussing other parables that have little relevance for understanding the Bible.

---

51. Flusser, *Parable*, 176–97.
52. Landry and May, "Honor," 287–309.
53. Wailes, *Allegories*, 247–53.

Confessum:
The Accused is Guilty—Fecit[54]

All the above-mentioned interpretations share a basic assumption: Jesus cannot recommend unethical, deceitful behavior. His exegetical defense lawyers have only chosen different strategies among the four options. Thus they share the basic weakness: for anybody reading or hearing the parable for the first time it becomes obvious that the steward acted in an immoral way, and Jesus recommends him to his audience as a role model. Thus Jesus, too, crosses the line.

In all biblical exegesis, fabricated evidence is to be suspected when the interpreter attempts to defend Jesus, to soften or explain away his hyperbolic sayings or incomprehensible behavior. Since the author presents the problematic expressions and incidents they must have a function, a purpose regarding the audience. Perception of that function is possible only when the exceptional feature is taken seriously. Thus some modern scholars are dissatisfied with the defense strategies presented above.

Bernard Brandon Scott admits that in the Lukan narrative the steward's conduct is immoral, and Jesus recommends this very action. But even then his culpability is mitigated. The steward is a rogue, but so is his master. For Scott the parable reflects another world, based on a complex vision of "new coordinates for power, justice and vulnerability."[55] However, neither Jesus' audience nor Luke's hearers are given any signs of the culpability of the master, nor is the complicated vision of the "new coordinates" easily discernible by the recipients. This explanation, too, requires alterations in the story line.

A straightforward interpretation of the parable would claim that stealing from the rich—and making friends by means of this

---

54. Lausberg, *Handbook*, §87.
55. Scott, *Parable*, 66.

money—is commendable in a crisis.⁵⁶ While this is unacceptable for modern Western Christianity, which is well integrated unto the society, the position of Jesus' poor lower-class hearers may have been different. In fact, Luke's gospel in particular abounds with criticism of the rich. Thus Mary Ann Tolbert sees the parable as rejecting traditional ethics for the sake of individual well-being.⁵⁷ Jesus advocates behavior that is unethical and wrong in principle but still advisable in practice. This interpretation avoids most pitfalls of the previous explanations. No new material is added to the text, external characters do not intrude on the story, Jesus is no longer defended, and the message remains simple enough to be understood by the audience. This reading should not be rejected because of a later image of Jesus as a pillar of Christian morality.⁵⁸ As S. I. Wright demonstrates, in the gospel narratives Jesus does not exclusively recommend unselfish ethics.⁵⁹

By encouraging the audience in financial arrogance, this interpretation takes the surprising reaction of the κύριος seriously. Instead of omitting it or explaining it away, it acknowledges that the master does what he is not expected to do. He does not whip or cut the steward in pieces, nor is he so weak that he has to face the facts and simply attempt to save face. Instead, the master praises the steward's dishonorable action as shrewd or prudent. Jesus the Narrator then recommends a similar unauthorized use of other's property, μαμωνᾶς τῆς ἀδικίας, to his hearers.⁶⁰

Unfortunately, the following verses (16:10-13) explicitly contradict this interpretation. Jesus emphasizes high morals and

---

56. S. I. Wright, "Parables," 230.
57. Tolbert, *Perspectives*, 88. For other corresponding explanations see Snodgrass, *Stories*, 720–21 n. 93.
58. *Contra* Snodgrass, *Stories*, 720, according to whom "one shudders to think of the implications of these arguments."
59. S. I. Wright, "Parables," 224–30.
60. The expression is here parallel to "other people's property" in v. 12.

fidelity to the master. This fits the rest of the document. An exhortation to steal money, to break the Seventh (Eighth) Commandment, would be unique in Luke. There are no corresponding examples. The closest resemblance is Matthew's parable of the treasure in the field (Matt. 13:44), but there no actual crime takes place. The idea of calling rich people to account belongs to God, as in the parable of the *Rich Fool* (Luke 12:13-21) or in the *Magnificat* (1:53). Jesus' hearers are exhorted to give away their *own* property rather than that of others.

Thus straightforward advice to an earthly criminal mind is hardly the answer, despite many advantages.[61] But could it have a religious counterpart? There are some faint hints at this in the text. In the immediate interpretation of the parable Jesus refers to *eternal tents* (v. 9), and to the steward as a son of this world and the hearers as the *sons of light* (v. 8b).[62]

Although the parable and its framework story recommend unrighteousness, a *general* attitude is not mentioned. The parable concentrates on describing what kind of ἀδικία is meant. Only a specific course of action is advocated. One should use the master's property for one's own benefit—and for that of other people as well. By giving away part of this property to people who have no right to receive it, one's own position is assured: in the parable financial future is meant, in the framework, eternal salvation. This is a win-win situation, except for the poor κύριος whose assets are diminished. But why is *he* content with this course of action?

---

61. If vv. 10-13 are not assessed as an integral part of the parable they do not affect the interpretation. However, such an assessment means a novel reconstruction of the document.
62. *Sons of light* are usually understood as denoting the audience. References to Essenes (Flusser, "Parable," 176–97) or Pharisees (Schellenberg, "Master," 280) are less probable, as the Lukan audience is not given any hint of such a meaning.

Is Jesus the Steward?

The connection with the situation in Luke 15 is frequently perceived.[63] Some scholars have therefore suggested an alternative hypothesis whereby the parable is Jesus' presentation of his own, allegedly unjustified, proclamation of grace. The parable is read as autobiographical. Jesus defends his own behavior, continuing his speech in the previous chapter.[64] He tells the story to the Pharisees and scribes and describes how he is nullifying the religious tradition by forgiving sins, that is, remitting the debts people owe to God. William Loader[65] and Eckart Reinmuth[66] present well-thought-out versions of this reading. For both, the story does not deal with Christian behavior. Instead, it defends Jesus' own conduct, or "die Praxis Jesu."[67]

To interpret the parable as referring to Jesus' controversial religious program has several advantages and avoids most of the problems connected with other interpretations. In particular it respects the existing text, as it requires only minor omissions or additions. For most advocates of this interpretation the annoying references to the culpability of both the steward and Jesus are not challenged; on the contrary.[68] Moreover, this interpretation does not extract the parable from its explicit context. Luke's recipients would find no difficulty in relating the parable to the preceding criticism of Jesus in 15:2.

---

63. Kenneth Bailey, *Poet*, 109; Nolland, *Luke*, 796; Schellenberg, "Master," 277.
64. For Kamlah, "Parabel," 293, the parable is told against the Pharisees, but the details remain unclear: "Klar ist die Parabel so noch keineswegs." Paliard, *Lire l'Ecriture*, 60–62, sees a reference to Christ but resorts to allegorical theology. Brown, "Steward," has difficulties with vv. 9–13, which he has to describe as a later Lukan addition. See also Baulder, "Gleichnis," 1985.
65. Loader, "Jesus."
66. Reinmuth, "Verwalter."
67. Ibid., 643.
68. Loader, "Jesus," 527–31, however argues that there is an "ironical twist," as Jesus is "no rogue at all."

Despite these benefits, the reference to Jesus' own behavior has been vehemently criticized, most recently by Snodgrass.[69] First, he dismisses any reference to Jesus' previous action by asking whether he really was about to be dismissed like the steward in v. 2. However, 15:2 indicates that he actually was. Luke does not specify the threat caused by the grumbling, but in view of the wider context the charges against Jesus were not petty. The social, religious, and physical danger was real. If the Pharisees and scribes were to succeed in proving that Jesus was a sinner he would no longer be able to continue his preaching.[70]

Snodgrass's second objection is more interesting: Why does the master not defend his steward against the charges reported in v. 1 "if an accusation of squandering forgiveness were the point?"[71] Particularly if the master denotes God and Jesus the steward, this appears odd indeed. To be sure, the same question can be asked concerning most interpretations of the parable. Many guesses can be offered: Perhaps the κύριος did not bother to investigate the case and gave the steward no opportunity to answer? Or what if the charges were true? As the story does not tell, the audience can never be sure. More importantly, such an answer hardly fits the narrator's plot.

Third, the reference to Jesus' behavior is further refuted by arguing that the steward's monologue in vv. 3-4 does not fit Jesus' situation. However, as Reinmuth shows, it describes a similar threat of losing status.[72] The steward's situation vis-à-vis the κύριος and the debtors allegedly resembled what Jesus faced in relation to God and the

---

69. Snodgrass, *Stories*, 410: "Nothing in the parable encourages us to accept this view"; Hultgren, *Parables*, 152 n. 31, simply declares it "unpersuasive" without any arguments.
70. The threat posed by the Pharisees is a known theme for the addressees. In 5:21, Luke as an omniscient author reveals their attitude, which is displayed also in 5:30; 6:2, 7; 11:53-54; 15:2.
71. Snodgrass, *Stories*, 410.
72. Reinmuth, "Verwalter," 643.

sinners; both positions were threatened by the charges brought against them.

A fourth question deals with the amount whereby the debts were reduced. If the steward represents Jesus, why not forgive all the debts?[73] The remark is based on an allegorical view of the parables in which each detail must carry a message. Since the story describes the steward's cunning or prudent operation, the existing version is more realistic and thereby more effective.

The fifth objection must be sustained, although Snodgrass's other objections can be overruled. The reference to Jesus' own behavior omits the parable's basic setting: unlike in chapter 15, he is now addressing his disciples. Even if the Pharisees overhear the parable, Luke does not present them as the main audience. Thus although the parable continues the theme of chapter 15, dealing with an alleged violation, its tenor must be different. Thus the function of the parable as Jesus' introspective autobiography remains vague. What kind of affect is pursued? How should the disciples react?

In order to find a more convincing target for the parable, Joachim Degenhardt suggests that Jesus tells the story to religious leaders who are about to lose their status, and advises them on how to cope with the situation.[74] Unfortunately no such hearers are named or hinted at in the text. This explanation too fails to envisage the parable's explicit audience. Again v. 9 is disregarded. There Luke implies that Jesus addresses the parable to his *disciples*. The steward faces a situation similar to that of Jesus in 15:1-2, but the emphasis is on his audience.

The steward is hardly an alias for Jesus. In general, parables do not report reality with the help of cover names. One should abstain from an allegorical determination of *who is who* in the story. The characters

---

73. Mathewson, "Parable," 31. He also criticizes Loader for ignoring the financial context and emphasis of the story. However, if debts refer to sin (see below), this criticism is invalid.
74. Degenhardt, *Lukas*, 118.

are fictional individuals within the story line, and only after hearing the whole story can the audience assess its relevance to the current situation.[75] In the same way, the κύριος is not God (or Jesus), and the anonymous critics are not Pharisees—although the hearers can hardly avoid seeing some similarities.

Instead of merely defending Jesus or presenting his theology, the parable urges the disciples to action.[76] This is typical of Luke. In fact, the whole document focuses on deeds, namely, what to do in order to inherit eternal life (10:25). Action, not definitions or theories, is what is crucial: he who did the right thing was the neighbor (10:37); one should do likewise in order to live (10:28, 37). In the current parable the steward wonders what to do (τί ποιήσω, 16:3); then he decides on a course of action (τί ποιήσω, 16:4); the κύριος praises him because he did it (ἐποίησεν, 16:8) shrewdly (16:8); finally, Jesus commands his disciples to do likewise (ποιήσατε, 16:9). This final exhortation is not an addition, which can be omitted, but reveals the goal of the parable.[77] The story is explicitly aimed at the disciples. It shows them a role model who makes friends by questionable means. They ought to do likewise.

The exhortation to the disciples, taken together with the general emphasis on action, indicates that the parable is neither a static christological description nor a retrospective autobiography. It seeks to persuade a certain audience to adopt a specific mode of behavior. The story also contains several theologically interesting messages, but no interpretation may exclude this central focus. In Luke 15, although the main goal was to influence the Pharisees and scribes,

---

75. Snodgrass rightly states that "interpreting parables does not mean assigning correspondences to the elements" and that the characters do not "stand for" anyone. However, he is simultaneously shooting himself in the foot by requiring such a close and complete match in the "biography of Jesus" explanation before it would be thinkable at all (Snodgrass, *Stories*, 410).
76. Ibid., 417.
77. *Contra* Reinmuth, "Verwalter," 634, 636.

important views of both Jesus and God were transmitted as well. In a similar way, in interpreting this parable it is essential to discern a general persuasive goal regarding the audience along with any inherent christological and theological message. Particularly in regard to the latter, allegorical readings are to be avoided.

To sum up, perception of Luke 16:1-9 as referring to Jesus' agenda involves a major step forward, providing helpful principles and ideas for a plausible understanding of the content. It fits the central narrative and persuasive conventions. It connects the parable to 15:1-2 and to the previous chapters, in which Jesus forgives sins and is therefore criticized. Moreover, this interpretation rightly treats the parable as a story with a point instead of emphasizing allegorical resemblances. It correctly sees the objectionable, if not shocking, features as functional devices aimed at gaining the audience's attention and ensuring that its members are emotionally involved.[78] But the explanation misleadingly identifies the steward with Jesus. The hub of such identification, the function of the parable for the *audience*, remains unclear and so must be carefully examined in scrutinizing the parable further.

Reading Luke 16:1-9 in Context

Any interpretation should begin with the context: Why is the narrator telling the story; what has provoked him; to whom is he speaking? The answers to these questions provide a necessary point of departure in the search for the function of the parable.

---

78. Ibid., 645.

Referring to Luke 15:1-2

My reading of the parable draws on the observations by Loader, Schellenberg, and Reinmuth but seeks to follow the text more closely and to let the implied audience play a central role in its assessment. Their ability to comprehend the story should be the criterion for the plausibility of the explanation. Moreover, the parable must have a specific persuasive goal in their regard.

Luke 16 begins with a brief comment by the author: "Then Jesus said to the disciples . . . ." The major break before this verse is artificial. For the Lukan recipients the setting presented in 15:1-2 remains the same, with the exception of the immediate audience. There Jesus was criticized by the Pharisees and scribes for welcoming sinners and feasting with them. After an immediate response to these critics in 15:4-32, Jesus now turns back to his disciples in 16:1. Moreover, he resumes the topic of money and discipleship, which he had raised in 14:25-35.[79] There he recommended careful calculation of what it costs to follow him.

Immediately after the parable and its explanations we learn that "the Pharisees were listening to all these things. They loved money and ridiculed him" (16:14). The audience is thus twofold: the parable is addressed primarily to the disciples, but the Pharisees—the main target of the previous parables—happen to hear it as well.[80] The modification of the audience signifies a modification in the setting, and thus also of the function of the parable, compared to those in Luke 15. As this is the context provided by the author, it should not be overlooked, no matter how one assesses the historical background of the individual stories. At least for the audience Luke has in mind

---

79. S. I. Wright, "Parables," 217–39, esp. 224–30.
80. Nolland, *Luke*, 796, argues that καί only widens the audience, but the mention of the disciples only and the observation that the Pharisees overheard the story (16:14) shows that the first group is the essential audience.

THE UNJUST STEWARD (16:1-9)

this context provides the most natural framework in which the parable is to be understood.

The steward is criticized for squandering his master's property as Jesus was criticized for squandering the forgiveness of God. In 15:2 the antagonists are specified while their audience remains unclear; in 16:1 the reverse applies. But in both chapters the accused individual is put in a difficult position and is not saved by divine intervention. Thus the audience cannot avoid seeing the connection.

In 15:4-32, Jesus replies to the Pharisees' and scribes' criticism as he invited guests in a precise but controversial way. He accepted disreputable individuals and feasted with them. In view of the religious references (15:7, 9) this indicates that, according to Jesus, God also accepts such individuals. However, the three parables in Luke 15 present neither an allegorical autobiography nor a counterattack on the Pharisees and scribes. Jesus does not demonstrate the stupidity of the Pharisees and scribes, but extends to his antagonists a kind invitation to join the feast.[81]

In 16:1-13 Jesus is not primarily describing his own situation, but exhorting the disciples. They should emulate the steward's behavior. His problems in vv. 3-4 refer to the difficulties they are expected to confront, and just as the master does not help him in v. 2, the disciples should not look for support from heaven (cf. 9:54, where they consider such an option). The disciples of Jesus are facing hard times—no matter whether these are brought on by the current opponents, the Pharisees and scribes, or by an eschatological crisis. The reference to "eternal tents" suggests a wide theological *cum* eschatological perspective. In this situation it is important for them to act swiftly and rapidly. Luke 12:54-59 gives another example of how to act in a crisis, using corresponding vocabulary. However, the

---

81. For a more detailed analysis see chap. 3 above.

central idea of dishonesty is not mentioned there. Thus it must be studied carefully.

Understanding the steward primarily as the disciples' target for identification meets the criticisms against a reference to 15:1-2 even better than does comparing him with Jesus. In the text, the parable serves as a background for Jesus' exhortation to follow the steward's example. It should convince the hearers that the steward acted admirably in his situation, and they should do likewise in their own lives, which are in some respect analogous. In other words, the disciples (and perhaps also the Pharisees) should identify with the steward and regard him as a role model, just as the father constituted an acceptable role model for them in the previous parable. Nevertheless, in both parables the role model corresponds to Jesus' own behavior as well, inasmuch as he not only tells his audience to forgive sins on God's behalf but himself follows this principle.

The Wider Lukan Context

Not only chapter 15, but other previous stories have prepared the audience to understand the parable in 16:1-9. Central themes and concepts occurring earlier in Luke affect their ability to perceive its message.

Several scholars have demonstrated how central Lukan topics—forgiveness of sins or debts and acceptance of outsiders—create a background for understanding the parable in 16:1-9.[82] Correspondingly, the Scripture text read by Jesus in Nazareth (Luke 4:18-19, citing Isa. 61:1-2; 58:6 LXX) is often seen as his opening proclamation. Jesus' mission is to proclaim good news to the poor, release captives, and announce the year of Lord's favor. The

---

82. Loader, "Jesus," 527–31; Brown, "Steward," 133–38.

Lukan description of Jesus' behavior and teaching reflects this Jubilee imagery: healing of illness, remission of debts, and forgiveness of sins.[83] Luke 6:32-36 in particular emphasizes the financial dimension. Moreover, the Pharisees often criticize details of this program, and do so also in the immediate context in 15:1-2. Thus the audience is prepared to see a connection between the steward and Jesus, both of whom were criticized for unauthorized use of their master's property. Thus although the steward does not represent Jesus, his situation and behavior illustrate the situation and recommended behavior of anyone who implemented Jesus' controversial Jubilee program.

While the original claims against the steward are not specified, his offense as depicted in 16:4-8 consists in reducing the debts of the debtors, which ought to save his own future. Thus it is important to assess the audience's ability to connect the image of debts with that of sin. Indeed, apart from this parable the same metaphor is used in Luke almost exclusively for sins. In 7:41-42 there are two debtors (χρεωφειλέται) whom the creditor (δανειστής) forgives everything. A natural reaction, defined with a rhetorical question, is that they will "love" the creditor. Jesus then explains the parable: the debts are sins, and as the woman's sins are forgiven (*passivum divinum*), she loves much. In addition, Jesus himself assures the woman that her sins are forgiven in 7:47-48.

In 11:4 the disciples are told to pray to God for forgiveness of their *sins* as they forgive everyone who is *indebted* (ὀφείλοντι) to them. In 12:54-59 the disciples are enjoined to pay their debts to others in order to avoid punishment by the judge in an (apparently) eschatological crisis. In 13:4 Jesus asks whether those killed at Siloam were worse ὀφειλέται than all those living in Jerusalem. The metaphor of debts refers to sin against God, allegedly punished by the

---

83. For examples and discussion, see Schellenberg, "Master," 275–78.

accident. Only 17:10, which follows our parable, lacks this directly negative theological connotation: the slaves owe (ὠφείλομεν) their master their daily labor.

Thus for the Lukan audience the use of the metaphor of debt has a specific connotation. Individuals *owe* God because of their sins, either directly as in chapters 11 and 13 or, in a parable, to a creditor who proves to refer to God, as in chapter 7. This is not an *ad hoc* allegorical interpretation but the most probable connotation created for the audience, as well as the first semantic choice because of the previous occurrences of the word in the document.

In the parable the steward counts on the debtors' willingness to take care of him when he is dismissed. The motivation is not explicit and thus is irrelevant. Similarly, new friends won by squandering God's forgiveness will receive the audience into their eternal tents. This *breviloquium* is not further explicated and so has prompted several interpretations.[84] An accurate allegorical explanation is hardly necessary; it suffices to say that following Jesus' Jubilee program of forgiving sins helps the members of the audience to secure their own future as well. The closest parallels are 12:54-59, where good relations with others help the audience to avoid the judge's verdict in an eschatological situation, and the following *Rich Man and Lazarus* in 16:19-31.

Summarizing the Function of Luke 16:1-9

On the basis of the above observations it is possible to arrive at a comprehensive explanation. How does the parable sound to the Lukan recipients, and to Jesus' auditors? They have just heard Jesus'

---

84. Snodgrass, *Stories*, 415, suggests that "they" refers to the poor, to angels, or to God. However, as in v. 4, the new friends are meant (thus correctly Nolland, *Luke*, 804).

emotional response to the criticism leveled by the Pharisees and scribes. This criticism is a common topic in Luke: "The Son of Man has come eating and drinking, and you say, 'Behold, a gluttonous man and a drunkard, a friend of tax collectors and sinners!'" (7:34); "and when they saw it, they all beganto grumble [διεγόγγυζον, as in 15:2], saying, 'He has gone to be the guest of a man who is a sinner'" (19:7).

In the three previous parables in Luke 15, Jesus attempted to persuade his critics that his eating with sinners is not just inappropriate feasting, but—what may be even worse—means the unconditional acceptance of sinners back into the community. Moreover, he claims that this corresponds to both human and divine ideals. Even if it is not legally requisite or especially rational, he insists that even his critics should feel deep compassion and joy for the returning individuals (τίς ἄνθρωπος ἐξ ὑμῶν . . . οὐ, 15:4). Jesus claims that God must act likewise (οὕτως χαρὰ ἐν τῷ οὐρανω, 15:7; οὕτως . . . ἐνώπιον τῶν ἀγγέλων τοῦ θεοῦ, 15:10), as God obviously cannot be worse than ordinary mortals. Thereby Jesus has not only defended his behavior but has appealed especially to his critics to act likewise: would not you do as I do? At least God would!

In 16:1 Jesus then (δὲ) turns to his disciples. Naturally, he will add another aspect. He no longer answers his critics, but refers to the criticism in the passive voice (διεβλήθη). Instead, he now focuses on the insiders. Since the Pharisees are not excluded, the verse does not imply their negative reaction to the previous parable.

Thus v. 2 refers to the situation described in 15:1-2 from a different angle. A steward is criticized for squandering his master's property, as *de facto* in the previous chapter, but this time a worst-case scenario is presented—as if the three defense speeches (15:3-32) had failed. In a sense, Jesus the Narrator is giving the Pharisees and/or the critical elder brother another chance by admitting that perhaps they are right after all. What if Jesus indeed squanders God's property? Contrary to the father in 15:28-32, the master in this parable takes the charges seriously, and the steward is dismissed.

Although the master does not represent God, in one respect he plays a similar role for the audience: he is in the position of deciding what happens to the chief character in the story. This is a typical feature: in the previous parables, the sheep owner, the woman, and the father were compared to the Pharisees, to Jesus, and to God in different respects. In chapter 18 a wicked judge is compared to God in one respect. Thus these figures are not identical with God, but for the hearers they share a specific role. The story is after all a parable, not a report on the situation.

Correspondingly, the accused and dismissed steward is not Jesus, although they share a similar role: both run the risk of losing their status between their master and the debtors/sinners.[85] However, as the parable is told to the disciples, the steward offers a good target for them as well as for the Lukan recipients. He is the protagonist in the story who in the beginning gets into trouble, then makes a plan, and finally emerges as a hero. Whereas the other individuals stand aloof, the audience has access to the steward's thoughts and feelings. Thus it is natural that any hearer identifies with him, follows his destiny anxiously, and feels great relief at the end. This identification is due to a general narrative custom that the hero's immoral solution cannot eliminate.[86] Enticing the audience to such identification may be unethical, but it is highly effective as persuasion.

The parable warns the audience that they may face a corresponding crisis, either due to religious criticism or in an eschatological situation. They too need a survival plan. The emphasis

---

85. Cf. Reinmuth, "Verwalter," 642–43.
86. For the general narrative conventions of the "adventure of the hero," see the classic study by Campbell, *Hero*.

of the story is neither on demonstrating *that* the hero managed to survive in the crisis nor that he reacted *quickly*. The lengthy description of the *measures* he adopted focuses the audience's attention on this feature: the steward secured his future by an illegal use of his master's property.[87] The κύριος praises not the steward's speedy reaction but his prudence or cunning.[88]

Thus the narrator and the author provide the audience with an allegedly clever solution and ensure that the audience understands this message correctly by articulating an explicit commandment in v. 9: "Make friends for yourselves by means of *the mammon of unrighteousness* so that when it fails, they may welcome you into the eternal dwellings." Likewise, the audience should use God's property without proper authorization. They too should take part in Jesus' Jubilee program to forgive debts, that is, sins, without proper authorization. For a reason not specified, the new friends are necessary in order to enter the eternal tents. In other words, with their help the addressees ensure their own future, when God's property is no longer at their disposal.

The Aftermath: Luke 16:10-13

If the above interpretation offers a plausible approach to reading the parable in 16:1-9, the function of vv. 10-13 becomes particularly interesting. To be sure, they are not included in the parable or the immediate exhortation based on it, yet these commands are clearly connected to the parable, as the same concepts are discussed: faithfulness in the use of unrighteous mammon and service of two

---

87. The steward's solution is not presented as identical with the crime of which he was accused in v. 1. There the accusation referred to non-specific squandering, perhaps as in 12:45. It is only now that the steward conceives of a means of making friends.
88. Irrespective of the word's general semantic field (see the discussion in Schellenberg, "Master," 278 n. 34), it here refers to the word ἀδικία and the steward's resolution of his situation.

masters. However, the verses recommend behavior that is diametrically opposed to the model promoted in the parable and its explanation.

Thus the high morality recommended in 16:10-13 could be used as the weightiest argument against reading the previous parable as recommending fraud. Although the master there praises his steward, this cannot be because the latter lived up to the ideals of vv. 10-13. Nor is dishonest use of other people's property praised; on the contrary. Moreover, the steward's solution meant in practice that he began to serve other masters, the debtors. Thus in the light of v. 13 he despised his own master.

It would be an easy solution to omit these verses and claim that Luke accidentally added these sayings to the parable because they treat similar themes. This would mean that Luke did not know what he was doing, as these verses seem to supersede the previous message. It is more likely that the verses have a premeditated function here.[89] In fact, vv. 10-13 offer an intriguing aftermath to the parable.

In 16:1-9 the audience is urged to an allegedly unauthorized use of God's forgiveness, not other peoples' property. The parable focuses on one point; no other "criminality" is recommended. Verses 10-13 are necessary to prevent the audience from misunderstanding Jesus, as if the parable concerned worldly money, wheat, and oil. "This world" and "light" represent different spheres; worldly debts and debts to God are not identical. The "moral holiday" is over. Hence the multifaceted, morally-based defense of Jesus by numerous scholars appears to be in vain. No ethical attorneys are needed. The Lukan Jesus succeeds in refuting the possible moral charges against himself by presenting strict principles in vv. 10-13. The immoral behavior of the steward remains within the world of the parable. This, however, by no means exonerates Jesus.

---

89. For discussion of Luke's ability as an author see Schellenberg, "Master," 263–64.

THE UNJUST STEWARD (16:1-9)

Was Jesus' Theology Illegal?

The crux of the parable and its explanation is ἀδικία. If, based on vv. 10-13, Jesus cannot be charged with promoting financial dishonesty, the alternative charge is more fatal: he is inciting his audience to theological ἀδικία. In the parable the steward was exonerated by his master's surprising praise. An explanation would shed light on the question of whether through the parable Jesus actually accepts the theological charges brought against him.

Why Was the Steward Praised?

The hub of any explanation of the parable reads: Why did the κύριος praise the steward, and why does Jesus also recommend the steward's course of action? Again, the answer cannot be far-fetched, but must be feasible for the audience implied in the text. Are the hearers given any clues to a deeper understanding of the master's decision? Sympathy for the underdog, or malicious delight in the loss of property by the rich and success on the part of the poor hardly justify the steward's plan,[90] as the text does not support such ideas. The master's verdict is the only explicit argument to prove that the steward was right after all, and thus the audience should see him as a role model in religious matters: he bursts into praise (ἐπῄνεσεν, aorist, 16:8) because of the steward's shrewdness.

The master has suffered substantial losses because of the steward, who in addition has deceived him, at least for now. Speculations suggesting that the master was rich enough to be magnanimous and show appreciation of a smart move, or that he was delighted when a man who had put him to shame succeeded in saving his reputation,[91] or that the praise was ironic and threatening[92] are based

---

90. Kenneth Bailey, *Poet*, 105.

on the interpreters' imagination and lack substantiation in the text. As it cannot be guaranteed that the audience was expected to think likewise, such explanations are to be dismissed, however attractive they may seem.

An attempt to alleviate the surprise is to say that the master had "however grudgingly" to acknowledge the steward's cleverness, as he could neither retrieve his property nor dismiss the steward again. He had no other options.[93] But of course he had! The audience has just heard another story of a deceitful steward and his κύριος in 12:42-48. There the steward did not squander his master's goods; he merely mistreated the slaves and drank to excess. Nevertheless, the punishment was outrageous: the κύριος cut him in pieces. Ordinary slaves receive lashes (12:47-48). Thus the audience must expect a harsh, violent reaction. Later parables in Luke only show them that this interpretation is correct: deceitful farmers in 20:16 are destroyed by the owner of the vineyard, ἄνθρωπός τις. The nobleman, ἄνθρωπός τις, in 19:11-27 is no better: he too is known as an austere (αὐστηρός) man and acts according to his reputation. The unexpected and uncontrolled violence of κύριοι is thus well known to Luke's audience. Masters had a sovereign right to do as they pleased, and the peasants could not complain or to ask for more, as emphasized in 17:7-10, the *Useless Servant*. The fate of deceitful business partners was no better.

Luke 12:37 and 16:8a are further examples of a master's autocratic decision, but in a positive light. A similarly unwarranted positive solution based on the master's sovereign right to manage his property is described in Matthew 20:1-15, where the owner of the vineyard pays a day's wage even to workers arriving at the last hour. But if

---

91. Landry and May, "Honor," 309.
92. Scott, *Parable*, 263–66.
93. Nolland, *Luke*, 802, based on a peculiar understanding of ἐπῄνεσεν.

Luke's audience is expected to understand the verse in this way they should be prepared by previous communication.

Luke 6:27-36 sheds some light on the master's positive decision. Even there Jesus discusses debts and their payment.[94] He suggests that his audience should not act like Gentiles, but ". . . lend, expecting nothing in return. Your reward will be great, and you will be sons of the Most High; for he is kind to the ungrateful and the wicked" (6:35). Why, then, does God love the wicked? Whereas in Matthew 5:45 God is compared to the nature, sun and rain, which do not discriminate between good and bad people, Luke refers to the human level. He attempts to prove that God cannot be worse than bad people (Luke 11:5-13; 15:4-32; 18:1-8).

If the sovereign master is better than the Gentiles, and good as God, the steward implemented his financial policy by reducing his debtors' debts on the master's behalf. The steward's high-handed action proved to be the right course.[95] However, he is *not* said to have been aware of such a guiding principle. Thus formally he was unjust and committed a crime. It is important to note that the steward's deceit was not annulled by his master's praise. He did not prove to be a faithful, honest steward who fulfilled the requirements stated in 16:10-13. The master did not praise him because of his integrity but because of his shrewdness or prudence.[96]

A simplified Toulminian version of the argumentation is shown in figure IV.1.

---

94. Cf. Schellenberg, "Master," 277.
95. Schellenberg, "Master," 278, more explicitly sees the steward as fulfilling the master's mission, but identifies the latter with Jesus on the meta-level. Such an unwarranted identification is not necessary for explaining the master's praise. As argued above, it is more likely that the audience notices a certain connection between the accused Jesus (15:2) and the accused steward, whereas the master, as having the highest authority, plays the role of God.
96. Thus correctly Schellenberg, ibid., 278–79. However, he argues that the steward's unrighteousness as based on "his plan is calculated to elicit reciprocation from his newly generated 'clients.'" Yet, as the steward's ἀδικία is his central trait to be followed by the audience, this can hardly be the right description.

Figure IV.1

Backing: The parable as an example

▼

Warrant: Breaking the rules for specific reasons is commendable

▼

Data: You have been entrusted with God's property ▶ *Claim*: You should forgive God's "debtors" even if not authorized to do so

The example is relevant since a typical emphasis of the Lukan Jesus is that God cannot be worse than human beings (11:5-13 *Friend at Midnight* and *Father and Son 2*; 15:4-32 *Lost Sheep, Lost Coin, Prodigal Son*; 18:2-6 *Unjust Judge*).

A Rare Window on Jesus' Theology

In the parable Jesus does not withdraw the original charges in 15:2. Instead, the steward's recommended action is explicitly described as unauthorized, and the man is labeled as οἰκονόμος τῆς ἀδικίας. When Jesus appeals to his disciples by this parable and exhorts them to follow the same pattern in religious matters the parable resembles a confession: *feci*. This renders the defense attorneys' task impossible.

The confession was hardly made without intent. Thus in order to understand the parable, and Jesus' own program behind it, it is important to ask: What is the message of the steward's dishonesty or immorality? Moreover, as the steward's solution for alleviating his master's debtors' situation resembles Jesus' own action, the parable conveys an interesting glimpse into the core of Jesus' own theology.

THE UNJUST STEWARD (16:1-9)

Jesus' only direct justification is that, after all, the master praised the steward's actions. However, he does not reveal the master's motivation. Likewise, v. 8b onward does not base the encouragement to forgive people's sins in God's name on any specific claim concerning God, save that God happens to like this and God does what God pleases. As a response to the presented criticism this is far weaker than the appeal in the previous chapter. Whereas 15:11-32 at least appeals to the audience's compassion to enable them to understand his acceptance of sinners, 16:1-9 makes the critics' viewpoint even more reasonable. Why would God praise his acceptance of sinners and forgiveness of their debts even if such an action appears high-handed?

The audience's assessment must be based on the previous context. In the parable of the Prodigal the motivation of unconditional acceptance of immoral individuals is discussed in greater detail. Depending on how the Lukan audience's view of Jewish culture is assessed, one could claim that the father is actually squandering the elder brother's half of the estate (v. 31), or at least his inheritance, when celebrating his returning son.[97] But in any case, when attempting to persuade his audience that the father's decision was advisable, Jesus refers not to the Torah but to the father's emotion (ἐσπλαγχνίσθη, 15:20, cf. 10:33), which—against the *per se* rational arguments of the elder brother—ought to touch the deep feelings of his hearers.

Thus Jesus does not claim even in 15:4-32 that his program of accepting sinners was legal. He does not allege that "all the tax collectors and sinners" around him have first repented, or that the Prodigal did so, before they were accepted back into society. The

---

97. This is the message explicit in the story. Later explanations claiming the father's sole right to the remaining property not only contradict the text (15:31b) but introduce information not known to the audience implied by Luke.

former just "came near [Jesus] to listen to him," whereas the latter planned to get something to eat. Zacchaeus did not decide to rectify his wrongdoing before celebrating with Jesus (19:1-10).

Jesus' critics were right: according to the Torah and the other Scriptures, merely to proclaim public sinners to be righteous (*iustificatio impii*) was accursed (Exod. 23:7; Isa. 5:22-23; Prov. 17:15; 24:24).[98] Isaiah 5:22-23 is particularly important, as it combines the two main charges against Jesus: wine-drinking and justifying the wicked (Luke 7:34). Moreover, the wrongful justification in Isaiah is effected in order to obtain personal profit, just as in Luke 16:1-9.

Consequently, when the disciples acknowledge sinners as righteous they are acting against the Law and the Scriptures. They are abusing God's property as μαμωνᾶς τῆς ἀδικίας, unrighteously. The surprising climax of the parable, the master's reaction to the steward's plan, is intended to assure the audience that such conduct is not only acceptable but worthy of praise. Thereby it also serves as a model for the audience's behavior.[99] The topic is known to the audience from the discussion between Jesus and the Pharisees and scribes in 5:17-26, especially the charge of blasphemy in v. 21: "Who is this who is speaking blasphemies? Who can forgive sins but God alone?"[100] In early Judaism the eschatological forgiveness of sins by God was expected, but God's role could hardly be assumed by a human being.[101] Jesus here unavoidably admits that the criticism leveled against him by the Pharisees and scribes in 15:1-2 was correct,

---

98. Exodus 23:7: "I will not justify the wicked"; Isa. 5:22-23: "Woe to men mighty at drinking wine, woe to men valiant for mixing intoxicating drink, who justify the wicked for a bribe"; Prov. 17:15: "He who justifies the wicked, and he who condemns the just, both of them alike are an abomination to the Lord"; Prov. 24:24: "He who says to the wicked, 'You are righteous,' him the people will curse; nations will abhor him."
99. However, the audience is not told whether or not the steward was reinstalled, as this is irrelevant to the point of the story.
100. Forgiving sins was considered an exclusive right of God and an eschatological sign. See Nolland, *Luke*, 235.
101. For discussion see ibid., 236.

THE UNJUST STEWARD (16:1-9)

at least on some level—and so will their criticism of the disciples be. They have no formal right to forgive sins on God's behalf.

How does Jesus asses his own mission, based on this information? In Luke 5 he claims the right to forgive sins, but instead of referring to the Scriptures he heals a lame man as an argument in the discussion. Probably the implicit claim is that since healing can happen only by God's authority, God must accept Jesus' power to forgive sins.[102] Simultaneously, Jesus shows understanding of the opponents' position. When responding to their criticism he characterizes them as "healthy" and "righteous" (Luke 5:31-32), with no hint of sarcasm or irony.[103] But he explains his action by referring to common sense: it is not reasonable to heal the healthy or to seek what is not lost. The reasoning in Luke 15 is a modified version of this common sense or custom, as it assumes that the sick has been healed and the lost found: it is not normal to celebrate what is not lost rather than the lost. Finally, in the present parable Jesus argues that his Jubilee program, which involves the unauthorized forgiving of human debts to God, will nevertheless find favor with God, as God is both a sovereign master not bound by the Law and "kind to ungrateful and evil men" (6:35).

To sum up: 16:1-9, the *Unjust Steward*, and corresponding previous texts in Luke provide us some information about Jesus' view of theology. The program he is implementing and advocating to his disciples, namely, proclaiming God's forgiveness freely to sinners, does not comply with a vital principle of the Torah and the Scriptures. From this point of view its condemnation is justified.

---

102. Cf. the discussion in 11:14-26.
103. *Contra* Schellenberg, "Master," 280, who argues that in 15:7 also "righteous" is ironic, as a part of Jesus' "ongoing debate" with the Pharisees. However, Jesus' logic is sensible without any irony or sarcasm: The healthy do not need a healer, and those who are safe do not cause as great joy as those lost and then found. Despite a common preoccupation, Jesus in Luke 15 is trying to persuade the Pharisees, not to vilify them.

However, the program is allegedly accepted by God, who is a sovereign master and not bound by the Law. God's goodness is to be compared to the human experience of love and mercy in certain situations, in Matthew also to universal features in nature such as sun and rain.

It is interesting to note that Luke later presents another parable in which a wicked individual's behavior is depicted in a positive light. In the light of the *qal wahomer* reasoning, the judge in 18:1-8 illustrates God's behavior: If an uncaring individual can do good on certain occasions, why not God? If the interpreters diminish the judge's bad character they also reduce the persuasive force of the parable. An allegorical reading enables one to apply the same idea to 16:1-9, the *Unjust Steward*. If this kind of individual is praised for expending his master's property, why not the master's own son? Jesus, after all, is not acting in his own right, but as God's beloved Son (3:22), whom God has anointed (4:18). According to this admittedly allegorical line of thought, Jesus did not assess his message as illegal after all.

The goal of the parable is not to describe Jesus but to exhort the disciples. They will possess the same authorization when sent by him. Just as the master can accept and even praise without explanation an individual who causes him considerable financial losses, so will God praise anyone usurping the sovereign divine right to forgive sins. Their eternal status will thereby be secured as well. This bold theological foundation is, in my opinion, clear to the hearers of Luke's gospel on the basis of the previous chapters—if the astonishing end of the parable and the culpability of the steward and Jesus are not explained away.

THE UNJUST STEWARD (16:1-9)

Referring to Paul?

According to an interesting ancient interpretation by Theophilus of Antioch, the steward points toward the apostle Paul.[104] The steward, or at least a model disciple following the commandments according to the parable, calls the apostle to mind. Paul's Gentile mission and its foundations indeed resemble the steward's arrogant solution. His major theological dilemma corresponds to the steward's economic solution. He was criticized by "Judaizers" for proclaiming the Gentiles δίκαιοι without their fulfilling the requirements of the Torah. He advocated justification of the sinners, which can be interpreted as squandering God's property.

It is interesting to note that Luke and Paul share a common vocabulary.[105] Paul calls himself a *steward* (1 Cor. 4:1-4; 9:17; cf. Gal. 4:2). This is not to say that the steward in the parable *is* Paul. But as Paul is a hero of Luke's later book, the Acts of the Apostles, a connection is not inconceivable: he can be seen as a disciple who followed Jesus' exhortation. Continuing along these lines, one could surmise that he thereby won new friends who welcomed him into their "dwellings" when he was no longer accepted in the synagogue or in Jerusalem, and he hoped to gain access to the "eternal tents" as well.[106]

There is, however, a major difference between Paul and the Lukan Jesus. Paul at least attempts to prove that he has a full right to his proclamation. At any rate, Pauline trajectories must remain speculations, and the audience was scarcely assumed to perceive the connection at this stage. However, the parable may prepare the Lukan readers for the presentation of Pauline theology and his controversies in Acts as well. If there is a connection, this may reflect

---

104. According to Jerome (*Hier. ep.* 121, 6). See Reinmuth, "Verwalter," 644.
105. Ibid., 641.
106. 1 Cor. 3:10-15 reflects this imagery.

his understanding of the parable, or Luke may apply Paul's imagery to the story. In any case the image of the steward rapidly gained popularity in early Christianity.[107]

Conclusion

I hope I have proved that an unplugged reading of "the most difficult parable of Jesus" is worthwhile. The narrative becomes easier to understand when the existing text is respected: nothing is censored—even if the story makes one "shudder"[108]—and additional information is kept to a minimum. This rule cannot be absolute, as we do not know exactly how much extraneous information the two audiences are assumed to possess, but their image is more or less clear from the text, which "must reveal its context."[109] The most reliable source of their knowledge is the context, what Luke has told them in the previous chapters. The implied audience must be the judge: its mode of understanding the parable is the ultimate criterion.

All attempts to exonerate the dishonest steward and his inventor, Jesus, are misleading, as the story concentrates on describing his crime and explicitly calls him οἰκονόμος τῆς ἀδικίας. The parable is not a static description of Jesus but a piece of his *paraenesis*. It does not illustrate a financial reality but a precise mode of religious arrogance. The steward as a role model on the religious level is set before the sons of light, that is, the disciples of Jesus: they too should distribute their Master's property and thereby help not only the debtors but also themselves.

---

107. Baergen, "Servant," 28–30, and Reinmuth, "Verwalter," 641 refer to 1 Tim. 1:4; Titus 1:2; Eph. 1:10; 3:2, 9; Col. 1:25; 1 Pet. 4:10, and several church Fathers.
108. Snodgrass, *Stories*, 720.
109. Sloane, "Rhetoric," 798–99.

The parable may cause some theological unease, as Jesus accepts in some measure the charges brought by his critics. Although not supported by the Law, he and his disciples claim to execute God's sovereign will. If the wicked steward's unauthorized use of his master's property was accepted and praised by him, how much more can God's beloved Son and his followers act accordingly? Lucid arguments along this line are not presented. However, as observed by the early Fathers, the steward's behavior may have a bearing on the theology of Luke's other hero, the apostle Paul. He is far more explicit when providing a theoretical foundation for the problematic concept of justification of the impious.

5

The Wicked Tenants (20:9-19)

The parable of the *Wicked Tenants* suffers from the too-obvious christological interpretation and too-alluring intertextual and historical connections, which have left the actual story in the shadow. Thus the attempt to look behind all the extraneous material to see how the story is designed in order to persuade its actual recipients, the audience of the Lukan Jesus and the readers of the Lukan work, is intriguing.

External Factors Dominate the Interpretation

There are at least eight factors that influence how the parable is currently understood, although these factors do not appear in the text:

1. The influence of the *Old Testament background* on the parable's imagery and story line is evident, especially Isaiah 5:1-7, Psalm 118:22-23, and Daniel 2:44-45.[1] On the basis of these traditions

the owner of the vineyard is axiomatically identified as God, the vineyard as Israel or Jerusalem, and the servants as the prophets.

2. On the basis of *later Christian documents* most readers axiomatically identify the son with Jesus, who was killed,[2] since he was the rejected cornerstone.[3] This interpretation neatly fits into the OT background.

3. The parable is often connected to *later historical information*, such as the defeat of Herod Antipas's army in 36 CE,[4] the death of Nero in Rome in 68 C.E. after his alleged persecution of the Christians, and the destruction of the Temple at Jerusalem in 70 C.E. Since the parable is usually read with some or all of these factors in mind, the christological interpretation has gained strong support, albeit currently with different modifications and with anti-Jewish overtones.[5]

4. The close *parallels in the Synoptic Gospels* and the *Gospel of Thomas* invite scholars to reconstruct an original version,[6] since each document has its own emphasis. For example, a non-allegorical proclamation of the "gospel to the poor" has been reconstructed on the basis of Mark and the *Gospel of Thomas*,[7] yet there is no consensus on the original wording of the parable.

5. Other *ancient documents* provide additional information about the details.[8] There are, for example, reports on how ambassadors,

---

1. Other possible allusions can be found, e.g., in Gen. 37:20; 1 Kgs. 21:1-29; 2 Chr. 24:17-21; 26:10; Ps. 1:3; Isa. 3:14-15; Jer. 12:7-17; and Song 8:11-12.
2. Luke 23:66–24:49 already supports this reading.
3. Luke lets Peter make this connection in Acts 4:11; the same idea is attributed to Peter in 1 Pet. 2:4-8.
4. Schürer, *History*, 350.
5. Thus Nolland, *Luke*, 953, argues that the reassignment of the vineyard refers to "the Christian leadership of the renewed People of God." See also Oldenhage, "Spiralen," 352; Snodgrass, *Stories*, 293–94, 296–97.
6. Matt. 21:33-46; Mark 12:1-12; *GThom*. 65-66.
7. Jeremias, *Gleichnisse*, 59, reads the parable as a gospel to the poor. This interpretation is supported by the sociohistorical information in point 8 below.
8. Snodgrass, *Stories*, 277–80.

heralds, and tax collectors were killed on several historical occasions. This supposedly enhances the *street credibility* of the story.

There are modern ethical values that have made three essential features in the parable unbearable for contemporary readers:

6. The current *sympathetic view of Judaism* makes the parable difficult, since it has given impetus to anti-Semitic attitudes alleging that it prophesies the fall of Jerusalem and the Jews' loss of God's favor.[9]
7. The *contemporary view of Christianity,* with a strong emphasis on peace, is hardly compatible with the unbearable amount of escalating violence in the parable.[10] Perhaps Jesus was only giving a monitory example?
8. By *modern ethical standards* the owner's behavior is unacceptable, and one can feel a certain sympathy for the tenants. When this is combined with sociohistorical information about Galilee at the time the parable can be seen as the peasants' riot against a rich landowner. In this interpretation the owner appears as the villain of the story.[11] Moreover, the parable can simply be seen as a tragic story of a murder.[12]

Although aspects 6 through 8 are not unanimously accepted, they have managed to challenge the axiomatic christological interpretation. However, they do not escape the essential problem

---

9. Schottroff, *Gleichnisse*, 27–47, and Oldenhage, "Spiralen," 352–66, show how modern scholars strive for a politically correct interpretation.
10. Newell and Newell, "Parable," 226–37; Schottroff, *Gleichnisse*, 15–28; Oldenhage, "Spiralen."
11. For example, Scott, *Parable*, 251–53; Kloppenborg, *Tenants*, 134–59; J. David Hester, "Socio-Rhetorical Criticism," 27–57.
12. Cf. different interpretations in this vein presented by Evans, *Mark*, 221.

that is common to aspects 1 through 5: that the interpretation of the parable is heavily influenced by aspects outside the text[13] since both the narrator's audience and Luke's recipients were unaware of them.

My claim is that because of the attractive possibilities and alternative viewpoints offered by these eight extraneous factors the actual story within its textual framework has been overlooked. Although these factors may influence modern ways of understanding the parable, this may not necessarily be true concerning the audience(s) as implied by the text. It is important to note that the external factors are secondary, if not detrimental, to the parable's interpretation.

To the people listening to Jesus in the Lukan story, aspects 2 through 4 are purely anachronistic, and the influence of aspects 1 and 5 is in doubt as well. The way Luke's own recipients are designed to perceive the parable cannot be influenced by these factors either, at least not to a great extent.

1. The importance of the Old Testament references for the implied audience(s) is difficult to assess. Some general concepts, such as the vineyard as a metaphor for Israel, may be known to readers with a Jewish background or to people interested in Judaism. However, even then the same reservation has to be made as with the parable about sheep and their owners in Luke 15. We are reading the story in the Bible, but those listening to Jesus were not. Neither did the Lukan readers know that this text was going to be a part of the Holy Writings. A vineyard was such a common *topos* throughout Mediterranean culture that Israel hardly came to mind each time it was mentioned. Only

---

13. For example, out of Snodgrass's seven "issues requiring attention" only one or two discuss the meaning of the parable in the text: (5) "Is this parable an allegory . . . ?" and (7) "Does this parable . . . teach that God has rejected Israel by giving the kingdom to Gentiles?" (Snodgrass, *Stories*, 276–77).

the direct reference to Psalm 118 points to the Scriptures with certainty.

2. The fate of Jesus is not crucial for understanding this parable, since it is not mentioned until Luke 23. Even if Luke's audience is not supposed to be unaware of Jesus' death, this does not automatically have an impact on their reception of the text.[14] The audience of Jesus the Narrator is even less cognizant of his forthcoming passion and crucifixion. It might also be of interest that when Jesus, shortly before the parable, actually prophesies his own suffering and death (18:31-34) he does *not* accuse the Jewish leaders for what will happen; rather the contrary. Instead, the Son of Man "will be handed over to the Gentiles; and he will be mocked and insulted and spat upon. After they have flogged him, they will kill him."[15]

3. The same incognizance applies to later historical information about the fate of Jerusalem, Antipas, Nero, and so on. Applying each detail, such as killing the son "outside the vineyard" (Luke 20:15, cf. Heb. 13:12), to Jesus may be an interesting allegorical exercise for the church but was hardly intended as such for the audience listening to the Lukan Jesus, and probably not even for the readers of Luke.[16]

4. Synoptic references play no significant role when the goal is to understand Luke, since his recipients are not supposed to be aware of them[17] and since Luke the Author is thought to be

---

14. In a corresponding way it can be exciting to read a detective story for the second time, even though the result is already known, since a reader "agrees" to stay within the world of the narrative in order to be able to enjoy it; no direct connection to the real world is needed (see Segal, "Fictional Narrative," 70–71).
15. However, earlier in 9:22 it is prophesied that the religious leaders will reject the Son of Man and make him suffer.
16. Although both Luke 20:15 and Matt. 21:39 (not necessarily Q) make this change to Mark 12:8, Luke's implied readers are not aware of it.
17. To be sure, 1:1 refers to previous material about Jesus, but it does not suggest that the reader is cognizant of its closer contents. See above, chap. 1.

responsible for the story in every detail and not only for his own alterations of previous material. The "gospel to the poor" or any other explanation neglecting the emphasis on Jesus' authority typically makes it meaningless in the context, as if Jesus abruptly changed the subject to some political, financial, or other issue. Why would Luke have chosen such a topic in his presentation?[18]

5. When attempting to understand the text from the perspective of the recipients to whom it is told, general sociohistorical details play a role, but only insofar as the recipients are supposed to be aware of them. For example, absentee owners and lease arrangements are known issues, making the story easy to listen to from the outset.[19] However, a good story does not need to reflect on ordinary reality in every detail: flying carpets and speaking lamps can also occur in oriental stories without distracting the mind of the listener.

The modern perspectives 6 to 8 are even more dubious if the goal is to understand the meaning of the ancient text and not a religious or political application thereof.[20]

6. The later use of the parable for anti-Semitic purposes does not pertain to the question of how it was originally meant to be understood. Since it was based on prophetic material its language stays within Judaism.[21] Yet even if the parable turns out to be directed from the outset against the Jewish people it should not be censored, since the goal of an academic study is not to make the Bible politically correct.

---

18. Snodgrass, *Stories*, 276, calls these interpretations "banal."
19. See Hengel, "Gleichnis," 1–39; Snodgrass, *Stories*, 284.
20. To be sure, contemporary hermeneutical applications can consider them, but since applying any biblical text to the interpreters' own life requires a religious attitude to the text it cannot be a part of an academic reading that applies controllable methods only.
21. Cf. Milavec, "Analysis," 109.

7. The same applies to the question of the overwhelming violence in the story. No matter how horrible it seems to us, Luke's text is thoroughly colored by contemporary reality. Uncontrolled ferocity is an integral part of his story, and Luke's audience is accustomed from the outset to the use of brute strength. Individuals are mutilated in reality and metaphorically: it is predicted that Mary's heart will be pierced by a sword (2:35); people try to throw Jesus down a cliff (4:29), which he actually manages to do with some pigs (8:33), and the Son of Man is predicted to suffer and be killed (9:22), as happened to the prophets (11:49-51). Correspondingly, a man coming down from Jerusalem was stripped and beaten until he was half-dead (10:30) and another individual was similarly attacked and robbed (11:22). A typical character in the parables is a master or a strong man, who, like this owner, may slaughter bad servants (12:46) and enemies (19:27), or at least he beats the servants either lightly or severely (12:47-48).

There are also prophecies about divine violence. Capernaum will be thrown down to Hades (10:15), just as Sodom was destroyed by fire and sulfur from heaven (17:29)—an act the disciples want to repeat (9:54). All who do not repent will perish (13:3, 5). Every tree not producing good fruit will be cut down and thrown into the fire (3:9); the chaff will be burned with inextinguishable fire (3:17), and Jesus wishes that this fire were already kindled (12:50). To conclude, in Luke severe violence is an integral part not only of the parables but also of real life. Jesus and his disciples are not only victims of aggression but are aggressive themselves, though the most vehement destruction is carried out by God. Thus irrespective of the function of Luke's description of violence, by chapter 20 his audience was already accustomed to it.

8. Although not tolerable in modern Western business and working life, the owner's harsh and autocratic conduct was not unconventional in ancient societies, and Lukan readers were already accustomed to such behavior. The character of a landowner or master may not only show uncontrolled violence, as discussed above. He does not even need to treat his a servants especially well (17:7-10), since he can fire people without a proper hearing (16:2).

Attempts to see the parable as just a sad story, a warning to bad landowners, manage to de-allegorize it, but they simultaneously and completely remove it from the context, leaving the parable with "no real justification for preservation or retelling."[22] To be sure, there is a remarkable non-christological reading that partly escapes the problem of poor relevance to the audience by identifying the owner with Rome and the tenants as Zealots.[23] This interpretation suits the Lukan Jesus, who actually makes prophetic predictions against Jerusalem (19:41-44; 21:5-6, 20-24; 23:28-30). Moreover, the political threat was recognizable even without knowledge of the Jewish war. If Jerusalem were to be destroyed, the Romans were the best candidates for the task. Unfortunately, this allegory fits poorly with the story line, in which the founder of the vineyard destroys the tenants. The Romans did not found Jerusalem or rent it to the Jews.

It is thus problematic to base the interpretation on material that was unknown to the two audiences of the text. Such readings use the Lukan story as a basis for other, typically later ideological constructions but do not reflect the message and function of the story as it appears in the document.

---

22. Evans, *Mark*, 221, *contra* several American scholars working with modern methods.
23. Newell and Newell, "Parable."

THE WICKED TENANTS (20:9-19)

Does the Son Refer to Jesus?

Could the audience of Jesus the Narrator or Luke the Author understand the parable as referring to Jesus and his death? In other words, is the parable compatible with the traditional christological interpretation, if read unplugged? There are at least eight points that speak against connecting the son with Jesus.

1. According to the christological interpretation the religious leaders were charged with the murder of Jesus, since the parable accuses the tenants of murdering the son. Indeed, Luke says that the religious leaders were irritated because they felt that the parable was about them (πρὸς αὐτοὺς in 20:19). Thus they allegedly had something to do with the murder of the son. However, this can hardly refer to Jesus, who was alive and well at the time. A dead person would have made a better candidate for the murder victim.
2. According to the christological interpretation Jesus identified himself through the parable with the Son of God. Even if not referring to a specific Messianic title,[24] the son in the story is far more important than the servants, who are traditionally interpreted as prophets. If Jesus claimed to be such a super-prophet, this would probably have aroused fury. Indeed, the religious leaders were irritated with the framework of the story, but not because of Jesus' prophetic or christological claims.[25]
3. The tenants' aggression toward the son is based on their awareness of his identity, their confidence that the owner was unable to retaliate and was close to death, and their hope to inherit the vineyard once the son was gone. In the christological

---

24. See later in this chapter.
25. This is not done until 22:70, referring to Son of Man.

interpretation this means that the religious leaders, who realized that the parable was about them, knew that Jesus was God's only Son and that God was unable to react.

4. The christological interpretation leaves the persuasive function of the parable unclear. If it simply prophesies the death of Jesus and accuses the leaders of his murder it is but an assertion. Presenting it in the form of a parable does not provide any additional support to the assertion; moreover, it would be an exception. The Lukan parables seldom contain any specific information about reality and most of them exemplify a general rule. However, it could be a warning against killing Jesus.

5. If the parable aimed to stigmatize the leaders in the eyes of the people, their immediate negative reaction, μὴ γένοιτο (20:16), indicates that it was unsuccessful. It is unlikely that the people suddenly began to favor the leaders, who simultaneously are reported to be uncertain of their own popularity and afraid of the people (20:5-6, 19).[26] According to an alternative explanation, the people's negative reaction indicates that they thought the parable was about them. This, however, is not stated by the omniscient author, who instead lets the readers know (20:19) that the parable is about the religious leaders.

6. As a prophecy against Jerusalem or Israel the parable would repeat an Old Testament topic (as in 19:41-44; 21:5-6, 20-24; 23:28-30) and especially attract Luke's readers; however, in that case the emphasis on the son is pointless.

7. As predicting the death of Jesus (as in 9:22; 13:33; 18:31-34), the brutal climax of the parable is difficult to combine with the Lukan story of Jesus. The death of the son is avenged by the owner with overwhelming aggression: he will destroy the

---

26. Contra Nolland, *Luke*, 952, who argues that the people here suddenly defend the leaders "despite their enthusiasm for Jesus."

tenants (ἀπολέσει, 20:16) and a stone will crush them (λικμήσει, 20:18). As vengeance for the murder of Jesus, Jerusalem will be destroyed. However, the last point especially is a poor fit with Luke's message, since for him Jesus' death will bring Jerusalem the forgiveness of sins (24:47).

8. Finally, the traditional interpretation separates the parable from its near context. It means that Jesus introduces a new topic out of the blue. However, his partners in discussion, the scribes and the high priests, are mentioned both before and after the parable (19:47-20:8 and 20:19 (and vv. 20-26); this *inclusio* indicates a coherent framework. It is most natural to seek the function of the parable within this entity. Before any high-level theological theories are developed, the parable should make sense to the characters appearing in the discussion.

To avoid the difficulties as mentioned above it is high time to unplug the parable from the extraneous data and reconnect it to its context: the discussion about the authority (ἐξουσία) of Jesus and John the Baptist (20:1-8).

Does the Son Refer to John the Baptist?

Before we focus on the story as such and its function in persuasion an additional fascinating allegorical hypothesis deserves attention. According to an old reading the son refers to John the Baptist instead of Jesus. It would be odd if Jesus revealed his divine status to his antagonists before telling his disciples, and immediately after refusing to answer the question about his authority.[27] According to Malcolm Lowe, "if, however, the assumption is abandoned that Jesus himself was supposed to be the owner's son, there is a much more obvious

---

27. Gray, "Parable," 42–52; esp. 45.

alternative which appears not to have been entertained, namely that he was speaking of John the Baptist."[28]

I shall first discuss the reasons for the almost complete rejection of this alternative and then estimate its plausibility for the audiences of Luke and his Jesus.

Counterarguments

Klyne Snodgrass, a specialist in this parable, states that a reference to John the Baptist has "found relatively little support" and emphatically rejects it.[29] He presents four grounds for doing so:[30]

1. The interpretation involves "a desperate attempt to avoid a self-reference on the part of Jesus."
2. No hearer of the parable would think John the Baptist was its subject, even though he appears in the "preceding context's question," since the central term ἐκεφαλίωσαν in Mark 12:4 is a "far cry from decapitation and is no allusion to John [the Baptist]."[31]
3. John is never referred to as *son*.
4. The killer of John was Herod Antipas, not the religious leaders.[32]

To me the weakness of these arguments indicates that the hypothesis that the parable refers to John indeed deserves further study.

---

28. Lowe, "Parable," 257. Most of Lowe's article concentrates on reconstructing a hypothetical Baptist sequence in Proto-Matthew.
29. Snodgrass, *Stories*, 285 n. 115. Both he and Kloppenborg have published monographs on this parable. According to the latter the reference to John would solve some problems, but he still rejects the possibility (Kloppenborg, *Tenants*, 87–88).
30. Snodgrass, *Stories*, 294.
31. Ibid., n. 170. Cf. Evans, *Mark*, 232.
32. For Kloppenborg, *Tenants*, 87–88, this is "the obvious objection."

THE WICKED TENANTS (20:9-19)

1. The reference to John does not exclude a self-reference by Jesus, in fact rather the contrary. In Luke 20:3-4, 8 he combines the question of John's authority with that of his own. He suggests that John's status in some way resembles his own position.
2. The reference to John does not require a close allegorical description of his death. A reference to Mark is out of place; Luke does not use the verb ἐκεφαλίωσαν here. What happened to the head of the servant or the son is not reported, since the son was simply thrown out of the vineyard and killed. Nevertheless, an allusion to Mark 12:4 is feasible.[33]
3. The claim is incorrect. John is called "son" (υἱός) four times in Luke: 1:13, 36, 57; 3:2. Moreover, as many scholars have pointed out, "Son of God" (which actually does not appear in the parable) is not a notably messianic, apocalyptic, or theological concept, but may refer to a righteous person in general (for example, in Wis. 2:10).[34] Even if the reference to Jesus as God's only Son becomes commonplace in Christian theology later (for example, μονογενὴς υἱός in John 1:18 A, C³, Θ, ψ, and so on), the Deity was hardly in mind every time someone was called "son." Although Luke mentions that a heavenly voice called Jesus "beloved son" (Luke 3:22) after his baptism by John, Luke does not explicitly return to this theme.
4. It is even more difficult to charge the religious leaders with the murder of Jesus, since he is alive whereas John is dead. Luke explicitly refers to the leaders' negative attitude toward John, which was well known to the people (20:5-6), who considered

---

33. Evans, *Mark*, 233, argues against Crossan, "Parable," 452, that the somewhat obscure verb referring to the mutilation of the head has nothing to do with John, who was beheaded. However, to require such an exact match with reality would make it impossible to tell parables.
34. For example, according to Jeremias, *Gleichnisse*, 56–57, no Jew would have interpreted "son" here as a messianic title. However, Hengel, "Gleichnis," and Dunn, *Christology*, 12–22, demonstrate that the concept "Son of God" was more ambiguous in early Judaism.

John a prophet. But can the leaders be accused of an execution committed by Herod? Actually, the recipients must remember that Luke has declared such a general guilt earlier: "This generation may be held accountable for the blood of all the prophets that has been shed since the beginning of the world," 11:50. In 11:47-51 Jesus charges the experts in law with killing all the prophets and apostles sent to them by God. Thereby he makes use of an old topic (Jer. 7:25-26; 25:4, 29:19) that can clearly be found behind the parable of the tenants as well.[35] Who actually performed the killing is irrelevant when the goal is to accuse the leaders. The audience has heard that the Pharisees and the experts in the law declared John's proclamation useless or set his message aside (ἠθέτησαν, Luke 7:30). Immediately after the parable Jesus speaks of a stone that is similarly "set aside" or "declared useless" (ἀπεδοκίμασαν, 20:17), referring to Psalm 118:22. This is presented as an alternative to "killing" (ἀπέκτειναν) the son in the parable (20:15):

7:30	The Pharisees and the experts in law / οἱ Φαρισαῖοι καὶ οἱ νομικοί	ἠθέτησαν	God's plan proclaimed by John the Baptist
11:47-51	The experts in law / οἱ νομικοί	ἀπέκτειναν (x2), ἀποκτενοῦσιν, ἀπολομένου	The prophets, the apostles, from Abel to Zechariah
20:15	The tenants / οἱ γεωργοί	ἀπέκτειναν	The son of the owner
20:17	The builders / οἱ οἰκοδομοῦντες	ἀπεδοκίμασαν	The stone

In each case the audience is made culpable for killing God's messenger, even though technically they were not responsible. In

---

35. E.g., Nolland, *Luke*, 951.

the same way, in Acts 2:23 Luke lets Peter accuse his fellow Jews in Jerusalem of Jesus' murder. Although this happened "by the hands of those outside the law" (διὰ χειρὸς ἀνόμων προσπήξαντες ἀνείλατε) the Jews are held responsible for his death. But unlike John's death, this had not yet taken place at the time the parable was told.

Snodgrass's reasons for excluding a reference to John the Baptist in the parable are thus either misleading or insufficient. But a more thorough reading of the narrative is required to see whether the implied audiences could actually identify the son with John. Moreover, since some allusion to Jesus himself may also be plausible, the function of the parable in its context becomes interesting indeed.

John in Luke

Would it be plausible that the audience primarily connects the son in the story with John? Does he outshine the prophets as the son did when compared with the servants?

John plays a specific role for the Lukan Jesus, since the two are intertwined. Luke presents a miraculous childhood narrative of both and combines these stories. John and Jesus are introduced as cousins (1:5-80). John's own proclamation is presented in 3:1-19, and their last communication is reported in 7:20-23. The following section, 7:24-35, contains Jesus' comments on John, including a comparison of their style (vv. 33-34). But most importantly, according to Jesus, John "is a prophet and far more than a prophet" (v. 26: προφήτην; ναὶ λέγω ὑμῖν, καὶ περισσότερον προφήτου). In 9:7-9 it is said that Jesus reminds Herod of John, whom Herod had executed. Other people are said to make the same connection in 9:19 (and 11:1). Finally, 16:16 contains Jesus' obscure statement: "The law and the prophets were until John." Nowhere does Jesus present himself as being more important than John. Instead, he wants to get a share of John's fame, as can be seen in his answer in 20:4.

Throughout his text Luke presents John as being almost equal to Jesus, and the two are compared to each other not only by other people, including Herod, but also by Jesus himself. John is not only the greatest "among those born of women" (7:28), he is the last prophet, and far more than just a prophet. God sent his prophets to the people several times, and they have all been mistreated and killed. John was the last in the sequence, but simultaneously something more than any of his predecessors, and yet he faced the same destiny they did.

Since John has repeatedly been presented to the Lukan audience as an outstanding character and as the final super-prophet he may well fit the role of the son in the parable. In view of the preceding discussion on John's authority it is most natural to think that at least the listeners to the Lukan Jesus understand the parable as illuminating the question of John's authority and fate. Without any closer allegorical connections they can see that John is the ultimate prophet and more, and that he was ill-treated and killed, like the preceding prophets. Thus those who are guilty can reckon with the God's coming and retaliation.

Yet such a fixed allegorical identification would destroy the flexibility of the parable. For the audience the reference to John hardly excludes a simultaneous allusion to Jesus. On the contrary, since Jesus in 20:3-8 combines his own and John's authority, a certain identification with Jesus and the son in the story can be assumed: If John were the last prophet, who was killed and whose message was rejected, what would happen to Jesus? Thus it can serve as a warning, and not as a description of future events. The audience hears even this parable within Luke's story world, a world in which Jesus is still alive.[36]

Is the Parable an Allegory at All?

Homogenizing Jesus' narration with that of Luke is the equivalent of resorting to allegory. This means finding "real life" counterparts to the parable's characters, events, ideas, or other details. The risks and benefits of this approach have been discussed in the Introduction above.[37] The allegorical reading of the story of the tenants is based on intertextual connections that would never have occurred to the audience(s) implied in the text. The approach transforms the parable to a theological or ethical proclamation with neither a persuasive role nor the means of appealing to the audience. In brief, a one-sided allegorical reading is, for the implied audience, hardly the primary way of understanding the parable. On the other hand, the resemblances between the story and the context should not be overlooked either, since they are visible for any audience. Thus the parable's narrative and persuasive dimension must be integrated by observing the clear signals connecting it to the context.

The choice between Jesus and John has been discussed above without an exclusive answer, but both audiences more easily observe further allegories. Thus the servants may remind the audiences of the Old Testament prophets, and the owner may refer to God. The vineyard may create more than one allusion: it can refer to Israel, Jerusalem, or even a specific religious status.[38] This can be said to be true no matter whether Luke's audience is well-versed in the Scriptures or not, since the idea of sending servants who are ill-treated reminds them of God sending the prophets and of the apostles in Luke 11. Separating religious and political interpretations

---

36. See more fully in chap. 1.
37. See more in detail in chap. 1.
38. Snodgrass, *Stories*, 293.

is anachronistic; the parable also includes a warning to Jerusalem, as can be seen in 21:5, 20-24, which is likewise derived from Old Testament tradition and does not simply describe the history *ex eventu*.

However, no allusions suffice for understanding the meaning and function of the parable. If they determine the parable's meaning it becomes an unwarranted accusation against the religious leaders. Then the parable also retells the real situation from the speaker's perspective. If the message is "you have killed the son" (John or Jesus), saying this in the form of a parable does not make the accusation any stronger. It would not have any persuasive force in itself, and the people's reaction would indicate its failure. Moreover, accusing the leaders of John's death would perhaps be too late, and for Jesus' death, too early. A warning could be a better choice. But in general it can be said that the allegorical references have no clear connection to the context; their relevance to the discussion on authority in the previous verses still remains obscure. Thus the function of the parable must be sought elsewhere.

Above I have referred to some attempts to liberate the parable from allegory. According to these readings the owner is not axiomatically seen as God, the tenants are not always Jesus' opponents, and the son is not Jesus (or even John). However, most of these readings have no relevance within the context.

The Parable as Persuasion

The following discussion will take a different approach. The parable is first studied without any allegory, but also without separating it from its context. Only after that is its message connected to the context by observing some allusions that are obvious to the implied audiences.

THE WICKED TENANTS (20:9-19)

Reading the Story in Context

The goal of an unplugged reading is to see the parable as its implied audience would. Thus after purifying the story of external and anachronistic information it is time to read it in its immediate context and ask how it is designed to function there. Toulmin's model for analyzing argumentation can be used for this purpose. First, some particular observations concerning the narration can be made:

1. The parable is told specifically to the people, while the religious authorities overhear it; this setting resembles the double audience of the previous story in 16:1-9, the *Unjust Steward*, which is told to the disciples but overheard by the Pharisees.
2. The audience's most natural perspective or object of identification is the tenants, although this is not self-evident. The servants and the son lack their own will, since they are almost solely go-betweens in the owner's and tenants' business; only the owner and tenants have the freedom to make choices. However, the owner is dissociated from the scene both spatially and temporally, since he goes abroad for a long period and most of the time he is not present. Moreover, his obscene wealth and unpredictable behavior make him a difficult object for identification.[39] Thus it is most natural for the addressees to follow the story from the tenants' perspective.
3. The story line is rather conventional, except for the multiple strong signals at the end. As in any good story, some escalation can be observed regarding the treatment of the servants.[40]

---

39. To be sure, in 12:16-21, the *Rich Fool*, and 16:19-31, the *Rich Man and Lazarus*, a wealthy man is the protagonist of the story and therefore the best object of identification.
40. Contra Nolland, *Luke*, 951, according to whom "escalation is retained exclusively for the case of the son."

However, the variation is not significant: the first servant is beaten (δείραντες, 20:10), the second is beaten and insulted (δείραντες καὶ ἀτιμάσαντες, 20:11), the third is wounded (τραυματίσαντες, 20:12), and the beloved son is killed (ἀποκτείνωμεν, 20:14). Following narrative conventions, one would expect the high point of the story to be connected with the third servant, since the son as the fourth messenger comes as a surprise. However, the audience is not reported as reacting until the owner's vehement retaliation, which they find is the actual climax of the story.

4. The retaliation in the end is remarkable. The owner not only destroys the tenants (ἀπολέσει, 20:16) but, as the climax of the story, gives the vineyard to other people, as if the latter were even worse. In Jesus' parables the catastrophe resulting in negative behavior or attitude may be physical (for example, in 12:46-48), social (for example, in 14:29-30), financial (for example, in 19:24), or spiritual (16:22-31). These alternatives are not differentiated in any special way: shame may be as terrible as death; losing property is just as awful as ending in Hades. Thus even here Jesus does not even say whether the tenants are killed or not.[41]

5. The people's emphatic reaction to the climax of the story, the (typically Pauline) exclamation μὴ γένοιτο (20:16), is noteworthy since their attitude toward Jesus is extremely positive: they are reported to "hang on" to him (ἐξεκρέματο, 19:48). In contrast, they are told not to esteem the leaders too highly. If the goal of the story were to stigmatize the leaders, the people's reaction to it would be unwarranted. It hardly speaks

---

41. Nolland, *Luke*, 952, remarks that *destroying* the tenants could, in principle, refer to a court process instead of killing them.

of the people, either, since the omniscient author says otherwise. Obviously they understood it in another way.[42]

Second, the topic of the parable can be delineated by looking at the context. The preceding verses (20:1-8) discuss the legitimacy not only of Jesus' program but also that of an alleged prophet, John. When the parable, with its aftermath (20:9-19), then rephrases Scripture's recurring accusation that the prophets were received badly and killed, it is more natural to see these two sections hanging together than to argue that the parable introduces a completely new topic.

Luke's readers are already accustomed to both themes—the antagonists questioning Jesus' authority for proclaiming his Gospel and Jesus accusing them of killing the prophets. This background thereby guides their understanding of the text. In chapter 15 Jesus defended and explained his right to act (ἐξουσία) by telling the parables of the Lost Sheep, Coin, and Son; he emotionally tried to convince the critics that his behavior was justified. In 16:1-9, the *Unjust Steward*, Jesus argued that God favors his high-handed program, irrespective of its lacking formal justification. When Jesus now, in chapter 20, returns to this issue, the readers not only recognize the topic but can expect Jesus to be more outspoken.

When asked in 20:2 about his right to act, Jesus replies, in his typical way, with a counter-question about the authority of John: Was his baptism from heaven or was it of human origin? The omniscient author lets the readers listen to the antagonists' negotiations. Since they realize that the question is impossible to answer, they resort to expressing ignorance. Soon after this discussion they challenge Jesus with a formally identical Catch-22, the question

---

42. I have refrained from synoptic comparisons. However, in this case the contrast to Matt. 21:41 could not be stronger. There the audience urges the master to do what in Luke they abhor!

of taxes (20:26), where both answers are also equally wrong. But in both cases Jesus has the last word.

Jesus' answer in v. 8 has several functions. First, it does not explicitly reveal his opinion about the source of his authority, but implicitly it claims a heavenly, prophetic power, since everybody knows about his high respect for John. Second, it brings the character of John and his destiny into the discussion. Now Jesus can make use of both themes. As with all the cases in which he is asked an impossible question, he not only manages to defend himself but also uses the situation to teach and warn his interlocutors. Luke's audience is already familiar with this habit and can thus expect more from him than just avoiding a straight answer to a dangerous question. In this situation close allegorical resemblances are hardly required.

Analyzing the Argumentation

Now the text can be studied with Toulmin's model. We have seen that many parables function as the *backing* for a *warrant*, that is, referring to the audience's general knowledge, confirming the rule by which they ought to move from *data* to *claim*, being persuaded by the speaker. Could this parable have such a role, despite the axiomatic allegorical interpretations with all the variations? Delineating a Toulminian structure of argumentation is challenging, since the only explicit argumentative factor is the parable itself (presumably a *backing*).

THE WICKED TENANTS (20:9-19)

Figure V.1

Backing: The parable of the Wicked Tenants

▼

Warrant: [a general rule combining Data and Claim]

▼

Data: [something presumably accepted by the audience] ► *Claim*: [the hoped-for new opinion or action by the audience]

We can start by attempting to explicate the *warrant*, the general rule illustrated by the parable. If no allegory or even context is observed, what is the general lesson the story tries to teach? There are several non-exclusive alternatives. If the story is seen from the owner's viewpoint[43] it could teach: "never trust the tenants" or "don't be credulous, react to the first warning." If, however, the tenants are the most natural protagonists, the lesson could read: "the messengers of the landowner should not be mistreated but obeyed" or, more generally: "the messengers of a distant strong man should be taken seriously and respected," "underestimating the strong man's capability of retaliation may lead to destruction," or the like. The climax, the surprise at the end, is not only the death of the son but especially the vehement retaliation by the owner, who, despite the tenants' belief, arrives after all. Other parables in Luke illustrate the furious arrival of a master (12:46-48; 19:15-27). In any case, no allegory is needed in order to recognize this message.

---

43. As stated above, the servants and the son are poor protagonists or targets for identification, since they lack any volition.

Figure V.2

Backing: The parable of the Wicked Tenants

▼

Warrant: The messengers of a distant strong man should be obeyed

▼

Data: [something presumably accepted by the audience] ▶ *Claim*: [the hoped-for new opinion or action by the audience]

This *warrant* (or its alternatives as presented above) guides the search for the *data* and *claim*, and it should show why anybody accepting the *data* naturally arrives at the *claim*. At this point we have to return to the context.

In our search for the *data* we should look at the people's opinions, since they are the explicit audience (20:9). Is there anything they hold to be true, anything that would function as the point of departure for the argument? This should be clearly stated or strongly implied in the text, so that not only they but also Luke's readers could follow the reasoning. Indeed, such a statement can be found in 20:6, where the omniscient author informs the audience about the thoughts of the religious leaders. According to the leaders, the people were persuaded (πεπεισμένος) that John was a prophet. This statement in itself may serve as *data*. Alternatively, since the topic is authority, the people's belief may be rephrased: John's authority came from God. Thus the leaders should have obeyed him. This is actually what the leaders suspect that the people think (v. 5).

If the strong Old Testament tradition behind the story is considered, the *warrant* can be seen more directly as referring to the fate of the prophets. God punished those who not only did not accept their message but also mistreated them. Then the *data* can be more precise as well: John acted with prophetic authority based neither on his high social status nor on his religious education but on his sender, God.[44] This corresponds to the authority of the servants sent by the owner: the tenants were supposed to obey them, not because of their personal qualities but because of the authority of their master.

Figure V.3

Backing: The parable of the Wicked Tenants

▼

Warrant: The messengers of a distant strong man should be obeyed / Mistreating and neglecting them leads to punishment

▼

Data: John was God's prophet ▶ *Claim*: John should have been obeyed

If the *data* is accepted, the recipients should also accept the *claim*, the actual message put forward by Jesus. This implicit goal depends on the *data*. Insofar as it refers to John, the *claim* must deal with John as well. A plain accusation such as "John should have been taken seriously" does not call for any action. Another charge, "Those who rejected John will suffer retaliation," sounds more dynamic, and accords with the listening leaders' reaction in v. 19 "because they realized he had told this parable against (or with reference to, πρὸς αὐτοὺς εἶπεν) them." However, as the discussion actually deals with the authority of Jesus, his claim in v. 8 to share authority with John opens new possibilities for the *claim*. If the *data* read "Jesus' authority

---

44. Thus, e.g., Nolland, *Luke*, 944, according to whom the possibility of their immediate divine authorization nullifies the claims of the people representing the institutional religious framework.

comes from God," then the *claim* can look forward instead of just blaming the antagonists: "Jesus' proclamation should be accepted" or "Jesus must not be mistreated." Thereby it attempts to change the audience's behavior, no matter whether they represent the people or the leaders.

Figure V.4

Backing: The parable of the Wicked Tenants

▼

Warrant: The messengers of a distant strong man should be obeyed

▼

Data: John's and Jesus' authority comes from God ▶ *Claim*: The audience must accept Jesus' proclamation

Moreover, the parable refers to God with a *qal wahomer* structure: If a landowner will avenge himself on people harming his messengers, how much more will God?

Figure V.5

Backing: The parable of the Wicked Tenants (*4)

▼

Warrant: A distant strong man will retaliate against those offending his messengers / God is not weaker than earthly strong men

▼

Data: John and Jesus are God's prophets ▶ *Claim*: God will retaliate against those offending them

When the parable is interpreted from the leaders' viewpoint the most significant change is that they do not accept the *data*, namely, John's (or Jesus') prophetic authority. This may make the whole persuasion collapse. However, the purpose of leaving some elements implicit in the argumentation is to cover its weaknesses. If the recipients agree on everything else they may swallow the implicit factors as well. Typically the *warrants* are such elements, but this time the major question discussed (the *data*) may function in this way. Jesus does not reveal the source of his ἐξουσία, but he attempts to confirm his thesis about his divine authority not only by connecting himself to John but also by telling the parable. Thereby he calls his antagonists, at least hypothetically, to think about the possibility that John *was* and he *is* God's messenger. In that case severe punishment threatens everyone who does not accept their message. Thus the obvious conclusion is that the recipients ought to accept them and their message and to act accordingly.

Conclusion

Liberation of the parable from anachronistic and other extraneous information and subsequent interpretations challenges the traditional axiomatic understanding. The story of the *Wicked Tenants* is neither a christological prophecy nor does it chiefly accuse the Jews or predict the destruction of Jerusalem. Modern substitutes for the traditional interpretation, such as a reference to Galilean social turmoil, are also misleadingly based on information unknown to the implied audience. Other alternative interpretations suffer from weak contact to the situation and the topic discussed; they imply that Jesus suddenly changed the subject.

No allegorical allusions are required for understanding the parable and its primary function. It simply emphasizes a principle according to which the envoys of a distant business partner or strong man should be taken seriously. This idea appeals to financial and political common sense; the story is aimed at enhancing this principle.

Allusions to Old Testament prophets, as mentioned earlier by Luke, and further allusions to John and Jesus indicate how the principle should be applied. Seen in its actual context, the parable is an integral part of the ongoing discussion between Jesus and the religious leaders. It belongs to the final plea to listen to his message. He challenges them to at least think about the possibility that the famous John, and he as well, are God's ultimate messengers. Their authority is not based on their status, wisdom, or education, but on their sender, just as was the case with the prophets referred to in the corresponding stories in the Old Testament tradition.

On a higher ideological, which is to say theological level, the parable and its framework story create the climax of the Lukan discussion about the legitimacy of Jesus' radical Jubilee program of forgiving sins and proclaiming God's acceptance to those not deserving it. The placement of this parable as the last of the narrative parables gives Lukan readers a signal for its interpretation. The opening childhood stories (Luke 1–2) and the encounters with John and the devil (Luke 3–4) indicate that Jesus is God's beloved (only) Son. This is further strengthened by his presentation of the Jubilee program in Nazareth (4:18-21). Although Luke does not continue to emphasize this idea, this closing parable may be seen as an *inclusio* that finalizes the theme.

Meanwhile, Jesus has attempted to persuade his antagonists in several ways to accept his program and join it. He has admitted that legally they are right in their criticism, but he first appeals to their feelings (Luke 15) or God's autonomy (Luke 16). Now he finally states as clearly as possible that he is fulfilling a mission from God; he works with a prophetic, that is, a divine authority that surpasses any other.

Despite the invitation to the audience to reassess their opinions, the tone is more severe than before. The warning undertone is not unique in Luke. In 12:36-38, the *Watchful Slaves*, a servant acts against his distant master's will and is punished. However, the emphasis on the messengers in Luke 20 is new. When the principle is applied to the discussion it supports the implicit claim that the rejection of John by the leaders will have serious effects on Jerusalem and its religious elite. Listening to Jesus is their last chance to survive. This means that not even by this fierce parable is Jesus simply mocking or attacking his antagonists. Instead, he strongly appeals to both the people and the leaders, and he is still attempting to change their point of view.

The unplugged interpretation of the parable of the wicked tenants escapes the problems typical of a basic allegorical reading. It seamlessly connects the parable to the context and the ongoing discussion. As the threat at the end remains rather stereotypical and unspecific, it is not to be seen as an accurate prophecy of the fate of the antagonists—or Jews in general. Instead of such an anti-Semitic message, we can find here a serious attempt to influence the partners in the discussion.

The traditional christological interpretation is not excluded by this reading. However, on the level of Jesus the Narrator and his audience it remains somewhat veiled, like the prophecy in 18:31-34. For the Lukan readers a clearer reference to Jesus can be assumed, especially after they have studied the subsequent chapters.

PART III

6

The Overall Mapping of the Parables

No general hypothesis about the Lukan parables is reliable if it is based on a selective reading.[1] Therefore, after the previous deep analysis of some key parables, the next step is to create a comprehensive presentation of all Jesus' parables in Luke.[2] I will do this in two interrelated parts. chapter 6 will provide a synopsis of the parables. I will examine how to identify them and their essential qualities, such as length, type, images, audience, exigency, credibility, and references. The overall results for each question and their most interesting correlations will be displayed. One specific aim of this chapter is to create Spreadsheet 1,[3] which illustrates all the Lukan

---

1. Forbes (*God*, 16–23) presents a review of major studies on the parables in Luke. These, similar to his own book, make conclusions about Luke's theology based on Luke's *Sondergut* only. However, Luke's readers could hardly distinguish such a selection. Moreover, it cannot be proven that the historical author preferred sources unknown to Matthew (whom he hardly knew) to the others.
2. This study follows the principles presented in the introduction. Briefly, the ideal way of reading the parables is to know nothing more and nothing less than the audience at which they are aimed.
3. Visit fortresspress.com/thuren and click on the "Additional Supporting Resources" tab to view and download the spreadsheets.

parables and their most prominent characteristics. This database will allow one to make several comparisons and cross-references in order to see which features are linked cto each other.

All this paves the way for chapter 7, where I will scrutinize the formal features, contents, and functions of every Lukan parable. This chapter serves as a practical handbook to these texts. Analyzing particular parables simultaneously supports the general results presented in chapter 6. Together, these chapters provide an overview of the messages of the Lukan parables, their persuasive function, and the theology, which will be presented in chapter 8.

Introduction

This all-encompassing study of the Lukan parables aims at a better understanding of both particular stories and their general features.

First, in order to understand any single parable it is useful to ask how and why Luke and his Jesus usually tell them. If we can identify some typical characteristics they can be detected even when they are less evident. In other words, general knowledge of Lukan parables will serve as a heuristic tool guiding the interpretation when a particular case is obscure. Any information may be valuable, since gathering *big data*[4] may reveal important issues unnoticed by specific questions. Eventually, general observations regarding the way Luke and his Jesus use the parables may yield profound theological results as well.

Second, an essential prerequisite for any dependable general characterization is that all parables are included. In earlier research there is no shortage of attempts at overarching descriptions, but too often these studies omit problematic cases.[5] However, Lukan parables

---

4. See http://en.wikipedia.org/wiki/Big_data. To be sure, the number of qualities discussed in this study remains limited. Nevertheless, we may gain new insights into the parables.

are so multifaceted that one can even make mutually exclusive characterizations and give good examples in the text if other cases are set aside. Thus references to only a few parables do not suffice for reliable general observations.

A holistic view of all the parables requires specific techniques. In chapters 2 through 5, I discussed this thoroughly regarding earlier research on some key parables. Now I will mainly refer to some recent and illustrative studies. Since there are around sixty distinct parables in Luke, and in each case more than a dozen factors deserve attention, they cannot all be discussed here at length, even if in some cases a deeper examination would be desirable. This has to do with delineating the material—the parabolic nature of some cases is disputed among scholars—as well as assessing their different attributes. Accordingly, the overview presented here can hardly be fault-proof, but it can be fault-tolerant. Since the aim is to get a preliminary rough image of the Lukan parables, single cases are not too significant. Disagreement with one or even several details does not yet disqualify the general view. After all, the Lukan parables are so various and manifold that exceptions from almost any convention can be found.

What is a Parable and Where Can They Be Found?

The Lukan text abounds with parabolic narratives, parabolic rules extended by some narrative elements, and shorter corresponding sayings, as well as different metaphors and figures of speech using images. This diversity means that an absolute definition of a *parable* is difficult to achieve. There will always be some disputable cases that do not exactly fit the rule. In order to detect all Lukan parables

---

5. There are, however, some good exceptions, which will be discussed below (especially Drury, *Parables,* 108–57, and Merz, "Einleitung").

we need a reasonable working definition covering most cases usually understood as parables. The result must be compatible with other studies; an idiosyncratic definition is hardly useful.

Older exegetical definitions are typically based on formal features. They may contain unnecessary factors such as pious theological ideas[6] or require that a parable must be vivid and simple.[7] Often such descriptions limit parables to metaphors or narratives only.[8] Dictionaries cannot do any better, as they refer to moral or religious uses of the word.[9] Instead of discussing them I will start with the views of the three perhaps most prominent contemporary scholars in parable studies.

1. Klyne Snodgrass aptly focuses on function when defining the parable. His definition is supposed to resemble the ancient Greek use of the word and cover the cases found in the gospels: *A parable is an expanded analogy used to convince and persuade.*[10] Contrary to the dictionaries, Snodgrass emphasizes the aim of the parables and omits references to their spiritual and fictitious characteristics. His definition, however, has two critical problems. First, in Luke 13:1-4 Jesus refers to Galileans killed by Pilate and people killed by a tower in Siloam. This case, too, is an expanded analogy used to convince and persuade the audience. However, it is hardly a parable. Second, the requirement of a persuasive function is problematic as well. When Jesus speaks to God, referring to the family relationship (10:22, *Father and Son*), Luke presents this as a parable, not as an explicit christological statement.[11] But does this mean that Jesus uses it "to

---

6. Manson, *Teaching*, 65.
7. Dodd, *Parables*, 15–16.
8. Thus Snodgrass, *Stories*, 7–8.
9. Merriam-Webster: "A usually short fictitious story that illustrates a moral attitude or a religious principle" [http://www.merriam-webster.com/dictionary/parable]; Oxford: "A simple story used to illustrate a moral or spiritual lesson, as told by Jesus in the Gospels" [http://www.oxforddictionaries.com/definition/english/parable?q=parable].
10. Snodgrass, *Stories*, 9.

convince and persuade" God? Alternatively, is he only pretending to pray to God while actually persuading his audience?

2. Charles Hedrick, another prominent parables scholar, avoids the problem of references to reality by emphasizing that parables are "freely invented fiction narratives."[12] Nevertheless, both *invention* and *narrative* are difficult to delineate. Many brief rules the evangelist identifies as parables are excluded, since they neither contain a proper story (e. g., 4:23, *Healer 1*) nor any fiction. Moreover, there are longer problematic rules as well. Is the exhortation to settle with the opponent (12:58-59, *Going to Judge*) fiction? Hedrick correctly assesses it as a narrative.[13] It displays four people, three stages, and several forms of action. Yet Luke presents it as an exhortation, a practical piece of advice to the audience, not actually a story invented by Jesus.

Corresponding advice, neither based on reality nor fictitious, is given to banquet guests and their host (14:8-14, *Guidelines 1 and 2*), yet the message of these "instructions" is hardly limited to those people only. The instructions undeniably refer to some religious issues as well. Some other stories do not include guidelines but just describe typical behavior, such as 11:5-8, the *Friend at Midnight* and 17:7-10, the *Useless Servant*. Even these are actually non-fictional narratives that, however, do not refer to reality either but to general habits or observations.

For a more precise definition of a parable Hedrick correctly dismisses formal grounds by which "similes, similitudes, metaphors, aphorisms, and example stories" could be identified. Indeed, such criteria fit poorly with the language of the Synoptic evangelists, who can present the same stories in different forms.[14] Even the *function* is a

---

11. See van der Watt, "Meisterschüler," 745–54.
12. Hedrick, *Parables*, 5.
13. Ibid., 12–13.

difficult criterion as, according to Hedrick, not all parables call for a comparison.[15]

For identifying a *narrative*, Hedrick uses a simple classic standard: There should be "a structural plan, consisting of beginning, middle, and end."[16] However, he admits to including several stories that lack a proper beginning (11:5-8; 12:58-59; 17:7-9), as they "give clear evidence of a plot," stories that "no longer exist."[17] Unfortunately, no evidence is provided. Hedrick appears to base his solution on nonexistent versions reconstructed by himself. If, however, one is free to alter or invent stories inspired by the actual document there is no limit to finding parables.

Hedrick's results remain arbitrary. Of the sixteen cases explicitly signaled by Luke as parables, Hedrick discusses only six.[18] Some are omitted by classifying them with vague terms such as "traditional proverb" (4:23) or "aphorism" (6:39), while some are not discussed at all (e. g., 12:39). To be sure, these parables are not narratives, and narrative is Hedrick's main interest. Nevertheless, 21:29-31 is hardly just a "simple image," as it involves both people and action.[19] Peculiarly enough, 14:8-14 is dismissed as "teaching" or "instruction,"[20] although there is a clear story with an "opening, middle, and end," and Luke calls it a parable. The solution appears to be made on the basis of formal criteria: Jesus seems to give guidelines only. However, in the following verses his sayings are interpreted as an ordinary parable. The external form cannot be decisive: the parables can be questions (typically τίς ἐξ ὑμῶν), exhortations (4:23;

---

14. Ibid., 11–15.
15. Ibid., 16–17.
16. Ibid., 11.
17. Ibid., 12–13.
18. Hedrick does not observe that 5:37-39, *Wine 1 and 2*, and 15:8-10, the *Lost Coin*, are clearly (καί, ἤ) connected to the previous cases explicitly designated as parables.
19. Ibid., 14–15.
20. Ibid., 94.

THE OVERALL MAPPING OF THE PARABLES

10:2; 12:24, 27-28, 58-59; 13:24-29), claims (beginning, e.g., with οὐδεὶς) and so on, but they still have several other features typical of parables.

3. Referring to Rüdiger Zymner's suggestions,[21] Ruben Zimmermann makes the third recent attempt to define a parable. His criteria are based on a thorough theoretical discussion, and they result in a useful list of parables in Luke.[22] In general I find his criteria well-founded and helpful for defining the parabolic material in Luke. Moreover, they fit the evangelist's use of the word παραβολή. In order to reach an even more dependable definition, some comments and critical observations still need to be made.

According to Zimmermann, a parable is:

1. *Narrative*: At least one action sequence or change of status is involved; thus simple comparisons ("You are the salt of the earth") without any evidence of plot are excluded. This criterion is broader than Hedrick's "opening-middle-end" and better fits the Lukan material.
2. *Fictional*: References to examples presented as historical (Jonah in the belly of a sea monster), are excluded. This criterion is necessary as well, but it requires reshaping, as there are several parables that are neither fictional nor refer to any historical case (see my comments on Hedrick above). Thus it is better to say that a parable does not refer to allegedly historical events.
3. *Realistic*: Impossible things, such as apocalyptic visions, are excluded. The parables could have happened. This criterion 3 is superfluous. The parable in 18:25, *Camel* fulfills the other criteria but not this one. It is highly unrealistic, yet it functions just as

---

21. Zymner, "Parabel," 502.
22. Zimmermann, "Gleichnisse," 25–28; "Paradigm Shift," 172–73.

any other parable does. Thus there is no need to exclude it at the outset.

4. *Metaphoric*: A parable points to a statement outside the primary level of meaning. This criterion is well formulated.

5. *Active in appeal and interpretation*: A parable wants to be interpreted; it calls for taking a position, insight, deeper understanding, or action. This criterion is a more sophisticated version of Snodgrass's idea of the parable's purpose as "to convince and persuade." Yet similar problems are involved, especially regarding the parable presented to God (10:22). Although not persuading to action, it still aims at affecting the hearer in some way, perhaps by deepening previous insights, attitudes, or values. Yet Zimmermann's formulation is essentially more applicable than that of Snodgrass.

6. *Co-text- and context-related*: The literary setting is essential for a proper reading. This criterion is somewhat problematic. There are several parables in Luke that contain general instructions but are too loosely connected to a situation, especially the six parables included in the Sermon on the Plain (6:20-49).

When these criteria are applied to Luke's text, some cases remain perplexing. Zimmermann and the German *Kompendium*-collective count the apocalyptic vision in 17:34-35 as a parable,[23] going against criterion 3. Luke presents these cases as true examples of what will happen, not as fictitious stories. The *Kompendium* counts the reference to little children (18:17) as a parable,[24] but this contradicts criterion 1. The narrative aspect is too weak. The verse is a parallel to *GThom.* 22, which could indeed be a parable. This, however, does not make it a parable in Luke.

---

23. Labahn, "Alternative," 227–33.
24. Standhartinger, "Einssein," 883–87.

There are two parabolic expressions not included in the *Kompendium* that are worth considering. Besides 18:25, the *Camel*, discussed above, Jesus refers to a popular image of a prophet in 4:24: "And he said, 'Truly I say to you, no prophet is accepted in the prophet's hometown.'" The saying is metaphorical and does not describe a historical case, even if it is supported by the stories about Elijah and Elisha. If Jesus is not directly claiming that he is a prophet[25] he simply refers to a general principle according to which one cannot make a similar impact on people who know one compared to a foreign audience. Moreover, the image presented calls for interpretation and action. The crucial criterion is the first one: is there a narrative element, or is this a static saying? The change of status is at stake: will the prophet be accepted (δεκτός) or not? Although the answer is negative, the basic idea of Zimmermann's first rule is fulfilled. Admittedly, this verse and the reference to little children in 18:17 are both borderline cases. Although the latter also refers to an action, receiving, its Lukan version is so short that it does not even explicitly connect a verb to the main character, παιδίον.

One criterion needs to be added to Zimmermann's list when analyzing the Lukan parables: *The parable is presented by Jesus*. Otherwise the Sadducees' parable in 20:29-33 would have to be counted as well. In this regard Luke's first parable, 4:23, *Healer 1*, is somewhat problematic, as Jesus suggests that it will be uttered by his audience in Nazareth.

John Drury offers an interesting alternative to Zimmermann, as he finds in Luke fifty-three parables, almost as many as the *Kompendium*.[26] Some of them (3:7, 17; 7:24) have no narrative

---

25. See the analysis below.
26. Drury, *Parables*, 108–10. Despite some good results, his criteria for identifying a parable are peculiar. Quoting John Creed, he claims that there is "an analogy to a spiritual truth" (Creed, *St. Luke*, 134). Creed further argues: "The point of the parable lies in the analogy, not in the

element or they are not told by Jesus (3:9). Perhaps 6:45, which tells about the abundance of the heart, could be interpreted as a separate parable, parallel to 6:43-45, the *Bad Tree,* but "heart" is hardly a living metaphor here. Drury misses eight cases that are mostly brief parables, for example, 17:37, the *Vultures.*[27]

In general, the line between metaphors and brief parables is not always clear, and several cases can be assessed as separate. However, a preliminary working definition at least for Luke can be formulated as follows:

> *A parable is a narrative, non-historical, and metaphorical saying (by Jesus) appealing to an audience.*[28]

With these criteria in place, the material for studying the parables in Luke can be identified.[29] The list largely resembles that of the *Kompendium,* but instead of fifty-four parables I find fifty-seven. Besides the verses discussed above, I have treated three double parables as separate units. Moreover, 5:39, *Wine 2,* and 14:12-14, *Guidelines 2,* could be additional examples, increasing the number to fifty-nine. However, both cases not only continue to use the same image as the previous parable, but their functions appear similar as well; thus they can be assessed as a single parable.

Differences compared to the *Kompendium:*
- 4:24, *Prophet* fulfills the criteria of a parable, since Jesus does not explicitly claim that he is a prophet.

---

story itself" (ibid., 150–51). However, the grade of spirituality is difficult to measure since the very concept lacks clear borders.

27. Other missing parables are 4:24; 6:38; 10:2; 11:1-13; 16:13; 18:25; and 21:29-31.
28. An extended version of this definition is presented in chap. 8 below.
29. To be sure, this formulation does not answer some essential questions, such as the suggested argumentative and rhetorical function of the parables, their possible common message, or other important features pertaining to their function or contents. Such issues cannot be addressed until a thorough and comparative study of the material is carried out.

- 5:34-35, *Groom*, and 5:36, *Garment*, are treated as two separate parables, just like 15:4-7, *Lost Sheep*, and 15:8-10, *Lost Coin*, since the images are different.
- 12:24, *Ravens*, and 12:27-28, *Lilies*, are correspondingly treated as two separate parables.
- 14:28-30, *Tower*, and 14:31-32, *Warring King*, are treated as two separate parables.
  - 17:34-35, referring to the Rapture, is not assessed as a parable.
  - 18:17, referring to small children, is not assessed as a parable.
- 18:25, *Camel*, fulfills the criteria, except for the unnecessary criterion 3.

Table VI.1
Jesus' Parables in Luke (in order of appearance)

	Verses	Name
1	4:23	Healer 1
2	4:24	Prophet
3	5:31	Healer 2
4	5:34-35	Groom
5	5:36	Garment
6	5:37-39	Wine 1 and 2
7	6:38	Measure
8	6:39	Blind
9	6:40	Teacher
10	6:41-42	Speck in the Eye
11	6:43-45	Bad Tree
12	6:48-49	Two Builders
13	7:32-34	Playing Children
14	7:41-43	Two Debtors
15	8:5-8	Sower
16	8:16	Lamp 1
17	10:2	Harvest
18	10:22	Father and Son
19	10:30-37	Samaritan
20	11:5-8	Friend at Midnight
21	11:11-13	Bad Fathers
22	11:17	Kingdom
23	11:21-22	Protecting House
24	11:24-26	Unclean Spirit
25	11:33	Lamp 2
26	11:34-36	Eye as Lamp

THE OVERALL MAPPING OF THE PARABLES

27	12:16-21	Rich Fool
28	12:24	Ravens
29	12:27-28	Lilies
30	12:36-38	Watchful Slaves
31	12:39	Master and Thief
32	12:42-48	Unfaithful Servant
33	12:54-56	Weather
34	12:58-59	Going to Judge
35	13:6-9	Barren Fig Tree
36	13:19	Mustard Seed
37	13:21	Leaven
38	13:24-29	Closed Door
39	14:8-14	Guidelines 1 and 2
40	14:16-24	Great Dinner
41	14:28-30	Tower
42	14:31-32	Warring King
43	14:34-35	Crazy Salt
44	15:4-7	Lost Sheep
45	15:8-10	Lost Coin
46	15:11-32	Prodigal Son
47	16:1-9	Unjust Steward
48	16:13	Two Masters
49	16:19-31	Rich Man and Lazarus
50	17:7-10	Useless Servant
51	17:37	Vultures
52	18:2-6	Judge
53	18:10-14	Pharisee and Tax Collector
54	18:25	Camel
55	19:12-27	Minas

PARABLES UNPLUGGED

| 56 | 20:9-16 | Wicked Tenants |
| 57 | 21:29-31 | Fig Tree 2 |

Does Size Matter?

In order to compare the parables we must first define their exact magnitude. Some have a framework story whereas others do not. This could unduly distort the comparison. Therefore the framework stories have been excluded from the list, although their importance for interpreting the parables is highly valued.[30] In some cases an exact line cannot be drawn. Luke 8:5-8, the *Sower*, contains Jesus' lengthy and independent explanation, which is not counted in, unlike the brief explanatory utterances in 15: 7, 10; 18:6, 10, which provide new information about the parable's emphasis or characters. For the sake of clarity I refer to whole verses only rather than 1:1a or the like. The size of the parables is, however, counted by including the stories only, according to the number of Greek words in the Nestle-Aland 28th edition. In the following table all Lukan parables told by Jesus are presented according to their length.

---

30. *Contra* Hedrick, *Parables,* 5, and other scholars seeking the original form and meaning of the parables, I assess the setting provided by Luke the Author to be a more dependable basis for understanding them than any imaginary reconstruction of some historical setting. See chap. 1.

THE OVERALL MAPPING OF THE PARABLES

**Table VI.2
Length of Parables**

	Verses	Name	Words
1	4:23	*Healer 1*	3
2	4:24	*Prophet*	8
3	5:31	*Healer 2*	10
4	5:34-35	*Groom*	31
5	5:36	*Garment*	29
6	5:37-39	*Wine 1 and 2*	45
7	6:38	*Measure*	10
8	6:39	*Blind*	10
9	6:40	*Teacher*	14
10	6:41-42	*Speck in the Eye*	22
11	6:43-45	*Bad Tree*	34
12	6:48-49	*Two Builders*	65
13	7:32-34	*Playing Children*	21
14	7:41-43	*Two Debtors*	26
15	8:5-8	*Sower*	68
16	8:16	*Lamp 1*	21
17	10:02	*Harvest*	21
18	10:22	*Father and Son*	27
19	10:30-37	*Samaritan*	106
20	11:5-8	*Friend at Midnight*	82
21	11:11-13	*Bad Fathers*	48
22	11:17	*Kingdom*	11
23	11:21-22	*Protecting House*	33
24	11:24-26	*Unclean Spirit*	55
25	11:33	*Lamp 2*	20
26	11:34-36	*Eye as Lamp*	63

27	12:16-21	Rich Fool	88
28	12:24	Ravens	25
29	12:27-28	Lilies	44
30	12:36-38	Watchful Slaves	58
31	12:39	Master and Thief	16
32	12:42-48	Unfaithful Servant	128
33	12:54-56	Weather	43
34	12:58-59	Going to Judge	49
35	13:6-9	Barren Fig Tree	78
36	13:19	Mustard Seed	27
37	13:21	Leaven	15
38	13:24-29	Closed Door	122
39	14:8-14	Guidelines 1 and 2	140
40	14:16-24	Great Dinner	159
41	14:28-30	Tower	43
42	14:31-32	Warring King	41
43	14:34-35	Crazy Salt	29
44	15:4-7	Lost Sheep	81
45	15:8-10	Lost Coin	53
46	15:11-32	Prodigal Son	389
47	16:1-9	Unjust Steward	182
48	16:13	Two Masters	28
49	16:19-31	Rich Man and Lazarus	244
50	17:7-10	Useless Servant	68
51	17:37	Vultures	8
52	18:2-6	Judge	81
53	18:10-14	Pharisee and Tax Collector	98
54	18:25	Camel	16
55	19:12-27	Minas	253

THE OVERALL MAPPING OF THE PARABLES

56	20:9-16	Wicked Tenants	120
57	21:29-31	Fig Tree 2	20

Shorter parables prevail; half of the cases remain under thirty-five words and only eighteen percent are longer than one hundred words. Yet these are Jesus' best-known parables. The linear curve is illustrative:

Tables VI.3 and VI.4
Comparison of Length

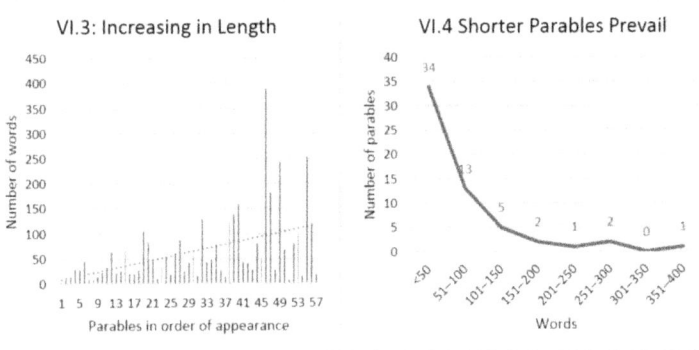

Counting the Characters

A minor criterion that relates rather well to the length is the number of different characters appearing in the story. By "character" I mean human actors. A unified group of humans, such as "people," is interpreted as one character. Most cases are obvious, whereas some require more interpretation; for example, servants are counted as one character whereas an individual standing out of the group is another (e.g., in 19:12-27, the *Minas*). This rather formal criterion can indicate to a certain extent the narrative nature of the parable.

		Table VI.5 Characters		
	Verses	Name	Words	Characters
22	11:17	Kingdom	11	0
51	17:37	Vultures	8	0
1	4:23	Healer 1	3	1
2	4:24	Prophet	8	1
5	5:36	Garment	29	1
6	5:37-39	Wine 1 and 2	45	1
11	6:43-45	Bad Tree	34	1
15	8:5-8	Sower	68	1
16	8:16	Lamp 1	21	1
26	11:34-36	Eye as Lamp	63	1
33	12:54-56	Weather	43	1
36	13:19	Mustard Seed	27	1
37	13:21	Leaven	15	1
43	14:34-35	Crazy Salt	29	1
54	18:25	Camel	16	1
57	21:29-31	Fig Tree 2	20	1
4	5:34-35	Groom	31	2
7	6:38	Measure	10	2
8	6:39	Blind	10	2
9	6:40	Teacher	14	2
10	6:41-42	Speck in the Eye	22	2
12	6:48-49	Two Builders	65	2
13	7:32-34	Playing Children	21	2
21	11:11-13	Bad Fathers	48	2
23	11:21-22	Protecting House	33	2
27	12:16-21	Rich Fool	88	2

THE OVERALL MAPPING OF THE PARABLES

28	12:24	Ravens	25	2
30	12:36-38	Watchful Slaves	58	2
31	12:39	Master and Thief	16	2
35	13:6-9	Barren Fig Tree	78	2
41	14:28-30	Tower	43	2
50	17:7-10	Useless Servant	68	2
53	18:10-14	Pharisee and Tax Collector	98	2
3	5:31	Healer 2	10	3
14	7:41-43	Two Debtors	26	3
17	10:02	Harvest	21	3
18	10:22	Father and Son	27	3
24	11:24-26	Unclean Spirit	55	3
25	11:33	Lamp 2	20	3
44	15:4-7	Lost Sheep	81	3
45	15:8-10	Lost Coin	53	3
48	16:13	Two Masters	28	3
20	11:5-8	Friend at Midnight	82	4
29	12:27-28	Lilies	44	4
32	12:42-48	Unfaithful Servant	128	4
34	12:58-59	Going to Judge	49	4
39	14:8-14	Guidelines 1 and 2	140	4
52	18:2-6	Judge	81	4
42	14:31-32	Warring King	41	5
47	16:1-9	Unjust Steward	182	5
19	10:30-37	Samaritan	106	6
46	15:11-32	Prodigal Son	389	6
38	13:24-29	Closed Door	122	7
49	16:19-31	Rich Man and Lazarus	244	7
55	19:12-27	Minas	253	7

| 56 | 20:9-16 | Wicked Tenants | 120 | 7 |
| 40 | 14:16-24 | Great Dinner | 159 | 9 |

Table VI.6

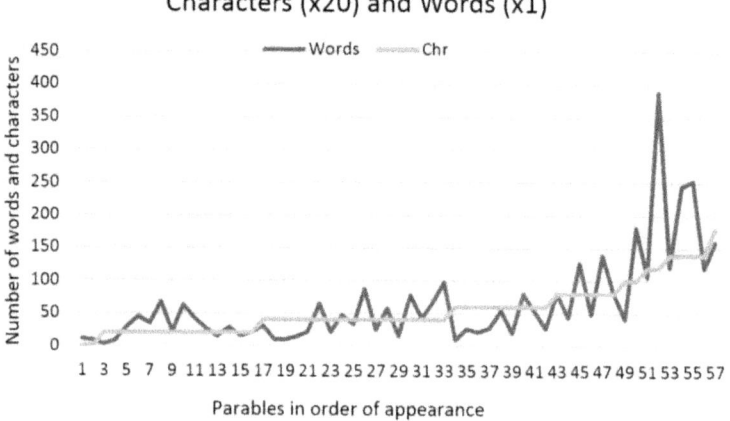

Characters (x20) and Words (x1)

Three Types of Parables

The general concept of parable includes different cases, ranging from a simple reference to a healer to a colorful story of the Prodigal Son and his family. Some formal division into subtypes is obviously needed in order to identify their typical features.

Scholars are usually interested in the longest parables, since they are the most beloved and most difficult, but drawing a line between categories based only on length would be arbitrary.[31] Several other suggestions for formal criteria have been made. However, the flexible nature of the parables means that they easily evade any external categories. Since all parables include *per definitionem* some form of

---

31. Thus Snodgrass, *Stories*, overlooks several important parables such as 5:37-39, *Wine 1 and 2*; 12:36-38, *Watchful Slaves*; 17:7-10, *Unworthy Servant*, without any proper explanation.

THE OVERALL MAPPING OF THE PARABLES

narration, variations in this regard offer a natural criterion for categorizing them. Three categories will suffice. In what follows I will divide the Lukan parables into *Simple Rules*, *Extended Rules*, and *Narratives*.[32] The limits, which will be defined below, are not absolute, and the characterization of some cases may be debatable, but this general partition serves as a practical tool for further analysis. All these types must be studied as parables, since Luke applies the label παραβολή to all of them. This word can designate a *Simple Rule* (4:23; 5:36, 37-39; 6:39; 12:39), an *Extended Rule* (14:8-14; 21:29-31), or a *Narrative* (8:5; 12:16-21, 3; 13:6-9; 15:4-7, 8-10; 18:2-6, 10-14; 19:12-27; 20:9-16).

Table VI.7

Types of Parables

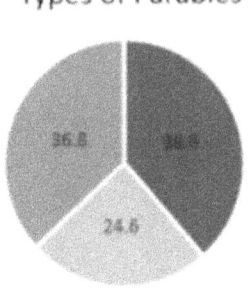

• Simple   • Extended   • Narrative

In what follows, a telling example of each type will be displayed, followed by a brief characterization of the type and a list of corresponding parables.

---

32. From now on the capitalized word *Narrative* will refer to a parable in this category. In addition I will still refer to narrative devices, etc.

201

Simple Rule

A blind person cannot guide a blind person, can he? Will not both fall into a pit? (6:39)

First, there are twenty-two general parabolic sayings or rules in which the narrative element is weak or only hinted at. This means that an "action sequence or change of status" can be detected, but it is simple. There is only one scene and little development in the plot. The three basic parts of the story, beginning-middle-end, are hardly distinguishable. These sayings are neither fictive nor personal but present a typical course of action. Half the cases are negative: nobody acts this way. These parables are short (typically 21 words, one-third of an average parable in Luke consisting of 64 words); and only 1.7 characters on average are involved (compared to the 2.8 average in all parables). None of the cases belongs to Luke's own material.[33]

---

33. I refer to the list of L-parables in the *Kompendium*, 518–21.

THE OVERALL MAPPING OF THE PARABLES

	Table VI.8 Simple Rules		
	Verses	Name	Words
1	4:23	Healer 1	3
2	4:24	Prophet	8
3	5:31	Healer 2	10
5	5:36	Garment	29
6	5:37-39	Wine 1 and 2	45
7	6:38	Measure	10
8	6:39	Blind	10
9	6:40	Teacher	14
10	6:41-42	Speck in the Eye	22
11	6:43-45	Bad Tree	34
16	8:16	Lamp 1	21
18	10:22	Father and Son	27
22	11:17	Kingdom	11
25	11:33	Lamp 2	20
28	12:24	Ravens	25
29	12:27-28	Lilies	44
31	12:39	Master and Thief	16
33	12:54-56	Weather	43
43	14:34-35	Crazy Salt	29
48	16:13	Two Masters	28
51	17:37	Vultures	8
54	18:25	Camel	16

Extended Rule

Thus when you go with your accuser before a magistrate . . . (12:58–59)

Second, there are fourteen general parabolic rules; here the narrative element is more evident in comparison to the *Simple Rules*. Typically, more characters are presented (2.5, which is close to the overall 2.8 in all parables). In the *Extended Rules* the basic principle is expanded with some course of action. In contrast to the *Narratives* proper, this action is presented as typical or general; no particular fictive cases are displayed. The presentation stays on a hypothetical level. The stories are static and involve little development. Some cases, however, lean toward the *Narratives*, as the story contains more action and details.

The *Extended Rules* are twice as long as the *Simple Rules* (typically 47 words, three-fourths of an average parable).

Table VI.9 Extended Rules			
	Verses	Name	Words
4	5:34-35	Groom	31
13	7:32-34	Playing Children	21
17	10:02	Harvest	21
21	11:11-13	Bad Fathers	48
23	11:21-22	Protecting House	33
24	11:24-26	Unclean Spirit	55
26	11:34-36	Eye as Lamp	63
30	12:36-38	Watchful Slaves	58
34	12:58-59	Going to Judge	49
39	14:8-14	Guidelines 1 and 2	140
41	14:28-30	Tower	43
42	14:31-32	Warring King	41
50	17:7-10	Useless Servant	68
57	21:29-31	Fig Tree 2	20

Narrative

There was a rich man who had a steward . . . (16:1-9)

Third, there are twenty-one parables that present a particular fictive story. They typically begin with the phrase ἄνθρωπός τις. The *Narratives* are long (on average 117.4 words, making them 84% longer than the average parable of 63.7 words). Of the nineteen longest parables, seventeen are *Narratives*, but the shortest of them (13:21, the *Leaven*) has only fifteen words. Almost half the *Narratives* are derived from Luke's own material.

	Table VI.10 Narratives		
	Verses	Name	Words
12	6:48-49	Two Builders	65
14	7:41-43	Two Debtors	26
15	8:5-8	Sower	68
19	10:30-37	Samaritan	106
20	11:5-8	Friend at Midnight	82
27	12:16-21	Rich Fool	88
32	12:42-48	Unfaithful Servant	128
35	13:6-9	Barren Fig Tree	78
36	13:19	Mustard Seed	27
37	13:21	Leaven	15
38	13:24-29	Closed Door	122
40	14:16-24	Great Dinner	159
44	15:4-7	Lost Sheep	81
45	15:8-10	Lost Coin	53
46	15:11-32	Prodigal Son	389
47	16:1-9	Unjust Steward	182
49	16:19-31	Rich Man and Lazarus	244
52	18:2-6	Judge	81
53	18:10-14	Pharisee and Tax Collector	98
55	19:12-27	Minas	253
56	20:9-16	Wicked Tenants	120

THE OVERALL MAPPING OF THE PARABLES

So Many Images

The next step is to classify the images referred to in the parables. Finding common features for different images is important in several ways for understanding the parables.

It is usual to categorize the parables based on the images used in them. Thus Hedrick divides the parable stories in the gospel literature into four main categories: (1) natural processes, such as farming; (2) individual human action, involving domestic activities, food production, construction, military activity, and crime; (3) society, including business, labor relations, landlord/tenant, feud, food production, domestic, legal, religion, and construction; and (4) mythological.[34] There are twenty-five different subcategories altogether, most of which are represented in Luke. I find these categories less helpful since, for example, the title "construction" appears twice and "food production" three times.[35]

Indeed, the parables cannot be classified by images or themes only since some involve several images and could be placed in more than one group. At the very least one should estimate what image in the parable is the key factor designed to affect the audience. Thus although 12:16-21, the *Rich Fool*, tells about agriculture, the rich man's occupation plays no major role in the story. He could be anyone hoarding possessions. Instead, the story focuses on the effect of death on one's property and gives preference to riches in heaven. The decisive point is God's unpredictable action. A viable solution is to put it among the rare religious parables in Luke.[36]

In order to be useful, the classification cannot consist of too many categories. As most parables refer to what is natural, typical, or

---

34. Hedrick, *Parables*, 259–61.
35. Building a tower belongs to individual images, whereas building two houses belongs to images referring to society.
36. However, de-theologizing the story would not affect it much; see chaps. 6 and 8.

207

possible in a certain setting, whether in nature, at home, or in various occupations, this perspective provides an operational way of categorizing them. To be sure, the result of such endeavor can never be objective. Debatable cases remain. Again, a rough estimation will suffice; occasional disagreements will hardly challenge the overall image.

Based on the point of reference, the Lukan parables can be divided into four themes and eight subcategories. These refer to typical or possible observations made (a) in nature (5); (b) at home (12); or (c) regarding various occupations (36), including a master (8 or more) and a healer (6). Only a few are based (d) on slightly religious themes (3). The exceptional *Samaritan* (10:30-37) remains unclassified at this point. This categorization is presented in the tables below. Moreover, particular parables will be further discussed when their argumentation is analyzed in chapter 7.

a. Nature (5)

These parables are based on observation of nature. They are 12:24, *Ravens*; 12:27-28, *Lilies*; 12:54-56, *Weather*; 17:37, *Vultures*; and 18:25, *Camel*. These brief parables (typically 27 words; 1.6 characters) are *Simple Rules*; there are no *Narratives* among them.

b. Domestic (12)

Many parables are based on common domestic life. They point to ordinary behavior at home by different members of the household on different occasions. These are 5:34-35, *Groom*; 7:32-34, *Playing Children*; 8:16, *Lamp 1*; 10:22, *Father and Son*; 11:5-8, *Friend at Midnight*; 11:11-13, *Bad Fathers*; 11:21-22, *Protecting House*; 11:33,

Lamp 2; 13:21, *Leaven*; 14:34-35, *Crazy Salt*; 15:8-10, *Lost Coin*; and 16:13, *Two Masters*. These parables are longer than those referring to nature (typically 34 words; 2.3 characters). All three classes are present, as there are five *Simple Rules*, four *Extended Rules*, and three *Narratives*.

To be sure, a central character of the Lukan parables, the master, appears in at least two of the domestic stories. However, differently from the other master-parables, this role is not crucial. In 11:21-22, *Protecting House*, the person could be a servant, and in 16:13, *Two Masters*, the focus is on the servants in their attitudes and behavior, not on the master. Therefore these parables perhaps fit better among domestic issues. Some other stories, like 15:11-32, the *Prodigal Son*, could be placed among the domestic parables. However, the main point of reference in this parable is not conventional behavior at home. Thus 10:22, *Father and Son*, is commonly seen as referring to a craftsman's occupation,[37] but the Lukan version does not specify any occupation, just family relationships.

c. Various Occupations (9)

Several parables are based on typical behavior in various occupations or professions. They refer to the way skilled people normally work. Before separately discussing the three major categories (healer, agriculture, and master), I will first deal with the professions having a clear function: prophet (4:24, *Prophet*), tailor (5:36, *Garment*), merchant (6:38, *Measure*), teacher (6:40, *Teacher*), builder (6:48-49, *Two Builders* and 14:28-30, *Tower*), king (11:17, *Kingdom* and

---

37. For example, van der Watt, "Meisterschüler." Indeed, the Johannine parallel (John 5:19-23) presents it as a description of transferring an artisan's skills. In Luke the image is more general but still parabolic: Jesus compares his relationship to God the Father with that of a father and son, but this does not indicate any high Christology.

14:31-32, *Warring King*), and sheep owner (15:4-7, *Lost Sheep*). These parables are as short as the domestic ones (34 words, 2 characters). Typically they are *Simple Rules* (5), but *Extended Rules* (2) and *Narratives* (2) are also present. Some cases are ambivalent. The parable in 19:12-27, the *Minas*, speaks of a king and could therefore be placed in this group. However, the focus of that story is not on politics but on another role of the nobleman, as the master of his servants.

d. Healer (6)

This is a specific case, as there are six parables referring to the same occupation: 4:23, *Healer 1*; 5:31, *Healer 2*; 6:39, *Blind*; 6:41-42, *Speck in the Eye*' 11:24-26, *Unclean Spirit*; 11:34-36, *Eye as Lamp*. These parables are short (typically 27 words, 2 characters), yet there are both *Simple Rules* (4) and *Extended Rules* (2). The classification of some parables is far from self-evident. Thus there are various interpretations of 11:24-26, *Unclean Spirit*, which will be discussed in chapter 7. In brief, I assess this parable as referring to the experience of an exorcist.

e. Agriculture (6)

Farming is a particular occupation, depicted in six parables: 5:37-39, *Wine 1 and 2*; 6:43-45, *Bad Tree*; 8:5-8(15), *Sower*; 10:2, *Harvest*; 13:19, *Mustard Seed*; 21:29-31, *Fig tree 2*. These parables are roughly as long as the ones referring to domestic issues or various occupations (typically 36 words, but only 1.3 characters). They present customs and phenomena typical of producing wine, fruits, herbs, or crops. All three classes are represented: there are two *Simple Rules*, two *Extended Rules*, and two *Narratives*.

f. Master (15)

A specific character in Lukan parables is the master. With small variations he appears as the protagonist in at least eight parables, but seven others can be counted in this group. Moreover, in 16:13, *Two Masters,* his role is less dominant. The master is typically a rich landowner. In addition, a king (19:12-27, the *Minas*) and two judges (12:58-59, *Going to Judge*; 18:2-6, *Judge*) act in a way that so resembles a master's behavior that they can be counted here as well. Thus this group is characterized by the similar social and professional roles of different occupations rather than the actual profession. The parables include 7:41-43, *Two Debtors*; 12:36-38, *Watchful Slaves*; 12:39, *Master and Thief*; 12:42-48, *Unfaithful Servant*; 12:58-59, *Going to Judge*; 13:6-9, *Barren Fig Tree*; 13:24-29, *Closed Door*; 14:8-14, *Guidelines 1 and 2*; 14:16-24, *Great Dinner*; 15:11-32, *Prodigal Son*; 16:1-9, *Unjust Steward*; 17:7-10, *Useless Servant*; 18:2-6, *Judge*; 19:12-27, *Minas*; and 20:9-16, *Wicked Tenants*. These parables are very long (typically 125 words; 4.6 characters), and 70% of the twenty longest parables tell about a master. Two-thirds of the proper master-parables are *Narratives,* and half of them come from Luke's own sources.

In general I find more refined attempts to delineate stereotypical characters in the parables less helpful.[38] Not all fathers or servants are alike. Importing features from other parables into the story at hand damages the process of interpretation by diminishing the possibility of understanding the story in its own right. This can be compared to the traditional habit of importing historical or ideological data into the story. Moreover, there is a risk of allegorization, as if the characters lived their own lives outside the stories and could be compared directly to features of real life.

---

38. Such presentations include Skinner, ed., *Characterization*; Burnett, "Characterization"; Marguerat and Bourquin, *Stories*, 58–76; Resseguie, *Narrative Criticism*, 121–65.

Having said this, I suspect that the character of master in Luke is an exception. The master is the least stereotypical character in the text, as he can be extremely demanding and cruel as well as incredibly generous and forgiving: the person managing to maintain the capital is punished (19:12-27, *Minas*), whereas those losing everything are forgiven (7:41-43, *Two Debtors*). Nevertheless, this is precisely the point. The logic of parables referring to the master is the opposite of that in the parables referring to other trades. Whereas the latter are based on typical, ordinary behavior in each profession, the master's main attribute is that he is unpredictable. Thus this character deserves specific analysis in the next chapter, where the persuasive functions of the parables are studied.

g. Religious (3)

Only three parables in Luke are based on religious matters: 18:10-14, *Pharisee and Tax Collector*; 12:16-21, *Rich Fool*; 16:19-31, *Rich Man and Lazarus*. These are long (typically 143 words; 3.7 characters); 67% are of Lukan origin. To be sure, 12:24, *Ravens* and 12:27-28, *Lilies* mention God as well, but God could easily be replaced by *nature* or by a non-personal passive voice. Even the three stories counted here are only faintly theological or distinctly Jewish. God's role in *Rich Fool* could be eliminated without doing any harm to the parable, just as God is absent in the closely allied parallel of the *Rich Man and Lazarus*. The remaining *Pharisee and Tax Collector* is more intriguing; if it only claims that it is better to be humble than proud no specific theology need be inferred: "I tell you, this man went down to his house as a better person than the other." The maxim could work in social or religious contexts. If, however, some type of *doctrine of justification* is found in the story it would become the only dogmatic parable in Luke.

h. The Samaritan (1)

This long (106 words; 6 characters), distinctly Lukan parable remains unclassified. It does not refer to any typical observation, whether in nature, at home, or in some occupation; there are no religious matters involved. The story mentions some professions (priest, innkeeper, robbers) and nationalities or classes (Levite, Samaritan). The focus, however, is not on any typical behavior but on the Samaritan's particular, surprising—even if not impossible—course of action. In this sense the parable resembles the master-parables, but the Samaritan is by no means depicted as an almighty autocrat. The persuasive force may be found in his emotional reaction, identical with that of the father of the Prodigal (see chap. 7).

Table VI.11
Images

Verses		Name	Words		Image	Type
6	5:37-39	Wine 1 and 2	45	1	Agriculture	Simple
11	6:43-45	Bad Tree	34	1	Agriculture	Simple
15	8:5-8	Sower	68	1	Agriculture	Narrative
17	10:02	Harvest	21	3	Agriculture	Extended
36	13:19	Mustard Seed	27	1	Agriculture	Narrative
57	21:29-31	Fig Tree 2	20	1	Agriculture	Extended
4	5:34-35	Groom	31	2	Domestic	Extended
13	7:32-34	Playing Children	21	2	Domestic	Extended
16	8:16	Lamp 1	21	1	Domestic	Simple
18	10:22	Father and Son	27	3	Domestic	Simple
20	11:5-8	Friend at Midnight	82	4	Domestic	Narrative
21	11:11-13	Bad Fathers	48	2	Domestic	Extended
23	11:21-22	Protecting House	33	2	Domestic	Extended
25	11:33	Lamp 2	20	3	Domestic	Simple
37	13:21	Leaven	15	1	Domestic	Narrative
43	14:34-35	Crazy Salt	29	1	Domestic	Simple
45	15:8-10	Lost Coin	53	3	Domestic	Narrative
48	16:13	Two Masters	28	3	Domestic / Master	Simple
19	10:30-37	Samaritan	106	6	Emotion	Narrative
1	4:23	Healer 1	3	1	Healer	Simple
3	5:31	Healer 2	10	3	Healer	Simple
8	6:39	Blind	10	2	Healer	Simple
10	6:41-42	Speck in the Eye	22	2	Healer	Simple
24	11:24-26	Unclean Spirit	55	3	Healer	Extended
14	7:41-43	Two Debtors	26	3	Mast/Moneylender	Narrative
26	11:34-36	Eye as Lamp	63	1	Healer	Extended

THE OVERALL MAPPING OF THE PARABLES

30	12:36-38	Watchful Slaves	58	2	Master	Extended
31	12:39	Master and Thief	16	2	Master	Simple
32	12:42-48	Unfaithful Servant	128	4	Master	Narrative
34	12:58-59	Going to Judge	49	4	Master / Judge	Extended
35	13:6-9	Barren Fig Tree	78	2	Master/Agriculture	Narrative
38	13:24-29	Closed Door	122	7	Master	Narrative
39	14:8-14	Guidelines 1 and 2	140	4	Master	Extended
40	14:16-24	Great Dinner	159	9	Master / Emotion	Narrative
46	15:11-32	Prodigal Son	389	6	Master/Emotion/Domestic	Narrative
47	16:1-9	Unjust Steward	182	5	Master	Narrative
50	17:7-10	Useless Servant	68	2	Master	Extended
52	18:2-6	Judge	81	4	Master /Judge	Narrative
55	19:12-27	Minas	253	7	Master / King	Narrative
56	20:9-16	Wicked Tenants	120	7	Master	Narrative
28	12:24	Ravens	25	2	Nature	Simple
29	12:27-28	Lilies	44	4	Nature	Simple
33	12:54-56	Weather	43	1	Nature	Simple
51	17:37	Vultures	8	0	Nature	Simple
54	18:25	Camel	16	1	Nature	Simple
53	18:10-14	Pharisee and Tax Collector	98	2	Religious / Emotion	Narrative
27	12:16-21	Rich Fool	88	2	Religious/Master	Narrative
49	16:19-31	Rich Man and Lazarus	244	7	Religious/Master	Narrative
7	6:38	Measure	10	2	Var: Business	Simple
12	6:48-49	Two Builders	65	2	Var: Construction	Narrative
41	14:28-30	Tower	43	2	Var: Construction	Extended
22	11:17	Kingdom	11	0	Var: Politics	Simple
42	14:31-32	Warring King	41	5	Var: Politics	Extended

PARABLES UNPLUGGED

2	4:24	Prophet	8	1	Var: Prophet	Simple
44	15:4-7	Lost Sheep	81	3	Var: Sheep Owner	Narrative
5	5:36	Garment	29	1	Var: Tailor	Simple
9	6:40	Teacher	14	2	Var: Teacher	Simple

Putting the Parables in Context

After assessing the parables' basic technical features—their length, type, and the image used—we need to study their immediate context. In order to scrutinize each parable's message and function it is essential to know to whom the story is told and what is its general type of exigency. Moreover, I will ask how each parable appeals to the audience and how credible it is. These analyses pave the way for the most important study in the next chapter, where the parables' particular messages and the specific argumentative roles are examined.

Audience

The hearers are usually easy to identify, as Luke typically attaches a framework story or other information to the parables.[39] Thus there are (a) thirteen parables aimed at the general public, (b) six addressing the general public or the disciples, and (c) fifteen aimed clearly at the disciples;[40] (d) ten parables are told to opponents and (e) three are addressed to the general public and the opponents.[41]

Furthermore, the audience can be an imprecise group (in three cases *some*) or an individual (in two cases *someone*), guests (in two

---

39. In 60% of the cases Luke describes the parable's context.
40. Actually, 17:7-10 *Useless Servant* is told to "apostles," but they are also called "disciples" in the context.
41. For a comprehensive list see *Spreadsheet 1*. Visit fortresspress.com/thuren and click on the "Additional Supporting Resources" tab to view and download the spreadsheets.

cases), or various individuals (in five cases), including an expert in law, a ruler, Simon, and God (10:22). A peculiar instance is 4:23, *Healer 1*, which Jesus claims will be spoken to him in the future by the people of Nazareth. This parable is assessed here as aimed at the public.

At times the story glides from one situation to another, with the result that the audience may also change. Moreover, even if one group is the main audience, others overhear the parable (for example, tax collectors and sinners in 15:4-32 and the Pharisees in 16:1-13).

The audience correlates with the length of the parables in an interesting fashion:

Table VI.12

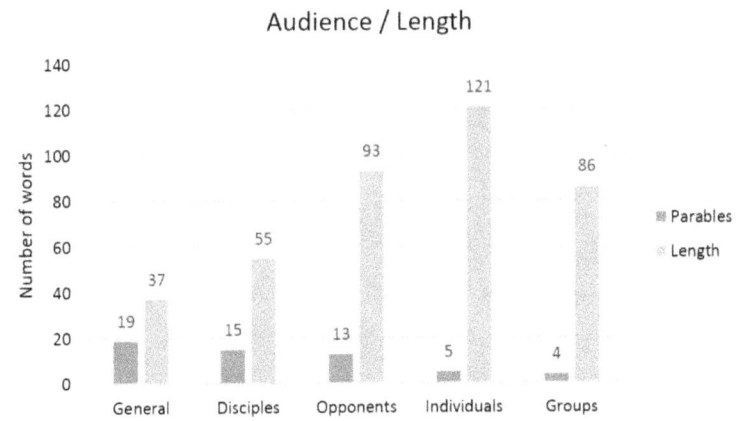

Apparently Jesus makes the most effort to persuade different outsiders such as the Pharisees, scribes, high priests, "some," or unspecified guests. Not all of these groups are designated as antagonistic to him and his message. Simon the Pharisee and different unnamed individuals (a ruler, an expert in law, "someone") are told shorter parables. The education of the disciples receives still fewer words and the general public has to make do with brief sayings. An exception is 12:16-21, the *Rich Fool,* with eighty-eight words.

The audience correlates to the image referred to as well. The general public is told parables mainly referring to various occupations, but only once to a master. Only one of these is of Lukan origin (14:28-30, the *Tower*), and three belong to the *Narratives*.

Table VI.13

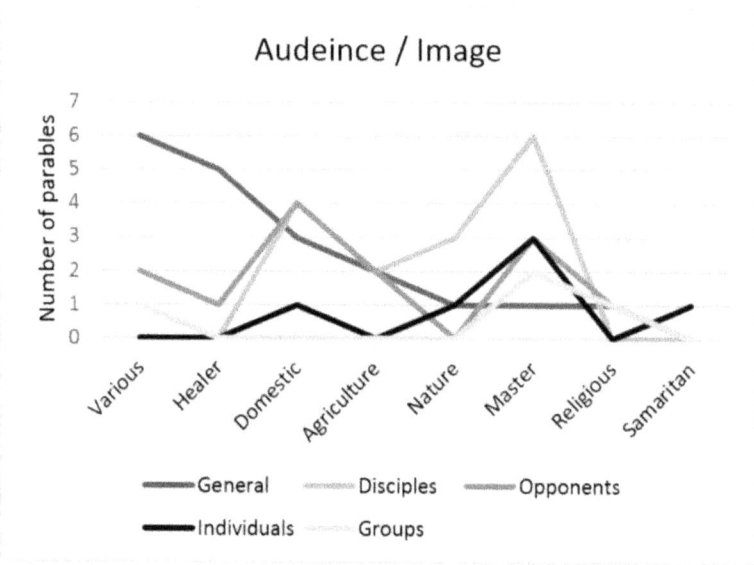

Moreover, the audience correlates to the type of parable:

Table VI.14
Audience / Type

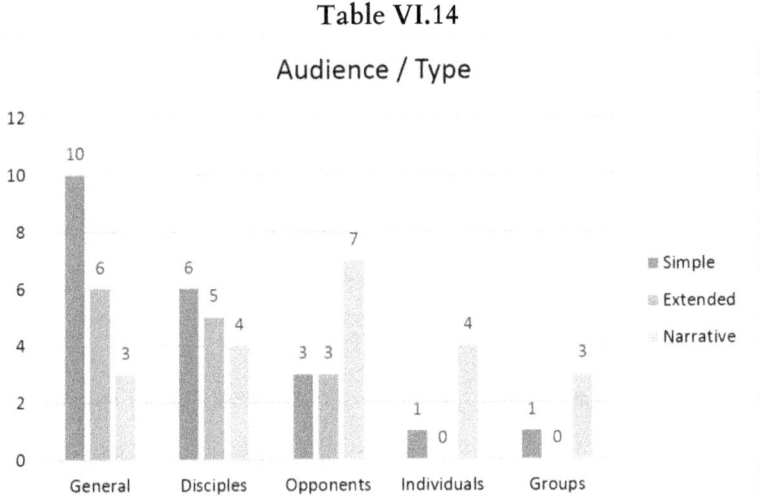

Simple Rules are aimed at all types of groups, whereas *Extended Rules* are never told to individuals or unspecified groups. Instead, these groups hear more *Narratives* than the other audiences.

The disciples hear each type of parable (6 + 5 + 4), and half of these refer to a master. Half of the parables told to the antagonists (Pharisees, scribes, and high priests) are *Narratives*, and 40% of them tell about a master. Most parables told to other groups or individuals are also *Narratives*, and half of them tell about a master. In other words, 33% of the master-parables are told to "others," 40% to the disciples, and only 20% to the "antagonists" and 7% to the general public.

Exigency

In 60% of the parables Luke gives particular information about the situation prompting the story. This provides a good basis for understanding their persuasive function. The cases can be roughly divided into situations in which Jesus defends himself (12 parables) and those in which he teaches in some other particular situation (21 parables); moreover, there is one prayer. In the remaining 40% (23 parables) the parables contain general teaching without a clear immediate impetus.

General teaching is usually brief (36 words; 2.1 characters). It uses a variety of images and is aimed at all audiences, except individuals and imprecise groups. One-third of these parables are included in the Sermon on the Plain (6:20-49). Half of the cases (12 of 23) are *Simple Rules*; there are also six *Extended Rules* and five *Narratives*. In other words, fewer than one-third of the *Narratives* in Luke are told without an immediate reason. The introductory rhetorical question τίς ἐξ ὑμῶν is not used, and ἄνθρωπός τις appears only twice. Instead, half of these parables are introduced with the negative οὐ, or with other references to typical behavior. Four instances are called "parable" by Luke.

The *Defensive* category consists of twelve parables prompted by a situation in which at least a hint of controversy can be observed.[42] Their number equals 21% of the parables. They are shorter than other particular parables (typically 68 words); there are four *Narratives* (20% of Lukan *Narratives*), six *Simple Rules*, and two *Extended Rules*. The antagonists (Pharisees, scribes, high priests) are naturally the most typical audience (in two-thirds of the cases), and the rest are told to the general public. All the opening formulas are used. Like the general parables, the defensive ones are typically short (30 words), except for the long stories 15:11-32, the *Prodigal Son* and 20:9-16, the *Wicked Tenants* (which increase the average length to 68 words). Most images used refer to general occupations; only two speak of a master.

---

42. These, to be sure, do not refer to the German *Streitgespräche*, as Jesus' goal is not to win against or vilify his antagonists but to persuade them. The three parables in Luke 15 are a good example see chap. 3.

Parables involving *Particular Teaching* are all different. They are long (89 words; 3.6 characters), and mostly *Narratives* (55%). To put it differently, 60% of the *Narratives* are aimed at a particular situation and 40% lack a clear reason. There are only four *Simple Rules* and only four of this group are aimed at a general audience or at the opponents. In addition, there are six *Extended Rules*. Luke's favorite character, the master, appears in half of the cases (11 of 22). The parables are aimed at the disciples (7 of 22) or different individuals (8 of 21), but only twice at the antagonists. ἄνθρωπός τις is presented eight times but the negative introduction only once. However, three cases refer to typical behavior and four use the rhetorical question τίς ἐξ ὑμῶν. One specific parable does not fit in any of these groups; 10:22, *Father and Son*, consists of Jesus' prayer to the Heavenly Father. This can neither be described as teaching nor as defensive.

	Table VI.15 Exigency		
	Verses	Name	Exigency
1	4:23	Healer 1	Defense
2	4:24	Prophet	Defense
3	5:31	Healer 2	Defense
4	5:34-35	Groom	Defense
5	5:36	Garment	Defense
6	5:37-39	Wine 1 and 2	Defense
22	11:17	Kingdom	Defense
23	11:21-22	Protecting House	Defense
44	15:4-7	Lost Sheep	Defense
45	15:8-10	Lost Coin	Defense
46	15:11-32	Prodigal Son	Defense
56	20:9-16	Wicked Tenants	Defense
7	6:38	Measure	General
8	6:39	Blind	General
9	6:40	Teacher	General
10	6:41-42	Speck in the Eye	General
11	6:43-45	Bad Tree	General
12	6:48-49	Two Builders	General
13	7:32-34	Playing Children	General
15	8:5-8	Sower	General
16	8:16	Lamp 1	General
24	11:24-26	Unclean Spirit	General
25	11:33	Lamp 2	General
26	11:34-36	Eye as Lamp	General
28	12:24	Ravens	General
29	12:27-28	Lilies	General

THE OVERALL MAPPING OF THE PARABLES

30	12:36-38	*Watchful Slaves*	General
31	12:39	*Master and Thief*	General
33	12:54-56	*Weather*	General
34	12:58-59	*Going to Judge*	General
36	13:19	*Mustard Seed*	General
37	13:21	*Leaven*	General
48	16:13	*Two Masters*	General
50	17:7-10	*Useless Servant*	General
52	18:2-6	*Judge*	General
14	7:41-43	*Two Debtors*	Particular
17	10:02	*Harvest*	Particular
19	10:30-37	*Samaritan*	Particular
20	11:5-8	*Friend at Midnight*	Particular
21	11:11-13	*Bad Fathers*	Particular
27	12:16-21	*Rich Fool*	Particular
32	12:42-48	*Unfaithful Servant*	Particular
35	13:6-9	*Barren Fig Tree*	Particular
38	13:24-29	*Closed Door*	Particular
39	14:8-14	*Guidelines 1 and 2*	Particular
40	14:16-24	*Great Dinner*	Particular
41	14:28-30	*Tower*	Particular
42	14:31-32	*Warring King*	Particular
43	14:34-35	*Crazy Salt*	Particular
47	16:1-9	*Unjust Steward*	Particular
49	16:19-31	*Rich Man and Lazarus*	Particular
51	17:37	*Vultures*	Particular
53	18:10-14	*Pharisee & Tax Collector*	Particular
54	18:25	*Camel*	Particular
55	19:12-27	*Minas*	Particular

| 57 | 21:29-31 | Fig Tree 2 | Particular |
| 18 | 10:22 | Father and Son | Prayer |

Are the Parables Credible?

An interesting quality of the parables is their credibility. Does Luke the Author or Jesus the Narrator assess the recipients' willingness to accept the way people act in the parable? Correspondingly, is the audience assumed to assent to the reasoning presented in the parable? Estimating this credibility with numeric codes would support a comparative analysis. It would be good to know how the variations in credibility correspond to the other attributes, since knowledge of regular combinations can guide the interpretation of obscure cases. Moreover, parables with low credibility may indicate the sore points of Jesus' theology. Are there cases in which he is on such thin ice that he has to resort to risky parables?

Estimating the credibility of the parables may appear difficult, but certain good markers in the text make the task easier.[43] Rhetorical questions are not supposed to be answered, since the answers are assumed to be self-evident. Otherwise the reasoning would collapse. Thus their credibility is assessed as high. The goal of a rhetorical question is to make the audience react in a way that in itself is not problematic for them but that makes further persuasion easier.[44] Typically, Jesus can ask: Who of you (Τίς ἐξ ὑμῶν)? An even better signal revealing the narrator's confidence in the parable is a negative claim referring to an absurd thing nobody would ever do (Οὐδεὶς δὲ λύχνον ἅψας καλύπτει . . .) or that in some other way sounds illogical. Poor credibility has clear markers as well. At times Luke

---

43. To be sure, in many cases the precise assessment of credibility remains somewhat subjective. Small variations are not, however, fatal, since the goal is to identify general trends among the parables.
44. For different types of rhetorical questions see Gideon Burton, *Silva Rhetoricae* (http://rhetoric.byu.edu/figures/R/rhetorical questions.htm).

THE OVERALL MAPPING OF THE PARABLES

has recorded the audience's negative reaction: When they heard it they said "No way! (μὴ γένοιτο)" (20:16). The estimates remain rough: distinguishing between Luke's and Jesus' audiences would be arbitrary, and the distances between the grades may not be equal. Yet classifying the parables based on their credibility and comparing the results with other features may provide some interesting information. In order to enable numerical analysis I will estimate the grade of credibility with numbers, as follows:

(*4) *Indisputable,* self-evident cases, where no objections are expected;

(*3) *Credible* cases, where objections are theoretically possible but hardly plausible;

(*2) *Conceivable* cases that, however, can be disputed; and

(*1) *Controversial* cases, where the audience is expected to be highly suspicious.

Indisputable Parables (*4)

Those who are well who have no need of a physician, but those who are sick. (5:31)

No one after lighting a lamp hides it under a jar. (8:16)

The most credible and evident parables, signaled here with the code (*4), refer to pure reason or to very general experiences. There are thirteen parables of this kind, or 23%. They are exceptionally short (typically 20 words); 69% are *Simple Rules,* yet, for example, 14:28-30, the *Tower,* is an *Extended Rule.* On average only 1.9 characters or groups are involved. The indisputable parables are used in all three exigencies. They are often introduced with a negative rhetorical question (5 cases). This device indicates that the speaker is confident about the audience's answer.

These parables highlight something characteristic of different occupations (6 cases, 4 of which speak of healers), domestic issues (3 instances), or nature (2 instances). They refer to how things are normally done. Four parables are extended with a minor narrative element, but proper *Narratives* are absent. Thus these parables are clear and acceptable in themselves. Their only problem is relevance: Does the audience agree that the rules presented or illuminated suit the case discussed, or are there counterproductive factors? These parables are aimed at a general audience (62%), disciples (23%), and one each to opponents and to a "ruler."

Table VI.16 Indisputed Parables (*4)							
Nr	Verses	Name	Words	Image	Type	Audience	Exigency
1	4:23	Healer 1	3	Healer	Simple	All (Jesus)	Defense
3	5:31	Healer 2	10	Healer	Simple	Opponents	Defense
8	6:39	Blind	10	Healer	Simple	All / Disc	General
9	6:40	Teacher	14	Var: Teacher	Simple	All / Disc	General
10	6:41-42	Speck in the Eye	22	Healer	Simple	All / Disc	General
16	8:16	Lamp 1	21	Domestic	Simple	Disciples	General
23	11:21-22	Protecting House	33	Domestic	Extended	All	Defense
25	11:33	Lamp 2	20	Domestic	Simple	All	General
41	14:28-30	Tower	43	Var: Construction	Extended	All	Particular
42	14:31-32	Warring King	41	Var: Politics	Extended	All	Particular
51	17:37	Vultures	8	Nature	Simple	Disciples	Particular
54	18:25	Camel	16	Nature	Simple	I Ruler	Particular
57	21:29-31	Fig Tree 2	20	Agriculture	Extended	Disciples	Particular

Summing up, the indisputable parables, referring to some general observation or to reasonable, conventional behavior in some occupation, can be described as the basic type of parables. They present self-evident or generally accepted phenomena or modes of behavior. The audience does not have to believe Jesus because he simply refers to something already known.

The type of these parables is important: they present some rule that is natural or reasonable in the case at hand. This is true regardless of their grammatical form: exhortation, question, or statement. Their applicability is based on generalizing the rule. What pertains to lighting a lamp (8:16) applies to other corresponding issues as well—nobody does unreasonable things. Thus the rule illuminated by the parable is only an example of a more general rule.

Credible Parables (*3)

No one tears a piece from a new garment and sews it on an old garment; otherwise the new will be torn, and the piece from the new will not match the old. (5:36)

The next category, signaled with the code (*3), consists of twenty-one parables (37%) referring to the audience's experience and knowledge. They discuss typical behavior in different known professions or at home, or natural phenomena. This is often done in a negative form: for example, no winemaker or gardener would do that. The credibility of this group is good.

This second category is not as obvious as the previous one, but the line is not sharp. These parables suit all purposes and audiences. Contrary to the previous category, the contents could be challenged in principle; thus some further narrative element is needed. Thereby, these cases are not self-evident, but still credible. There are no essential factors compromising the credibility. These parables can be described as a developed version of the basic parables.

The *Credible* parables are 80 percent longer than the *Indisputable* category, typically thirty-six words. In this case, expanding the story does not diminish its reliability. The audience does not need to believe that the storyline is plausible, as it merely describes further the issue. This is true regarding the four proper Narratives, too. One is not presumed to challenge the plausibility of 13:21 *Leaven* or 13:19 *Mustard Seed*; they but describe a natural process. 15:8-10 *Lost Coin* and 15:4-7 *Lost Sheep* refer to social conventions at home or in the pasture, but they are introduced with a rhetorical question expecting no objection: who would not act like this?

Although the parables as such are not considered problematic, their application to the situation may prove challenging. The audience may well approve of the story but not find it relevant in the situation. For example, 15:8-10, the *Lost Coin*, sounds reasonable as such, but its relevance to the criticism leveled against Jesus is not obvious.

References to domestic issues prevail (7); other topics are various occupations (4), agriculture (4), nature (3), masters (2), and a healer (1). They are *Simple Rules* (12), *Extended Rules* (4) or short *Narratives* (4). The opponents (33%) and the disciples (33%) are the main audiences. Most parables (48%) involve general teaching, but 35% are aimed at defense as well. It is interesting to note that only three parables (14%) target a particular situation, compared to 38% in the previous group. There are two exhortations; the rest refer to typical phenomena in nature or at home.

Table VI.17
Credible Parables (*3)

2	4:24	Prophet	8	Var: Prophet	Simple	All	Defense
4	5:34-35	Groom	31	Domestic	Extended	Opponents	Defense
5	5:36	Garment	29	Var: Tailor	Simple	Opponents	Defense
6	5:37-39	Wine 1 and 2	45	Agriculture	Simple	Opponents	Defense
11	6:43-45	Bad Tree	34	Agriculture	Simple	All / Disc	General
17	10:02	Harvest	21	Agriculture	Extended	Disciples	Particular
18	10:22	Father and Son	27	Domestic	Simple	I God	Prayer
21	11:11-13	Bad Fathers	48	Domestic	Extended	Disciples	Particular
22	11:17	Kingdom	11	Var: Politics	Simple	O Some	Defense
26	11:34-36	Eye as Lamp	63	Healer	Extended	All	General
28	12:24	Ravens	25	Nature	Simple	Disciples	General
29	12:27-28	Lilies	44	Nature	Simple	Disciples	General
31	12:39	Master and Thief	16	Master	Simple	Disciples	General
33	12:54-56	Weather	43	Nature	Simple	All	General
36	13:19	Mustard Seed	27	Agriculture	Narrative 9	Opp / All	General
37	13:21	Leaven	15	Domestic	Narrative 10	Opp / All	General
43	14:34-35	Crazy Salt	29	Domestic	Simple	All	Particular
44	15:4-7	Lost Sheep	81	Var: SheepOwner	Narrative 13	Opponents	Defense
45	15:8-10	Lost Coin	53	Domestic	Narrative 14	Opponents	Defense
48	16:13	Two Masters	28	Domestic / Master	Simple	Disciples	General

THE OVERALL MAPPING OF THE PARABLES

| 50 | 17:7-10 | Useless Servant | 68 | Master | Extended | Disciples | General |

Summary of Categories (*4) and (*3)

Together the two easy categories include thirty-four parables, 60% of all Jesus' parables in Luke. They refer to reason or the audience's general knowledge and experience; thus their credibility is high. In these categories a typical parable is a *Simple Rule* (62%) consisting of thirty words; only 12% are *Narratives*. A parable of this type functions as general teaching (44%). It is aimed at a general audience (13) or the disciples (10), whereas eight cases are specifically told to the antagonists. Two characters (or groups) are usually involved.

Despite their overall common characteristics as general, credible, and noncontroversial, moving from category *4 to category *3 means that the parables get longer, more defensive, or are aimed at the disciples in a particular situation.

Table VI.18
Indisputable and Credible Parables

Category	*4 Indisputable	*3 Credible	Overall
Cases	13	21	34
Length (words)	20	36	30
Typical image	Healer 31%	Domestic 33%	Domestic 29%
Characters	1.9	1.8	1.9
Audience	General 62%	General or Disciples 33%	General 38%
Function	General /Particular	General 69%	General 40%

Conceivable Parables (*2)

In a certain city there was a judge who neither feared God nor had respect for people . . . (18:2-6)

The third category consists of twelve parables that appear conceivable and possible but not necessarily compelling. They do not rely on the audience's general knowledge of what is customary or reasonable. Instead, they are based on some claim made by the narrator; the audience may accept or reject it. A rhetorical question or negative statement is rarely used, as the audience's reaction is not evident. Thus these parables are more risky than the previous groups. Their effect depends not only on their applicability to the case at hand but also on the audience's willingness to accept the claim. Most of these parables are *Narratives*.

The parables describe some course of action that may or may not happen. Thus the behavior of the judge in 18:2-6 is understandable, but there is no guarantee that all wicked judges will act as he did. In a somewhat similar story, 11:5-8, the *Friend at Midnight,* the reference to "one of you" as the main character implies that Jesus expects his story to be accepted. However, additional assurance, λέγω ὑμῖν in vv. 8 and 9, indicates some doubt. Indeed, it does not appear necessary that the friend will get his bread. Differently from the basic parables, the course of action described is not the only option.

THE OVERALL MAPPING OF THE PARABLES

		Table VI.19 Conceivable Parables					
7	6:38	Measure	10	Var: Business	Simple	All / Disc	General
12	6:48-49	Two Builders	65	Var: Construction	Narrative 1	All / Disc	General
13	7:32-34	Playing Kids	21	Domestic	Extended	Opp / All	General
14	7:41-43	Two Debtors	26	Mast/ Moneylender	Narrative 2	I Simon	Particular
15	8:5-8	Sower	68	Agriculture	Narrative 3	All	General
20	11:5-8	Friend at Midnight	82	Domestic	Narrative 5	Disciples	Particular
24	11:24-26	Unclean Spirit	55	Healer	Extended	All	General
34	12:58-59	Going to Judge	49	Master / Judge	Extended	All	General
35	13:6-9	Barren Fig Tree	78	Mast/ Agricult	Narrative 8	O Some	Particular
38	13:24-29	Closed Door	122	Master	Narrative 11	I Someone	Particular
39	14:8-14	Guidelines 1 and 2	140	Master	Extended	Opponents	Particular
52	18:2-6	Judge	81	Master /Judge	Narrative 18	Disciples	General

Parables in this category *2 are still longer than the previous ones (typically 66 words and 3.2 characters). They come close to the average parable in Luke (64 words and 2.8 characters). Some 58% are *Narratives* and 58% include general teaching. Half of them refer to the behavior of a master, whereas in category *3 there were but two such instances and none in category *4. None of the stories is told exclusively to the antagonists. A total of 42% are of Lukan origin.

Only 6:38, Measure, is a *Simple Rule*. Compared to the previous group, the lower credibility is due to the bold claim. Fair habits in the marketplace are nothing extraordinary,[45] but it is not self-evident that practicing them creates a reciprocal response. Except for this parable, the weaker credibility in this category is compensated for with a longer presentation, typically a *Narrative*.

Controversial Parables (*1)

When they heard this, they said, "May it never be!" (20:9-16)

The eleven heaviest parables belong to the *Controversial* category. This means that their credibility is essentially challenged; not even Luke believes that the audience will agree. In the example above Luke quotes the audience's immediate reaction to the parable: μὴ γένοιτο.[46]

These parables are almost exclusively *Narratives*; they are very long (typically 166 words), and several characters are involved (5.2). They present the typical character, ἄνθρωπός τις (with two exceptions), and 45% originate from Luke's own sources. Numerous audiences are represented, but only one parable is told to the general public. Most stories (73%) present a master-character; they refer to religious or emotional factors. The previously typical different occupations or natural phenomena are absent. A total of 73% are aimed at a particular situation.

The profile of these parables is thus striking. In comparison to all other categories they are long and complicated. Instead of referring to what is obvious or typical they make strong claims about a master behaving in an unpredictable way. Thus their success must depend on factors other than pure logic or custom. Typical such factors are rhetorical and narratological devices and tactics. These help the

---

45. *Pace* Nolland, *Luke*, 301. See more detail in chap. 7.
46. The reason for this exclamation is not clear, however. See below chap. 5.

narrator to camouflage the weakness of the basic idea behind the story.

Also typical for these parables is the audience: they are often addressed to an obscure, unnamed individual or group. Many are of Lukan origin. Moreover, these parables are typically situated toward the end of the Lukan text. It will be interesting to study what kind of message Jesus is promoting with these stories.

			Table VI.20 Controversial Parables				
19	10:30-37	Samaritan	106	Emotion	Narrative 4	I Nomikos	Particular
27	12:16-21	Rich Fool	88	Religious/ Master	Narrative 6	All	Particular
30	12:36-38	Watchful Slaves	58	Master	Extended	Disciples	General
32	12:42-48	Unfaithful Servant	128	Master	Narrative 7	Disciples	Particular
40	14:16-24	Great Dinner	159	Master / Emotion	Narrative 12	I Someone	Particular
46	15:11-32	Prodigal Son	389	Mast/ Em/Dom	Narrative 15	Opponents	Defense
47	16:1-9	Unjust Steward	182	Master	Narrative 16	Disciples	Particular
49	16:19-31	Rich Man and Lazarus	244	Religious/ Master	Narrative 17	Opponents	Particular
53	18:10-14	Pharisee & Tax Collector	98	Religious / Emotion	Narrative 19	O Some	Particular
55	19:12-27	Minas	253	Master / King	Narrative 20	O Guests	Particular
56	20:9-16	Wicked Tenants	120	Master	Narrative 21	Opponents	Defense

Table VI.21 Conceivable and Controversial Parables (Categories *2 and *1)			
Credibility	*2 Conceivable	*1 Controversial	*2 and *1 Overall
Cases	12	11	23
Average length (words)	66	166	114
Typical image	Master 50%	Master 82%	Master 65%
Average number of characters	3.2	5.2	4.1
Class	Narrative 58%	Narrative 91%	Narrative 74%
Audience	All 42%	Various 36%	Various 30%,
Exigency	General 58%	Particular 73%	Particular 57%

Conclusions

Several factors display a clear escalation from category *4 to category *1. The length, characters involved, percentage of master-stories, *Narratives*, and Lukan origin, and most of all, the difficulty of accepting the parables, essentially grow.

An additional criterion, the parables' possible reference to God, can preliminarily be added to this data, although it will not be discussed in full until the next chapter. The result corresponds neatly to some other factors.

THE OVERALL MAPPING OF THE PARABLES

Table VI.22 Correlations of Credibility				
Credibility	*4 Indisputable	*3 Credible	*2 Conceivable	*1 Controversial
Cases	13	21	12	11
Length in words	20	36	66	166
Characters	1.9	1.8	3.2	5.2
Narratives	0 %	19 %	58%	91%
Referring to God	0 %	29 %	75 %	91%
Speaking of master	0 %	5 %	50 %	82 %
ἄνθρωπός τις	0 %	0 %	17 %	82 %
Lukan origin	8 %	10%	42 %	45 %

In this diagram the number of characters and grade of credibility are multiplied by ten for the sake of clarity. The result reveals interesting connections. The poor credibility of the basic idea correlates to several factors, such as the length of the parable, references to the master-character and to God, as well as the Lukan origin.

PARABLES UNPLUGGED

Table VI.23

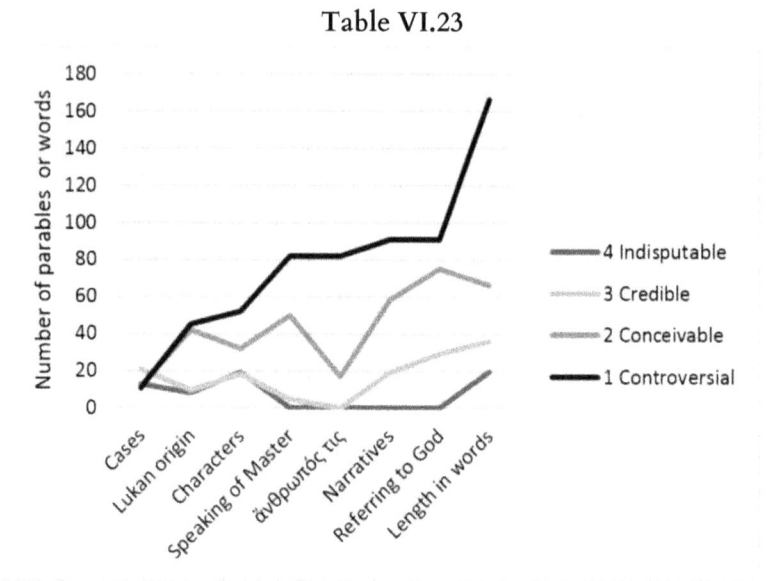

Strategic Function of the Different Types: A Hypothesis

The difference between categories *3 and *1 is well demonstrated by the three parables in Luke 15, which respond to the same exigency. These parables are discussed in detail in chapter 3, but now they can be studied as representative of two different groups.

The *Lost Sheep* (15:4-7) and the *Lost Coin* (15:8-10) are told in the same context and for the same audience as the *Prodigal Son* (15:11-32). The credibility of the first parables is high (*3), as the narrator uses rhetorical questions referring to typical, reasonable behavior in a profession or at home: "Who of you would not seek what is lost and not have a feast until it is found?" The third parable exceeds the previous ones in almost every sense: it is longer and involves more property, characters, narrative turns, and emotions.

However, there is one weakness, namely, the main idea put forward. The narrator would hardly dare present his basic thesis behind the story as a rhetorical question: "Who of you would not have a great feast when your arrogant son who has wasted half of your property returns home?" Differently from the first two parables, there are several possible answers, as the end of the story shows. Thus all the other factors need to be augmented and a master-figure, the father, has to be introduced.

This leads to a hypothesis: the factors displayed above serve as indicators of the qualities of the issue discussed in a parable. When illuminating a weak warrant, and thereby a weak case, with a parable, the narrator needs to compensate with persuasive narrative elements such as interesting characters, colorful descriptions, a good story line, and some *pathos*-effect. By using these, he or she attempts to circumvent the feebleness of the embedded claim she or he wants to make.

Typically these difficult or implausible parables deal with God. They explain how God acts or thinks and why the audience should act likewise. In comparison, when referring to himself with a parable Jesus uses much shorter and stronger images. Parables telling how the addressees should behave are likewise brief and forceful. This lets us presume that the weak or crucial point of Jesus' preaching was neither in his ethical message nor in his own status or self-image, but in his *theo*-logical vision. In other words, at least in his parables the Lukan Jesus does not make overly incredible claims about himself. However, his theses about God are more perplexing. In attempting to persuade his audience he had to resort to long and fascinating stories instead of merely uttering a proverb or two.[47]

---

47. Forbes, too, notices God's essential role in the Lukan parables, but unfortunately overemphasizes it (*God*, esp. 279–306).

This hypothesis, as well as other possible observations based on the data in this chapter, will be further tested in chapter 7 when analyzing the argumentation in each parable, using Toulmin's argumentation analysis.

To What do the Parables Refer?

One of the most interesting—and most difficult—questions is: what issues do the parables seek to illustrate? Identifying these targets of the parables and comparing them to other features may reveal interesting and important connections and typical combinations. In some cases the message or issue illustrated by a parable is obvious, while for some the interpreters' opinions are greatly divided; sometimes the number of different explanations is immense. Thus the question of reference must be narrowed down.

First, I will not look for any message, but instead will focus on the issue at hand in each parable. The proximate context is decisive: the issue must be relevant and have meaning to the audience reported by Luke in that specific situation.

Second, no precise theme will be examined; focus will be on a more general *topos*: does the parable refer to the audience, to the disciples, or to the opponents? Alternatively, does it say something about Jesus himself? or about a third party, such as God or the Kingdom?

Third, some parables appear to refer to several things. For example, 15:11-32, the *Prodigal Son*, formally explains Jesus' behavior for the Pharisees, but at the same time it deals with the Pharisees themselves.[48] In many other parables theological overtones are easy to detect as well; by this I do not mean allegorical readings but

---

48. For a fuller discussion see chap. 3 above.

issues essential for the reasoning in the immediate context. Yet the ultimate goal of any parable is hardly just to share information about theological issues; references to God also serve a more practical goal: to affect the behavior of the audience.

The most obvious secondary meanings will be marked.[49] This means that tables VI.24 (a and b), **Target,** and VI.25, **Comparing the Targets,** are not fully compatible with other tables in this chapter, since the same parable may appear several times.

The results of the following comparison are based on the argumentation analysis in chapter 7, which enables controllable explication of the unexpressed claims. Several parables refer to multiple targets. Further discussion and grounds for the interpretations made here can be found in that chapter.

In order to remain on a general level I have divided the targets of the parables into five main types. They may illustrate some feature connected solely to God, or to God as a secondary target, to the opponents, the disciples, other recipients, Jesus, and the Kingdom. Some parables clearly overlap. The following conclusion can be drawn:

---

49. No higher resolution is necessary for the present task. My aim is again to find an overall fault-tolerant characterization, the credibility of which does not collapse over a few disagreements.

Table VI.24a

	GROUP I	
TARGET	Opponents	God (all)
Cases	7	24
Length	150	114
Characters	4.6	4.3
"Parable" %	57	38
Lukan %	57	38
Narrative %	71	71
Audience	To opponents only	Seldom to general
Exigency %	43% not defensive	58 % particular
Credibility	1.9	1.7

Table VI.24b

	GROUP II			GROUP III		
TARGET	Disciples	Other recipients	God (primary)	Jesus	Kingdom	
Cases	8	24	4	10	7	
Length	74	63	50	21	18	
Characters	2.9	2.9	3	1.8	1	
"Parable" %	25	29	0	30	14	
Lukan %	38	21	25	0	0	
Narrative %	38	46	25	0	29	
Audience	Mostly disciples	67% to all	To disciples only	None to disciples	57% to disciples	
Exigency %	G/P	General/Particular, none defensive	General/Particular	80% defensive	14% defensive	
Credibility	2.1	2.5	2.8	3.4	3.3	

Table VI.25

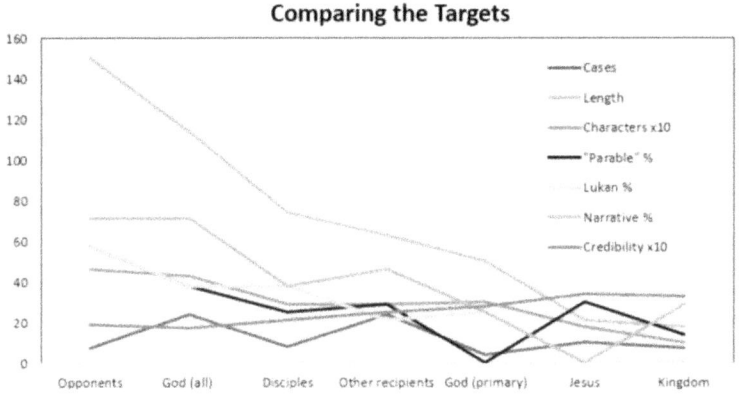

Comparing the Targets

This comparison leads to several interesting observations. There are three distinct, somewhat surprising groups based on the subject to which they refer: (1) the opponents and general references to God, (2) specific references to God, disciples, and other recipients, (3) Jesus and the kingdom.

(1) References to the opponents and to God (primary and secondary) stand out as the clearly longest parables. They involve most characters, most *Narratives*, and they are called "parable" by Luke more often than the other cases. Neither type is usually told to the general public. Finally, yet importantly, these are the most difficult parables. However, these two groups seldom overlap: only 17% of parables speaking of God are told solely to the antagonists. They are more often of Lukan origin. Further conclusions can be drawn with caution. Luke appears to be fond of long, difficult *Narratives* dealing with God and the opponents. A major message and theological direction of his Jesus may thus be found in these parables.

However, it must be kept in mind that all other *Narratives* are just as "Lukan" for his recipients.[50]

(2) The intermediate group consists of parables dealing only with God, or with the disciples and other recipients. The length, number of characters, and credibility within this group are roughly the same. However, those speaking of God differ in some ways: they are not called "parables" and they are more seldom *Narratives*. Typical for parables speaking of the disciples is that the only image used is that of the master. This perhaps suggests that Jesus, as the leader of the group, identifies with that figure to some degree.

(3) Parables speaking of Jesus and the Kingdom resemble each other and differ radically from those discussed above. They are short and involve the fewest characters. Luke seldom calls them parables, and they are not of Lukan origin. Their credibility is excellent. They have their own characteristics as well. Parables referring to Jesus are never *Narratives* but most often *Simple Rules*, and they are not told to the disciples, whereas the Kingdom-parables are seldom defensive. In Spreadsheet 2^{51} the parables are presented according to the target they illustrate.

Comparison to Other Texts

The characteristics of Lukan parables are usually related to parallel Synoptic texts and other corresponding documents. Such comparison yields interesting observations, but to use them for interpreting Luke is questionable.

Scholars have suggested several outstandingly Lukan features in his parables. Annette Merz gathers the essential observations and makes

---

50. For discussion, see later in this chapter.
51. Visit fortresspress.com/thuren and click on the "Additional Supporting Resources" tab to view and download the spreadsheets.

some new ones. The parables are often situated in dinner scenes or other closed environments, and they are presented in groups. Most of them are told during the great Travel Narrative (Luke 9:50 [sic!]–19:27). Several parables are sex-balanced, that is, a story about a male has a female counterpart. They are often introduced with phrases such as ἄνθρωπός τις or τίς ἐξ ὑμῶν,[52] and they typically include internal monologues, international perspectives, city environment, and provocative imagery.[53] Regarding the message, *paraenesis*, forgiveness of sins or return to earlier status, economic issues, and eschatology are prominent.[54] John Drury adds that the stories have a crisis in the middle instead of at the end, they describe the world of human beings, and they have many allegorical features.[55]

Most of these observations are well rooted in the text, but they are not without problems. They are typically based on redaction criticism, that is, comparison to other Synoptic sources. In this, features differing from parallel documents are thought especially to represent Luke's own specific conventions, message, or theology. Such an approach easily leads to a biased characterization of Luke, since he hardly presupposed recipients who had the opportunity to read a synopsis. For them the whole text, not only features different from other sources, contains Luke's message. This applies to the parables, too. Narratological and rhetorical observations, not redactional ones, reveal their main ideas. A hypothetical "network of intertextual references (*intertextuelle Vernetztheit*)" including different Old Testament and early Jewish traditions[56] has little bearing on people not aware of those texts, or on those who did not consider

---

52. Even more specific descriptions, such as "dramatic triangle," have been suggested, but Merz, "Einleitung," 514, correctly rejects them as not very helpful.
53. Ibid., 514–16. Many of these features are discussed by other scholars as well.
54. Ibid., 516.
55. Drury, *Parables*, 112–17.
56. Merz, "Einleitung," 516.

Jesus' stories holy at the outset. Similarities may be accidental rather than genealogical.

The prevalence of journey parables has little informative value, since the Travel Narrative (9:51–19:27) covers in any case half of the document, and one can hardly expect to find many parables in the narratives of Jesus' childhood or passion. Reference to dinner settings and groups of parables is correct, but this technique is not prominent unless compared with other documents, since most of the parables are told outside these settings. The same applies to the parables' female counterparts: the phenomenon goes unnoticed when reading Luke only, since most male parables lack them. Furthermore, not all ἄνθρωπός τις and τίς ἐξ ὑμῶν parables are of Lukan origin, and only some 10% of the parables have international color or take place in a city. Not all images refer to human beings; there are vultures, ravens, and lilies as well. However, although only a few images are provocative "immoral heroes," these definitely need more attention, since these simultaneously good and bad characters may be striking for any reader.[57] Finally, the allegorical interpretation of particular characters and themes is hardly based on the story and its context, but derives from later Christian traditions. I suggest that the parables make perfect sense for their audiences when presented in their context without any allegorical additions. This idea will be further tested in the argumentation analysis (chap. 7).

In general, although a synoptic comparison or search for broader intertextual connections is interesting, the value for interpreting the Lukan parables from the perspective of their implied recipients remains questionable. External connections do not play a role for an audience not aware of them. Moreover, issues not different from the parallel texts may be just as important to the author as those typical

---

57. See in more detail Drury, *Parables*, 149.

of only his own text. Thus it is more promising to focus on the texts as the audience hears them. In this study I have marked the parables occurring in Luke only, but no far-reaching conclusions are based on these.

Nevertheless, simple comparisons especially between Luke (57 parables), Matthew (55 parables), and Mark (23 parables) reveal that some general features are not specific to Luke. In each document the length of the parables grows toward the end, as can be seen in the following table.[58] In Matthew the trend is slightly stronger than in Luke. The Lukan parables are also longer than the others. Moreover, in each document, toward the end the parables become not only longer but also less credible. Mark is clearly different, demonstrating the slowest growth in length but the fastest decline in credibility. However, this is mainly due to the dominance of easily acceptable simple rules. Luke has the most difficult parables, Mark the easiest ones.

---

58. For the sake of readability the development is presented by linear trendlines. The parables were identified and measured by my students at the University of Eastern Finland, Mr. Markus Finnilä (Matthew) and Mr. Petri Tiusanen (Mark). The data were gathered according to the principles presented in this chapter. In order to improve the comparison the number of Mark's parables was multiplied by 2.5.

Table VI.26 and VI.27

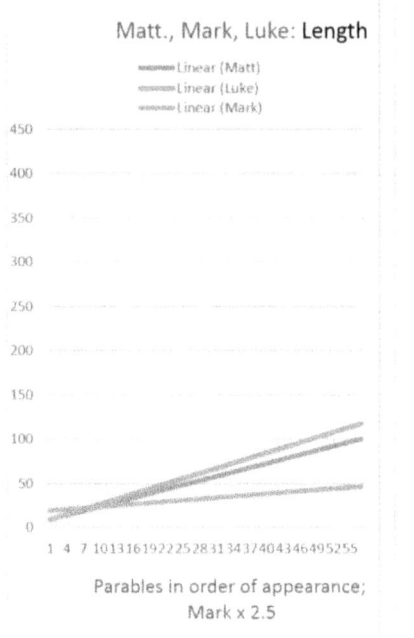
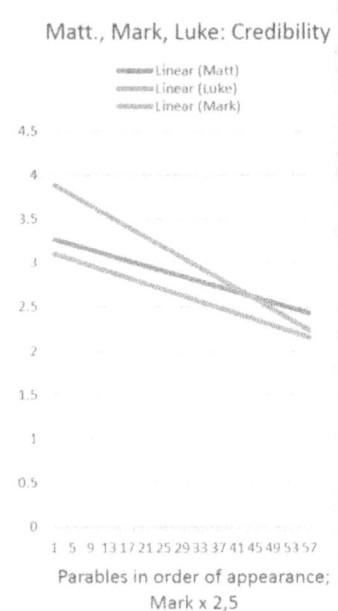

The formal analysis of all Lukan parables has illuminated in several ways how Luke and his Jesus tell parables. Several correspondences between various characteristics have been found. Perhaps the most interesting observation pertains to the correlation between length and credibility. Jesus appears to compensate for problems with the message's credibility through multifaceted narrative artistry. In other words, the weaker the claim, the longer the parable.

A combined general view of the results presented in each section can be found in Spreadsheet 1.[59] Based on this study, I can now proceed in the following chapter to the most important question about the parables' role in persuasion. There I will present a close argumentation analysis of each parable in its context.

---

59. Visit fortresspress.com/thuren and click on the "Additional Supporting Resources" tab to view and download the spreadsheets.

7

The Parables as Persuasion

The most important challenge when interpreting any parable is recognizing its function: How is it intended to convince its audience? Only thus can its meaning or message can be accurately perceived. Together with the story line, contextual factors such as the speaker, the audience, and the exigency determine the function of a parable. The argumentative structure is just as important. This chapter presents a comprehensive unplugged analysis of every Lukan parable told by Jesus, focusing on these issues.

Introduction

An unplugged approach to the argumentation means that only the function in the written context, lacking any reconstructed Lukan or other early Christian setting, will be pursued. Fascinating but uncontrollable allegorical interpretations will be avoided. What matters is how the story as a whole seeks to influence the audience as portrayed or implicit in the text. This can be revealed by modern argumentation analysis.

Still, the force of a parable does not lie in rational discourse only, but also in its poetic qualities, human experience, the interesting plot, and the fascinating characters.[1] Classical rhetoric studied human reasoning as interaction of *logos* and *pathos*, intellectual and emotional factors. The poetic dimension of a story supports its aim. Although these features remain somewhat subjective since they touch different readers in diverse ways, they can be successfully studied, as Charles Hedrick has demonstrated.[2] However, poetics should not overshadow the basic goal of the parables, namely, to convince their audience. Although the brief argumentation analysis of each parable provided here does not cover all the poetic dimensions, it by no means opposes or neglects them. Focusing on this dimension can undeniably enhance our understanding of the persuasive effect especially of the longer parables, but the results can scarcely contradict their basic rational structures as revealed by modern argumentation analysis. I maintain that no interpretation of a parable can be trusted if it results in inappropriate reasoning with respect what is inherent to it.

Instead of diving into the sea of deep theological explanations I will use a precise, controllable tool, as suggested in the Introduction: a modern approach to argumentation analysis developed by Stephen Toulmin.[3] This method not only helps to illustrate the essential content of each parable; it also enables transparent explication of the elements implicit in it. One of the best features of Toulmin's model is that the results are transparent and open to criticism, although the execution of the analysis requires some expertise.

---

1. These dimensions of narration are studied, for example, by Fludernik, *Narratology*, and Hogan, *Narratology*.
2. For example, Hedrick, *Parables*, 187–207, shows what kinds of reactions 18:2-6, the *Judge* can evoke.
3. See chap. 1.

In brief, every argumentation consists of the following elements:

- *Claim* is the opinion put forward, presumably not wholly accepted by the audience.
- *Data* denotes known and accepted specific grounds that should assure consent to the *claim*.
- *Warrant* signifies a general rule connecting *data* and *claim*, indicating why the *data* are relevant to the question.
- *Backing* consists of general, non-case-specific information guaranteeing the credibility of the *warrant*. Typically, it is made up of expert opinions, statistics, experience, examples, universal attitudes, and so on.

Any single missing element can usually be identified with precision, since Toulmin's model informs us about many of its attributes. In fact, normal argumentation seldom defines all the elements. The persuasive strategy can convince by introducing implicit ideas without articulating them.

Another way to gain controllable information about unspoken elements and, especially, the implicit purposes of a parable is to compare it with other parables in the same text. This lets us know what the implied audience expects when hearing a new parable.

In the Introduction I submitted a hypothesis according to which a parable illuminates a general rule that is then applied to the case discussed. In other words, a parable is a *backing* supporting a *warrant*. The long *Narratives* analyzed so far support this belief, but does it apply to all the Lukan parables, or do they share other typical methods of influencing the audience?

Luke starts appropriately with brief, simple, and credible parables. Not until the sixth parable (6:38, *Measure*) do difficulties arise. My working assumption is that corresponding persuasive features can be found in the longer, more complex parables as well, although they may be concealed by several persuasive devices designed to cause a stronger *pathos* effect among the recipients. Therefore the scrutiny of a large number of the shortest and simplest parables may prove fruitful for attempting to understand the longer, more intriguing parables. Presumably the basic way a parable is aimed at affecting the audience does not change when such factors as length or emotional devices are added to it. Thus knowledge of how a parable typically functions helps also to explain those that are complicated. This generates a hermeneutical circle in which a survey of all parables leads to a sharper image of a single parable, which in turn yields a more reliable vision overall.[4]

This chapter will be based on the formal observations in the previous chapter. The estimations provided there will be further illuminated. This creates a practical resource for further studies of any of these parables; chapters 2 through 5 provide examples of such exercises. Moreover, the results open new possibilities for corresponding studies of all other parables by Jesus in the New Testament or in non-canonical documents.

A Comprehensive Argumentation Analysis of the Lukan Parables

In what follows, the argumentative function of every Lukan parable attributed to Jesus will be discussed. This occasionally requires a deeper interpretation, which cannot be presented here for lack of space. For the sake of uniformity the parables examined in the previous chapters will be summarized here as well.

---

4. In such an approach, however, circular reasoning must be avoided.

I will begin with a brief review of the technical details of the parable discussed in chapter 6: the verses, the title, the type (*Simple Rule, Extended Rule,* or *Narrative*), the length in the Greek, the number of characters involved, the type of image used, and the primary audience to which the parable is addressed. In obscure cases the motive for the assessment is briefly stated. Perhaps the most difficult of these formal topics pertains to the target, mentioned in passing in the previous chapter: What does the parable seek to illustrate? To whom or to what does it refer? I am convinced that Toulmin's model will shed some light on this question, too.

Second, the main objective of this chapter, the discovery of the persuasive function of each parable, will be identified and the argumentative structure clarified. Comparison with earlier scholarship will mainly be limited to the best, most comprehensive recent presentations by Klyne Snodgrass and Ruben Zimmermann, and to John Nolland's illustrative commentary on Luke.[5] Finally, I will arrive at a variety of conclusions.

(1) 4:23, Healer 1

Doctor, cure yourself!

This *Simple Rule* is the first and shortest parable in Luke, consisting of but three words and one character, yet it fulfills the minimum requirements of a parable.[6] The image refers to a profession, and the credibility is excellent (*4), as the validity of the idea is not expected to be challenged. A sick physician is hardly trustworthy. But who are the audience? Allegedly the people of Nazareth are about to tell[7] the

---

5. Snodgrass, *Stories*; Zimmermann, ed., *Kompendium*; Nolland, *Luke*.
6. The saying has a narrative structure; it is non-historical, metaphoric, and appeals to the audience. See chap. 6 and Esch-Wermeling, "Heimvorteil," 523.
7. Nolland, *Luke*, 199, rightly states that ἐρεῖτε does not mean "prophesy."

parable to Jesus, but in reality Jesus tells it to them! The setting is hostile and the function defensive. The parable is applied to Jesus.[8]

Formally, the sentence consists of exhortation. However, although Jesus is assessed in the context as a healer, people allegedly do not bid him be healed. Thus this is a parable. Nothing in the text implies that Jesus was, or claimed to be, sick.[9] Instead, the parable urges him to heal some of his hearers.[10] Despite the common image, the exhortation refers to a general principle. It fits the injunction to heal the sick not only in foreign cities but also in the hometown. A similar *backing* could be, for example, "The shoemaker's children go barefoot," leading to a general *warrant*, "One should not neglect those closest to oneself." Such a rule indicates that Jesus should perform a miraculous healing in Nazareth. Since this reading fits the context, deeper theological or christological interpretations would be superfluous.

The argumentative function of the parable is not a general rule (*warrant*) combining known facts (*data*) with the thesis put forward (*claim*). Instead, it is a known example (*backing*) supporting such a general rule.

---

8. More precisely, the reasoning containing the parable seeks to persuade the audience about an attribute of Jesus. Thus the ultimate goal of the parable is to modify or change the audience's opinions or values (and even behavior) regarding him.
9. Contrary to this verse, Jesus would need help in the similar 23:35, ἄλλους ἔσωσεν, σωσάτω ἑαυτόν.
10. *Contra* Nolland, *Luke*. However, he rightly perceives that no reference to a prophetic future is required.

Figure VII.1

Backing: **Doctor, cure yourself!** (*4)[11]

▼

Warrant: One should not neglect those closest to oneself

▼

Data: Jesus has healed people in Capernaum ▶ *Claim*: He should heal people in Nazareth, too

(2) 4:24, Prophet

No prophet is accepted in the prophet's hometown.

This *Simple Rule* is not much longer (eight words and one character); it, too, describes an occupation.[12] The credibility is still good (*3), but apparently adjudged weaker as additional support referring to Elijah and Elisha (4:25-27) is presented. The parable is addressed to a general audience and has a defensive purpose. It, too, refers to Jesus.

This parable, 4:24, *Prophet*, is Jesus' counter-parable to 4:23, *Healer 1*, seeking to nullify it: Jesus cannot heal any resident in Nazareth. There are two feasible interpretations. The first builds on explicit *data* accepted by the recipients.[13] The additional examples, concerning the prophets of old, support the reasoning as *backing*. But the parable itself cannot constitute a general *warrant*, since it does not combine the *data* with the proposed *claim*. Thus a more general implicit *warrant* has

---

11. The number with an asterisk (*) refers to the grade of credibility discussed in the previous chapter. Reference to the parable will be presented in **bold**.
12. The *Kompendium*, 518, does not assess the saying a parable. However, the requirements for a parable are fulfilled. See more fully in chap. 6.
13. For example, Schürmann, "Traditionsgeschichte," 190, favors this option.

to be deduced. Indeed, "No prophet is welcome in his home town" could be expressed more generally as "familiarity reduces authority."

Figure VII.2

(I)

Backing: The examples of Elijah and Elisha

Backing: **No prophet is accepted in the prophet's hometown.** (*3)

▼

Warrant: Familiarity reduces authority

▼

Data^1: Jesus has healed people in Capernaum
Data^2: Jesus grew up in Nazareth and is known as Joseph's son
▶ *Claim*: He cannot heal the sick in Nazareth

However, there is a bolder possibility. If the parable itself is a *warrant* combining the *data* and the *claim* the verse is not a parable but implies that Jesus actually is a prophet. Apparently this hidden idea aroused more resentment among the hearers than his reluctance to heal the sick.[14]

---

14. This is the typical interpretation; see Nolland, *Luke*, 200–1.

Figure VII.3

(II)

Backing: The examples of Elijah and Elisha

▼

Warrant: **No prophet is welcome in his hometown** (*3)

▼

Data: Jesus is a prophet ▶ Claim: He cannot heal the sick in Nazareth

Which interpretation is to be preferred? In alternative (I) Jesus does not boldly state that he is prophet; he remains a healer. Alternative (II) is based on a similar thesis but involves a change of subject and requires an addition to the explicit text. As an interpretation of Isaiah 61 it is not impossible for the Lukan readers, but hardly their first choice. Moreover, it would constitute a poor point of departure for the reasoning, as the audience is not presumed to agree. Since alternative (I) is at least as intelligible, builds on existing text, and contains a feasible starting-point, it is the primary, albeit not the only possible meaning.[15] Hence this saying is a parable and functions as a *backing*. In any case, further theological implications are scarcely based on the Lukan text.

(3) 5:31, Healer 2

Those who are well have no need of a physician, but those who are sick.

---

15. Acceptance of the implied secondary interpretation as primary not only derives from barely acceptable *data* but also ruins the narrative plot, in which Jesus' seemingly polite answer covers his bold message.

The third *Simple Rule* is of similar length (10 words, 3 characters). It too refers to an occupation and has excellent credibility. The defensive purpose and the reference to Jesus remain the same, but the audience are the Pharisees and scribes, that is, the antagonists.

The parable is again self-evident. The commonly accepted point of departure (*data*) is Jesus' meal with sinners, and he argues that this is acceptable, even commendable (*claim*). The two factors are combined with a general rule (*warrant*), expressed in 5:32: "One should not call the righteous to repentance, but sinners," or in other words, "if it works, don't fix it." Applying this general *warrant* to the data implies that fellowship with sinners is the same as summoning them to repentance.

This rule is confirmed (*backing*) by an example from the healer's profession. It is often axiomatically read as an allegory so that Jesus is the healer, the sinners are the sick.[16] However, such an equation is misleading. In the text Jesus is not healing any sick people. Instead, the parable supports the *warrant*, combining the *data* and the *claim*. The parable itself cannot serve as a *warrant*, since it does not combine the *data* and the *claim*. The credibility is excellent (*4), since no objections are envisaged.[17]

---

16. Esch-Wermeling, "Heimvorteil," 529.
17. The analysis could be extended, since several implicit issues can be found. For example, why is a common meal interpreted as a call for repentance? Obviously if Jesus, as a respected religious individual, shared a common meal with known sinners that would indicate reacceptance into the religious community, which, in turn, requires repentance. This, however, is not explicitly stated in the text.

Figure VII.4

Backing: **It is not those who are well who need a physician, but those who are sick**
(*4)

▼

[*Backing¹*: One should not help those who are not in need]

▼

Warrant: One should not call the righteous to repentance, but sinners (5:32)

Data¹: Jesus has table-fellowship with sinners (v. 30)
Data²: Eating with them means calling them to repentance (v. 32) ▶ *Claim*: Jesus' behavior is reasonable

(4) 5:34-35, Groom

You cannot make wedding guests fast while the bridegroom is with them, can you?

This parable is the first Extended Rule, since it includes a clear narrative element. It is markedly longer than the previous parables (31 words, 2 characters), but the Pharisaic audience, the defensive purpose, and the reference to Jesus all remain the same.

The antagonists criticize Jesus' disciples for their failure to fast (data). Jesus argues that the disciples' behavior is reasonable since it is time to feast (claim). The parable uses the image of a bridegroom and his attendants, who are often axiomatically identified with Jesus and his disciples. However, as with the previous parables such an allegorical solution involves problems, since it converts the parable into a statement describing reality in figures and thereby minimizes its persuasive force in the framework story. There Jesus is not entering into marriage. Moreover, he is not dead, and to see here a prophecy of his death can hardly serve as the primary interpretation.[18] Although Jesus' audience can be suspected of awareness of the theological marriage imagery,[19] they do not know that this story will end in a biblical reference. In other words, using the word bridegroom did not automatically assume theological connotations. Thus no allegorical identification between Jesus and the bridegroom, messianic claims, or prophecy concerning his death are required, not to speak of later Christian fasting practices.[20] Instead, the image simply emphasizes that the disciples are in the middle of something important, and the time of fasting will come later. Thereby the parable is in essence an example supporting a general rule.

The difference from John, highlighted by the Pharisees, hints toward the eventual purpose of Jesus' answer. The famous John's presence did not imply a feast, whereas the presence of Jesus does. Thus he claims to be something more, and his disciples' behavior demonstrates this claim.

---

18. *Contra* Drury, *Parables*, 125. The audience is not supposed to read Luke backward. See also chap. 5 above.
19. See, e.g., Kern, "Fasten," 268–69. Perhaps this pertains to Luke's readers, too.
20. For discussion see Nolland, *Luke*, 248, who rightly dismisses messianic readings but axiomatically favors an allegorical interpretation.

THE PARABLES AS PERSUASION

Figure VII.5

Backing: **You cannot make wedding guests fast while the bridegroom is with them... (*3)**

▼

Warrant: Fasting is not suitable during a feast. [*Warrant*: The reason for a feast is something great]

▼

Data: Jesus' disciples do not fast; John's disciples do ▶ *Claim*: Jesus is more than John

However, just as in 4:24, Prophet, there is an implicit connection between Jesus and the bridegroom. In that case the rule is not a parable but a warrant. The claim suggests that Jesus is the messianic Bridegroom. This hidden message should not overshadow the primary meaning of the saying as a parable.

Figure VII.6

Warrant: **You cannot make wedding guests fast while the bridegroom is with them...**

Data: Jesus' disciples do not fast ▶ *Claim*: Jesus is the Bridegroom

(5) 5:36, Garment

No one tears a piece from a new garment and sews it on an old garment.

This Simple Rule has twenty-nine words and one character, referring to a tailor. The credibility is good (*3) but not self-evident, as it is unclear whether all share the experience described. The parable is told to the Pharisees. The exigency is no longer defensive but approaches ordinary teaching. The parable still refers to Jesus and his message, but no allegorical reading is necessary.[21]

This and the following two instances in 5:37-39, Wine 1 and Wine 2, illustrate the belief that a parable supports a general rule, or in Toulminian terms serves as a backing for a warrant. Their parallel nature is indicated by καί. Some scholars argue that Jesus here favors the old against the new,[22] but that is a misleading allegorical reading. Instead of merely considering the details one should focus on the principle they illustrate: the incompatibility of old and new.[23]

Unfortunately, both the precise data and the claim remain implicit. We only have the backing and the reconstructed warrant, but no clear point of departure (data) or goal (claim). The issue can no longer be simply the disciples' fasting. It is presumed that they will fast again, but that is hardly regarded as returning to something old. It is more likely that Jesus' whole message and mission are at stake. Since the author does not state the scope more precisely, to do so would mean unnecessary, unwarranted theologizing. At this point Luke as a good narrator leaves the question open: Jesus is involved with something new, but its actual nature remains to be seen. Thus both data and claim remain on a general level. References to later groups or the relationship between the church and Judaism are not based on the text.[24]

---

21. According to Nolland, *Luke*, 249, the parable stresses the continuity between Judaism and Christianity. Such an idea would hardly occur to the minds of Jesus' audience.
22. For example, Good, "Jesus," 19–36.
23. Thus correctly Dupont, "Vin," 286–304.
24. Contra Drury, *Parables*, 126–27.

Figure VII.7

Backing: **No one tears a piece from a new garment and sews it on an old garment; otherwise...** (*3)

▼

Warrant: Old and new should not be mixed

▼

Data: Jesus' message means something new ▶ *Claim*: Old rules do not apply to Jesus' message

(6) 5:37-39, Wine 1 and 2

And no one puts new wine into old wineskins . . .

And no one after drinking old wine desires new wine . . .

These two almost identical parables together form the longest Simple Rule in Luke (45 words, 1 character), but this is due to their double nature.[25] They can be treated together since they share not only most characteristics (image, type, audience, exigency, credibility, and so on) but also the same persuasive function. Both exemplify the same rule: old and new should not be mixed. They refer to agriculture and to people's experience with wine. These examples are introduced with a negative rhetorical question like the previous parables; this indicates the author's trust in their acceptance. Therefore their credibility is good (*3), albeit not self-evident. Like the previous parable they are aimed at the Pharisees and scribes. The exigency and target, Jesus and his message, remain the same. As above, allegorical references would only cause unnecessary problems.[26]

---

25. They could be analyzed as two separate parables as well.

Figure VII.8

Backing: **No one puts new wine into old wineskins; otherwise... (*3) / No one after drinking old wine...**

▼

Warrant: Old and new should not be mixed

▼

Data: Jesus message has a new meaning ▶ *Claim*: Old rules do not apply to Jesus' message

(7) 6:38, Measure

A good measure, pressed down, shaken together, running over, will be put into your lap.

This brief parable (10 words, 2 characters) describes business, but unlike other Simple Rules the credibility is not so good (*2), since a statement replaces the usual opening rhetorical question. Moreover, the content of the saying is not self-evident. It graphically describes generous measures in the marketplace. These are not exceptional or impossible. Even today, farmers at the market actually practice this rule when selling potatoes, peas, and so on.[27]

The said custom supports the general rule (warrant) expressed in 6:38b: "By your standard of measure it will be measured to you in return." The same rule recurs in several versions in the teaching starting at 6:27, for example, the Golden Rule, or actually *ius talionis*, "Just as you want people to treat you, treat them in the same way"

---

26. For example, Drury's reference to "the complacently traditionalist Jewish drinker" (*Parables*, 128) sounds elegant but is not based on the text.
27. *Contra* Nolland, *Luke*, 300, who finds here a reference to "superabundant generosity." My own experience from the marketplace in my hometown of Turku, Finland corresponds to Jesus' description. This is hardly due to the Finnish merchants' familiarity with the parable.

(6:31). The parable envisages a general audience and the disciples, and is free of context. Thereby it is the first non-defensive parable in Luke, and the first lacking a mention of Jesus.

As in the previous parables, the data and the claim are difficult to discern. In the context Jesus not only advocates reciprocity but argues that doing good to those unable to repay is not an exception to this rule. It will be rewarded by God (passivum divinum),[28] who also does good to those unable to repay. The obscurity of these factors does not, however, affect the parable's persuasive nature.

Figure VII.9

Backing: **Generous measuring practices in the marketplace** (6:38a) (*2)

▼

Warrant: By your standard of measure it will be measured to you in return. (6:38b)

▼

Data: You give generously to others ▶ *Claim*: People/God will give generously to you

(8) 6:39, Blind

A blind person cannot guide a blind person, can he? Will not both fall into a pit?

This is the first in a series of four similar parables in 6:39-45. It is a brief (10 words, 2 characters) Simple Rule, referring to the healer's vocation with excellent credibility (*4), introduced with the negative statement μήτι. The audience or exigency is not specified. This causes some problems for the interpretation.

---

28. Tannehill, *Sword*, 109.

Without taking a stand on the audience or the meaning of the parable, we can first analyze its basic persuasive function or "logic" in a comparison with the next three parables. A common general rule (warrant) can be formulated in different ways, such as "one cannot help anyone without being his or her superior." The same idea is found in 4:23, Healer 1. But is the rule now aimed at those who seek leadership or to benefit others,[29] or at those who are helped?[30] The commentators offer diverse versions of both solutions, often referring to comparisons with Matthew or to the later situation of the church. However, since we are reading the Lukan text the best context is found therein.

In 6:41-42 Jesus is addressing "you," who must first improve in order to be fit to help others, since a poor source cannot produce anything good. This idea is reiterated in 6:39 and in 6:43-45. To see here a warning against other transgressors, such as false teachers, hardly befits this neat combination, not to speak of any anachronistic explanations. When nothing is added to the context, 6:39 suggests that the hearers must learn to see before guiding others. The hearers' nearer identity is not even implied—Luke does not mention whether they are the opponents, the disciples, or merely a general audience. Choosing a specific group would do violence to his presentation.

The warrant can be formulated in association with the following parables in 6:40, the Teacher, 6:41-42, the Speck in the Eye, and even 6:43-45, the Bad Tree. They all illustrate the same rule with images taken from several different areas: "the copy is never better than the original" or "one must be good in order to do good to others."[31]

---

29. Several options have been presented: Jesus is talking to the disciples who wish to be leaders, to Jewish teachers, to teachers of the church, or to bad teachers. For an overview see Nolland, *Luke,* 306–7.
30. Based on Matt. 15:14, Nolland, *Luke,* 307, claims that the parable is undoubtedly addressed to those being led, and the *claim* is: "Do not be led by blind leaders."

The common claim of these four parables is implicit. However, behind every instance there is a general exhortation (claim): You must first mend your ways yourselves. A corresponding point of departure (data), expressed with the images lead (v. 39), teach (v. 40), heal (vv. 41-42), and bear fruit (vv. 43-44), could read: "you want to help others."

Figure VII.10

Backing: **A blind person cannot guide a blind person, can he? Will not both fall into a pit? (*4)**

▼

Warrant: You cannot help anybody unless you are his or her superior

▼

Data: You want to help others ▶ *Claim*: You must first improve yourselves

(9) 6:40, Teacher

A disciple is not above the teacher, but everyone who is fully qualified will be like the teacher.

This second version of the parable is a Simple Rule having fourteen words and two characters. It refers to an occupation. The credibility (*4), the audience, the exigency, and the reference all remain the same.

As in the previous parable, the exigency is implicit. Nevertheless, this is hardly an injunction to avoid false teachers.[32] Since in this

---

31. Actually, the same warrant would fit the first parable of a healer as well: "Physician, heal yourself!" (4:23), but as there is no reference to any illness in Jesus it must rather be interpreted in light of its actual context.
32. Contra Nolland, *Luke*, 307.

context (6:41-45) "you" are the ones who must improve, the same audience requires amendment even here. The reference to teaching provides a clue to the audience. The general audience is excluded, and allusions to later church leaders would be anachronistic. Perhaps Jesus is training his disciples,[33] but a warning to actual teachers among the audience, namely, the Pharisees and scribes, is also feasible.

Figure VII.11

Backing: **A disciple is not above the teacher... (*4)**

▼

Warrant: The copy is never superior to the original

▼

Data: You want to teach others ▶ *Claim*: You must first improve yourselves

(10) 6:41-42, Speck in the Eye

Why do you see the speck in your brother's eye . . .

Despite its length, this third version is a Simple Rule (22 words, 2 characters), actually a rhetorical question. It refers to the healer's occupation with an excellent (*4) credibility. The audience, the exigency, and the reference remain constant. The exhortation in 6:42b to remove the log from your own eye is part of the parable and not the actual claim. It does, however, hint at how the claim can be formulated.

---

33. Kern, "Grössenwahn?!," 73.

Figure VII.12

Backing: **You cannot find the speck that is in your neighbor's eye with a long in your own eye (*4)**

▼

Warrant: You cannot help anybody if you are worse than she or he is

▼

Data: You wish to help others ▶ *Claim*: You must first help yourselves

(11) 6:43-45, Bad Tree

No good tree bears bad fruit . . .

This fourth and final version is a Simple Rule consisting of thirty-two words and one character. It pertains to the experience of agriculture with good (*3) credibility.[34] The audience, the exigency, and the references remain constant as before.

All four parables serve as backing for the ultimate warrant. Thus examples of fig trees, thorn bushes, grapes, and briars support the rule "No good tree produces bad fruit and vice versa," which in turn is generalized into "Each tree is known by its own fruit." The data and claim are not self-evident. On the one hand, the previous theme continues: One who desires to do good (data) must first be good (claim). However, the principle can be considered also from the opposite angle: good deeds demonstrate that an individual is good. Both trajectories, with several specifications, are assessed in the primary goal (claim) of the parable.[35] A theoretical acceptance of the

---

34. The credibility is perhaps not excellent (*4), since Jesus needs to support his opening statement with several examples. One could argue that occasionally even a good tree produces some bad fruit.

inseparability of the outer and inner sides of a human being has also been suggested,[36] but the simpler, general idea is to be preferred in the context. The ambiguity of the data and claim do not obscure the reasoning of the parable.

Figure VII.13

Backing[3]: **Examples of different plants (8:44b)**

▼

Backing[2]: **No good tree bears bad fruit, nor does a bad tree bear good fruit (*3)**

▼

Backing[1]: **Each tree is known by its own fruit**

▼

Warrant: A bad person cannot do good

▼

Data: You want to do good ▶ *Claim*: You must first improve yourselves

The credibility of this parable is somewhat weaker than that of the previous three because it postulates some experience of gardening or farming. Therefore additional support for the rule "each tree is known by its own fruit" is required. Yet no objections are expected. To whom is the parable told? Once again Luke does not tell and

---

35. Nolland, *Luke*, 308–9, presents several options, such as an attack on false teachers, a call to true inner goodness over against hypocrisy (favored by Nolland), or a call for the teachers to demonstrate their goodness.
36. Starnitzke, "Früchten," 86, 90–91.

so we should not know. The disciples and the antagonists are good candidates, but no recipient can consider himself or herself excluded.

Verse 45 applies the above image to good and evil treasures of the heart. It could be assessed as an additional parable,[37] but it suffices to regard it merely as describing real life with some metaphors. The sentence supports an explicit metaphorical rule, "The mouth speaks what the heart is full of."

(12) 6:48-49, Two Builders

. . . a man building a house . . . dug deeply and laid the foundation on rock . . .

The first Narrative in Luke is longer (65 words, 2 characters) and less credible (*2) than the previous parables. It refers to a construction worker's occupation. It, too, is aimed at a general audience and contains general teaching, illuminating their attributes.

This proper story lacks an obvious ending. In contrast to Matthew 7:24-27, the audience is not told at the outset that the second builder was foolish; thus such a prejudgment should not skew the interpretation. In fact, his project was easier and cheaper. Unfortunately, he risked a bad outcome that eventually materialized. This, however, comes as a surprise to the audience. The story could have had a far different ending. What if the man had been living comfortably in his house when the rainy season began, while the other was still digging and laying the foundation? Such a story would imply that avoidance of all risks yields a poor result, as in 19:12-27, the Minas. Since the ending of Jesus' story is only one of several options, the story line is possible but not self-evident.

The parable has inspired several allegorical interpretations, such as identifying the crisis with God's judgment, allusions to the Temple, Israel, and so on.[38] These additions are superfluous. The parable is best

---

37. So Drury, *Parables*, 108.

regarded as illustrating a general rule that is applied to the addressees' situation.

Indeed, despite its length and lower credibility, a general rule can be identified behind this story, too. It could be formulated: "sweat saves blood" or "making a great effort to follow the right way pays off in the end." This principle is not self-evident; one could argue that in every project some risks must be taken and excess effort avoided. The parable with its vivid, dramatic story seeks to cover the very objections or other problems inherent in the principle it exemplifies. Nobody is insinuated to be identical with the man who lost his house.

Figure VII.14

Backing: **Narrative of two men building houses (*2)**

▼

Warrant: A major effort to follow the right way finally proves worthwhile

▼

Data: You hear teaching ▶ *Claim*: You must act accordingly, despie the costs

(13) 7:32-34, Playing Children

> *... children sitting in the marketplace and calling to one another, 'We played the flute for you ...'*

This Extended Rule consists of twenty-one words, being the second shortest (together with 10:2, Harvest). It describes a familiar incident involving two groups. It refers to the audience and it is aimed at the Pharisees and scribes, but without any immediate exigency.

---

38. Snodgrass, *Stories,* 334–37, discusses several options, including an eschatological interpretation. See also Nolland, *Luke,* 310. Most of them require massive additions to the simple Lukan text.

The parable describes children playing wedding and funeral.[39] They criticize each other for not joining in both sides' activities. The narrator claims that this reflects the audience's reaction to John's and Jesus' opposite modes of behavior: John was fasting, Jesus is feasting (data). The credibility of the example is low (*2), since the children's behavior is feasible but not inevitable. Despite the vivid image, the message of the parable is obscure. It has provoked numerous interpretations, most of which can be divided into two categories: either the parable displays the children's failure to play together or it describes a popular game.[40] The latter can be ruled out, since Luke does not give his recipients any further information about such play. Instead of pondering hypotheses built on external factors, I will analyze merely the argumentation in the text.

The basic problem is that too many elements remain implicit. Most importantly, the opinion proposed (claim) is missing. What we do have is the accepted point of departure (data)—the audience is condemning both John and Jesus, albeit for opposite behavior—and the parable, in which the children similarly criticize each other. Starting from the hypothesis that both long and short parables perform the same function, we can identify the following explicit elements of the argumentation:

---

39. Cf. Nolland, *Luke*, 343.
40. See ibid., 343–44. There are some explanations outside these categories as well.

Figure VII.15

Backing: **Children criticizing each other for not dancing and not weeping**

▼

Warrant: ?

▼

Data: Antagonists criticize Jesus for not drinking and Jesus for drinking ▶ *Claim*: ?

Toulmin's scheme provides us with some information on the implicit elements. The warrant must be a general rule, it must connect data and claim, and it must be supported by backing. Correspondingly, the claim expresses a principle asserted by the speaker and not agreed upon at the outset by the audience. It must also fit the data and the warrant. Any interpretation of the parable that violates these requirements is misleading. On the other hand, several compliant options are possible, since Luke does not explicitly state the correct answer. Nevertheless, the sentence about the "children of Wisdom" in 7:35 may well guide the interpretation. The players' inconsistent criticism demonstrates their immature, ill-advised behavior; they are not among the children of Wisdom. To be sure, such a negative claim is hardly the ultimate goal, as the parables usually advocate some action as well. Probably the audience is prepared for an implicit exhortation: "Be consistent" or "Accept the message of John and Jesus," but it is not articulated at this time.

Figure VII.16

Backing: **Children criticizing each other for not dancing and not weeping (*2)**

▼

Warrant: Inconsistent criticism is unwise

▼

Data: This generation criticized John and Jesus for opposite behavior ▶ *Claim*: This generation is not wise

(14) 7:41-43, Two Debtors

A certain creditor had two debtors; one owed five hundred denarii, and the other fifty . . .

This second Narrative consists of twenty-six words, being the second shortest. Unlike in the previous parable, a distinct storyline can be identified. It describes commercial practices and involves three characters, one of whom is a moneylender, a typical unpredictable master-character. It refers to two individuals (a sinful woman and Simon the Pharisee) and responds to a particular exigency. This is the first parable derived from Luke's own sources[41] and the first one told to an individual. The Narrative depicts the moneylender in a way that may be feasible but is by no means inevitable. Thus the credibility is not so good. However, Simon accepts the story (7:43), which indicates that it is far-fetched.

No allegorical explanations are necessary:[42] The debtors are not Simon and the woman, and the moneylender is not Jesus or God.[43] Such identifications not only complicate the interpretation by

---

41. According to the list of L-parables in in the *Kompendium*, 518–21.
42. Moreover, glorifying statements like "ranked with the most revealing stories of the Christian faith" (Snodgrass, *Stories*, 77) only make the interpretation more difficult.

provoking irrelevant questions; they also deprive the parable of its persuasive force. If the parable bluntly stated that God forgives more sins for the woman than for Simon the audience could raise an objection. However, as a true parable, it presents an example against which they cannot protest. The principle highlighted by this parable is then applied to the actual case. The abundance of love shown by the woman indicates that she actually is forgiven much. The reasoning shown in figure VII.17 is lucid.

Figure VII.17

Backing: **Two debtors are forgiven different amounts of money, resulting in different quantities of love (*2)**

▼

Warrant: The value of the gift correlates with the amount of gratitude [The quantity of love shown correlates to the extent of the sins forgiven (7:43, 47)]

▼

Data: The woman showed moe love to Jesus than Simon (7:37-38, 44-46) ▶ *Claim*: The woman is forgiven more sins than Simon (7:47-48)

To be sure, there are strong theological undertones indicated by the passivum divinum in 7:47-48 and expressed in the following reaction: "Who is this man who even forgives sins?" (7:49). Thus the real-world story about the woman performs a function similar to that of the parable, with the claim referring to God's forgiveness. Luke, however, does not so postulate.

---

43. *Contra* Snodgrass, *Stories*, 87, and most commentators. Roose, "Rollenwechsel," 533, is more reluctant to identify the characters.

(15) 8:5-8, Sower

A sower went out to sow his seed; and as he sowed, some fell on the path ...

The third Narrative contains sixty-eight words. The story is told to a general audience and refers to its ability to maintain the message (and implicitly the Kingdom of God). Only one character is involved, and no particular exigency is present.

Attempts to interpret the parable are extensive, and not all can be presented here.[44] They include at the extreme Rudolf Bultmann's despair of ever perceiving the meaning of the parable.[45] However, most of the problems discussed and the interpretations offered are based on external factors such as Synoptic comparisons, searches for the original story, extensive agricultural details, later Christian allegorical interpretations, and so on. When the purpose is to understand how the text was meant to be understood, all these can be ignored, since the audience to whom Luke wrote was unaware of them. To be sure, a general knowledge of ancient farming may be possessed by the audience, but not by us. Therefore the exclusion of external information cannot be absolute. The result, an unplugged reading focusing solely on the Lukan text and its argumentation yields a simple and clear reading.[46]

Luke (and his predecessors) supplement the parable with an allegorical explanation by Jesus. Since the extension belongs to the text it must be read as just as original as the parable. Thus the variation of the soil compares to differences in perseverance, even if the story as such offers other possibilities as well. The explanation

---

44. Good presentation and discussion from different perspectives can be found in Hedrick, *Parables*, 164–86 (including his own poetic reading); Snodgrass, *Stories*, 145–76; and Dronsch,"Fruchtbringen," 297–311.
45. Bultmann, *Geschichte,* 199–200; Nolland, *Luke,* 374–75.
46. To be sure, the parable offers unusually tempting possibilities of reconstruction based on Synoptic comparison and suggestions of an Aramaic origin, but such imaginary parables are beyond the focus of this analysis.

also indicates how the readers are supposed to make some allegorical interpretations of other parables. However, Jesus explains only the details and does not allude to the parable's function as a narrative. The surprise at the end stands without comment. In this way Jesus' explanation provides additional support to the persuasiveness of the story.

The parable begins by describing a typical agricultural practice with good credibility (*3). Anyone who has sown seed by hand knows that it is not a work of precision.[47] Moreover, an impossible image at the beginning of a Narrative would be unusual and ruin the rest of the story. However, the ending is excessive: one hundred times as great a crop is far beyond normal,[48] which lowers the credibility (*2). Thus two different warrants are supported by the parable: (1) Grade of perseverance correlates to the result; (2) Good perseverance produces an abundant result. The interpretation depends on the nature of the parable: the former is based on interpreting tit as an Extended Rule referring to what is normal or typical. The latter can be seen when the parable is observed as a proper Narrative with a surprise at the end. Since there is such an ending, this option is to be preferred. See figures VII.18 and VII.19.

---

47. The parable also exaggerates the proportion of lost seed, but this is hardly its focus and should not lead to any allegorical interpretations (*contra* Nolland, *Luke*, 371). For (needlessly precise) discussion of ancient Palestinian agricultural conventions see Snodgrass, *Stories*, 166–67.
48. Some scholars argue that one hundred grains per seed was possible, albeit abnormal (see Nolland, *Luke*, 371–72). However, this evaluation is based on ancient hyperbolic rhetoric rather than biological facts. See, e.g., http://pods.dasnr.okstate.edu/docushare/dsweb/Get/Document-6695/PSS-2149pod.pdf.

Figure VII.18

Backing: **Variations in the soil's ability to sustain growth produces different crops** (*3)

▼

Warrant: Grade of perseverance correlates to the result

▼

Data: People hear God's word (and hope for a good result) ▶ *Claim*: They should retain the message in perseverance

Figure VII.19

Backing: **Story revealing that good soil produces an abundant crop** (*2)

▼

Warrant: Perseverance is rewarded to excess

▼

Data: People hear God's word (and hope for a good result) ▶ *Claim*: They should retain the message in perseverance

(16) 8:16, Lamp 1

No one after lighting a lamp hides it under a jar ...

This Simple Rule consists of twenty-one words and illustrates a domestic issue. The credibility is good (*4), indicated by a negative introduction (οὐδείς). At most one character is involved, and no particular exigency is at hand. The parable is told to the disciples, but its reference to the real world is not explicit. According to a typical allegorical explanation the light is the word of God or the message of Jesus, which the audience should not hide.[49] However, such an allegorical interpretation gives rise to a needlessly problematic situation, since the one who lights the lamp and the one who omits to cover it are the same individual, who thus cannot be both Jesus and his hearers. Instead of seeking such allegorical correspondences it is simpler and easier to read the parable as emphasizing the principle explicit in the following 8:17: All secrets must come out.

Although the parable itself is clear, its application is not evident. Verse 17 refers to the secrets of the Kingdom. This saying as such lacks credibility; why can some matters not remain secret? However, inasmuch as Jesus has revealed the secrets to the disciples (8:10), this may be a warrant, reflecting the parable: When shared, any secret will be made known. Again, extensive theological or other allegorical explanations are superfluous.

Figure VII.20

Backing: **No one, after lighting a lamp, covers it** (*4)

▼

Warrant: All secrets must come out (8:17) [when shared]

▼

Data: You have been shown the secrets of the Kingdom (8:10) ▶ *Claim*: You must make them known

(17) 10:2, Harvest

The harvest is plentiful, but the laborers are few . . .

---

49. For example, Dronsch, "Leuchte," 136–37, states that the question is left open in Q, but regarding Luke he argues allegorically that the light is the word of God, which should not be covered by people sympathetic to Jesus' message.

This parable is among the three shortest Extended Rules (21 words, three characters). Although formally an exhortation, it describes a typical situation in agriculture with fairly good credibility (*3).[50] The command is given to seventy disciples in a particular situation. It refers to preparation for the tour planned by Jesus, or more generally to the proclamation of his message of the Kingdom (10:1).

Any eschatological or other theological exaggeration of the parable itself is unnecessary.[51] The parable merely exemplifies a principle: if the task exceeds the labor force available, more workers are needed. This principle must then be applied to the situation presented in the context.

Figure VII.21

Backing: **The need for additional workers in the field due to a rich harvest (*3)**

▼

Warrant: The number of workers must match the increased amount of work

▼

Data: There are too many people in Galilee to be reached ▶ *Claim*: The disciples must pray to God for additional coworkers

(18) 10:22, Father and Son

No one knows who the son is except the father . . .

---

50. Owners of large estates did not live on the farm and thus needed information about the number of harvesters required. The situation is not specific to Palestine and could thus be well understood by the Lukan recipients; cf. Zimmermann, "Folgenreiche," 111–14.
51. Nolland, *Luke*, 550–51, rejects any attempt to avoid allegory and claims that the *lord* and the *harvest* must have at least some theological and eschatological bearing and refer to the OT background. For more overt theological readings see Zimmermann, "Folgenreiche," 114–16. However, the ancient Jews scarcely referred to OT theology every time they spoke of harvest. Such literary and theological reading is not the first option, especially when the image functions well without additions.

This Simple Rule contains of twenty-seven words and three characters. Unlike the Johannine parallel (John 5:19-21), which refers to delivery of a father's skills to his son,[52] and unlike any profound christological definition, Luke explicitly depicts only a general domestic image emphasizing the close relationship between the two.[53] As usual, the parable is best understood without a theological supplement.[54] To the audience following the world of the story, Jesus is not yet known to be divine. The credibility of the parable is fairly good (*3): A father knows his son better than other people do, and vice versa. However, since the nature of "knowing" remains obscure, the Johannine counterpart is more credible.

However, the audience is unusual. Unlike all other parables, this one is explicitly addressed to the Lord of heaven and earth. To be sure, the text may appear to be aimed at outsiders, but in the context (10:21) it is a prayer to God. Oddly enough, another parable (18:10-14, the Pharisee and the Tax Collector) contains a corresponding thanksgiving to God that is apparently aimed at the bystanders!

The specific audience does not exclude analysis of this parable together with the others. It refers to Jesus and supports the claim that his knowledge of God is exceptional. To be sure, the parabolic image here is fading, as the opening phrase 10:22a ("All things have been handed over to me by my father") sounds like a statement relating to the real world, not a parable. This prayer plays a key role in Luke, as it presents Jesus in an extraordinary light. However, as a parable it is exceptional in many ways.

---

52. See van der Watt, "Meisterschüler."
53. No references to Greek or Egyptian gods are needed; see Nolland, *Luke*, 573–74.
54. Nolland, *Luke*, 573–75, discusses far-reaching theological and intertextual references.

Figure VII.22

Backing: **A son knows his father better than anyone else** (10:22b) (*3)

▼

Warrant: Close kinship to an individual confers trustworthy knowledge

▼

Data: Jesus has a specific relationship with God ▶ *Claim*: Jesus' message about God is trustworthy

(19) 10:30-37, Samaritan

A man was going down from Jerusalem to Jericho, and fell into the hands of robbers . . .

This is the first long Narrative in Luke (the tenth longest)[55], consisting of 106 words and involving six characters. The imagery is unique, as it does not refer to a typical feature of any phenomenon or occupation or to a likely occurrence, but merely to a peculiar incident. Instead, the behavior of the protagonist is presented as atypical; the parable alleges that 67% of people would not act in the same way. Thus the credibility must be adjudged weak (*1). The parable's persuasive force is based not on the application of common practice to another issue but on its ability to arouse emotions.

The parable is aimed at a single individual (νομικός) in a specific situation, which is not offensive. The reference of the Narrative is complex: formally it seeks to illustrate the definition of the concept of neighbor. This, in turn, is needed in order to know how to "inherit eternal life." It may be assumed that a theological message underlies

---

55. See the detailed discussion in chap. 2.

the whole story. Here only the structure of the final argument is presented in figure VII.23.

Figure VII.23

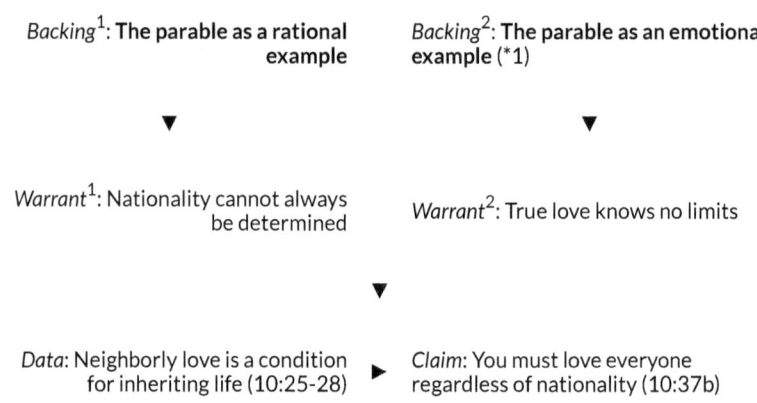

Backing[1]: **The parable as a rational example**

Backing[2]: **The parable as an emotional example** (*1)

▼ ▼

Warrant[1]: Nationality cannot always be determined

Warrant[2]: True love knows no limits

▼

Data: Neighborly love is a condition for inheriting life (10:25-28) ▶ *Claim*: You must love everyone regardless of nationality (10:37b)

There is also an underlying theological principle, as shown in figure VII.23.

Figure VII.24

Warrant: God is true to God's own rules

▼

Claim/Data[1]: Unconditional neighbor love ▶ *Claim*[1]: God loves everyone unconditionally

(20) 11:5-8, Friend at Midnight

Suppose one of you has a friend, and you go to him at midnight . . .

Luke's fifth Narrative consists of eighty-two words and four characters. It presents a domestic image with satisfactory credibility (*2). It is the first τίς ἐξ ὑμῶν parable in Luke, suggesting the audience's own conduct; yet despite the rhetorical question it is not self-evident that all would behave as the characters in the story do. The parable is aimed at the disciples with a particular exigency. It refers explicitly to God's behavior and comes from Luke's own sources.

Scholars and translators typically diminish the story's exaggeration by ruthlessly softening the negative attribute attached to the begging friend, ἀναίδεια, shamelessness.[56] Such an attempt, however, misses the point of the story. This can be seen by scrutiny of the parallel parables. Just as in the following 11:11-13, Bad Fathers, the hearers are bluntly described as "bad," and as the judge in 18:2-6 respects neither God nor other people, 11:5-8, the Friend at Midnight, describes one of the most irritating situations one could encounter.

Rhetorical exaggeration is common to these stories: indeed, the worst possible individuals, even when trapped in a very annoying situation, will help others. Why? Not because of social customs (about which especially the judge did not care), not because of their ethical quality (the said father was bad, not good), and not because of any positive feelings toward the person in need (who would like to be disturbed in the middle of the night?). No references to ancient Middle-Eastern patterns of hospitality are needed; on the contrary.[57] At least the friend and the judge are prompted simply by the desire to get rid of the begging individual as soon as possible. All these cases are based on *qal wahomer* reasoning, as stated in 11:13. If the worst or most irritated individual will help those in need, how much more will God give you anything you lack, since God must be better than they are.

---

56. See, e.g., Nolland, *Luke*, 625–26. Snodgrass, *Stories*, 444–45, correctly rejects such readings.
57. For such explanations see Merz, "Freundschaft," 558–60.

The parable illustrates a general principle warrant. The claim is found in 11:9, but the data remain implicit. Apparently God is equated with the person irritated by a nocturnal visitor.

Figure VII.25

Backing: **The behavior of friends at midnight (*2)**

▼

Warrant: Even an irritated individual helps others when entreated

▼

Data: God cannot be inferior to an irritated individual ▶ *Claim*^{1}: God will certainly help you (11:9)

▶ *Claim*^{2}: You must ask for God's help shamelessly

(21) 11:11-13, Bad Fathers

Is there anyone among you who, if your child asks for a fish . . .

This is simpler than the previous parable and can be classified as an Extended Rule, consisting of forty-eight words. It is also more credible (*3), although it, too, refers to the audience's own imaginable behavior. Other characteristics, such as the type of image used, the audience,[58] the exigency, and the subject cited, are identical.

---

58. *Contra* Kenneth Bailey, *Poet*, 140–41, who assumes that the audience consists of Pharisees.

Figure VII.26

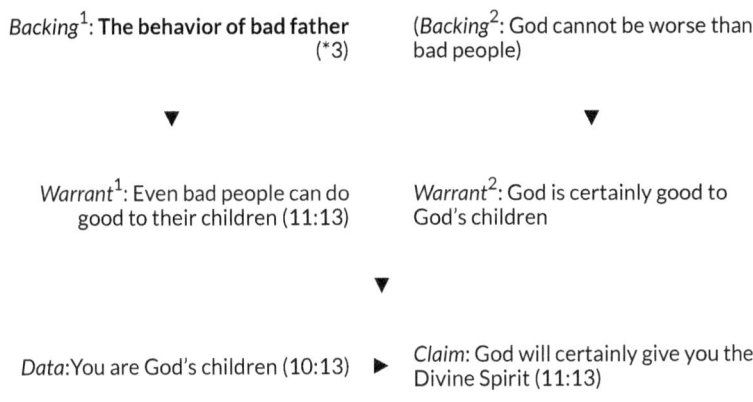

(22) 11:17, Kingdom

Every kingdom divided against itself becomes a desert, and house falls on house.

This Simple Rule consists of only eleven words and has no human characters. It envisages a political scenario, which is plausible and indeed actually happened later in Jerusalem in 70 C.E. Yet the rule is not self-evident (*3). It is intended as a defense against anonymous antagonists (ἕτεροι) among the people, and it refers to Jesus' own actions.

Figure VII.27

Backing: **The image of a civil war** (*3)

▼

Warrant: An individual cannot fight against himself or herself

▼

Data: Jesus drives out demons ▶ *Claim*: Jesus cannot represent Beelzebul, but God

(23) 11:21-22, Protecting the House

When a strong man, fully armed, guards his house, his property is safe . . .

This Extended Rule consists of thirty-three words and two characters. The image is both domestic and military, and despite the narrative element the credibility is high (*4), as the story is self-evident: you will lose a fight with an opponent stronger than you, and when this happens your goods and your armor are lost. As always, the figures are not to be identified allegorically with anyone else in the context or in theology.[59] Instead, the story illustrates a principle: the winner takes all. The point of the story is not only that the stronger defeats the weaker but that he or she also despoils the weaker's house.

The exigency is no more defensive than in the previous parables; the teaching has declined to a more general level, as demonstrated by a woman's reaction in 11:27. The actual relevance of the principle illustrated by the parable is not overt. The closest reference is the previous exorcism. It emphasizes the absolute difference between the two masters: after the exorcism by Jesus, nothing will be left for the

---

59. Typically the "strong one" is identified with Satan, an individual, or Israel, and the stronger with Jesus or Satan. For discussion see Nolland, *Luke*, 642.

former master. This interpretation does not require any identification of Jesus and Beelzebul with the characters in the story.

Figure VII.28

Backing: **The victor plundering the loser's possessions (*4)**

▼

Warrant: The winner takes all

▼

Data: Jesus casts out demons ▶ *Claim*: Beelzebul has nothing left

(24) 11:24-26, Unclean Spirit

When the unclean spirit has gone out of a person, it wanders through waterless regions looking for a resting place . . .

This parable too is an Extended Rule, but somewhat longer, consisting of fifty-five words and three characters. The applied image may sound odd or transcendent, but demons and evil spirits were a regular part of the ancient worldview.[60] Thus the story describes the experience of a healer, in this case an exorcist, just as other parables refer to a farmer or a builder. If nothing replaces the demon it may return. Perhaps the audience will not accept this rule as easily as those pertaining to agriculture. Thus the grade of credibility can be adjudged somewhat weaker (*2): it is feasible, but not necessarily true. As with the previous parable, the exigency may be assessed as somewhere between a plea to the antagonist and general teaching to a wider audience. This time the latter dimension is stronger.

---

60. Labahn, "Raum," 128–29.

The idea exemplified by this parable is disputed. John Nolland finds here an illustrative warning against "the temporary windfalls of life" and rejects any connection with exorcism.[61] Indeed, if the text merely claimed that a person can be possessed again after exorcism it would not be a parable at all, but merely a statement concerning reality. Then its persuasive force would remain weak: the audience may choose whether or not to believe. But as a parable it refers to an attribute typical of a profession. When deducing a general rule from this experience, objections are rare.

To be sure, there are actually two consecutive parables, which complicates the interpretation. There is a house vacant after the tenant has left and a person vacant after the departure of an evil spirit. Both, however, illustrate the same principle. A room cannot remain unoccupied forever, and the same applies to a person's mind: someone or something will always fill the vacuum.

New images or ideas, such as "soap, paint, bad penny," or "false hope" should not be attached to the parable, since they distort the image.[62] Instead, it is better to seek the parable's function in the immediate context. It primarily explains Jesus' previous maxim in 11:23: "Whoever is not with me is against me," which serves well as a *warrant* illustrated by the parable. An individual who has been touched by Jesus' message cannot remain neutral. Although both *data* and *claim* are somewhat obscure, the following factors within the context constitute a rational structure (see figure VII.29).

---

61. Nolland, *Luke*, 645–46, argues diametrically against the existing text: "The story has nothing to do with the threat of repossession after exorcism."
62. *Contra* Nolland, *Luke*, 647.

Figure VII.29

Backing: **Experience of an empty room / an exorcist's patient (*2)**

▼

Warrant: A religious vacuum is not possible (whoever is not with Jesus is against him (11:23)

▼

Data: Jesus is proclaiming a message ▶ *Claim*: The hearer must take a stand (11:28)

(25) 11:33, Lamp 2

No one after lighting a lamp puts it in a cellar, [or under the bushel basket . . .]

This Simple Rule consists of twenty words and three characters. It repeats the parable Lamp 1 (8:16) and cites a domestic image. The credibility is high (*4). It is interesting that the audience has changed: while 8:16 was told to the disciples, now the hearers belong to the general public. In other words, Jesus re-uses the parable in a new situation.[63] The exigency is general teaching. This is the last parable to refer chiefly to Jesus and his proclamation. However, the issue of revealing secrets is less clear.

Interpreters usually connect the image of the lamp with the subsequent discussion about light in a body. However, the preceding reference to the sign, which individuals should observe, offers the audience a more natural link, as the parable ends by emphasizing a lamp's proper function: it should be seen by those who enter the house.

---

63. Such circulation is historically probable; it is reasonable to re-use the same stories for different audiences. This, in turn, must be taken into account when reconstructing the original parable.

Figure VII.30

Backing: **A lamp should be seen by those entering the house (*4)**

▼

Warrant: A sign must be perceived

▼

Data: Jesus' proclamation is a sign to people and it is more important than the sign of Jonah (11:29-33) ▶ *Claim*: Jesus' message must be observed

(26) 11:34-36, Eye as Lamp

Your eye is the lamp of your body. If your eye is clear, your whole body is full of light . . .

This Extended Rule contains sixty-three words and two characters. The physical image refers to a healer's profession. Although the idea may seem strange to modern readers, in ancient times it was normal.[64] Thus this is one of the few parables for which some knowledge outside the text is required in order to assess the credibility as good (*3). It is aimed at a general audience with no particular exigency. But to what general rule does the parable refer, and how is this to be invoked? It argues that a dysfunctional (πονηρός) eye makes the whole body dark, which is to be avoided. This can be interpreted as saying that the purpose of the eye is to watch, for example, for signs (11:29-33). The inability to perceive a sign endangers the whole person.

Physical blindness illustrates a rule that is associated with spiritual blindness. Both the data and the claim are obscure, yet no further

---

64. There are good examples showing that the eye was widely assumed to emit light (Popkes, "Auge," 139–42; Nolland, *Luke*, 657–58).

issues such as "moral and spiritual illumination" should be added.[65] The context speaks of Jesus as a vital sign; this parable concerns seeing the sign. The two images go together: if an individual cannot see the sign represented by Jesus, the lack will be fatal for his or her whole being. The exhortation in 11:35 serves as the claim.

Figure VII.31

Backing: **A dysfunctional eye makes the whole body dark** (*2)

▼

Warrant: Inability to observe the sign endangers an individual

▼

Data: Jesus is an important sign ▶ *Claim*: Take care of your ability to see (Jesus)

Alternatively, one could assume that the "bad eye" refers to a malicious or critical approach to other people or objects. Disapproval of Jesus' healing activity (11:15-16) would be such an approach. However, the connection with criticism is obscure.

(27) 12:16-21, Rich Fool

The land of a rich man produced abundantly. And he thought to himself . . .

The first *Narrative* reporting on an ἄνθρωπός τις is also the second-longest so far, consisting of eighty-eight words and two characters. The agricultural story is credible as it stands; there was nothing

---

65. *Contra* Nolland, *Luke*, 658.

immoral in the rich man's intentions.⁶⁶ The only problem he faces is God's intervention and the warning of his death.

The story would remain the same if the supernatural aspect were omitted. It would suffice to mention that the man died the next night. The question concerning earthly riches after his death would be just as harsh. Actually, God's role weakens the credibility of the parable (*1), as it was not typical for God to speak directly to people rather than angels—even in parables.⁶⁷ If it did not mention God the story would merely describe a possible course of action and be more credible (*3). The story is aimed at a general audience, but the exigency is specific, prompted by an individual's request in 12:13.

Depending on whether or not God's role is emphasized, alternative *warrants* can be derived from the parable. Consequently, two applications can be envisaged. These, however, are not mutually exclusive.

---

66. Hedrick, *Parables*, 158, raises unnecessary questions such as "How . . . had he failed to foresee the need for additional storage space *some weeks* prior to the harvest?" (emphasis supplied). The problem is caused by incorporating new information into the text. Snodgrass, *Stories*, 395, reports several correspondingly artificial interpretations.
67. In fact, God does not utter a single explicit line in the New Testament. Snodgrass, *Stories*, 394, observes that this is the only New Testament parable in which God "appears as an actor."

Figure VII.32

(I)

Backing: **The rich fool's example** (*3)

▼

Warrant: Earthly riches cannot be trusted

▼

Data: You want to secure your future ▶ Claim: Seek divine riches. (12:21)[68]

(II)

Backing: **The rich fool's example**

▼

Warrant: God can intervene in your plans

▼

Data: You have important plans for your life ▶ Claim: Beware of God

(28) 12:24, Ravens

Consider the ravens: they neither sow nor reap, they have neither storehouse nor barn . . .

This Simple Rule has only twenty-five words and two characters. It refers to a natural phenomenon, even though God is mentioned. The credibility is good (*3) since the parable relies on the recipients' own

---

68. The idea of θησαυρίζειν has an interesting parallel in Rom. 2:5, where a treasure of wrath is accumulated before God.

observation. Although it continues the previous theme, the audience now consists of the disciples. The change of audience indicates that the exigency has also changed, from the particular to the general. The message of the parable deals explicitly with God. It responds to the challenges of discipleship instead of simply promoting a relaxed way of life.

In fact, two arguments are combined. First there is an explicit claim in 12:22: "Do not worry about your life, what you will eat, or about your body, what you will wear." Jesus urges his audience to observe the ravens in order to prove that they are not anxious. See figure VII.33.

Figure VII.33

(I)

Warrant: Whoever does not sow is not anxious about eating

▼

Data: Observing the ravens ▶ *Claim*: Ravens are not anxious ▶ Ravens do not sow, etc.

Second, he uses the ravens' example to illustrate a general rule. See figure VII.34.

Figure VII.34

(II)

Backing: **Ravens are not anxious about life, yet God feeds them**

▼

Warrant: Anxiety is not required for maintaining life

▼

Data: You want to maintain your life (eat, etc.) ▶ Claim: You must not be anxious about your life

Third, a *qal wahomer* structure boosts the effect of the reasoning. See figure VII.35.

Figure VII.35

(III)

Backing: General concept of *qal wahomer*

▼

Warrant: One takes better care of valuable possessions

▼

Data: God takes care of the ravens and you are more valuable than the birds ▶ $Claim^1$: God certainly takes care of you

▶ $Claim^2$: Do not be anxious for your life

(29) 12:27-28, Lilies

Consider the lilies, how they grow: they neither toil nor spin . . .

The sister parable is also a Simple Rule, but the second longest of these rules (44 words and 4 characters). It, too, refers to observation of nature, despite the theological dimension. The credibility is thus good (*3); also the audience, exigency, and reference remain the same. Again a combined structure, including the *qal wahomer* reasoning, can be displayed:

Figure VII.36

(30) 12:36-38, Watchful Slaves

Be like those who are waiting for their master to return from the wedding banquet . . .

This is an Extended Rule, but its surprising ending resembles a Narrative. It contains fifty-eight words and two characters or groups. As in 8:5-8, the Sower, two messages are embedded. If the ending is not considered, the basic story is a conventional Extended Rule. It refers to what is normal and typical, emphasizing the need for constant alertness. The credibility is good (*3). However, one can also focus on the narrative convention of adding a surprise at the end. The credibility is then weaker, even poorer than in 7:41-43, Two Debtors. This time the master surprisingly waits on his servants at table, in contrast to the typical behavior described in 17:7-10, the Useless Servant. This message does not further alert the audience; it claims that the master will be unusually generous to his watchful servants (*1).[69]

See figures VII.37 and VII.38.

Figure VII.37

Backing: **Servants waiting for their master in the middle of the night (*3)**

▼

Warrant: Servants must be alert at all times

▼

$Data^1$: You are God's servants
$Data^2$: God can intervene in your life at any time   ▶   *Claim*: You must be alert at all times

---

69. Nolland, *Luke*, 36, holds the switching of the roles as "not at all true to life," whereas Gerber, "Sklavinnen," 576, finds Roman parallels.

Figure VII.38

Backing: **Master waiting on his watchful servants (*1)**

▼

Warrant: A master can reward good works beyond measure

▼

Data: You are God's servants ▶ *Claim*: God will reward our alertness to excess

Thus the parable has two different trajectories. It speaks of the recipients and praises them for alertness, but it also focuses on the master and his exceptional benevolence. The eventual function remains implicit: the audience is not told how to react to the master's unexpected, unconventional kindness. From this point on, such a double role becomes typical of the Lukan parables. The master-character is reminiscent of God, but no allegory is needed. If an earthly master can act thus, how much more God in heaven?!

In many other ways, too, this parable involves a turning point in Luke's work. With some generalization it can be said that the brief, easily acceptable parables using images from nature or from different occupations now yield to longer, more challenging parables that refer to an unpredictable master and, second, cite an attribute of God. A comparative diagram may illustrate this change:

Table VII.1
Parables in the Two Parts of Luke

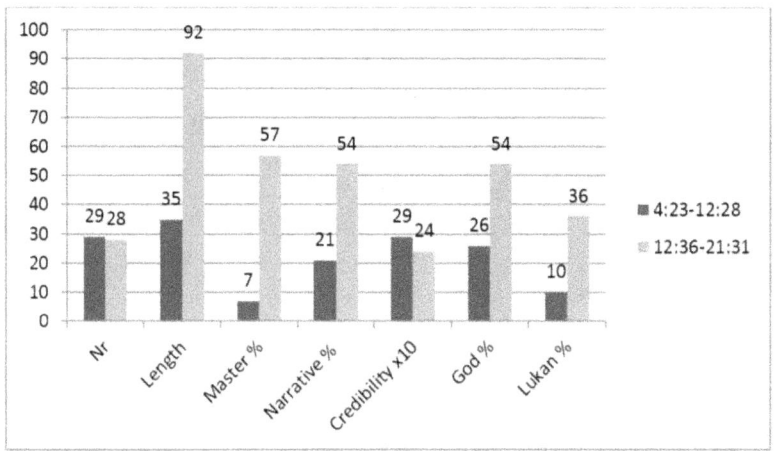

(31) 12:39, Master and Thief

If the owner of the house had known at what hour the thief was coming . . .

This Simple Rule, which is not to be confused with the previous one, consists of a mere sixteen words and two characters. No protests are expected; the credibility is good (*3).[70] The parable portrays a master, but his behavior is again conventional. The parable is aimed at the disciples—although Peter is doubtful of this (12:41!)—and the exigency remains general. Unlike the surrounding master-parables, this one refers to the disciples' behavior, and in contrast to the former there is no double message. The context (12:40) refers to the coming of the Son of Man, which makes this story one of the few truly eschatological parables in Luke.[71]

---

70. διορυχθῆναι could in principle refer to Palestinian building technique (thus Nolland, *Luke*, 702), but a thief can dig under any type of wall.
71. See more fully in chap. 8. Many parables are commonly interpreted as eschatological. However, they can be better understood as referring to daily life or some personal disaster.

Figure VII.39

Backing: **Master does not expect a thief at night (*3)**

▼

Warrant: One must be alert at all times if the time of arrival is unknown

▼

Data: The time of arrival of the Son of Man is unknown ▶ *Claim*: You must be alert at all times

(32) 12:42-48, Unfaithful Servant

Who then is the faithful and prudent steward, whom his master will put in charge of his slaves . . .

This Narrative is the seventh-longest in Luke (128 words, 4 characters). It tells an incredible (*1) story about a cruel master who not only punishes his servant but also chops him into pieces.[72] It is aimed at the disciples, as mentioned in 12:41, and can be classified as particular teaching since it is prompted by Peter's question. It relates not only to the audience, who should be alert as in the previous parables. The exceeding severity of the peculiar master apparently illustrates an attribute of God as well. Without the exaggeration at the end the credibility would be much higher (*3), as in the first version (8:42-44). Thus the parable contains three interrelated messages.

---

72. Snodgrass, *Stories*, 502–3; and Nolland, *Luke*, 704, correctly warn against softening the hyperbole.

Figure VII.40

(I)

Backing: **An account of a good servant (*3) [12:42-44]**

▼

Warrant: Good servants are richly rewarded

▼

Data^1: You are God's servants ▶ Claim: You must obey God's will
Data^2: You want to be rewarded

The main story in 12:45-46 is more complicated and includes two warrants, as shown in figures VII.41 and VII.42.

Figure VII.41

(II)

Backing: **An account of an arrogant servant and his cruel master (*1) [12:45-46]**

▼

Warrant: Even the absent master must be taken into account

▼

Data: You are servants of an absent God ▶ Claim: You must still obey God's will

Figure VII.42

(III)

Backing: **An account of an arrogant servant and his cruel master (*1) [12:45-46]**

▼

Warrant: A master's vindictiveness knows no limits

▼

Data: God is your master ▶ *Claim*: God can be extremely harsh ▶ You must obey God's will

The extension in 12:47-48 displays yet another warrant, as shown in figure VII.43.

Figure VII.43

IV *Backing*: **An account of an innocent and a perceptive servant (*3) [12:47-48]**

▼

Warrant: From everyone who has been given, much shall be required. (12:48)

▼

Data: You have been given much (12:10, 41) ▶ $Claim^1$: God will require much from you

▶ $Claim^2$: you must obey God's will diligently

The parable is typically interpreted as an eschatological prophecy or a warning against malpractice by church leaders.[73] However, the latter option in particular is anachronistic: in the text Jesus is not planning a church. God was commonly expected to take action, and the audience, as good Jews, were God's servants.[74] But no allegory is needed; neither God nor the Son of Man is the master. The parable merely exemplifies the *qal wahomer* reasoning manifested in 19:12-27, the Minas, and 20:9-16, the Wicked Tenants, as well: if an absent master will take action against his bad servants, how much more so will God take action against God's own?

(33) 12:54-56, Weather

> *When you see a cloud rising in the west, you immediately say, 'It is going to rain,' and so it happens . . .*

This Simple Rule consists of forty-three words and one character. The image is derived from nature, and the credibility is good, as it reflects the hearers' known perceptions (*3). It is aimed at a general audience and general teaching. The negative question, "Why do you not interpret this time?" can be translated into an exhortation to do so.

Figure VII.44

Backing: **A meteorological example** (*3)

▼

Warrant: You can interpret signs

▼

Data: There are signs anticipating this age ▶ *Claim*: You should interpret the signs of the time

---

73. Nolland, *Luke*, 703–4.
74. Snodgrass, *Stories*, 498–501, correctly refers to OT imagery.

PARABLES UNPLUGGED

To be sure, there is a theological hint, emphasized in the next parable, explaining how those signs should be interpreted.

(34) 12:58-59, Going to Judge

... when you go with your accuser before a magistrate ...

This Extended Rule has forty-nine words but no fewer than four characters (you, the opponent, the magistrate/judge, and the constable). The credibility is not very good (*2)—why could not the opponent lose the case and be thrown into jail instead? Indeed, 12:59 suggests that the quarrel concerns money, but inasmuch as an official verdict is required, the case is far from resolved.[75]

The story is aimed at a general audience lacking a particular exigency. It refers to the audience's behavior, but also to the nature of God. However, as in the previous parable, both data and claim remain implicit. Apparently the reasoning is founded on the belief that a judge's decision cannot be anticipated. An allegorical reading would lead to confusion: Is God the debtor, the judge, or the constable? Instead, we must consider the principle illustrated by the parable. There are many minor elements within it, such as assessments of the costs of settling the case in relation to the fines to be paid prior to release from prison. The time factor is also significant. In any case, the basic structure is clear, as shown in figure VII.45.

---

75. Contra Nolland, *Luke*, 714, who suggests that the "going" is involuntary and that the addressees are already presumed to be guilty before meeting the judge. Adding such extraneous information to a parable detracts from its proper understanding, as the story of the Samaritan illustrates (see more fully in chap. 2).

Figure VII.45

Backing: **Preparing for an unexpected court trial (*2)**

▼

Warrant: Better safe than sorry

▼

Data: You will face a rial by God in the near future ▶ *Claim*: Be prepared soon, although it may prove costly

The implicit theological version could read as shown in figure VII.46.

Figure VII.46

Backing: **Preparing for an unexpected court trial (*2)**

▼

| *Warrant*: Better safe than sorry | *Warrant*: If an earthly judge is to be avoided, how much more the heavenly judge |

▼

Data: You will face a trial by God ▶ *Claim*: Be prepared for it soon, although it may prove costly

(35) 13:6-9, Barren Fig Tree

> *A man had a fig tree planted in his vineyard . . .*

This Narrative (78 words and 2 human characters) refers to an agricultural image, but also to a sovereign master. The story is conceivable (*2), as it depicts an individual's (τις) behavior, which is feasible but not essential. As is typical of parables from Luke's own sources, it is told to an anonymous audience (τινες). Direct application to Israel is out of the question, since the story was not included in Scripture when it was written.[76] It simply emphasizes that a master may be tolerant, but his patience is limited. Again, explicit data and claim are missing, but they can be extrapolated from the previous verses. No allegory is needed, since a *qal wahomer* reasoning is more appropriate: if a tree-owner is impatient, how much more is God.

Figure VII.47

Backing: **The barren fig tree and its owner (*2)**

▼

Warrant: Individuals expecting results may be patient, but there is a limit

▼

Data: God expects good results from you ▶ *Claim*^{1}: God's patience may end

▶ *Claim*^{2}: Start providing results soon

(36) 13:19, Mustard Seed

It is like a mustard seed that someone took and threw into the garden...

This is one of the shortest Narratives, consisting of twenty-seven words and one character. It, too, refers to agriculture and is aimed at a general audience, perhaps the opponents mentioned in 13:17.

---

76. Snodgrass, *Stories,* 259, presents some OT material (such as Hos. 9:10 and Mic. 4:3), but Nolland, *Luke,* 718, notes that none actually fits this story. In any case people hardly referred to Scripture every time they spoke about figs.

THE PARABLES AS PERSUASION

It relates to a typical phenomenon with good credibility (*3) and refers to the Kingdom of God. The pejorative traditional role of the birds is unlikely, as it plays no role in the argumentation and would not be perceived by addressees unaware of Old Testament traditions. Moreover, it lacks a counterpart in the next parallel parable.[77] The reasoning is problematic, as not all small things grow large. Perhaps Jesus is suggesting that the Kingdom cannot less productive than mustard.

Figure VII.48

Backing: **A tiny mustard seed produces a tall tree (*3)**

▼

Warrant: Small things can become great

▼

Data: God's kingdom appears small ▶ *Claim*: God's kingdom will be very great

(37) 13:21, Leaven

It is like yeast that a woman took and hid in three measures of flour until all of it was leavened.

This is the shortest Narrative (15 words, 1 character), which also renders it shorter than any of the Extended Rules and the ninth-shortest parable in Luke altogether. Yet it is a real story with a main figure, a story line, and an ending. The other characteristics recall the previous parable: the audience is general and the credibility good (*3),

---

77. For discussion see Snodgrass, *Stories*, 224–25.

as it relates to the audience's experience.[78] The reasoning reflects the Kingdom.

Figure VII.49

Backing: **A small amount leavens the whole (*3)**

▼

Warrant: Small things can become great

▼

Data: God's kingdom appears small ▶ *Claim*: God's kingdom will be very great

The parable has prompted numerous allegorical interpretations that are not only impossible for the implied audience but also obscure the basic message.[79]

(38) 13:24-29, Closed Door

Strive to enter through the narrow door; for many, I tell you, will try to enter and will not be able . . .

This section is formally an exhortation supported by several assertions, predicting the consequences for the audience. However, it cites metaphorical images that isolate it from reality. Since it

---

78. Nolland, *Luke*, 730, argues that the leaven was not mixed in and therefore had to be abnormally effective. This, however, is based on a peculiar understanding of the woman's action (ἔκρυψεν), which may well describe a typical procedure. Thus the parable is not difficult to believe. Cultural "information" can be misleading: it is scarcely the case that leaven was automatically a pejorative word because of the Passover rituals, since it was in daily use year round (*contra* Snodgrass, *Stories*, 231). Jesus hardly meant that his message or the Kingdom was going to be spoiled.
79. For alternatives, from the Virgin Mary to women's leadership in the church, see ibid., 232.

constitutes a story with a change of status it can be classified as a Narrative, despite the fact that it is mingled with direct teaching.

This eighth-longest parable (122 words) involves no fewer than seven different characters.[80] It depicts the behavior of a master. This time his action is easy to believe. There is no admission to the feast after the guests are expected to have arrived and the door is closed (13:24-27). However, the subsequent discussion glides toward a theological theme and thereby to the application of the parable. The parable is aimed at "somebody" (τις) and includes particular teaching. It refers to God and the audience. The message is mixed: The reason for inability to enter is (1) lateness, (2) unfamiliarity with the master, and finally (3) bad behavior. It seems that but for these two additional criteria a late entry might have been possible after all. In other words, although guests arrived too late, the master could have let them in since he knew them or because their behavior was so good.

Figure VII.50

Backing: **The master closing the door to the feast (*2)**

▼

Warrant: Meeting the criteria is vital for acceptance

▼

Data: You desire to be saved (13:23) i.e., get inside (13:24) ▶ *Claim*: Strive to meet the criteria (13:24), i.e., act quickly / learn to know God / do good

An implicit theological version emphasizes the strict attitude of the master.

---

80. This is exceeded only by 14:16-24, the *Great Dinner*, which has nine characters.

Figure VII.51

Backing: **The master closing the door to the feast (*2)**

▼

Warrant: If an earthly master can be strict, how much more can God

▼

Data: You desire to be saved ▶ *Claim*: Strive to meet God's criteria

(39) 14:8-14, Guidelines 1 and 2

When you are invited by someone to a wedding banquet, do not take the place of honor . . .

When you give a luncheon or a dinner, do not invite your friends . . .

This parable is the longest Extended Rule (140 words) and the sixth-longest parable in Luke. Despite the four characters involved and a lively story, nothing actually happens. Instead, Jesus lays down guidelines for acceptable behavior. The text is a parable, however, as an implicit theological goal underlies the social imagery. The theological message is not fully explained until the third parable, 14:16-24, the Great Dinner.

    1. The first story employs a domestic image, but the master-character is also involved. As his behavior in the story is possible but cannot be taken for granted, the credibility is not very good (*2). The parable is told to undefined guests, and pertains to the addressees and to God. Although the reasoning includes no theology, it is hardly meant to be "prudential advice that might save us from humiliating shame in a social situation."[81] It is more likely that the

---

81. *Contra* Nolland, *Luke*, 749.

recommendation of humility recalls 18:10-14, the Pharisee and Tax Collector, designating God as the ultimate judge of honor and shame.

The warrant is an explicit rule in 14:11 "All who exalt themselves will be humbled, and those who humble themselves will be exalted." This can be understood as a passivum divinum. The data and the claim are not explicit in these verses, but can be reconstructed from the warrant.

Figure VII.52

Backing: **Guidelines for guests at a feast** (14:8-10) (*2)

▼

Warrant: Those who exalt themselves will be humbled, and those who humble themselves will be exalted (14:11)

▼

Data: You desire to be exalted [before God] ▶ *Claim*: You must be humble [before God]

2. Verses 12-14 instruct the organizer of the feast, a Pharisee.[82] They can also be considered as a separate parable that illustrates a general warrant: God will pay for those unable to pay for themselves. The credibility of this rule is weaker: the feast as a parable does not validate the narrator's promise regarding God's future action. However, the theological concept is interesting and will be expounded in the next parable and further, for example, in 16:1-9.

---

82. Perhaps the parable does not victimize the Pharisee. He has actually already followed the rule by inviting a man suffering from dropsy, in 14:2, albeit with bad intentions.

Figure VII.53

Backing: **Guidelines for organizing a feast** (14:12-14) (*1)

▼

Warrant: God will pay for those who cannot pay for themselves

▼

Data: You desire to be rewarded by God ▶ *Claim*: Be good to those who are not worthy

Indeed, the exhortation is specifically linked to the parable: "Invite the poor, the crippled, the lame, the blind." Thereby it, too, may contain parabolic language. Jesus' ultimate aim is not to control the quality of guests at the Pharisees' feast but to illustrate a principle: God seeks to benefit individuals who are not worthy. The next parable will then confirm this principle.

(40) 14:16-24, Great Dinner

Someone gave a great dinner and invited many . . .

This Narrative is the fifth-longest in Luke, consisting of 159 words and nine characters, far more than in any other parable. Its length, its complexity, and the traditional allegorical explanations connected to it complicate any attempt to focus on the text. Thus a longer discussion is required.

First some general characteristics may be presented. The parable portrays a master who acts in an unpredictable way, thus weakening its credibility (*1). The story is aimed at "someone," apparently at the Pharisees, scribes, and other guests present. The parable may be characterized as particular teaching, responding to a specific

THE PARABLES AS PERSUASION

comment, but its function is hardly defensive. Later allegorical interpretations relating to the fate of Israel cannot be drawn from the explicit text.[83] Likewise, reference to Gentile mission is hardly in the mind of Jesus' table-fellows. In the text Jesus is addressing them, so the parable should be understood primarily according to their way of hearing it.

The parable constitutes an intriguing story demonstrating that not the status of those invited but their actual response guarantees admission to the feast. The question in 14:15 refines the subject: Who shall eat bread in the Kingdom of God?

Figure VII.54

Backing: **Reluctant guests replaced by individuals with low social status (*1)**

▼

Warrant: Not the status but the response to the call guarantees admission

▼

Data: You are invited to the Kingdom of God ▶ (*Claim*: You may lose the right to entrance despite your status)

Perhaps the most interesting issue pertaining to this parable is its persuasive force. How is such an incredible story expected to ensure the approval of the warrant, so that the hearers will endorse the claim? It cannot refer to what is reasonable, logical, or customary, as do the Simple Rules and even many Extended ones. The master's decision is far from usual, and yet it is expected to convince the audience that a corresponding rule will apply for admission to the Kingdom of God. Apparently the lively story line is intended to cover the

---

83. Thus correctly Snodgrass, *Stories*, 316–17. However, he simultaneously claims that the parable "is about Israel's response to Jesus," ibid., 314.

problems inherent in the master's strange behavior. It emphasizes the master's emotional reaction (ὀργισθεὶς ὁ οἰκοδεσπότης) to the secondary explanations of the reluctant guests. He becomes so angry that he decides to replace them with just anybody. This emotion, more than anything else, is assumed to be experienced as genuine and gain sympathy; the audience should understand and even identify with the infuriated man let down by his friends. Such a resort to emotion instead of custom or reason can be found in other great parables, 10:30-37, the Samaritan, and 15:11-32, the Prodigal Son, as well. The Samaritan is not called good, but overwhelming sudden emotion (ἐσπλαγχνίσθη) made him do the right thing. The father of the Prodigal considers his son "dead" until he is filled with the same emotion. Here the master's emotion is negative but still designed to be felt as genuine and identifiable.

Figure VII.55

Backing: **Reluctant guests replaced by people with low social status (*1)**

▼

Warrant: Poor excuses irritate the organizer of a feast

▼

$Data^1$: Neighborly love is a condition for inheriting life
$Data^2$: Those worthy of the feast make poor excuses ▶ *Claim*: God will be irritated, punish those unwilling to obey, and invite unworthy guests

It is interesting to note that this parable combines the master's hyperbolical negative and positive features. His goodness toward the unworthy is presented as a consequence of his irritation with the decent people. If applied to Jesus' proclamation of grace, this makes it a tool of God's punishment!

The context, v. 15, suggests that the feast refers to a heavenly banquet and the master correspondingly to God. If an earthly master can act in this way, how much more can God? Thereby the parable fits the Lukan context, in which Jesus invites the unworthy to the Kingdom by healing the sick and proclaiming the Gospel to the poor (14:18-21). The parable seeks to justify his program and to invite the audience's participation.

Figure VII.56

Backing: **The parable explaining why a rich man may invite the poor to his feast**

▼

Warrant: Not status but the response to the call guarantees admission

▼

$Data^1$: Jesus invites sinners to heaven
$Data^2$ The sinners do not reject God's call
▶
Claim: Jesus' action is theologically correct

Nevertheless, the parable may encourage Lukan readers to envisage abstract theological interpretations as well. For a modern reader its theme recalls Paul's theological discussion about Israel and the Gentiles in Romans 9–11. However, the master's categorical exclusion of those invited first (Luke 14:24) fits poorly with this interpretation, since for Paul "the gifts and the calling of God are irrevocable" (Rom. 11:29). Although such trajectories are acceptable to later recipients, perhaps already Luke's readers, the primary meaning in the context is to be preferred.

(41) 14:28-30, Tower

For which one of you, intending to build a tower, does not first sit down . . .

This Extended Rule consists of forty-three words and two characters. It pertains to an occupation; a typical phenomenon is enhanced with a narrative element. Despite the supplement, the credibility is excellent (*4), indicated by the rhetorical question. The audience is general but the exigency particular: people follow Jesus and he proceeds to speak of the requirements for doing so. Direct theological interpretations cannot be based on the text.[84]

Figure VII.57

Backing: **Example of building a tower** (*4)

▼

Warrant: The costs of any project must be estimated

▼

Data: You desire to follow Jesus ▶ *Claim*: You must be prepared for heavy costs. (14:26-27)

(42) 14:31-32, Warring King

Or what king, going out to wage war against another king, will not sit down first . . .

This parallel parable shares most of the attributes of the previous 14:28-30, Tower; even the length is similar (41 words, but 5 characters). It is essential to realize that no real knowledge of

---

84. For discussion see Snodgrass, *Stories*, 383, 385. Hunzinger, "Unbekannte Gleichnisse," 213–16, suggests that that God, too, has precalculated his project with Jesus, whereas Louw, "Parables," 478, thinks that Jesus himself is depicted.

decision-making practices in royal courts or military headquarters is required to explain the parable. In a similar way, parables referring to other occupations or natural phenomena are expected by Luke to be understood by his audience, even without specific information about sociohistorical or other Palestinian details of the time.[85]

Figure VII.58

Backing: **The example of going into battle (*4)**

▼

Warrant: The costs of any project must be estimated

▼

Data: You want to follow Jesus ▶ *Claim*: You must be prepared for heavy costs (14:26-27)

(43) 14:34-35, Crazy Salt

Salt is good; but if salt has lost its taste how can its saltiness be restored?

This brief Simple Rule contains twenty-nine words and one obscure character or group. It is aimed at a general audience. The exigency is difficult to define. The parable shares the same reasoning as those preceding it, but its connection to the particular situation is obscure. In any case, the parable pertains to the audience.

Any historical or chemical attempt to explain this oxymoron,[86] how salt can become tasteless (lit. "crazy," μωρός), is doomed to fail, as Luke's audience would hardly be familiar with such a phenomenon.[87] Without supplementing the parable it must be stated

---

85. The war between Herod Antipas and Aretas IV in 36 c.e. could serve as a historical example (Jos. *Ant.* xviii, 5).
86. Lausberg, *Handbook*, §807.

that the image sounds impossible, not customary. Probably this is precisely the effect planned by the author.[88] A corresponding rhetorical technique is used in 18:25, Camel:[89] even if impossible things happen, the issue discussed will not. Nevertheless, differently from Matthew 5:13, Luke does not compare the audience with salt. Thus such an allegory is out of place. The purpose and quality of salt should not be applied to the audience. The parable focuses on what happens to salt.

Figure VII.59

Backing: **Salt becoming tasteless would make it useless (*3)**

▼

Warrant: Loss of essential characteristics causes nullity

▼

Data: You are disciples ▶ *Claim*: You will not lose the attributes of discipleship

▲

Counter-Rebuttal: Even if impossible things happen, this will not take place

The next four parables are discussed more fully in chapters 3 and 4. Only the technical details and the final argumentation structure are listed here.

---

87. Nolland, *Luke*, 765, presents the idea of impure salt stored in mountain cabins but rightly rejects it.
88. Drury, *Parables*, 138, correctly remarks on the absurdity of this parable.
89. See also Isa. 49:15 (a woman forgetting her nursing child) and 54:10 (mountains removed).

(44) 15:4-7, Lost Sheep

Which man among you, having a hundred sheep and losing one of them ...

This Narrative consists of eighty-one words and three characters.[90] It is told to the Pharisees and scribes, primarily as defense. The image refers to a customary incident in an occupation. The credibility is good (*3), as there is a rhetorical question, τίς ἄνθρωπος ἐξ ὑμῶν. The parable is applied to a multiple target: the audience, Jesus, and God.

Figure VII.60

Backing: **A story of a sheep, referring to the audience's own attitude and that in heaven (15:4-7) (*3)**

▼

Warrant: Finding something lost causes great joy

▼

Data: The tax collectors and sinners are lost and found ▶ *Claim*: It is natural to rejoice when finding the lost

When the *claim* is stated in 15:7, the data will refer also to the audience's attitude. See figure VII.61.

---

90. See more information in chapter three.

Figure VII.61

Backing: General conception of God

▼

Warrant: God cannot be worse than you

▼

Data: You rejoice when finding the lost ▶ *Claim*^{1}: God too will rejoice when finding the lost

When associated with the situation at hand, this *claim* yields further results:

▶ *Claim*^{2}: Jesus' feasting with sinners is accepted by God   ▶ *Claim*^{3}: The audience ought to join the feast

(45) 15:8-10, Lost Coin

Or what woman having ten silver coins, if she loses one of them . . .

This Narrative consists of fifty-three words and three characters.[91] It is told to the Pharisees and scribes, primarily as a defense. The image reflects a domestic setting. The credibility is good (*3), as it shares the rhetorical question with the previous parable. The parable is applied to a multiple target: the audience, Jesus, and God. The theological addition corresponds to the above.

---

91. See more detail in chapter three.

Figure VII.62

Backing: **A story of a coin, referring to the audience's own attitude and that in heaven** (15: 8-10) (*3)

▼

Warrant: Finding something lost causes great joy

▼

Data: The tax collectors and sinners are lost and found ▶ *Claim*: It is natural to rejoice when finding the lost

(46) 15:11-32, Prodigal Son

There was a man who had two sons . . .

This is the longest Narrative (389 words, 6 characters).[92] The story refers to agriculture and a domestic setting, but the main emphasis is on the master-character represented by the father. The credibility is essentially weaker than in the previous parables (*1). Just as in 10:30-37, Samaritan, and 14:16-24, Great Dinner, the father's emotion is assumed to be the main target of identification and thereby carry the persuasive force of the story. Whereas several additional claims can be detected, the basic argumentative structure, shown in figure VII.63, is clear.

---

92. See more detail in chapter three.

Figure VII.63

Backing: **The farmer giving a feast when his wicked son returns (*1)**

▼

Warrant: The return of a lost relative causes great joy, irrespective of his guilt [or: "Love covers all transgressions" (Prov. 10:12; 1 Pet. 4:8; Jas. 5:20)]

▼

Data: The sinners and tax collectors are lost and found ▶ *Claim*: You should join the feast

A theological implication may be based on the two previous parables, and is shown in figure VII.64.

Figure VII.64

Claim^1 (above) / *Data*: It is natural for compassionate people to celebrate returning sinners

▼ ◀ *Warrant*: God cannot be worse than compassionate people

Claim^2: God celebrates returning sinners

▼ ◀ *Warrant*: God's will is important to you

Claim^3: You should join the feast

(47) 16:1-9, Unjust Steward

There was a rich man who had a steward ...

This fourth-longest Narrative contains 182 words and five characters.[93] Like the previous story, it speaks of agriculture, but more important is the incredible (*1) behavior of the ἄνθρωπός τις, the master, whose surprising conduct is not explained, in contrast to the previous parable. This parable is aimed at the disciples and contains particular teaching. It refers to the disciples, but to a lesser degree to God and even to Jesus. It argues that if an earthly master can accept the described dishonest action, why would not God?

Figure VII.65

Backing: **A master praising his steward for misusing his property (*1)**

▼

Warrant: Misusing a master's property for a specific reason is commendable

▼

Data: You have been entrusted with God's property ▶ *Claim*: You should forgive God's "debtors" even if not authorized to do so

The theological alternative could read as shown in figure VII.66.

Figure VII.66

Backing: **A master praising his steward for misusing his property (*1)**

▼

Warrant: A master can accept forgiveness of debts

▼

Data: God cannot be worse than an earthly master ▶ *Claim*: God approves forgiveness of sins

---

93. See more detail in chapter four.

(48) 16:13, Two Masters

No servant can serve two masters . . .

This Simple Rule has twenty-eight words and three characters. It refers to a domestic setting, the servants' experience. Although two master-characters appear, their roles remain passive. This saying is the last parable to use a negative introduction (οὐδείς) indicating good (*3) credibility.[94] The parable is aimed at the disciples without any particular exigency. It refers to their own behavior.

The parable serves as *backing*, an example illustrating a more general rule. No allegory is required. Although not available to the implied audience, *GThom.* 47:1-2 offers an interesting parallel that does not invite a direct allegory either: "It is impossible for a man to mount two horses or to stretch two bows."

Figure VII.67

Backing: **No one can serve two masters, but hates the one and loves the other (*3)**

▼

Warrant: Two authorities cannot be held simultaneously

▼

Data: God and Mammon require your obedience ▶ *Claim*: You cannot serve both God and Mammon

(49) 16:19-31, Rich Man and Lazarus

There was a rich man who was dressed in purple and fine linen . . .

This parable is one of the most misunderstood, since its second part

---

94. However, *hatred* must be understood in a specific way.

THE PARABLES AS PERSUASION

is commonly depreciated. Due to the parable's length, complexity, cunning narrative turns, and diverse traditional explanations it calls for a thorough discussion.[95] Here only the basic information will be offered.

Luke's third-longest Narrative consists of 244 words and seven characters. The imagery is exceptional, as it may be defined as religious: the second act takes place after death. The use of a proper name, which is a strong signal in any story, is unique in the Lukan parables. Although the protagonist is ἄνθρωπός τις, and the first act—turning the tables after death—is stereotypical,[96] the Narrative as a whole by no means refers to what is customary. Thus its credibility is poor (*1). The type of exigency is obscure. The parable is not prompted by any request per se; however, it continues the hostile discussion with the Pharisees and pertains chiefly to the audience.

The structure of the parable resembles 15:11-32, the Prodigal Son.[97] According to the basic storytelling convention the punch line should stand at the end, not in the middle.[98] In both cases there is a touching story, but its climax does not end the whole parable; on the contrary. The essential feature is the long dialogue between the two main characters. Only a boring storyteller can fail to stop after the punch line. In the case of the Rich Man and Lazarus the second section, 16:23-31, is 167% longer than the somewhat conventional 16:19-22! How can this be explained?

---

95. Snodgrass, *Stories*, 419–36, and Leonhardt-Balzer, "Reicher," 647–60, provide excellent surveys of the earlier research.
96. For ancient similarities see Nolland, *Luke*, 826–27. Although no direct dependence can be demonstrated, the theme is hardly unique.
97. Thus also Drury, *Parables*, 149–51. But to call the second part of these stories a mere "explanation" is wide of the mark. In both cases the *scopus* does not appear until the last sentence.
98. Jeremias, *Gleichnisse*, 133, rightly claims that even in this story the focus is to be found in the ending. However, scholars are usually so interested in the colorful story that this basic convention is overlooked (for example, Snodgrass, *Stories*, 428–29).

The persuasive strategy is cunning: the audience is first attracted to the description of the "Lifestyles of the Rich and Famous." Then they feel Schadenfreude on seeing the fate of the villain who gave only meager alms. Gradually, perhaps, they wonder why Jesus does not know how to set an end. At this point the trap closes. The story ends with a surprise, turning the plot against the listeners, who, despite their virtuous conduct, are identified with the villain. After all, the parable is not another account of giving alms, let alone envisaging life after death, but concerns a more theological matter: obedience to the Scriptures.[99]

But why emphasize the Scriptures? If they merely stipulate that one must help the poor there is no incentive: according to hearsay, a man was punished after death because he did not give alms despite the exhortation in the Scriptures. Thus one must obey the Scriptures and give alms. If the audience does not recognize the importance of almsgiving in the first place, this fabrication would hardly persuade them. However, if the audience already judges almsgiving essential they must accept the story as well. It thereby functions as a parable: it describes commonly held values, as do references to different occupations or social practices in the shorter parables. The story illustrates the fate of those who neglect the Scriptures, just as 5:36, the Garment, demonstrates the consequences of putting a new patch on an old garment. Then, according to standard procedure, Jesus applies the principle embodied in the parable to a different situation.

While this situation is not explicit, the story presumably refers to Jesus himself. No prophecy needs to be seen here. Jesus' audience in the text is not aware of his forthcoming resurrection.[100] For them the reference to a dead man's resurrection denotes primarily such cases as

---

99. Thus rightly Leonhardt-Balzer, "Reicher," 657. However, she misses the function of this goal.
100. The Lukan audience might be different, but even for them a reference to later generations (Nolland, *Luke*, 833) is misplaced.

1 Samuel 28.[101] Nor is Jesus directly referring to messianic prophecies concerning him (as in John 5:39). Still, Luke may well intend this parable to prepare his audience for such prophecies. The Scriptures, especially the prophecy Jesus cited at Nazareth (Isa. 42:7 in Luke 4:18-19), surely guarantees the authority of Jesus' proclamation. If they do not suffice, nothing will. This issue will be considered later in Luke 20:2.

Figure VII.68

Backing: A rich man facing harsh treatment because he did not pay attention to Moses and the prophets (*1)

▼

Warrant: The Scriptures must be duly heard

▼

Data^1: Neighborly love is a condition for inheriting life
Data^2: They validate Jesus' proclamation
► *Claim*: You should heed Jesus' proclamation

This interpretation does not nullify the injunction in the first section of the parable, where the rich man consumed his treasure on earth, saving nothing for the afterlife. Correspondingly, the warm welcome of the Prodigal in the middle of the parable in Luke 15 has a message of its own. Both messages conform to other sections in Luke. The crux, however, is that such a preliminary meaning must not overshadow the proper function of the parable as a whole.

---

101. King Saul was not helped by the spirit of the late Samuel since he did not obey the prophet when he was alive.

(50) 17:7-10, Useless Servant

Who among you would say to your slave who has just come in from plowing or tending sheep . . .

This is the second-longest Extended Rule (68 words, 2 characters). Despite the vivid presentation, the parable is merely describing what is typical; no actual story line with real characters is envisaged. The credibility is assumed to be high (*3) since the parable begins with a rhetorical question, τίς δὲ ἐξ ὑμῶν. The story is told to the disciples, it refers to the audience, and there is no particular exigency.

The parable contains some peculiar features.[102] Not only is it formally an exhortation, but the identity of "you" is switched from the master to the slave. The reasoning is still lucid: if you own a slave you will expect certain behavior from him or her. Since you are slaves, you should act accordingly. The identity of their master together with their actual duties remain implicit. Since the story exaggerates the harsh demands imposed on a slave this tone should by no means be tempered, although it offends modern religious feeling.[103]

---

102. Thus Snodgrass, *Stories*, does not dare to lay hands on this story.
103. *Contra* Nolland, *Luke*, 843.

Figure VII.69

Backing: **The example of a servant (*3)**

▼

Warrant: Not even a good servant is entitled to extra privileges

▼

Data: You are God's servants ▶ *Claim*: You should not crave any extra bonus

(51) 17:37, Vultures

Where the corpse is, there the vultures will gather.

This Simple Rule is among the shortest parables (8 words, no human characters). The credibility is excellent (*4), as it refers to personal observation. The parable is told to the disciples in a particular situation, and it refers to the coming of the Son of Man and the Kingdom (17:20, 22). Like the previous parable, this one, too, has a gruesome tone.

Figure VII.70

Backing: **Vultures gathering where the corpse is (*4)**

▼

Warrant: Secrets can be revealed by observation

▼

Data: You want to know where the Son of Man will come ▶ *Claim*: Observe the signs

(52) 18:2-6, Judge

In a certain city there was a judge who neither feared God nor had respect for people . . .

This Narrative (81 words,[104] 4 characters) tells of a strange master-figure, the judge, and is aimed at the disciples. The credibility is average, since the judge's irritation appears feasible but not necessary (*2). Earlier, in 12:58-59, Going to Judge, Jesus showed no similar trust in the judge's just decision. The exigency is not specific unless the eschatological setting is emphasized. The story refers to the audience, who are urged to pray, but also to God, who is at least as virtuous as the judge is wicked. The vivid story has inspired diverse interpretations,[105] but the reasoning in the text is lucid. Two themes can be discerned.

First, the title in 18:1 emphasizes that the audience should persevere in prayer, as did the widow. To call this introduction "misplaced"[106] sounds odd, since it is written by the same author as the next parable.

Figure VII.71

Backing: **Even an indifferent judge will help a widow who perseveres (*1)**

▼

Warrant: Perseverance in prayer yields good results (18:1)

▼

Data: You need justice (18:7-8)   ▶   *Claim*: You should persevere in prayer

---

104. Verse 18:6 must be counted in, since it gives new information about the judge.
105. Snodgrass, *Stories*, 449–62; Hedrick, *Parables*, 187–207; and Merz, "Stärke," 667–80, offer good overviews.
106. Snodgrass, *Stories*, 449.

Second, the story actually focuses on the judge rather than on the widow.[107] It thereby continues the reasoning articulated in the similar 11:5-8, Friend at Midnight, and 11:11-13, Bad Fathers. In each parable unpleasant individuals are alleged to do good occasionally. The *qal wahomer* reasoning is then invoked: how much more will God be good to you. The burden of proof rests on those claiming that God does not help.

Figure VII.72

Backing: **An indifferent judge will help a widow who perseveres (*1)**

▼

Warrant: Even bad individuals do good when necessary

▼

Data: God cannot be inferior to bad individuals ▶ *Claim*: God will help you speedily

For those prone to allegories the parable is not only difficult but also blasphemous. Although the judge is not portrayed as "bad"—his professional skills are not condemned—he provides a less than promising metaphor of the Deity. This, however, is not a mistake, as the parallel parables indicate. Precisely because of its scandalous nature, the image confirms the persuasion.

(53) 18:10-14, Pharisee and Tax Collector

Two men went up to the temple to pray, one a Pharisee and the other a tax collector . . .

---

107. Thus correctly Hedrick, *Parables*, 187.

This eleventh-longest Narrative has ninety-eight words[108] but only two characters; no other long account has so few. It belongs to the rare religious parables, with 12:16-21, Rich Fool, and 16:19-31, Rich Man and Lazarus, the former also having but two characters. Regardless of the word δεδικαιωμένος, this is not a theological explanation of the Christian doctrine of justification.[109]

Despite the vivid description and a neat story line, the persuasive force and credibility are poor (*1). Jesus' claim that the virtuous man, revealed by his religious affiliation, and the bad man, indicated by his profession, switched attributes at the temple is bold and lacks valid proof. The story makes no attempt to prove that the Pharisees are in fact wicked and the tax collectors are good.[110] It simply refers to the audience's attitude to the case in point. It is told to "some," resembling the Pharisees but not so called. The exigency is particular, and the story refers not only to the audience but apparently also to God (as passivum divinum in the perfect participle) behind the surprising solution at the end.[111] The point of departure, the data, is clear, whereas several different claims can be postulated. A negative version could read: "you will be humbled" or "God will proclaim you unrighteous," whereas a positive response to the parable would be humility or repentance. The two versions do not exclude each other. If the goal is not merely to denigrate the audience, the positive call is to be preferred. God will proclaim righteous those who are humble and put their trust in God.[112]

---

108. Verse 14b must be counted in, since it gives new information about the characters.
109. Snodgrass, *Stories*, 473–75, is an example of such reading. See further below in chap. 8.
110. Thus correctly Nolland, *Luke*, 879.
111. Peculiarly enough Hedrick, *Parables*, 208, does not see whose prayer was accepted.
112. Cf. 2. Chr. 7:14; Jas. 4:6

Figure VII.73

Backing: **The story of a proud Pharisee and a humble tax collector at the temple (*1)**

▼

Warrant: Those who exalt themselves will be humbled, and vice versa

▼

Data: You trust in your righteousness ▶ *Claim^1*: God will proclaim you unrighteous

▶ *Claim^2*: Be humble and put your trust in God

(54) 18:25, Camel

Indeed, it is easier for a camel to go through the eye of a needle …

The last Simple Rule in Luke has sixteen words and refers to no human beings, but to one animal. The credibility is high (*4); no one is expected to cast doubt on the absurdity of the image. The parable is aimed at a "ruler"; it has a particular exigency, and comments on the audience.

The reasoning resembles 14:34-35, Crazy Salt: even if the impossible happens, this will not take place. Even if a miracle enabled a camel to go through the eye of a needle, a rich person will not enter the Kingdom. The interpretation is not based on an allegory; the camel is not on a par with a rich person. Instead, the imagery confronts a possible rebuttal[113] that involves an exception to the rule, for example: unless the rich person gives enough alms.

---

113. Toulmin et al., *Introduction*, 81–101.

Figure VII.74

Backing: A camel failing to pass through the eye of a needle (*4)

▼

Warrant: Excess size prevents access

▼

Data: Riches in some sense enlarge ▶ *Claim*: The rich cannot enter the Kingdom

▲

Counter-Rebuttal: Even if the impossible might come to pass, this will not

According to a basic rhetorical convention, *peroratio*, the central theme must be reiterated as briefly and clearly as possible at the end of the presentation.[114] Therefore it can be assumed that by presenting this simple proverb as the fourth-last parable of the gospel Luke probably has a specific goal. It must be more than merely a banal image against rich people.

Indeed, the parable can be judged the climax of the warnings against any form of "riches." Earlier, 18:10-14, Pharisee and Tax Collector, argued that one should not trust in the righteousness admired by others, or in anything else but God. Likewise, parables about a feast discourage the audience from inviting guests who issue a return invitation, and 12:16-21, Rich Fool, discourages them from putting grain in larger barns. All these parables refer to the accumulation of earthly assets. Jesus emphasizes that only the deeds

---

114. Lausberg, *Handbook*, §§431–42.

not paid back by anybody will be rewarded in heaven. Thus a general meta-parable can be identified.

Figure VII.75

Backing: Parables about economic, social, and religious investments

▼

Warrant: Only investments not yielding profit on earth will be rewarded in heaven
or: Good deeds will be recompensed, but only once.

▼

Data: You desire to obtain eternal treasures (inherit life, and so on) ▶ *Claim*: Focus on favors not repaid by others

The parable in 16:19-31, Rich Man and Lazarus (= God helps), further enlarges the warrant by arguing that the lack of benefits on earth will be compensated in the afterlife. There God will balance everyone's fortune. Apparently the divine reimbursement will surpass its earthly counterpart.

Figure VII.76

Backing: Parables about treasures on earth (economic, social, and religious)

▼

Warrant: In the Kingdom, God will balance to excess the fortunes of all

▼

Data: You desire prosperity ▶ *Claim*: Avoid seeking prosperity outside the Kingdom

(55) 19:12-27, Minas

A nobleman went to a distant country to get royal power for himself...

This Narrative is the second-longest in Luke, consisting of 253 words and six characters. It portrays a royal pretender and his servants. The parable is aimed at the "guests," the exigency is specific, and the story refers both to the audience and to God.

The credibility is low (*1). The master's order to take a mina from one servant and give it to another already possessing ten was not accepted by the bystanders (19:25). Furthermore, the master's shocking behavior at the end (19:27) was by no means conventional. The story would function well and be more plausible without this additional slayer-scene. To be sure, brutal and cruel deeds do not sound exceptional to Luke's audience (for example, 13:1 contains an account of Herod and the Galileans). Yet this supplement resembles other apparent exaggerations of a master's conduct: 12:37 displays one as extremely humble, waiting on the servants. These strange additions apparently record a significant feature of the master-figure.[115]

Once again the explanation of the parable has suffered from unduly allegorical references.[116] At least Jesus the Narrator cannot guide the church, since it does not yet exist. Nor can the parable refer to the fate of Jerusalem, since the city is far from destruction; thus the interpretation must do without these standard solutions, at least insofar as Jesus and his audience are considered. To be sure, Lukan readers probably knew better, but even they were reading a story

---

115. For example, Snodgrass, *Stories*, 540–41, attempts to moderate the harsh saying. However, it must be stated again that Jesus' deliberately offensive expressions should not be muted, as they apparently serve the author's purposes.
116. See Ibid., 528–29.

THE PARABLES AS PERSUASION

set forty years before the fall of the city. As with any good tale, the audience is hardly expected to import later ideas in order to understand it.[117]

Another detail, the kingdom received by the master from a distant country, has inspired allusions to Archelaus or someone else in Herod's family. However, no particular individual needs to be in mind, since a local king under Roman rule could seldom dispense with such a journey.[118] Moreover, an allegorical allusion to Jesus' "royal" arrival in Jerusalem is hardly in mind, since according to Luke he did not follow the ruthless example of the nobleman in the parable.

The function must be sought in the immediate context. Indeed, Luke presents his reason for telling the parable in 19:11: there were those who believed that the kingdom of God was going to appear immediately. Apparently Jesus disagreed, but where does the expectation go astray? And exactly how does the parable meet the exigency? The nobleman's absence and return resemble the absence and advent of the Kingdom. In the story, the mistake made by some of the servants was their failure to use the time effectively enough; they produced no profit. Thus the expectation of the approaching end is probably connected with such behavior, and the parable aims to correct the situation. Thus the following claim can be postulated:

---

117. See chap. 1 above and Segal, "Fictional Narrative."
118. See Nolland, *Luke*, 918.

Figure VII.77

Backing: **The exacting master demands a high profit** (*1)

▼

Warrant: The return of a distant master will mean great reward or severe punishment

▼

Data: The imminent arrival of the Kingdom is expected ▶ *Claim*: The remaining time must be used effectively

Moreover, several minor messages can be discerned. In particular, the characterization of the master may anticipate the returning Son of Man. If an earthly master may prove ruthless, how much more the heavenly ruler?

Figure VII.78

Backing: **The exacting master demands a high profit** (*1)

▼

Warrant: The return of a distant master will mean great reward or severe punishment

▼

Data: The Son of Man is a distant master ▶ *Claim^1*: The coming of the Son of Man will mean great reward or severe punishment /

▶ *Claim^2*: The remaining time must be used effectively

This interpretation, based on the context rather than external data, befits the status of the parable as the second-last longer parable in Luke. Any convincing presentation must escalate the pathos effect and urge the audience to act. Finally, the following parable raises the crucial issue behind especially the long and less credible parables in Luke: the ethos, that is, Jesus' personal credibility.

(56) 20:9-16, Wicked Tenants

A man planted a vineyard, and leased it to tenants …

This is the last of Jesus' Narratives.[119] It consists of 120 words and seven characters. It is set in an agricultural context, but the protagonist is a master-character. The credibility is poor (*1), since the audience's adverse reaction is reported by Luke in 20:16 (μὴ γένοιτο). The parable is aimed at Jesus' antagonists and the primary exigency is defensive, since Jesus is replying to a hostile question.

Due to the parable's complexity it has been scrutinized in chapter 5. I argue that this parable should be detached from the traditional christological reading and historical reconstructions and read in its actual context. Then it becomes an integral part of the argumentation structure beginning at 20:1, where the authority of Jesus and John the Baptist is discussed. Instead of the axiomatic allegorical anti-Jewish message, the parable confirms a general rule (alt I): The messengers of a distant strong man should be obeyed. This rule pertains to the leaders' reception of John, and correspondingly to that of Jesus himself. Moreover, the parable refers to God (alt II): If a landowner will punish those who offend his delegates, how much more will God? In any case, the parable does not prophesy Jesus' death but serves as a serious attempt to make him heard.

---

119. See more detail in chapter five.

Figure VII.79

(I)

Backing: **The story of the Wicked Tenants (*1)**

▼

Warrant: The messengers of a distant strong man should be obeyed

▼

Data: John's and Jesus' authority comes from God ▶ *Claim*: the audience must heed their proclamation

Figure VII.80

(II)

Backing: **The story of the Wicked Tenants (*1)**

▼

Warrant: A distant strong man will punish those offending his messengers / God is not weaker than earthly strong men

▼

Data: John and Jesus are God's prophets ▶ *Claim*: God will punish those offending them

(57) 21:29-31, Fig Tree 2

Look at the fig tree and all the trees ...

Surprisingly, the last parable in Luke is also the shortest Extended one, having but twenty words and one character. An allegorical reference to Israel is superfluous.[120] The parable merely presents a natural observation, along the lines of 17:37, Vultures, and 12:54-56, Weather. The credibility is excellent (*4). The parable is aimed at the disciples, the exigency is particular, and the parable visualizes the coming Kingdom.

Figure VII.81

Backing: **Trees putting forth leaves herald the summer** (*4)

▼

Warrant: Signs tell about the future

▼

Data: You will observe the signs. ▶ *Claim*: You will know that the Kingdom is near

Conclusions based on this comprehensive study of the argumentation will be drawn in the next chapter. This analysis of every parable by Jesus included in the Gospel of Luke may be used as foundation for detailed study. In this book a few such are presented in chapters 2 through 5.

---

120. Contra Nolland, *Luke*, 1008–9. The addition πάντα τὰ δένδρα indicates that no precise symbolism is meant.

8

Re-Plugging the Parables

In conclusion I shall ask how and why Jesus, as Narrator, uses parables in order to persuade his audience—and how Luke, as Author, has the same intent with respect to those who read his text. I shall begin by classifying and analyzing the messages supported by each particular parable. This is enabled by the above study of their argumentative structure. Do these messages have any bearing on classical topics such as theology, Christology, and eschatology—or on historical issues? If so, this would mean that the outcome of this book should be *re-plugged* to accommodate traditional theological and historical perspectives.

The Parables' Message

What do Luke and his Jesus strive for by telling parables? Although the parables themselves are seldom theological, the argumentation in which they occur often includes religious themes. Instead of far-fetched, poorly documented doctrinal hypotheses,[1] I will simply gather all the *warrants* and *claims* in the argumentation analysis above. These components of argumentation, as supported by the parables, either appear in the Lukan text or can be made explicit by Toulmin's model. Many of them resemble each other to the degree that some general categories can be suggested.

It would be misleading to narrow down the main message supported by the Lukan parables to a single theme. Instead, they can be divided into four great themes that for the most part correlate with the described target. The parables (1) exhort the audience, (2) support Jesus' authority, (3) proclaim God's excessive love, and (4), announce God's strict requirements.[2] Most parables refer to a simple message, but the above argumentation analysis detected nineteen complex parables with more than one target.

Since one parable may support several messages, it can be displayed under several themes. Therefore the number of parables in the groups (eighty) exceeds the number of Jesus' parables in Luke (fifty-seven). *Thus the figures and tables in this chapter are not fully compatible with those in chapter 6.*

---

1. Forbes, *God*, 225–60, presents an interesting overview of theological themes in Luke's parables. Unfortunately, their contact with the persuasive functions of the actual parables remains weak. It is not true that "each of the Lukan parables" concentrates on the image of God (*contra* Forbes, ibid., 305).
2. To be sure, the Lukan Jesus expresses his ideas in several ways, so only focusing on the parables gives but a narrow view. Still, it can contribute to a general assessment.

Table VIII.1

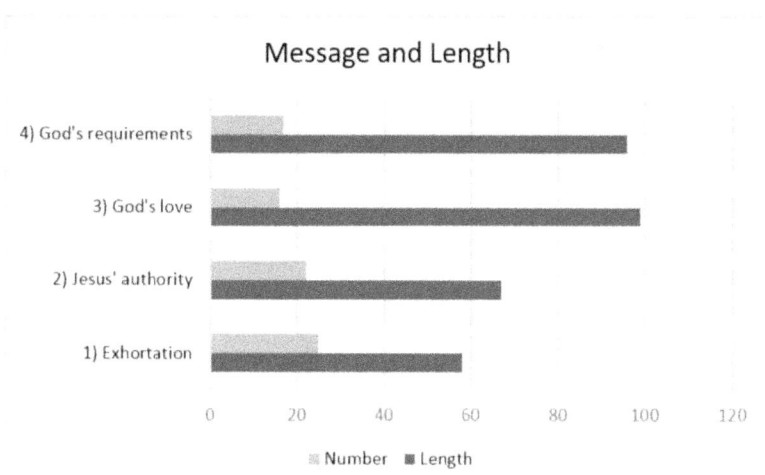

In the following table such alternatives are marked with I and II. Regarding two parables there is also an option III indicating a third possible message. Typically, a complex parable not only deals with those who hear or read it but also simultaneously supports a claim pertaining to God, or in some cases to Jesus, as well. The line between an implicit message and a more distant allusion is not sharp; in the following only the most obvious cases are discussed.

1. Exhorting the Audience

The largest group (25 parables) supports direct exhortation of the audience, including the disciples, opponents, and the general public. They must be humble (for example, 14:8-14), obedient (12:42-48), persistent (8:5-8; 14:34-35), and show impartial love (10:30-37). The typical length is fifty-eight words and the credibility is *2.5.

These parables do not just support some ethical standards. Typically, the members of the audience must put their trust solely in God and not in any material or social assets. Humility both before

God and other people is important. Perseverance and unconditional obedience to God are significant, but Jesus the Narrator does not present any particular ethics or moral programs.

	Table VIII.2	
4:23	Healer 1	He should heal people in Nazareth, too
6:38	Measure a	People will give generously to you
6:39	Blind	You must first improve yourselves
6:40	Teacher	You must first improve yourselves
6:41-42	Speck in the Eye	You must first improve yourselves
6:43-45	Bad Tree	You must first improve yourselves
6:48-49	Two Builders	You must act accordingly, despite the costs
7:32-34	Playing Children	This generation is not wise
8:5-8	Sower a	They should retain the message in perseverance
8:16	Sower b	They should retain the message in perseverance
10:30-37	Samaritan a	You must love everyone irrespective of nationality
10:30-37	Samaritan b	You must love everyone
12:16-21	Rich Fool a	Seek divine riches
12:42-48	Unfaithful a	You must obey God's will
13:6-9	Barren Fig a	Start providing results soon
13:24-29	Closed Door a	Strive to meet God's will
14:8-14	Guidelines a	You must be humble
14:28-30	Tower	You must be prepared for heavy costs
14:31-32	Warring King	You must be prepared for heavy costs
14:34-35	Crazy Salt	You will not lose the attributes of discipleship
16:13	Two Masters	You cannot serve both God and Mammon
17:7-10	Useless Servant	You should not crave any extra bonus
18:2-6	Judge a	You should persevere in prayer
18:10-14	Phar & Tax Coll a	Be humble and put your trust in God
18:25	Camel	The rich cannot enter the Kingdom

2. Supporting Jesus' Authority

Almost as many cases (22 parables) support Jesus' authority or his message on a general level. The average length (67 words) and credibility (*2.8) correspond to the exhorting parables (Group 1). Many of these parables have a defensive purpose, and four subgroups can be identified:

2.1.   Six parables simply seek to augment Jesus' authority.

		Table VIII.3
5:31	Healer 2	Jesus' behavior is justified
5:34-35	Groom b	Jesus is the Bridegroom
10:22	Father and Son	Jesus' message about God is trustworthy
11:17	Kingdom	Jesus cannot represent Beelzebul, but God
11:33	Lamp 2	Jesus' message must be observed
16:19-31	Rich and Laz A	You should heed Jesus' proclamation
20:9-16	Wicked a	The audience must heed Jesus' proclamation

2.2.   Six parables explain why Jesus' program is reasonable and not to be mixed with old patterns.

		Table VIII.4
4:24	Prophet a	Jesus cannot heal the sick in Nazareth
4:24	Prophet b	Jesus cannot heal the sick in Nazareth
5:34-35	Groom a	Jesus is more than John
5:36	Garment	Old rules do not apply to Jesus' message
5:37-39	Wine 1 and 2	Old rules do not apply to Jesus' message

2.3. Six parables urge the audience to accept Jesus' message.

Table VIII.5		
11:21-22	Protecting House	Beelzebul has nothing left
11:24-26	Unclean Spirit	The hearer must take a stand
15:4-7	Lost Sheep a	It is natural to rejoice when finding the lost
15:8-10	Lost Coin a	It is natural to rejoice when finding the lost
15:11-32	Prodigal a	You should join the feast
16:1-9	Unjust Steward a	You should forgive God's "debtors" even if not authorized to do so

2.4. Four parables say how the result of Jesus' program, the Kingdom, is small but will grow and become great.

Table VIII.6		
8:16	Lamp 1	You must make them known
10:02	Harvest	The disciples must pray to God for additional coworkers
13:19	Mustard Seed	God's kingdom will be very great
13:21	Leaven	God's kingdom will be very great

Groups 1 and 2 resemble each other in their strategic function. Together they prepare the audience for the double theological message in groups 3 and 4, which formally resemble each other as well.

3. Proclaiming God's Love

A distinguishable group (16 parables) emphasizes God's positive attitude toward the audience. These are longer on average (99 words) but less credible (*1.9) than the previous group. Many of these parables are *Narratives*. Two subgroups can be found:

3.1. Seven parables argue that it is natural for God to take good care of everyone. Anyone who doubts this bears the burden of proof.

Table VIII.7		
6:38	Measure b	God will give generously to you
11:5-8	Friend at Midnight	God will certainly help you
11:11-13	Bad Fathers	God will certainly give you the Divine Spirit
12:24	Ravens	God certainly takes care of you
12:27-28	Lilies	God certainly takes care of you
12:36-38	Watchful Slaves b	God will reward your alertness to excess
18:2-6	Judge b	God will help you speedily

3.2. Nine parables present a superlative version of the previous group. Many are secondary interpretations of other parables (marked with II). When seen from a theological perspective they argue that God especially loves those not deserving it; thus the audience should do likewise.

Table VIII.8		
7:41-43	Two Debtors	The woman is forgiven more sins than Simon
10:30-37	Samaritan c	God loves everyone unconditionally
14:8-14	Guidelines b	Be good to those who are not worthy
14:16-24	Great Dinner b	God will be irritated, punish those unwilling to obey, and invite unworthy guests.
15:4-7	Lost Sheep b	God too will rejoice when finding the lost
15:8-10	Lost Coin b	God too will rejoice when finding the lost
15:11-32	Prodigal b	God too will rejoice when finding the lost
16:1-9	Unjust Steward b	God approves forgiveness of sins
18:10-14	Phar & Tax Coll b	God will proclaim righteous those who trust in him

The message of Group 3 is exceptional. It has deep roots in the prophetic tradition, especially in Isaiah. According to these parables God is not only highly demanding but also extremely generous, and especially shows love to those not deserving it.

4. Proclaiming God's Requirements

Since many cases (17 parables) refer to the imminent threat caused by God's austere requirements, the audience is called upon to react to the situation immediately. These parables are also long on average (96 words) and difficult to accept; the average credibility rating is as low as *1.9. The direct warning stories are typically *Narratives* about a master.

4.1. Nine parables want to alert the audience: they should observe the signs and prepare for the imminent crisis.

	Table VIII.9	
11:34-36	Eye as a Lamp	Take care of your ability to see (Jesus)
12:36-38	Watchful Slaves a	You must be alert at all times
12:39	Master and Thief	You must be alert at all times
12:54-56	Weather	You should interpret the signs of the time
12:58-59	Going to a	Be prepared for it soon, although it may prove costly
14:16-24	Great Dinne a	You may lose the right to entrance despite your status
17:37	Vultures	Observe the signs
19:12-27	Minas a	The remaining time must be used effectively
21:29-31	Fig Tree	You will know that the Kingdom is near

4.2. Eight parables present an explicit warning or threat. They refer to God and argue that the audience must provide good results soon. God's patience is about to end, and the alternative is a severe punishment—no mercy will be given.

		Table VIII.10
12:16-21	Rich Fool b	Beware of God
12:42-48	Unfaithful c	You must obey his will
12:42-48	Unfaithful d	You must obey God's will diligently
12:58-59	Going to b	Be prepared for it soon, although it may prove costly
13:6-9	Barren Fig b	God's patience may end
13:24-29	Closed Door b	Strive to meet God's criteria
19:12-27	Talents b	The coming of Son of Man will mean great reward or severe vindication
20:9-16	Wicked b	God will punish those offending John and Jesus

Group 4 also serves as a reminder of many Old Testament prophets, but the message is the opposite of that of Group 3. The judgment is imminent. People should read the "handwriting on the wall"[3] and react to the threat as soon as possible. Jesus emphasizes the high demands, the sternness, and the unpredictability of God's forthcoming reckoning. The only reasonable response is a complete change of behavior. Any attempts to limit God's requirements are considered deceitful,[4] as is trust in one's religious achievements, not to speak of money or high social rank.

Despite the different messages, the parables referring to God (Groups 3 and 4) are parallel as far as their length and credibility are concerned, just as Groups 1 and 2 resemble each other. Thus Jesus' theological message is bifurcated: God is both more exacting and severe and more generous and forgiving than the audience is

---

3. Cf. Daniel 5.
4. As emphasized by 10:30-37, *Samaritan*, and its framework story; see chap. 2.

supposed to think. Although both messages apparently challenge the traditional religious views of the Lukan Jesus' antagonists, the second especially irritates them. They naturally ask for the justification, that is, the source of this radical information or the authority on which it is based. Accordingly, several parables attempt to support the message.

Both Groups 3 and 4 are usually long; they contain lively characters and a touching story. This is because the theological theses they support are weaker than those in Groups 1 and 2, which promote more general exhortations or Jesus' authority. But also the parables in the group urging the acceptance of Jesus' message (Group 2.3) and proclaiming God's impartial love (Group 3.1), support the idea of accepting outsiders and sinners. They appeal to the audience's reason and feelings: the hearers would also show mercy to people on certain occasions, so why not now? Since this line of persuasion does not seem to suffice, Jesus resorts to arguing (Group 3.2) that God, as a sovereign master, has the right to do whatever pleases him. In other words, Jesus at least indirectly admits that his proclamation has been legitimately criticized. The ultimate answer to the question of authority (Group 2.1) is, however, based on his claim to have a close familiarity with God; therefore his message ought to be accepted. This means that the hearers should maintain and practice his teaching: in other words, show unconditional love to everyone just as God does.

Luke does not clearly indicate how this message applies to his readers' contemporary religious and historical situations. Later readings of his text in the church made such applications, but assessing them goes beyond the limits of critical exegesis. The type of message correlates to its credibility in the following ways:

Table VIII.11: General Message and Credibility

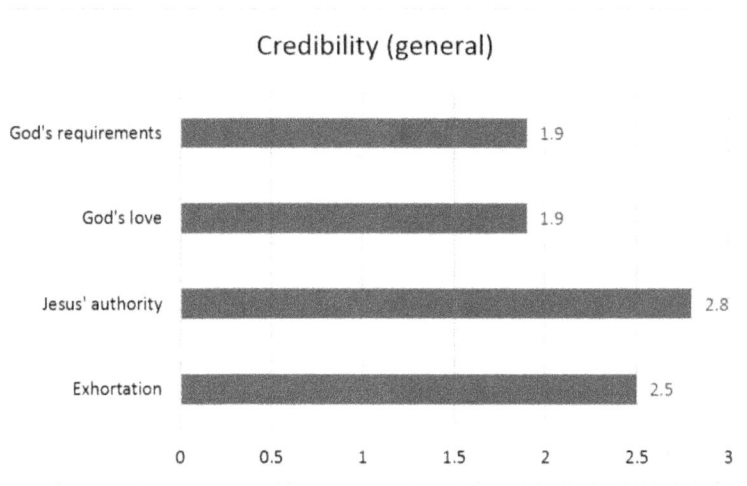

Table VIII.12: Specific Message and Credibility

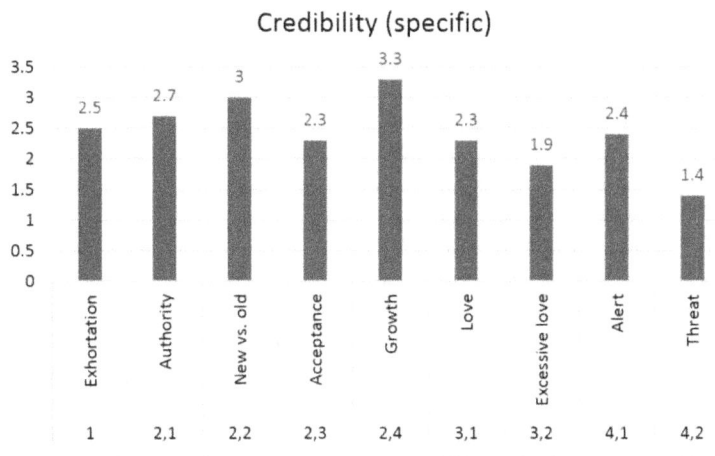

Theology After All

It has become obvious that many theological themes usually discussed in parables research are not prominent in Luke. Reading his parables as persuasive tools in their context shows that in themselves they are seldom religious. Only a few, if any, can be characterized as prominently christological, eschatological, prophetic, or theological at all. However, they illuminate a wide range of such religious topics, from known dilemmas in early Judaism to the sore point of Jesus' own theology. Thus when no theology is added to the stories they can still yield theological messages. Thereby they can be re-plugged into later theological discussions. However, if religious themes and details are axiomatically found everywhere in the parables themselves the stories become distorted and lose their contact with their actual religious context.

Non-Christian Reading?

The parables in Luke concentrate neither on the fate of Jerusalem nor of Israel, neither on the relationship between Jews and Gentiles nor on that of Jewish and Gentile Christians. They do not explicitly discuss any christological dogmas or regulate Christian congregations. Although there are some important clues about the specific relationship between Jesus and God (especially 10:22, *Father and* Son), detailed christological readings are anachronistic since they are incomprehensible within the world of the story; they require information that is unavailable to Jesus' audience. Nevertheless, by the parables Luke is sending a message to his own recipients as well. This message can by all means include Christology as well as bearing polemical theological overtones, but it cannot determine the parables' meaning in their primary literary setting.

Luke the Author invites his own recipients into the world of Jesus, who is telling stories to different audiences. This world is not identical with Luke's or his recipients' world, but it differs from real historical life in first-century Palestine as well, though similarities may be found. This world exists within Luke's story, and his readers are supposed to follow the story within its limits.[5] Only when first understood in a meaningful way in this context can the messages of the parables then be generalized so that they apply to the situation of Luke's recipients. This interpretation then opens the way to a hermeneutical perspective for any reader, including contemporary Christians.

Non-eschatological Reading?

Contrary to another common view, the parables seldom proclaim an imminent end. When they are studied without eschatological eyeglasses the looming threat may as well concern an individual recipient as the whole community. They speak of ordinary life or individual death rather than an ultimate national or global catastrophe. For example, 12:16-21, *Rich Fool*, portrays an individual man dying in the middle of the night, not universal destruction, and in 12:42-48, *Unfaithful Servant,* only one of the numerous characters faces difficulties. However, in some cases the context points toward a global interpretation. For example, 12:39, *Master and Thief*, refers to the coming of the Son of Man (12:40).

These parables are meant to warn the audience. The non-eschatological reading does not mean an individualized interpretation—only five or six parables are told to a single person. But to interpret them solely as prophecies against Jerusalem is based

---

5. This is the common way to read any novel. See above in chap. 1 and Segal, "Fictional Narrative," 64.

more on knowledge of later events than on the information provided by Luke. I do not deny the possibility of some eschatological messages, but they should not overshadow the primary message of the parables.

Non-religious Reading?

Compared to traditional interpretations, especially those by the early Fathers and by many modern critical readers as well, the unplugged reading of the parables as argumentation seems less religious and less christological. I have repeatedly argued that such interpretations are anachronistic, unduly allegorical, or otherwise superfluous for understanding any particular parable. Only a few parables clearly use theological imagery: God appears as a character only in 12:16-21, *Rich Fool*. Perhaps the references to God's care of nature in 12:24, *Ravens*, and 12:27-28, *Lilies*, should also be included. However, in all these cases *God* is not very personal, and the *passivum divinum* contains no necessary theological message; these parables could be told with an immanent reference to nature as well. Only 10:22, *Father and Son*, if seen as referring to God, deals with a personal Deity; 15:11-32, *Prodigal Son*, and 18:10-14, *Pharisee and Tax Collector*, refer to such a One obliquely.

Moreover, only four parables say something primarily about God. Despite the two references to nature, as mentioned above, the references to the unpleasant people in 11:5-8, *Friend at Midnight*, 11:11-13, *Bad Fathers*, and also perhaps 18:2-6, *Judge*, have an explicit theological message. Nevertheless, even this is unconventional. Instead of proclaiming some special attribute of God, these parables express by a *qal wahomer* reasoning that God cannot be worse than bad people are. If, in some cases, these people can do good, then God must be good by default. Thus the parables are not very religious *per se* and should not be read as such. "God," even when explicitly mentioned, could easily be replaced by other expressions.

For Jesus the Narrator there is a persuasive reason for the parables' secular style. The context typically describes a religious dilemma. The parable then aims at disconnecting the audience from the situation; it shows how a certain principle is reasonable or poignant. Only then can the audience apply the principle to the actual dilemma. After accepting a certain maxim in another context they ought to do the same even in the case of the theological or ethical problem discussed in the context.

Luke uses the same technique when writing to his audience. When he tells them about Jesus' discussion with people in a different context, several decades ago, this, too, may be seen as a *parable*. Luke first alienates his readers from their own situation and problems, whatever they may be. The tensions between Gentile and Jewish Christians, or other problems in the early church, are good guesses, but they are only guesses. In any case the audience is freer to accept certain principles and ideas within his story about Jesus. Only afterward can Luke ask them to apply the same principle within their own context. The same strategy functions well with any reader—unless it is compromised by direct allegorical application, which eliminates the necessary distance between the parable and the recipients.

The same applies to the framework of the narrative: what Luke says about Jesus and his audience belongs to Luke's story. It is a coherent entity and does not directly inform us about Luke's own situation. Only after the story has been allowed to have a meaning and purpose in its own context can the principles that are emphasized by it be applied to other situations. If something is applicable in the simple setting of Jesus and his audience it is, presumably, relevant to questions regarding the church (or any other later readers).

This *detheologization* of the parables by no means suggests that the parables do not carry a theological message. On the contrary, when read without additional religious factors the parables indicate that, for Luke and his Jesus, religious matters can be illustrated with earthly images, since God is not unnatural. God acts and feels as any of the hearers would, or as would a professional farmer, judge, or healer. However, God has an unpredictable, unconventional side as well; this is illustrated by references to a highhanded master who can be incredibly demanding and harsh as well as astonishingly compassionate and generous.

Glimpses of Jesus' Theology

A prominent feature of the Lukan parables is their development from short and credible parables to long and problematic ones.[6] Jesus begins with brief *Simple Rules*. These refer to various ordinary trades, to pure reason, or to the audience's experience. Thus their credibility is high. The next step takes him to *Extended Rules* and brief *Narratives* describing what is possible, but not necessary. Correspondingly, their credibility is somewhat weaker. They refer to domestic experiences, to natural phenomena, but also to the behavior of a master. They often lack any specific situation. Finally, there are mostly long *Narratives* about ἄνθρωπός τις, in some particular situation. Their credibility is poor, since they typically claim something unconventional about a master who in some way is reminiscent of God. Most of these stories are touching; the plot is carefully constructed with interesting characters. All these devices are

---

6. The phenomenon is somewhat weaker in Matthew, but different in Mark. See above, chap. 6.

necessary for overcoming the not-so-easily-acceptable message. These parables typically come from Luke's own sources.

Apparently Luke follows good rhetorical convention by moving from easy cases to difficult ones or from "light to heavy." After gaining credibility through simple parables he could then proceed to more difficult messages. It may be interesting that although 28% of the Lukan parables are called such by him, 50% of the first eight and 83% of the last six parables are given this description.

This concise study of the Lukan parables has revealed something about how his hero, Jesus, assessed his own theological mission and role. Several themes have emerged during this analysis; I will focus on only three of them.

First, especially in the exhorting parables (Group 1), Jesus advises his audience not to invest in earthly assets, by which he means the different actions reimbursed by other people. Doing good to people, or acting and speaking piously in front of them, produces money, grain, religious admiration, or social capital that all provide security and can be relied on for as long as one lives. According to Jesus, the problem with this strategy is that good deeds will not be compensated twice (e.g., 6:24-25; 16:25). In the afterlife God will only repay those who did not receive their lot on earth.

Second, many parables focus on Jesus' own authority, especially in Group 2.1. On several occasions he defends the legitimacy of his program to proclaim good news to the poor. At times he refers to the Scriptures in order to prove God's acceptance of his program.[7] Then he resorts to different parables, prompted by his habit of accepting sinners and eating with them, which was interpreted as receiving them back into the religious community, and suggesting that God favors this action.[8] When his actions are criticized, Jesus' parables

---

7. Isa. 42:7; Luke 4:18-19; 16:19-31.
8. For example, 15:1-2, 7, 10.

present several responses. He can appeal to the critics' customs and feelings: on certain occasions they would do the same, and from a certain perspective such behavior is the best option.

Third, the most intriguing solution is to admit the accusations: Jesus has no formal right to forgive sins on God's behalf. Thus he accepts the critics' viewpoint as correct. Nevertheless, he argues that God, as a sovereign master, accepts his agenda. Some crucial parables play a key role in this proclamation. They emphasize a master's sovereignty in regard both to immense generosity and to immense requirements. A master can destroy people who do not provide huge profits, but he can forgive enormous debts as well. If this applies to an earthly master, then how much more uncontrollable is God? God cannot be regulated by the scribes, and Jesus, as God's messenger, claims every right to proclaim freedom and forgiveness for those not deserving it. The master-character supports Jesus' double message for any recipient: both God's love and God's demands know no limits. Jesus is not so interested in people who live according to God's will. Instead, the parables often deal with those who are disobedient. God can show both extreme mercy and cruelty toward them.

Finally, Jesus can claim prophetic authority like that of John and the other prophets of Israel, arguing that his message has a divine source.[9] This line of thought is not emphasized by Luke, but it appears in certain key sections and thus is supposed to affect the audience. In the beginning Jesus is called "God's beloved son" (3:22) and "God's anointed one" (4:18-21). In the same vein, the last narrative parable suggests that he is God's beloved son (20:13).

---

9. For example, 10:22; 20:9-16.

Concluding Remarks

Finally, some key methodological findings of this study can be summarized, resulting in a more precise definition of a parable and prospects for further research. Especially important is the bearing of the unplugged reading on theological and historical questions.

The Parables Want to Persuade

The experimental reading of Jesus' parables as persuasion in their Lukan setting has, I hope, led to a renewed view of these overly interpreted stories. The purpose of this study has been to demonstrate how a transparent approach to the parables of Jesus provides a dependable basis for their interpretation. When these familiar stories are studied in their real—not reconstructed—context their actual meaning, function, and message are better observed.

The central conclusion to be drawn after scrutinizing all the Lukan parables is that the theoretical principles presented in the Introduction (chapter 1) have proven useful for illuminating parables that are either perplexing or axiomatically understood in a certain way. Moreover, applying observations regarding the simple parables to the complex ones and extending the analysis to include all the parables have proven to be beneficial.

Adolf Jülicher's old principle emphasizing the *scopus* or *punch line* or the end of the story matched the proper *Narratives* well. Especially the parables that seemingly suffer from poor storytelling still benefit from observing this principle. Thus in 16:19-31, *Rich Man and Lazarus*, and 15:11-32, *Prodigal Son*, Jesus appears not to know how to round up a parable—he goes on and on after passing the punch line or the decisive turn in the story. But the last sentences of that very extension indicate in both cases that the long wait was worthwhile and the rule still applies. To base the interpretation of these parables on some other part, against the narrative convention, leads to a misguided result. This principle applies also to the seemingly challenging 8:5-8, *Sower*, despite the narrator's allegorical explanation of its details in 8:10-15. However, in the shorter variants, the *Simple Rules* and *Extended Rules*, seeking such a decisive line is superfluous.

The idea of neither introducing any historical information into the text nor censoring anything as unoriginal has benefited the process of seeking the persuasive function. We have seen that the parables seldom need additional information in order to be understood. In several cases traditional interpretations can be set aside because they are based on an altered story. Typically they understand the parables as comments on the discussion between Christianity and Judaism, or as predicting the fate of Jerusalem in 70 c.e.. To be sure, when seeking the original message and function of the parables for the historical Jesus, or when creating hermeneutical interpretations, such perspectives may be justified. However, for analyzing the Lukan text they are misguided. I suggest that even for a purely historical study the function of the parable in its actual context proves more useful than any external information, the applicability of which is hard to prove.

Some examples can be mentioned. The messages of the grand parables 10:30-37, *Samaritan*, and 15:11-32, *Prodigal Son*, are better recognized when not too much Christology is added to them. Correspondingly, 14:16-24, the *Great Dinner*, 19:12-27, the *Minas*, and 20:9-16, the *Wicked Tenants* benefit from the liberation of axiomatic anachronistic anti-Jewish readings. Luke's allegedly most difficult parable, 16:1-9, the *Unjust Steward*, becomes understandable when left intact. When no verses are cut off, no external information is added, and the connection to the previous chapter is not overlooked, the parable becomes an effective and reasonable piece of persuasion. Even minor flourishes like the shepherd in 15:4-7, where no shepherds exist, can mislead the interpretation. The axiomatic introduction of this image and its Old Testament allusions to the story illustrates the scholars' habit of reading the parables as scriptural material with rich intertextual connections. Jesus' audience, however, only hear that he compares them with the owner of a hundred sheep.

The use of hyperbolic expressions is a perplexing feature of the Lukan parables. The master reacts unduly to his servants' unsatisfactory behavior but also rewards the good servants in excess. The returning prodigal is received in an unexpectedly friendly way, and the Samaritan's love has no limits. In fact, most of the longer parables in Luke contain some type of exaggeration. Even the poor woman's reaction to finding a coin by calling together her friends and neighbors appears exceptional.

From the perspective of argumentation this use of hyperbole is problematic. When the goal is to call to mind the audience's own behavior or known habits, any extraordinary elements serve only to weaken the reasoning. However, they do increase the parable's *pathos* effect. Since emotions play an essential role in an especially difficult parable's ability to persuade, the risk of overemphasizing them may be worth taking.

Despite the emphasis on emotions, almost all parables appeal to reason as well, rather than relying solely on good storytelling or appealing to the emotions. This is another central finding of this study. This aspect can be illustrated and scrutinized by use of modern argumentation analysis.

Where a parable is involved, it is typical to suppose that some factor remains implicit. To be sure, most human argumentation functions this way, but it causes special difficulties in interpreting the parables. Toulmin's approach, which provides important information about the missing components, has proven invaluable in reconstructing them, not least because it protects against inappropriate solutions.

In some cases the *warrant*, that is, the general rule the parable is supposed to support, is explicit. For example, "the measure you give will be the measure you get back" (6:38b) is such a rule, supported by the parable describing generous measuring habits in the marketplace in 6:38a. More often the rule must be deduced from the parable; then the essential criteria are that the rule (a) logically connects the point of departure, that is, the *data* agreed upon, and the opinion put forward, the *claim*, and (b), it remains on the general level and does not provide any particular information relating only to the actual case.

Usually Luke provides the starting point, the *data*. It can be a statement, a critical question, a description of the situation, or the like. Correspondingly, the thesis, the *claim* the audience should adopt, is often given. However, both can be missing. Thus in 6:38 we cannot know for sure what Jesus wants to achieve by his parable and the rule it illustrates. However, civilized guesses can be made based on the rule and the situation. Obviously, he promises that God will be generous to the hearers as they are generous to other people. This idea not only fits the parable but several other statements in the gospel as well. Unique claims presenting novel ideas should not be reconstructed.

The unplugged approach to the Lukan parables has posited their persuasive function. The analysis of all the cases supports the hypothesis put forward in the beginning: all parables in Luke are examples aimed at supporting some general rule. In Toulmin's terms, a parable is a *backing* that supports a *warrant*. A *warrant* is not a direct order and it never contains new, case-specific information. Instead, it is applicable to other situations as well.

The *warrant* supported by the parable is then applied to the situation. It shows why the facts at hand, the *data*, ought to lead to the conclusion, the *claim*, argued by Jesus. This means that the parables or any detail in them should not be applied primarily to the situation directly presented by the evangelist, even less to some later theological or ethical discussion. In other words, an allegorical interpretation contradicts the basic persuasive function of a parable. Thus my earlier definition of the parable can be complemented:[10]

> *A parable is a narrative, non-historical, and metaphorical saying (by Jesus), appealing to an audience. It illustrates a general principle to be applied in a particular context.*

This means that the parables seldom teach us any new information about God, Jesus, the disciples, or the antagonists. In principle such assertions would lack any persuasive function; claiming something about people by using cover names does not increase the credibility of the claim. On the contrary, Luke and his Jesus present conventional cases known and, they hope, accepted by the recipients, often instances typical of some occupation. Such examples are then refined into a rule that can be applied to religious or ethical issues as well. In more difficult cases the parable refers to a particular case that is presented not as typical but as possible. Several narrative devices, especially the appeal to the audience's feelings, are then used in order to win adherence. Thus the parables' typical persuasive function can be determined:

> *A parable alienates the audience from the issue under discussion. It is supposed to accept a general principle in a different context, and this principle is then applied to the original issue.*

---

10. See chap. 6 above.

The general conclusion needs to be specified in two ways. First, despite rejecting the allegory as a general model of explanation, it must be noted that Jesus encourages his recipients to accept his stories as allegorical as well. For example, in 8:9-15 Jesus' allegorical explanation of 8:5-8, the *Sower*, indicates how such additional messages can even be found in other stories. Indeed, details in some parables undoubtedly resemble the situation described by Luke. These allusions are always secondary and beneath the surface, often following the Jewish *qal wahomer* pattern of reasoning; they should never obscure the main message. Moreover, any allusion too difficult for Jesus' audience in the text must be ruled out. Thus one must be cautious when applying ideas containing future historical or theological details, especially regarding the fate of Jerusalem and Israel, as well as high Christology. The parable must always make sense to its recipients as presented in the text, even if it may have had an additional meaning for the Lukan audience. Only with these precautions in mind are these indirect messages of the parables worth studying.

In the argumentation analysis given above I have studied one such indirect message more closely: the way God is implied in the parables. Whereas only four parables directly aim at illuminating some rule concerning God, there are approximately nineteen parables carrying a corresponding message alongside their main function. Typically they use the master-figure. These references are not allegorical in the traditional sense of the word since they, too, illuminate a general rule. This means that they are not supposed to be directly applied to the case under discussion. However, they do not always follow the narrative convention of putting the sole meaning of the story at the end. Corresponding side-messages deal with Jesus and the Kingdom.

Second, in some cases the parable and the situation at hand are intertwined, so that the hearers become characters in the story. Such an especially confused story is 13:24-29, the *Closed Door*, in which Jesus makes specific claims about the audience. Since, however, the hearers want to be saved (13:23) and not to enter a house, this is not a prophecy describing real events in the future; it is an imaginary story about a feast in a house. Even in this case the persuasive function of the parable as a *backing* is not compromised.

On the whole, assessing the general function of the parables as *backing* helps us understand their meaning, message, and purpose, even in difficult cases. After we have observed this function in the brief and lucid cases, especially in the first part of Luke's text, it becomes possible to find a similar function in the longer and more complex ones as well.

Reconnecting to Theology and History

The Lukan parables play a double role. First, they are text-internal stories told by Jesus, the protagonist of Luke's work, and they aim to affect Jesus' listeners. Second, they are told to the more unspecified Lukan recipients. The latter situation in particular paves the way to their interpretation for any reader, including modern religious communities. In this, the unplugged interpretation does not seek to disconnect the Lukan parables from present-day uses, such as religious messages or historical inquiries. On the contrary, specifying the genuine meaning and purpose of any parable within its context and cleansing it from unwarranted allegorical or pseudo-historical readings may provide an inspiring platform for religious and historical uses as well.

The significance of this study for religious use of the Lukan parables depends to a great degree on the hermeneutical principles applied. Perhaps clarifying the *warrants* and *claims* in the document or, in other words, discovering what Luke and his Jesus want to say through the parables has some meaning for most religious communities. The findings can scarcely be replaced completely by later allegorical interpretations, which, despite their constant popularity (beginning with the early Fathers), are superfluous, if not harmful to one's understanding of Luke and his Jesus.

In practice, a sermon based on a Lukan parable will certainly benefit from the basic analysis in chapters 6 and 7, since it attempts to discover the actual message of each particular parable. On a more general level, the theological perspective of the Lukan parables may prove to be important because it opens access to perhaps the most vulnerable and most novel point of the theology of the Lukan Jesus. He attempts to justify his claim for God's unlimited love toward people unworthy of it by means of long and fascinating parables, but in the end he has to resort to comparing God with an unpredictable master who may use his property just as he pleases. This highhanded and unpredictable image of God is not unique; in this regard Matthew's *Workers in the Vineyard* (Matt. 20:1-16) may surpass all the Lukan stories. Thus it is possible that this vulnerable but fascinating theological focus was not invented by Luke but has roots in historical tradition.

Speaking of history, the reference to Matthew shows how a further unplugged study of Jesus' parables in any ancient collection, especially Mark, Matthew, Q, *Thomas*, and perhaps even John, and a general comparison between them, could shed more light on the historical figure of Jesus and his thinking. Although the present study does not venture to comment further on the relationship of the Lukan stories to the words of the historical Jesus, the results may contribute to such studies.

Too often Jesus' parables have been "reconstructed" in their allegedly original versions simply because they have been difficult to interpret. At times scholars have suggested that Luke, too, was confused by the material. Therefore some words or whole verses have been excluded as unnecessary Lukan additions; others have been added in order to reveal the original meaning—which the existing text is, allegedly, unable to convey. However, manipulating the material is the last resort when facing difficulties in its interpretation.

Reading the parables unplugged, as pieces of persuasion in their literary and argumentative contexts, has shown that each Lukan parable plays a distinctive role. More importantly, for the recipients implied by the evangelist this function is not hard to identify. These parables work well within Luke's presentation and fit the narrative world he presents, in which he describes how his protagonist interacts with different people. Therefore the Lukan parables are sufficiently polished to omit annoying seams or meaningless utterances that would necessitate historical reconstructions.

But did Jesus of Nazareth originally tell these stories? This survey has focused on the Lukan versions only. It has shown that they contain nothing outside the realm of understanding for a first-century Palestinian Jew, especially since each parable describes a story-world, not the contemporary sociohistorical reality. Therefore one does not have to assume that they were invented by Luke.

Yet 77% (44) of the parables are common to other Synoptic Gospels, and their versions are not identical with those written by Luke. Although no comparisons have been made here, combining the analysis with corresponding studies of the parallel texts would probably yield interesting results. For example, Matt. 7:24-27 is, essentially, inferior as a story compared to Luke 6:48-49, *Two Builders*.[11] Other parables are rather similar in the two documents,

---

11. Matthew's Jesus reveals at the outset that the man building on sand was stupid. Moreover, he does not emphasize the hard work of the other man. Both details diminish the narrative effectiveness of the story; there is neither any surprise nor a signal for perceiving the message of the parable. It seems as if Matthew tells the story to people who are already familiar with it.

but they are used for different purposes. Unlike Luke, Matthew does not even hint at Jesus in the parables *Crazy Salt* (Matt. 5:13; Luke 14:34-35), *Lamp* (Matt. 5:15; Luke 8:16), or *Eye as a Lamp* (Matt. 6:22-23; Luke 11:34-36). Correspondingly, *Bad Tree* (Matt. 7:16-20; Luke 6:43-45) refers to other people, not to the audience. However, both evangelists can reuse a parable (*Bad Tree* appears also in Matt. 12:33; *Lamp* also in Luke 11:33). It seems reasonable to suppose that Jesus, as a historical figure, reworked his best stories. Without further discussing the Synoptic redaction we can say that it seems plausible that several versions may be just as much—or as little—original.

* * *

A comprehensive, text-oriented approach to perhaps the best-known stories in the world is long overdue. This book has been an exercise in studying them as they exist in one of the earliest sources. I have tried to read them while respecting their original function as pieces of argumentation in their real context. I have asked what happens to them if nothing is added or excluded. Although the task sounds simple, it has been demanding indeed, due to the dominance and the abundance of religious and historical explanations. I hope this experiment will inspire other students of Jesus' parables to meet the challenge with an even sharper edge.

Bibliography

Aharoni, Yohanan. *The Land of the Bible: A Historical Geography*. 2d ed. Philadelphia: Westminster, 1979.

Albertz, Martin. *Die synoptischen Streitgespräche*. Berlin: Trowitzch, 1921.

Baergen, René A. "Servant, Manager or Slave? Reading the Parable of the Rich Man and his Steward (Luke 16.1-8a) through the Lens of Ancient Slavery." *SR* 35 (2006): 25–38.

Bailey, Kenneth E. *Poet and Peasant*. Grand Rapids: Eerdmans, 1976.

_____. *Through Peasant Eyes: More Lucan Parables, Their Culture and Style*. Grand Rapids: Eerdmans, 1980.

Bailey, Mark L. "Guidelines for Interpreting Jesus' Parables." *Bibliotheca Sacra* 155: 617 (1998): 29–38.

Bar-Efrat, Shimon. *Narrative Art in the Bible*. London: T & T Clark, 1989.

Barthes, Roland. "The Death of the Author." *Aspen* 5-6 (1967). http://www.ubu.com/aspen/aspen5and6/threeEssays.html#barthes.

Bauckham, Richard. "The Scrupulous Priest and the Good Samaritan: Jesus' Parabolic Interpretation of the Law of Moses." *NTS* 44 (1998): 457–89.

Baudler, Georg. "Das Gleichnis vom 'betrügerischen Verwalter' (Lk 16, 1-8a) als Ausdruck der 'inneren Biographie' Jesu: Beispiel einer existenz-biographischen Gleichnisinterpretation im religionspädagogischer Absicht." *TGeg* 28 (1985): 65–76.

Beavis, Mary Ann. "Ancient Slavery as an Interpretive Context for the New Testament Servant Parables with Special Reference to the Unjust Steward (Luke 16:1-8)." JBL 111 (1992): 37–54.

_____. "The Power of Jesus' Parables: Were They Polemical or Irenic?" *JSNT* 82 (2001): 3–30.

_____. "Feminist (and other) Reflections on the Woman with Seven Husbands (Mark 12:20-23)—A Neglected Synoptic Parable." Pages 603–17 in *Hermeneutik der Gleichnisse Jesu*. Edited by Ruben Zimmermann. Tübingen: Mohr Siebeck, 2008.

Berger, Klaus. "Hellenistische Gattungen im Neuen Testament." *ANRW*, 25/3. Berlin and New York: de Gruyter (1984): 1110–24.

Berlin, Adele. *Poetics and Interpretation of Biblical Narrative*. Winona Lake: Eisenbrauns, 1994.

Blomberg, Craig. *Interpreting the Parables*. Downers Grove: InterVarsity, 1990.

Booth, Wayne C. *The Rhetoric of Fiction*. 2d ed. Chicago and London: University of Chicago Press, 1983.

Bovon, François. *Das Evangelium nach Lukas*. EKKNT III/3. Zürich: Benziger; Neukirchen-Vluyn: Neukirchener, 2001.

Braun, Herbert. *Jesus–der Mann aus Nazareth und seine Zeit: Erweiterte Studienausgabe*. Stuttgart: Kreuz, 1984.

Brown, Colin. "The Parable of the Rebellious Son(s)." *SJT* 51 (1998): 391–405.

_____. "The Unjust Steward: A New Twist?" Pages 121–45 in *Worship, Theology and Ministry in the Early Church*. FS R. P. Martin. Edited by Michael J. Wilkins and Terence Paige. JSNTSup 87. Sheffield: Sheffield Academic Press, 1992.

Bruner, Jerome. *Acts of Meaning*. Cambridge, MA: Harvard University Press, 1990.

Bultmann, Rudolf. *Die Geschichte der synoptischen Tradition*. FRLANT 29. Göttingen: Vandenhoeck & Ruprecht, 1921.

Burke, Kenneth A. *Rhetoric of Motives*. Berkeley: University of California Press, 1969.

Burnett, Fred W. "Characterization and Reader Construction of Characters in the Gospels." *Semeia* 63 (1993): 3–28.

Burton, David J. "Groundwater in the Hashemite Kingdom of the Jordan." Pages 330–42 in *Assemblée générale de Rome 1954*. International Association of Hydrological Sciences, Publ. 37, Tome II. Louvain, 1954.

Burton, Gideon O. *Silva Rhetoricae*: http://rhetoric.byu.edu.

Campbell, Joseph. *The Hero with a Thousand Faces*. 3d ed. Bollingen series XVII. Novato, CA: New World Library, 2008 [1949].

Chatman, Seymour. *Story and Discourse: Narrative Structure in Fiction and Film*. Ithaca and London: Cornell University Press, 1978.

Clines, David J. A. *Job 1–20*. WBC 17. Dallas: Word Books, 1989.

Cortazzi, Martin. *Narrative Analysis*. London: Falmer, 1993.

Creed, John Martin. *The Gospel According to St. Luke*. London: Macmillan, 1930.

Crespy, Georges. "The Parable of the Good Samaritan—An Essay in Structural Research." *Semeia* 2 (1974): 27–50.

Crossan, John Dominic. "The Parable of the Wicked Husbandmen." *JBL* 90 (1971): 451–65.

_____, ed. *The Good Samaritan*. Semeia 2. Missoula: Scholars Press, 1974.

Culpepper, R. Alan. *Anatomy of the Fourth Gospel—A Study in Literary Design*. Philadelphia: Fortress Press, 1983.

Degenhardt, Joachim. *Lukas, Evangelist der Armen*. Stuttgart: Katholisches Bibelwerk, 1965.

Derrett, J. Duncan M. *Law in the New Testament*. London: Darton, Longman, and Todd, 1976.

Dodd, Charles Harold. *The Parables of the Kingdom*. London: Nisbet, 1936.

Donahue, John R. *The Gospel in Parable: Metaphor, Narrative, and Theology in the Synoptic Gospels*. Philadelphia: Fortress Press, 1988.

Dronsch, Kristina. "Vom Fruchtbringen (Sämann mit Deutung)." Pages 297–311 in *Kompendium der Gleichnisse Jesu*. Edited by Ruben Zimmermann. Gütersloh: Gütersloher Verlagshaus, 2007.

———. "Lieber eine Leuchte als ein unscheinbares Licht (Die Lampe auf dem Leuchter / Vom Licht auf dem Leuchter." Pages 133–38 in *Kompendium der Gleichnisse Jesu* (2007).

Drury, John. *The Parables in the Gospels—History and Allegory.* New York: Crossroad, 1985.

Dunn, James D. G. *Christology in the Making. A New Testament Inquiry into the Origins of the Doctrine of the Incarnation*. 2d ed. Grand Rapids: Eerdmans, 1989.

———. *Jesus Remembered. Christianity in the Making*, Volume 1. Grand Rapids: Eerdmans, 2003.

Dupont, Jacques. "Vinvieux, vin nouveau (Luc 5, 39)." *CBQ* 25 (1963): 286–304.

Eco, Umberto, et al. *Interpretation and Overinterpretation*. Cambridge: Cambridge University Press, 1992.

Eemeren, Frans H. van. *Strategic Maneuvering in Argumentative Discourse: Extending the pragma-dialectical theory of argumentation*. Argumentation in Context 2. Amsterdam: John Benjamins, 2010.

———, et al., eds. *Fundamentals of Argumentation Theory: A Handbook of Historical Backgrounds and Contemporary Development*. Mahwah, NJ: Lawrence Erlbaum, 1996.

Esch-Wermeling, Elisabeth. "Kein Heimvorteil für den Heiler." Pages 523–31 in *Kompendium der Gleichnisse Jesu* (2007).

Esler, Philip F. "Jesus and the reduction of intergroup conflict." *BI* 8 (2000): 325–54.

Evans, Craig A. *Mark 8:27–6:20*. WBC 34B. Nashville: Thomas Nelson, 2001.

Finnern, Sönke. *Narratologie und biblische Exegese*. WUNT 2d series 285. Tübingen: Mohr Siebeck, 2010.

Fitzmyer, Joseph A. "The Story of the Dishonest Manager (Lk 16:1-13)." Pages 161–84 in idem, *Essays on the Semitic Background of the New Testament*. Missoula: Scholars Press, 1974.

Fletcher, Donald R. "The Riddle of the Unjust Steward: Is Irony the Key?" *JBL* 82 (1963): 15–30.

Fludernik, Monika. *Towards a 'Natural' Narratology*. London and New York: Routledge, 1996.

_____. *An Introduction to Narratology*. London and New York: Routledge, 2009.

Flusser, David. "The Parable of the Unjust Steward: Jesus' Criticism of the Essenes." Pages 176–97 in *Jesus and the Dead Sea Scrolls*. Edited by James H. Charlesworth. New York: Doubleday, 1992.

Forbes, Greg W. *The God of Old: The Role of the Lukan Parables in the Purpose of Luke's Gospel*. JSNTSup 198. Sheffield: Sheffield Academic Press, 2000.

Foster, Edward Morgan. *Aspects of the Novel*. New York: Harcourt Brace Jovanovich, 1985.

Funk, Robert W. "The Good Samaritan as Metaphor." *Semeia* 2 (1974): 74–81.

_____. *The Poetics of Biblical Narrative*. FF: Literary Facets. Sonoma: Polebridge, 1988.

Genette, Gérard. *Narrative Discourse: An Essay in Method*. Translated by Jane E. Lewin. Ithaca: Cornell University Press, 1980.

_____. *Fiction and Diction*. Ithaca: Cornell University Press, 1993.

Gerber, Christine. "Wann aus Sklavinnen und Sklaven Gäste ihres Herren werden (Von den wachenden Knechten)." Pages 573–78 in *Kompendium der Gleichnisse Jesu* (2007).

Gerhardsson, Birger. *The Good Samaritan—The Good Shepherd?* Lund: Gleerup, 1958.

Gerwing, Walter. *Jesu Konfliktverhalten.* Berlin: Lit, 2009.

Good, R. S. "Jesus, Protagonist of the Old, in Lk 5:33-39." *NovT* 25 (1983): 19–36.

Gowler, David B. *What Are They Saying About the Parables.* Mahwah, NJ: Paulist Press, 2000.

Gray, Arthur. "The Parable of the Wicked Husbandmen." *HibJ* 19 (1920–21): 42–52.

Harnisch, Wolfgang. *Die Gleichniserzählungen Jesu: eine hermeneutische Einführung.* Göttingen: Vandenhoeck & Ruprecht, 1985.

Harrill, James Albert. "The Indentured Labor of the Prodigal Son." *JBL* 115 (1996): 714–17.

Hartman, Lars. "Galatians 3:15–4:11 as Part of a Theological Argument on a Practical Issue." Pages 127–58 in *The Truth of the Gospel. Galatians 1:1–4:11.* Edited by Jan Lambrecht. Rome: Benedictina, 1993.

Hawkes, Terence. *Structuralism and Semiotics.* London: Methuen, 1977.

Hedrick, Charles W. *Parables as Poetic Fictions: The Creative Voice of Jesus.* Eugene, OR: Wipf & Stock, 2005 [1994].

_____. *Many Things in Parables: Jesus and his Modern Critics.* Louisville: Westminster John Knox, 2004.

Hengel, Martin. "Das Gleichnis von den Weingärtnern: Mc 12:1-12 im Licht der Zenonpapyri und der rabbinischen Gleichnisse." *ZNW* 59 (1968): 1–39.

Hester, J. David. "Socio-Rhetorical Criticism and the Parable of the Wicked Tenants." *JSNT* 45 (1992): 27–57.

Hietanen, Mika. *Paul's Argumentation in Galatians: A Pragma-Dialectical Analysis.* LNTS 344. London and New York: T & T Clark, 2005.

Hogan, Patrick Colm. *Affective Narratology: The Emotional Structure of Stories.* Lincoln: University of Nebraska Press, 2011.

Hoppe, Rudolf. "Gleichnis und Situation: Zu den Gleichnissen vom guten Vater (Lk 15,11-32) und gütigen Hausherrn (Mt 20:1-15)." *BZ* 28 (1984): 1–21.

Hoy, David Couzens. "Legal Hermeneutics: Recent Debates." Pages 111–35 in *Festivals of Interpretation: Essays on Hans-Georg Gadamer's Work*. Edited by Kathleen Wright. Albany: State University of New York Press, 1990.

Hultgren, Arland J. *Jesusand his Adversaries: The Form and Function of the Conflict Stories in the Synoptic Tradition*. Minneapolis: Augsburg, 1979.

———. *The Parables of Jesus: A Commentary*. Grand Rapids: Eerdmans, 2000.

Hunzinger, Claus-Hunno. "Unbekannte Gleichnisse Jesu aus dem Thomas-Evangelium." Pages 209–20 in *Judentum-Urchristentum-Kirche. Festschrift für Joachim Jeremias*. Edited by Walther Eltester. BZNW 26. Berlin: Töpelmann, 1960.

Ireland, Dennis J. "A History of Recent Interpretation of the Parable of the Unjust Steward (Luke 16:1-13)." *WTJ* 51 (1989): 293–318.

Iser, Wolgang. *Der implizierte Leser: Kommunikationsformen des Romans von Bunyan bis Beckett*. Munich: Fink, 1972.

Jakobson, Roman. "Closing Statements: Linguistics and Poetics." Pages 350–77 in *Style in Language*. Edited by Thomas A. Sebeok. Cambridge, MA: MIT Press, 1960.

Jancovich, Mark. *The Cultural Politics of the New Criticism*. Cambridge: Cambridge University Press, 1993.

Jefferson, Ann, and David Robey, eds. *Modern Literary Theory. A Comparative Introduction*. London: B. T. Batsford, 1986.

Jeremias, Joachim. *Die Gleichnisse Jesu.* 2d ed. Zürich: Zwingli-Verlag, 1952.

Jülicher, Adolf. *Die Gleichnisreden Jesu: Zwei Teile in einem Band*. 2d ed. Tübingen: Mohr Siebeck, 1910.

Kamlah, Ehrhard. "Die Parabel vom ungerechten Verwalter (Luk. 16, 1ff.) im Rahmen der Knechtsgleichnisse." Pages 276–94 in *Abraham unser Vater:*

Juden und Christen im Gespräch über die Bibel. Edited by Otto Betz. Leiden: Brill, 1963.

Keesmaat, Sylvia C. "Strange Neighbors and Risky Care." Pages 263–85 in *The Challenge of Jesus' Parables.* Edited by Richard N. Longenecker. Grand Rapids: Eerdmans, 2000.

Kennedy, George A. *New Testament Interpretation through Rhetorical Criticism.* Chapel Hill: University of North Carolina Press, 1984.

Kern, Gabi. "Fasten oder feiern?—Eine Frage der Zeit (Vom Bräutigam / Die Fastenfrage." Pages 265–72 in *Kompendium der Gleichnisse Jesu* (2007).

_____. "Grössenwahn?! (Vom Schüler und Lehrer)." Pages 68–75 in *Kompendium der Gleichnisse Jesu* (2007).

Klawans, Jonathan. "Moral and Ritual Purity." Pages 266–84 in *The Historical Jesus in Context.* Edited by Amy-Jill Levine, et al. Princeton: Princeton University Press, 2006.

Klein, Hans. *Das Lukasevangelium.* MeyerK 1/3. Göttingen: Vandenhoeck & Ruprecht, 2005.

Kloppenborg, John S. "The Dishonoured Master. Luke 16, 1-8a)." *Bib* 70 (1989): 134–59.

_____. *The Tenants in the Vineyard.* WUNT 195. Tübingen: Mohr Siebeck, 2006.

Krämer, Michael. *Das Rätsel der Parabel vom ungerechten Verwalter, Lk 16.1-13.* Zurich: PAS, 1972.

Labahn, Michael. "Füllt den Raum aus—es kommt sonst noch schlimmer! (Beelzebulgleichniss)." Pages 126–32 in *Kompendium der Gleichnisse Jesu* (2007).

_____. "Die plötzliche Alternative mitten im Alltag." Pages 227–33 in *Kompendium der Gleichnisse Jesu* (2007).

Landry, David, and Ben May. "Honor Restored: New Light on The Parable of The Prudent Steward (Luke 16:1-8a)." *JBL* 119 (2000): 287–309.

Lausberg, Heinrich. *Handbook of Literary Rhetoric: A Foundation for Literary Study.* Translated by Matthew T. Bliss, et al. Edited by David E. Orton and Richard Dean Anderson. Leiden: Brill, 1998.

Leonhardt-Balzer, Jutta. "Wie kommt ein Reicher in Abrahams Schoss? (Vom reichen Mann und armen Lazarus)." Pages 647–60 in *Kompendium der Gleichnisse Jesu* (2007).

Loader, William. "Jesus and the Rogue in Luke 16:1-8a: The Parable of the Unjust Steward." *RB* 96 (1989): 518–32.

Longman Dictionary of Contemporary English. Edited by Paul Procter, et al. Harlow: Longman, 1978.

Louw, Johannes. "The Parables of the Tower-Builder and the King Going to War." *ExpTim* 48 (1937): 478.

Lowe, Malcolm. "From the Parable of the Vineyard to a Pre-Synoptic Source." *NTS* 28 (1982): 257–63.

Lüdemann, Gerd, et al. *Jesus After 2000 Years: What He Really Said and Did.* Amherst, NY: Prometheus Books, 2001.

Maier, Gerhard. *Mensch und freier Wille: Nach den jüdischen Religionsparteien zwischen Ben Sira und Paulus.* WUNT 12. Tübingen: Mohr Siebeck, 1971.

Malbon, Elizabeth Struthers. "Narrative Criticism: How Does the Story Mean." Pages 24–49 in *Mark & Method: New Approaches in Biblical Studies.* Edited by Janice Capel Anderson and Stephen D. Moore. Minneapolis: Fortress Press, 1992.

Manson, Thomas W. *The Teaching of Jesus: Studies of Its Form and Contents.* Cambridge: Cambridge University Press, 1939.

Marguerat, Daniel, and Yvan Bourquin. *How to Read Bible Stories: An Introduction to Narrative Criticism.* London: SCM, 1999.

Marshall, I. Howard. *The Gospel of Luke. A Commentary on the Greek Text.* NIGTC 3. Grand Rapids: Eerdmans, 1978.

Mathewson, Dave L. "The Parable of the Unjust Steward (Luke 16:1-13): A Reexamination of the Traditional View in Light of Recent Challenges." *JETS* 38 (1995): 29–39.

Mattill, A. J. "The Good Samaritan and the Purpose of Luke-Acts: Halévy Reconsidered," *Encounter* 33 (1972): 359–76.

McDonald, J. Ian H. "Alien Grace (Luke 10:30-36)." Pages 35–51 in *Jesus and his Parables: Interpreting the Parables of Jesus Today*. Edited by V. George Schillington. Edinburgh: T & T Clark, 1997.

Merenlahti, Petri. *Poetics for the Gospels? Rethinking Narrative Criticism*. London: T & T Clark, 2002.

Merz, Annette. "Einleitung." Pages 513–17 in *Kompendium der Gleichnisse Jesu* (2007).

———. "Freundschaft verplichtet (Vom bittenden Freund)." Pages 556–63 in *Kompendium der Gleichnisse Jesu* (2007).

———. "Die Stärke der Schwachen (Von der bittenden Witwe)." Pages 667–80 in *Kompendium der Gleichnisse Jesu* (2007).

———. "Last und Freude des Kehrens (Von der verlorenen Drachme)." Pages 610–17 in *Kompendium der Gleichnisse Jesu* (2007).

Milavec, Aaron. "A Fresh Analysis of the Parable of the Wicked Husbandmen in the Light of Jewish-Christian Dialogue." Pages 81–117 in *Parable and Story in Judaism and Christianity*. Edited by C. Thoma and M. Wyschogrod. SJC. New York: Paulist Press, 1989.

Newell, Jane E., and Raymond R. Newell. "The Parable of the Wicked Tenants." *NovT* 14 (1972): 226–37.

Niebuhr, Karl-Wilhelm. "Kommunikationsebenen im Gleichnis vom Verlorenen Sohn." *TLZ* 116 (1991): 481–94.

Nolland, John. *Luke 1:1–9:20*. WBC 35A. Dallas: Word Books, 1989.

———. *Luke 9:21–18:34*. WBC 35B. Dallas: Word Books, 1993.

———. *Luke 18:35–24:53*. WBC 35C. Dallas: Word Books, 2002 [1993].

Noyen, Carlos. "Teilt meine Freude: Exegetische Randbemerkungen zu Lukas 15,11-32." *Internationale katholische Zeitschrift* 22 (1993): 387–96.

O'Banion, John D. "Narration and Argumentation: Quintilian on *Narratio* as the Heart of Rhetorical Thinking." *Rhetorica* 5 (1987): 325–51.

Oldenhage, Tania. "Spiralen der Gewalt (Die böse Winzer) Mk 12,1-12." Pages 352–66 in *Kompendium der Gleichnisse Jesu* (2007).

Ollilainen, Vesa. *Jesus and the Parable of the Prodigal Son*. Ph.D. diss. Åbo: Åbo Akademi University, 2008.

Ostmeyer, Karl-Heinrich. "Dabeisein ist alles (Der verlorene Sohn) Lk 15,11-32." Pages 518–33 in *Kompendium der Gleichnisse Jesu* (2007).

Paliard, Charles. *Lire l'Ecriture, ecouter la Parole: La parabole de l'econome infidele*. Lire la Bible 53. Paris: Cerf, 1980.

Parrott, Douglas. "The Dishonest Steward (Luke 16.1-8a) and Luke's Special Parable Collection." *NTS* 37: (1991): 499–515.

Perelman, Chaïm, and Lucie Olbrechts-Tyteca. *The New Rhetoric: A Treatise on Argumentation*. Notre Dame, in: University of Notre Dame Press, 1969.

Piper, John. *'Love Your Enemies': Jesus' Love Command in the Synoptic Gospels and in the Early Christian Paraenesis*. SNTSMS 28. Cambridge: Cambridge University Press, 1979.

Popkes, Enno Edzard. "Das Auge als Lampe des Körpers (Vom Auge als des Leibes Licht)." Pages 143–47 in *Kompendium der Gleichnisse Jesu* (2007).

Porter, Stanley. "The Parable of the Unjust Steward (Luke 16:1-13): Irony *is* the Key." Pages 127–53 in *The Bible in Three Dimensions*. Edited by David J. A. Clines, et al. Sheffield: JSOT Press, 1990.

Powell, Mark Allan. *What Is Narrative Criticism?* Minneapolis: Fortress Press, 1990.

_____. *Chasingthe Eastern Star: Adventures in Biblical Reader-Response Criticism*. Louisville: Westminster John Knox, 2001.

Prince, Gerald. "Narratology." Pages 524–28 in *The Johns Hopkins Guide to Literary Theory and Criticism*. Edited by Michael Groden and Martin Kreiswirth. Baltimore: Johns Hopkins University Press, 1994.

Räisänen, Heikki. "The Prodigal Gentile and His Jewish Christian Brother: Lk 15,11-32." Pages 1617–36 in *The Four Gospels*. FS Frans Neirynck. Vol. 2. BETL 100b. Edited by Frans van Segbroeck, et al. Leuven: Leuven University Press, 1992.

Rau, Eckhard. "Jesu Auseinandersetzung mit Pharisäern über seine Zuwendung zu Sünderinnen und Sündern. Lk 15,11-32 und Lk 18,10-14a als Worte des historischen Jesus." *ZNW* 89 (1998): 5–29.

Reinmuth, Eckart. "Der beschuldigte Verwalter (Vom ungetreuen Haushalter) Lk 16,1-8." Pages 634–46 in *Kompendium der Gleichnisse Jesu* (2007).

Resseguie, James L. *Narrative Criticism of the New Testament: An Introduction*. Grand Rapids: Baker Academic, 2005.

Rhoads, David, Joanna Dewey, and Donald Michie. *Markas Story—An Introduction to the Narrative of a Gospel*. 2d ed. Philadelphia: Fortress Press, 1999.

Rhoads, David, and Kari Syreeni. *Characterizationin the Gospels: Reconceiving Narrative Criticism*. Edinburgh: T & T Clark, 2004.

Richards, Ivor Armstrong. *The Philosophy of Rhetoric*. London: Oxford University Press, 1936.

Ricoeur, Paul. *Time and Narrative*. Vol. 1. Translated by Kathleen McLaughlin and David Pellauer. Chicago: University of Chicago Press, 1984.

Robbins, Vernon K. "The Social Location of the Implied Author of Luke-Acts." Pages 305–32 in *The Social World of Luke-Acts: Models for Interpretation*. Edited by Jerome H. Neyrey. Peabody, MA: Hendrickson, 1991.

Robertson, D. W., Jr. "A Note on the Classical Origin of 'Circumstances' in the Medieval Confessional." *Studies in Philology* 4 (1946): 6–14.

Roose, Hanna. "Vom Rollenwechsel des Gläubigers (Von den zwei ungleichen Schuldnern)." Pages 532–37 in *Kompendium der Gleichnisse Jesu* (2007).

Schellenberg, Ryan S. "Which Master? Whose Steward? Metalepsis and Lordship in the Parable of the Prudent Steward (Lk. 16.1-13)." *JSNT* 30 (2008): 263–88.

Schottroff, Luise. *Die Gleichnisse Jesu*. Gütersloh: Gütersloher Verlagshaus, 2005.

Schürer, Emil. *The History of the Jewish People in the Age of Jesus Christ*. Vol. 1. Revised and edited by Geza Vermes, Fergus Millar, and Matthew Black. Edinburgh: T & T Clark, 1973.

Schürmann, Heinz. "Zur Traditionsgeschichte der Nazareth-Perikope Lk 4, 16-30." Pages 187–205 in *Mélanges bibliques*. FS Béda Rigaux. Edited by Albert-Louis Descamps and André de Halleux. Gembloux: Duculot, 1970.

Scott, Bernard Brandon. *Hear Then the Parable: A Commentary on the Parables of Jesus*. Minneapolis: Fortress Press, 1989.

Searle, Leroy. "New Criticism." Pages 691–98 in *The Johns Hopkins Guide to Literary Theory*. 2d ed. Edited by Michael Groden, Martin Kreiswirth, and Imre Szeman. Baltimore: Johns Hopkins University Press, 2005.

Segal, Erwin M. "A Cognitive-Phenomenological Theory of Fictional Narrative." Pages 61–78 in *Deixis in Narrative: A Cognitive Science Perspective*. Edited by Judith F. Duchan, Gail A. Bruder, and Lynne E. Hewitt. Hillsdale, NJ: Lawrence Erlbaum, 1995.

Sellin, Gerhard. "Lukas als Gleichniserzähler." *ZNW* 66 (1975): 19–60.

Siegert, Folker. *Argumentation bei Paulus gezeigt an Röm 9–11*. WUNT 34. Tübingen: Mohr Siebeck, 1984.

Skinner, Christopher W., ed. *Characters and Characterization in the Gospel of John*. Library of New Testament Studies. London: Bloomsbury, 2013.

Sloane, Thomas O. "Rhetoric." Pages 15: 798–803 in *Encyclopaedia Britannica*. 15th ed. Chicago and London: Encyclopaedia Britannica, 1974.

Snodgrass Klyne R. "From Allegorizing to Allegorizing." Pages 3–29 in *The Challenge of Jesus' Parables*. Edited by Richard N. Longenecker. Grand Rapids: Eerdmans, 2000.

_____. *Stories with Intent—A Comprehensive Guide to the Parables of Jesus*. Grand Rapids: Eerdmans, 2008.

Standhartinger, Angela. "Einssein an Gottes Brust (Stillkinder)." Pages 883–87 in *Kompendium der Gleichnisse Jesu* (2007).

Starnitzke, Dierk. "Von den Früchten des Bäumes und dem Sprechen des Herzens (Vom Baum und seinen Früchten). Pages 81–91 in *Kompendium der Gleichnisse Jesu* (2007).

Stibbe, Mark W. G. *John as Storyteller: Narrative Criticism and the Fourth Gospel*. SNTSMS 73. Cambridge: Cambridge University Press, 1992.

Tannehill, Robert C. *The Sword of His Mouth*. Semeia Supplements 1. Philadelphia: Fortress Press, 1975.

_____. "Varieties of Synoptic Pronouncement Stories." *Semeia* 20 (1981): 101–20.

_____. *The Narrative Unity of Luke-Acts. A Literary Interpretation*. Vol. 1: *The Gospel According to Luke*. Philadelphia: Fortress Press, 1986.

Thurén, Lauri. *The Rhetorical Strategy of 1 Peter; With Special Regard to Ambiguous Expressions*. Ph. D. diss. Åbo: Åbo Academy Press, 1990.

_____. *Argument and Theology in 1 Peter: The Origins of Christian Paraenesis*. JSNTSup 114. Sheffield: Sheffield Academic Press, 1995.

_____. "Is There Biblical Argumentation?" Pages 77–92 in *Rhetorical Argumentation in Biblical Texts*. Edited by Anders Eriksson, et al. Harrisburg, PA: Trinity Press International, 2002.

———. "Rhetoric and Argumentation in the Letters of Paul. *Oxford Handbook of Pauline Studies*. Edited by R. Barry Matlock. Oxford: Oxford University Press [forthcoming].

Tolbert, Mary Ann. *Perspectives on the Parables*. Philadelphia: Fortress Press, 1979.

Toulmin, Stephen Edelston. *The Uses of Argument*. Cambridge: Cambridge University Press, 1958.

———, et al. *An Introduction to Reasoning*. 2d ed. New York: Macmillan, 1984.

Trudinger, Paul. "Exposing the Depth of Oppression (Luke 16:1b–8a): The Parable of the Unjust Steward." Pages 121–37 in *Jesus and His Parables*. Edited by V. George Schillington. Edinburgh: T & T Clark, 1997.

Turrettini, Jean Alphonse. *De Sacrae Scripturae interpretatione tractatus bipartitus* [1728]. Whitefish: Kessinger, 2009.

Van der Watt, Jan. "Der Meisterschüler Gottes (Von der Lehre des Sohnes)." Pages 745–54 in *Kompendium der Gleichnisse Jesu* (2007).

Via, Dan Otto, Jr. *The Parables: Their Literary and Existential Dimension*. Philadelphia: Fortress Press, 1967.

Wailes, Stephen L. *Medieval Allegories of Jesus' Parables*. Berkeley: University of California Press, 1987.

Wilder, Amos N. *The Language of the Gospel: Early Christian Rhetoric*. Rev. ed. New York: Harper & Row, 1971.

Wimsatt, William, and Monroe C. Beardsley. "The Intentional Fallacy." *Sewanee Review* 54 (1946): 468–88.

Wolter, Michael. "Lk 15 als Streitgespräch." *ETL* 78 (2002): 25–56.

Wright, N. Thomas. *Jesus and the Victory of God*. Vol. 2. of *Christian Origins and the Question of God*. Minneapolis: Fortress Press, 1996.

Wright, Stephen Irwin. "Parables on Poverty and Riches (Luke 12:13–21; 16:1–13; 16:19–31)." Pages 217–39 in *The Challenge of Jesus' Parables*. Edited by Richard N. Longenecker. Grand Rapids: Eerdmans, 2000.

Zimmermann, Ruben. "Die Gleichnisse Jesu—eine Hinfügung." Pages 3–46 in *Kompendium der Gleichnisse Jesu* (2007).

———. "Folgenreiche Bitte! (Arbeiter für die Ernte)." Pages 111–18 in *Kompendium der Gleichnisse Jesu* (2007).

———. "Berührende Liebe Lk 10:30-35." Pages 538–88 in *Kompendium der Gleichnisse Jesu* (2007).

———. "How to Understand the Parables of Jesus: A Paradigm Shift in Parable Exegesis." *Acta Theologica* 29 (2009): 157–82.

———. *How to Understand the Parables of Jesus. A Postmodern Hermeneutic and Methodological Guideline for Parable Exegesis*. Minneapolis: Fortress Press [forthcoming].

———, ed. *Kompendium der Gleichnisse Jesu*. Gütersloh: Gütersloher Verlagshaus, 2007.

Zymner, Rüdiger. *Uneigentlichkeit. Studien zu Semantik und Geschichte der Parabel*. Paderborn: Schöningh, 1991.

———. "Parabel." Pages 502–14 in *Historisches Wörterbuch der Rhetorik*. Edited by Gerd Ueding. Vol. 6. Tübingen: Niemeyer, 2003.

Index of Names

Aharoni, Yohanan, 62
Albertz, Martin, 80

Baergen, Rene A., 146
Bailey, Kenneth E., 57, 60–61, 65, 73, 79, 92, 112, 117–18, 123, 137, 288
Bailey, Mark L.,18, 36–37
Bar-Efrat, Shimon, 16, 28
Barthes, Roland, 7
Bauckham, Rickhard, 64–65
Baulder, Georg, 123
Beardsley, Monroe C., 7, 28, 80
Beavis, Mary Ann, 44, 81, 115, 118
Berger, Klaus, 80
Berlin, Adele, 28
Blomberg, Craig, 16, 55, 78–79
Booth, Wayne C., 8, 27– 28
Bourquin, Yvan, 211
Bovon, François, 4, 77–78
Braun, Herbert, 56

Brown, Colin, 16, 77–78, 123, 130
Bruner, Jerome, 28
Bultmann, Rudolf, 80, 107, 279
Burke, Kenneth A., 61
Burnett, Fred W., 211
Burton, David J., 62
Burton, Gideon O., 224

Campbell, Joseph, 134
Chatman, Seymour, 27– 28
Clines, David J. A., 60
Cortazzi, Martin, 28
Creed, John Martin, 189
Crespy, Georges, 56
Crossan, John Dominick, 53, 161
Culpepper, R. Alan, 16, 27

Degenhardt, Joachim, 125
Derrett, J. Duncan M., 116
Dewey, Joanna, 16, 27–28
Dodd, Charles Harold, 184
Donahue, John R., 111, 118

Dronsch, Kristina, 279, 282
Drury, John, 20, 26, 78, 183, 189–90, 245–46, 262, 264, 266, 273, 322, 329
Dunn, James D. G., 4, 161
Dupont, Jaques, 264

Eco, Umberto, 9
Eemeren, Frans H. van, 13, 30, 32
Esch-Wermeling, Elisabeth, 255, 260
Esler, Philip F., 58–59, 61, 63, 66
Evans, Craig A., 151, 156, 160–61

Finnern, Sönke, 27–28
Fitzmyer, Joseph A., 116
Fletcher, Donald R., 116
Fludernik, Monika, 5, 28, 252
Flusser, David, 119, 122
Forbes, Greg W., 23–24, 57, 60, 85, 181, 239, 348
Foster, Edward Morgan, 28
Funk, Robert Walter, 16, 60–62

Genette, Gérard, 17, 27
Gerber, Christine, 301
Gerhardsson, Birger, 53
Gerwing, Walter, 45
Good, R. S., 264
Gowler, David B., 16
Gray, Arthur, 159

Harnisch, Wolfgang, 18, 80, 92, 95, 101
Harrill, James Albert, 79
Hartman, Lars, 4
Hawkes, Terence, 7
Hedrick, Charles W., 9, 16, 18, 53–54, 60–62, 185–87, 194, 207, 252, 279, 296, 334–36
Hengel, Martin, 154, 161
Hester, J. David, 151
Hietanen, Mika, 13
Hogan, Patrick Colm, 252
Hoppe, Rudolf, 79
Hoy, David Couzens, 8
Hultgren, Arland J., 23, 78, 80, 85, 87, 92–93, 96, 100, 124
Hunzinger, Claus-Hunno, 320

Ireland, Dennis J., 3, 107, 109, 115–16
Iser, Wolfgang, 8, 27

Jakobson, Roman, 8
Jancovich, Mark, 7
Jefferson, Ann, 42
Jeremias, Joachim, 4, 28, 57, 62, 82, 87, 110–12, 150, 161, 329
Jülicher, Adolf, 14–16, 21, 60, 84, 110, 367

Kamlah, Ehrhard, 123
Keesmaat, Sylvia C., 57–58, 68
Kennedy, George A., 12, 96
Kern, Gabi, 262, 270
Klawans, Jonathan, 65
Klein, Hans, 45
Kloppenborg, John S., 110, 112, 117–18, 151, 160
Krämer, Michael, 109

Labahn, Michael, 188, 291
Landry, David, 107, 109, 111–12, 116, 119, 138
Lausberg, Heinrich, 85, 90, 98, 101, 109, 115–16, 118, 120, 321, 338
Leonhardt-Balzer, Jutta, 329, 330
Loader, William, 123, 125, 128, 130
Louw, Johannes, 320
Lowe, Malcolm, 159–160
Lüdemann, Gerd, 96

Maier, Gerhard, 45
Malbon, Elizabeth, 28
Manson, Thomas W., 184
Marguerat, Daniel, 211
Marshall, Ian Howard, 45
Mathewson, Dave L., 125
Mattill, A. J., 53

May, Ben, 107, 109, 111–12, 116, 119, 138
McDonald, J. Ian H., 61, 67
Merenlahti, Petri, 17
Merz, Annette, 5, 80, 85, 183, 244–45, 287, 334
Michie, Donald, 16, 27–28
Milavec, Aaron, 154

Newell, Jane E., 151, 156
Newell, Raymond R., 151, 156
Niebuhr, Karl-Wilhelm, 78
Nolland, John, 23–24, 45, 53, 57, 60–61, 64, 66–68, 73, 78–79, 81–82, 84–87, 92–93, 103, 111, 112–13, 116–17, 123, 128, 132, 138, 142, 150, 158, 162, 167–68, 173, 234, 255–56, 258, 262, 264, 266, 268–69, 272, 274–275, 279–280, 283–284, 287, 290, 292, 294–95, 301, 303–4, 307, 308, 310, 312, 314, 322, 329–30, 332, 336, 341, 345
Noyen, Carlos, 95

O'Banion, John D., 115
Oldenhage, Tania, 150–51
Ollilainen, Vesa, 78, 94
Ostmeyer, Karl-Heinrich, 78–79

Paliard, Charles, 123
Parrott, Douglas, 115
Perelman, Chaïm, 13, 82
Piper, John, 72
Popkes, Enno Edzard, 294
Porter, Stenley E., 116
Powell, Mark Allan, 16, 25, 28, 41, 56
Prince, Gerald, 28, 42

Räisänen, Heikki, 78, 82, 97
Rau, Eckhard, 16, 81
Reinmuth, Eckart, 123–24, 126, 128, 134, 145–46
Resseguie, James L., 211
Rhoads, David, 16, 27–28
Richards, Ivor Armstrong, 7
Ricoeur, Paul, 17, 34
Robbins, Vernon K., 23
Robertson, D. W., Jr., 34
Robey, David, 42
Roose, Hanna, 278

Schellenberg, Ryan S., 107, 110–12, 114, 122–23, 128, 131, 135–36, 139, 143
Schottroff, Luise, 151
Schürer, Emil, 150
Schürmann, Heinz, 257
Scott, Bernard Brandon, 6, 16, 64, 120, 138, 151

Searle, Leroy, 7
Segal, Erwin M., 26, 153, 341, 361
Sellin, Gerhard, 53
Siegert, Folker, 13
Skinner, Christopher, 211
Sloane, Thomas O., 27, 28, 146
Snodgrass, Klyne R., 3, 5, 10, 15, 18, 29, 37, 41, 53, 59, 62–66, 73, 78, 83, 85, 87–88, 107, 109–11, 113–14, 116–18, 121, 124–26, 132, 146, 150, 152, 154, 160, 163, 165, 184, 188, 200, 255, 274, 277–80, 287, 296, 304, 307, 310–12, 317, 320, 329, 332, 334, 336, 340
Standhartinger, Angela, 188
Starnitzke, Dierk, 272
Stibbe, Mark W. G., 18
Syreeni, Kari, 16

Tannehill, Robert C., 16, 83, 267
Thurén, Lauri, 13, 29–31, 43, 74, 85, 101, 111
Tolbert, Mary Ann, 121
Toulmin, Stphen Edelston, 13, 16, 30–33, 57, 88, 104, 167, 170, 240, 252–53, 255, 276, 337, 348
Trudinger, Paul, 116
Turrettini, Jean Alphonse, 6–7

Van der Watt, Jan, 185, 209, 284
Via, Dan Otto, Jr., 4, 9, 77, 116

Wailes, Stephen L., 119
Wilder, Amos, 17
Wimsatt, William, 7, 28, 80
Wolter, Michael, 17, 80, 87, 92, 96
Wright, Nigel Thomas, 115

Wright, Stephen Irwin, 117, 121, 128

Zimmermann, Ruben, 3–4, 7, 17–18, 38–40, 53, 64, 73, 75, 187–89, 255, 283
Zymner, Rüdiger, 16–17, 187

Index of Subjects

Abraham, son of, 90, 103
Ad hoc, 58, 66, 132
Additions to the parables, 9, 37, 43, 45, 62, 123, 246, 273–74, 283, 340, 375
Addressees, *see* Audience
Afterlife, 46–47, 331, 339, 365
Aggression, 155, 157, 159
Agriculture, 207, 209–10, 214, 229, 265, 271, 279–80, 283, 291, 295, 309, 310, 325–26, 343
Alienation, 43, 363
Allegory, 5, 11, 14–22, 28, 35, 40, 47, 70, 78–79, 84, 86, 97, 110, 119, 123, 125, 127, 129, 132, 144, 152–53, 156, 159, 161, 164–66, 170–71, 176–77, 211, 240, 245–46, 251, 260–265, 273, 277, 279–83, 290, 302, 307–8, 310, 312, 316–17, 322,
328, 335, 337, 340–44, 362–63, 368, 371–74
Alpha privativum, 117
Ambiguity, 7, 18, 97, 99, 111, 161, 272
Ambivalent, 19, 210
Anachronistic, 19, 30, 41, 152, 166–67, 175, 268, 270, 306, 360, 362, 368
Analogy, 21, 22, 60, 130, 184, 189
Anti-Semitic (anti-Jewish), 150–51, 154, 177, 343, 368
Antipas, *see* Herod Antipas
Aphorism, 185, 186
Apocalyptic, 161, 187–88
Apostle, 145, 147, 162, 165, 216
Appeal, 17, 36, 37, 93, 102–3, 140–41, 176–77, 188, 216, 255, 358, 366, 369, 371
Aramaic original, 115, 279
Archelaus, *see* Herod Archelaus

Aretas IV, 25, 321
Argumentation, 14, 16, 20, 29, 30–32, 43, 46–47, 61, 65–67, 70, 82, 85, 101, 103, 170, 208, 253–254, 279, 311, 347, 362, 376
Argumentation analysis, 13, 30, 49, 98, 167, 175, 240–41, 244, 246, 251–52, 275, 348, 369, 372; *see also* Toulmin's model
Aristotle, on argumentation, 13, 30, 43
Attitude, 4, 12, 14, 24, 41, 48, 67, 71–73, 82–84, 88, 93, 96–97, 100–1, 104, 108–10, 122, 124, 151, 154, 161, 168, 184, 188, 209, 253, 313, 323, 325, 336, 354
Audience, see recipients
Author, 4–5, 10, 16, 19, 26–29, 38, 40, 46, 59, 61, 65, 71, 120, 124, 128, 135–36, 153, 157, 158, 169, 172, 194, 224, 246, 264, 322, 334, 347, 361; historical, 7–8, 17, 25, 27, 39, 80, 181; implied, 7–9, 17, 23–25, 34, 39, 49, 56; Luke the, 4, 19, 25, 27, 61, 153, 194, 224, 361
Authority, of God, 95, 139, 143; of Jesus, 45, 95, 143, 154, 159, 166, 169, 170, 173–77, 258, 331, 343, 344, 348, 352, 358, 365–66; of John the Baptist, 159–161, 164, 169, 172–77, 343–44, 348, 352, 366
Autobiography, 123, 125, 126, 129
Axiomatical interpretation, 8, 21, 34, 42, 49, 60, 72, 81, 84, 93, 150–51, 166, 170, 175, 260–62, 343, 360, 367–69

Backing, see Toulmin's analysis
Beelzebul, 290–91, 352–53
Big Data, 182
Blasphemy, 21, 86, 87, 142, 335
Breviloquium, 132

Catch-22, 169
Character, in parables, 8, 12, 17, 19–28, 35, 37–38, 44, 49, 58, 60, 62–68, 70, 79, 83, 90–91, 96, 101–2, 110, 118, 121, 125-26, 134, 155-56, 159, 164-65, 189, 194, 197–98, 200, 202, 204, 208–13, 220–21, 225, 231–34, 236–39, 242–44, 246, 252, 336, 340, 343, 358, 361–62, 364, 372
Characterization, 182–83, 201–2, 241, 245, 342
Christianity, 4, 79, 108, 113, 121, 146, 151, 264, 368, 372

Christology, 95, 161, 209, 347, 360, 368
Church, 10, 74, 77–78, 153, 264, 268, 270, 306, 307, 312, 340, 358, 363–64
Claim, *see* Toulmin's analysis
Complexity, 5, 91, 107, 120, 254, 285, 316, 329, 343, 348–49, 367, 373
Condemnation, 90, 143
Context, 4–5, 7, 9, 11–12, 16, 19–21, 27, 34, 40–41, 43–45, 48, 68, 71, 74, 78–79, 96, 101, 105, 113, 119, 123–25, 127–31, 141, 146, 154, 156, 159, 163, 165–67, 169, 171–72, 176–77, 216, 238, 240–41, 246, 249, 251, 256, 267–68, 269–70, 272, 283–84, 290, 292, 295, 303, 319, 341, 343, 360–61, 363, 367–68, 371, 373, 375–376
Convince, 11, 72, 102, 111, 125, 130, 169, 184–85, 188, 251, 252–53, 317, 343
Counter-parable, 257
Counterarguments, 160
Credibility of the parables, 49, 151, 181, 224–25, 228, 231, 233–34, 236–38, 241–42, 244, 247–248, 253, 349, 352, 355, 357–59, 364

Cultural, 3, 15, 24, 26, 41, 43, 45, 48, 59, 101, 141, 152, 312

Data, *see* Toulmin's analysis
David, king, 15, 22, 26
De-allegorize, 156
Demonstration, 11, 28, 129, 135, 161, 247, 271–72, 317, 367
Denigrate, 59, 97, 336
Detheologization, 207, 364
Doctrine, 77, 106, 212, 336, 347
Dogmatic, 78, 80–81, 94–95, 213

Early Church, 78, 113, 107, 146, 147, 251, 363
Early Fathers, 55, 59, 362
Early Judaism, 24, 40, 55, 58, 60, 64–65, 74, 78, 86, 92, 142, 146, 161, 245, 360
Ecclesiastes, 86
Egyptian, 284
Emotion, 8, 13, 50, 64, 69, 70–71, 83, 91, 104, 127, 133–134, 141, 169, 176, 213–15, 234, 235, 238, 252, 254, 285–86, 318, 287, 325, 332, 358, 366, 369, 371
Epideictic, *see* Rhetorical genre
Escalation, 151, 167, 236
Eschatology, 100, 110, 114–15, 129, 131–32, 134, 142, 245,

274, 283, 303, 306, 334, 347, 360–62
Ethics, 3, 12, 13, 20, 53–55, 68, 72–74, 78, 110, 121, 136, 151, 165, 239, 287, 349, 350, 363, 371
Ethnicity, 58, 59, 61, 78
Ethos, *see* Rhetorical dimension
Ex eventu, 166
Exaggeration, *see* hyperbole
Exhortation, 59, 67, 122, 126, 130, 135, 145, 185, 186, 227, 229, 256, 269, 270, 276, 283, 295, 307, 312, 316, 330, 332, 349, 358
Exigency, 4, 9, 11, 34, 96, 181, 216, 219, 222, 225, 227, 236, 238, 242, 251, 263, 265, 267, 269, 270–71, 274, 277, 279, 281, 287, 288, 290–91, 293–94, 296, 298, 300, 303, 308, 320–21, 328–29, 332, 334, 336–37, 340–41, 343, 345
Exordium, 96
Expert in Law, Jewish, 31, 54–72, 75, 217, 253
Extended rule, *see* Parable types
External information, 7–9, 11, 17, 20, 24–26, 42–43, 54, 63, 97, 121, 146, 149, 152, 159, 167, 175, 246, 275, 279, 308, 343, 368

Fairytales, 26, 41, 62
Fault-proof, 183
Fault-tolerant, 183, 241
Feeling, *see* emotion
Fiction, 14, 16, 20, 46, 59–60, 66, 118, 126, 184–85, 187–88, 202, 204, 205
Five W's, 34
Forgiveness, 74, 124, 129–32, 136, 141–43, 159, 245, 278, 327, 355, 366
Framework Story, 4, 9–10, 12, 17–23, 27, 34, 35, 39, 44–45, 47, 49, 54–59, 62–65, 69, 73, 78–80, 82–85, 90–91, 94–97, 99, 102–3, 109, 116, 119, 122, 129, 152, 157, 159, 173, 176, 194, 216, 261, 357, 363
Function of the parables, 4–5, 7–9, 11–17, 19, 24, 27–29, 34–37, 39, 42, 44, 46–50, 53–56, 59, 65, 74– 75, 79–80, 86, 91, 106, 108, 120, 125, 127–28, 132, 135–136, 156, 158–59, 163, 166–67, 170, 176, 182, 184–85, 190, 209, 216, 219, 231, 238, 251, 254–56, 265, 268, 275,

280, 292, 302, 317, 331, 340–41, 353, 367–68, 370–73, 375–76

Galilee, 25, 151, 175, 184, 283, 340
Gentiles, 58, 69, 139, 145, 153, 317, 319, 360
Gentile Christians, 97, 152, 360, 363
God's demands, 355–58, 366
God's forgiveness, 74, 132, 136, 143, 278
God's love, 73, 87–88, 354–55, 366
God's will, 305–6, 326, 351, 357, 366
Gospel of Thomas, 150, 188, 328, 374
Grace, 123, 319
Guidelines, 12, 22, 36, 49, 55, 108, 185, 186

Hades, 155, 168
Halakhic, 64, 65
Hellenistic, 24
Hermeneutics, 7, 37, 40, 42, 45, 49, 78, 154, 254, 361, 368
Herod Antipas, 25, 150, 160, 162–64, 321, 340–41
Herod Archelaus, 341

Heuristic, 182
High priests, 4, 73, 77, 90, 95, 107, 110, 112, 117, 119, 121, 136, 139, 159, 168, 170, 173, 209, 217, 219, 220, 224, 231, 238, 290, 293, 332, 337, 342, 357, 364
Historical research of the parables, 4–81, 97, 103, 106–7, 109, 113, 115–18, 128, 149–51, 153, 166, 181, 187, 189, 194, 211, 293, 321, 343, 347, 358, 361, 367–68, 372–76
Household, 79, 103, 208, 212, 273–74, 289, 290, 292–94, 303
Humiliation, 101, 102, 314
Hyperbole, 83, 93, 100, 102, 120, 280, 283, 287, 304, 318, 340, 369
Hypocrisy, 272

Identity, 58–64, 69, 96, 157, 268, 332
Ideology, 5, 16, 23, 27, 54, 78–79, 156, 176, 211
Idiosyncratic, 184
Illegal, 44, 109–10, 116, 135, 137, 144
Illogical, 114, 224
Immorality, 90, 107, 110, 120, 134, 136, 140, 141, 246, 296

Implied audience, hearers, recipients, readers, addressees, *see* recipients
Inclusio, 159, 176
Inherent, 8, 36, 44, 80, 93, 115, 127, 252, 274, 318
Intentional fallacy, 17, 27–28, 37–38, 59, 80
Interaction, 8–10, 17, 19, 40, 49, 81, 89, 252, 375
Intertextual, 20, 85, 149, 165, 245–46, 286, 369
Irony, 101, 116, 123, 137, 143, 371
Isaiah, 355
Israel, 85, 115, 150, 152, 158, 165, 273, 290, 310, 317, 319, 344, 360, 366, 372
Ius talionis, 266
Iustificatio impii, 142

Jericho, 53, 60, 62, 285
Jerusalem, 53, 60, 65, 131, 145, 150, 151, 153, 155, 156, 158–59, 163, 165–66, 175, 177, 285, 289, 340–41, 360–61, 368, 372
Jesus, historical, 4–5, 8, 17, 23, 35, 38–39, 42, 46, 48, 54, 78, 80, 106, 113, 368, 374, 376

Jesus' theology (Lukan), 9, 35, 44, 79, 126, 137, 140, 143, 224, 360, 364–66, 374
Jewish, 15, 18, 21, 40, 43, 46, 53, 55, 60, 64–65, 68, 72, 74, 79, 81, 83, 86, 92, 96–97, 141, 152–54, 156, 212, 245, 266, 268, 360, 363, 372, 375
Job, 60, 86
Johannine, 209, 284
John the Baptist, 159–77, 245, 255, 262–63, 275–77, 284, 292, 331, 343–44, 352, 357, 366
Jonah, 187
Jubilee program, 131–32, 140–44, 135, 143, 169, 176, 319, 352–53, 365
Judaism (general), 20, 23–24, 151–152, 154, 264, 368; *see also* Early Judaism
Judicial, *see* Rhetorical genre
Justification, 73, 141–42, 145, 147, 156, 169, 213, 336, 358
Jülicher's model, 14, 15, 16, 21, 60, 84, 110, 367

Kingdom, 36, 37, 152, 240–41, 244, 279, 282–83, 311–12, 317, 319, 333, 337, 341–42, 372

L-parables, 23, 181, 202, 247, 277

INDEX OF SUBJECTS

Law, 54–55, 64–65, 68, 79, 142–44, 147, 162–63, 217
Layman, 53, 57
Lazarus, 13, 132, 167, 193, 196, 199, 206, 212, 215, 223, 235, 328–29, 336, 339, 367
Legitimacy, 65, 169, 176, 358, 365
Levite, 63–64, 68–70, 118, 213
Linguistic, 25, 29, 38
Literary perspective, 5–6, 8, 16–19, 23, 27, 42, 45, 48, 63, 80, 116, 188, 283, 360
Logic, 30, 47, 57, 70, 74, 93, 143, 212, 234, 268, 317
Logos, *see* Rhetorical dimension
Love, 57–59, 62, 69, 70–75, 86–88, 93, 103–4, 131, 139, 144, 278, 286, 318, 326, 331, 348–49, 351, 354–55, 358, 366
Luke, *see* Author
Luke's theology, 35, 106, 181, 245
LXX, 130

Magnificat, 122
Mammon, 135, 328, 351
Manipulation, 24, 115, 375
Master-character, 108–147, 155–56, 169–71, 173, 177, 208–12, 218–21, 229, 234, 236–39, 244, 277, 290–91, 300–19, 325, 327–28, 332, 334, 340–43, 351, 355–56, 358, 361, 364, 366, 369, 372, 374
Master-parables, 209, 211, 213, 219, 236, 303
Messianic, 157, 161, 262–63, 331
Meta-level, 139, 339
Metaphor, 17, 131–32, 152, 155, 183–85, 188–90, 255, 273, 312, 335
Method, 7, 8, 13, 17–18, 22, 30, 38, 43, 49, 63, 154, 156, 252–53, 367
Middle-East, 287
Mina, 13, 197, 199, 210–12, 215, 273, 307, 340, 368
Moral, 84, 90, 97, 100, 107, 110, 116, 119, 121, 136, 184, 295, 350
Moses, 44, 331
Motivation, 64, 132, 141

Narratio, 115
Narrative parables, *see* Parable types
Narrative approach, 5–6, 10, 15–16, 19–29, 34, 38–39, 41–42, 49–50, 54–58, 62, 64–66, 68, 70–71, 73, 77–82, 108–12, 115, 118, 120, 127, 134, 146, 153, 163, 165, 167, 168, 176, 183, 185–90, 197,

403

201–2, 204–5, 211, 214–16, 226, 228, 230, 233–39, 242, 245–46, 248, 252, 255, 259, 261, 273–74, 277, 279–80, 285–86, 290, 295, 300–1, 304, 309, 311, 313, 316, 320, 323–26, 329, 334, 336, 340–41, 361, 363, 366, 368

Narrator, 6, 9–10, 16, 25, 27, 29, 34, 48, 65, 71, 75, 83–85, 91, 93–95, 99, 101–3, 108, 113, 118, 121, 124, 127, 135, 152, 157, 232, 235, 238–39, 264, 275, 315, 347, 368; implied, 48; Jesus the, 4, 6, 19, 27, 60–61, 64, 79, 82, 87, 89, 102, 111–12, 121, 133, 153, 177, 224, 340, 350, 363

Nathan, 15, 26

Nationality, 60–61, 67, 69, 71–72, 286, 351

Natural reading, 5, 28

Nazareth, 6, 8, 23, 130, 176, 189, 217, 255–59, 331, 351–52, 375

Nero, 150, 153

New Criticism 7, 8, 17, 48

Non-allegorical, 150

Non-canonical, 254

Non-case-specific, 253

Non-christian, 360

Non-christological, 156

Non-defensive, 267

Non-eschatological, 361

Non-exclusive, 171

Non-fictional, 185

Non-historical, 190, 255, 371, 373

Non-jewish, 24, 59

Non-orthodox, 20

Non-personal, 212

Non-religious, 362

Non-specific, 135

Noncontroversial, 231

Nonexistent, 186

Obedience, 72, 173, 305–6, 318, 328, 330–31, 349–51, 355, 357

Obscurity, 9, 54, 65, 70, 74, 81, 86, 98, 161, 163, 166, 182, 224, 235, 255, 267, 272, 275, 284, 292, 294, 295, 312, 321, 329, 372

Old Testament, 6, 149, 152, 158, 165, 166, 172, 176, 245, 311, 357, 369

Open-ended argumentation, 31

Opening-middle-end, 187

Opponents of Jesus (adversaries, antagonists), 18, 44–45, 80, 96, 129, 143, 166, 185, 216, 221, 226–227, 229–30, 233, 235, 240–43, 268, 290, 308, 310, 349, 371

INDEX OF SUBJECTS

Overemphasis, 23, 41, 101, 239, 369
Oxymoron, 116, 321

Palestine, 37–42, 48, 85, 87, 280, 283, 303, 321; first century 24–25, 361, 375
Parable, definition, 183–191; 371
Parable types: Simple rules, 108, 115, 121, 184, 186–87, 200–33, 244, 247, 253, 255, 257, 260, 263, 265–71, 274, 279, 281, 284, 289, 293, 297, 300, 303, 307, 317, 321, 328, 333, 337–38, 348, 364–65, 367, 368, 376; Extended rules, 183, 201–35, 255, 261, 274, 280, 283, 288, 290–91, 294, 300–1, 308, 311, 314, 317, 320, 332, 344, 364, 368; Narrative parables, 5, 16–17, 49, 62, 121, 183, 184–86, 201, 204–34, 236–37, 243–44, 246, 253, 310, 343, 354–55, 364, 367, 371–72, 375
Parabolic, 183, 187, 189, 202, 204, 209, 284, 316
Paraenesis, 146, 245
Passivum divinum, 131, 267, 278, 315, 336, 362
Pathos, *see* Rhetorical dimension

Patria potestas, 94
Paul, apostle, 17, 23, 34, 116, 145, 147, 168, 319
Peroratio, 338
Personification, 60–61, 92
Persuasion, 9–11, 14, 21, 33, 43, 56–105, 126, 133–134, 141, 143, 149, 159, 166, 175–76, 184–185, 188, 217, 220, 224, 239, 249, 251–347, 358–67, 369–75
Peter, apostle 150, 163, 303, 304
Pharisee, 6, 13, 17, 35, 42, 48, 62, 67, 77, 79, 80–87, 89, 91–96, 97, 99, 101–3, 105, 122–34, 142–43, 162, 167, 193, 196, 199, 206, 212, 215, 217, 219, 220, 223, 235, 240, 260–65, 270, 274, 277, 284, 288, 315–16, 323–24, 329, 335–38, 362
Plausibility, 16, 40, 128, 160, 228
Poetics, 16, 17, 28, 252
Point of departure, 27, 31, 46, 47, 57, 127, 172, 259–60, 264, 269, 275, 336, 370
Polemical, 360
Polyvalence, 19, 40
Postmodern, 19, 53, 376
Pragma-dialectical, 13, 30
Pragmatic, 38

405

Priest, 61–70, 74, 118, 213
Prodigal Son, 4, 13, 20, 35, 70,
    77–79, 83, 90, 93–94, 103, 105,
    140–41, 193, 196, 199, 200,
    206, 209, 211, 213, 215, 220,
    222, 235, 238, 240, 318, 325,
    329, 331, 353, 355, 362,
    367–69
Prophecy, 155, 158, 175, 177, 262,
    306, 330–31, 361, 373
Prophet, 15, 150, 155, 157,
    162–65, 169, 172–74, 176,
    189–190, 192, 195, 198, 203,
    209, 216, 222, 230, 257–59,
    263, 331, 344, 352, 357, 366
Propositio, 98
Protagonist, 80, 113, 134, 167,
    171, 211, 285, 329, 343, 373,
    375
Pseudonym, 23, 84
Punch line (scopus), 15, 20, 21–22,
    28, 34, 102, 112, 329, 367

Qal wahomer, 21, 67, 72, 75, 86,
    144, 174, 287, 299–300, 307,
    310, 335, 362, 372

Re-plugging, 48, 347, 349, 351,
    353, 355, 357, 359, 360–61,
    363, 365, 367, 370–71, 373,
    376

Reader, see recipients
Reader-response, 17
Rebuttal, *see* Toulmin's analysis
Recipients (audience, hearers,
    readers): implied 8– 9, 17,
    24–28, 34, 38–39, 41, 43, 49,
    54–55, 64, 74, 81, 89, 92, 108,
    111, 128, 137, 141, 146,
    152–53, 163, 165, 167, 175,
    246, 251–53, 312, 328, 375;
    Jesus', 6, 26, 35, 120, 122, 225,
    262, 264, 330, 360, 369, 372;
    Lukan (Luke's), 26, 27, 41,
    55–56, 58–59, 62–68, 72, 75,
    82, 84, 97, 99, 108–9, 117,
    122–23, 128, 132, 134, 138–39,
    141, 145, 152–53, 155–56, 158,
    164–65, 169–70, 172, 176–77,
    181, 259, 262, 283, 319, 321,
    330, 340, 361, 372–73;
    General, 221, 226, 231, 257,
    268, 270, 273, 279, 299, 307,
    308, 310, 321
Redaction criticism, 18, 23, 37, 38,
    245, 376
Refutatio, 98, 101
Repetition, 85, 100
Requirements, 103, 113, 139, 145,
    184, 255, 257, 276, 320, 348,
    355, 357, 366
Retaliation, 164, 168, 171, 173

INDEX OF SUBJECTS

Retelling, 11, 156, 166
Rhetorical approach, 12, 16, 19, 27–30, 34, 48–50, 61, 68, 78, 80–101, 109, 111, 115, 131, 146, 190, 220–21, 224, 226, 229, 232, 234, 238–39, 245, 252, 265–66, 270, 280, 287, 320, 322–24, 332, 338, 365
Rhetorical dimension: ethos 99–100, 343; pathos 10, 50, 56, 70, 85, 94, 99, 103, 239, 252, 254, 343, 369; logos 99, 252
Rhetorical genre, 96; judicial, 96; epideictic, 12
Roman, 62, 109, 115, 301, 341
Rome, 150, 156
Rule of three (regel-de-tri), 28, 62

Sadducees, 11, 14, 40, 44–47, 59, 189
Samaritans, 58, 66, 67, 72, 369
Samuel, 331
Sarcasm, 116, 143,
Satan, 290
Saul, king, 331
Schadenfreude, 330
Scopus, *see* Punch line
Scribes, 6, 17, 35, 62, 79–87, 91–94, 96– 97, 101, 103, 123–24, 126, 128–29, 133, 142, 159, 217, 219–20, 260, 265, 270, 274, 316, 323–24, 366
Scriptures, 40, 60, 85, 92–93, 130, 142–43, 153, 165, 169, 310, 330–31, 365, 369
Semantic, 16, 38, 79, 111, 132, 135
Semitic, 113
Sermocinatio, 101
Sermon on the Plain, 188, 220
Shame, 119, 137, 168, 287–88, 314–15
Sheepowner, 230
Shepherd, 6, 17, 40, 84, 85, 369
Siloam, 131, 184
Simple rule, *see* Parable types
Sinners, 33, 80–81, 84–86, 88–90, 94–96, 103–5, 124–25, 128, 133–34, 141–43, 145, 217, 260–61, 319, 323–26, 358, 365
Socio-historical, 38, 375
Sociocultural, 24
Sodom, 155
Solomon, king, 300
Son of Man, 4, 13, 20, 35, 69, 70, 77–79, 90, 92–94, 96–97, 102–3, 105, 113, 122, 133, 140–41, 144, 147, 150, 153, 155, 157–71, 176, 184, 192–93, 195–96, 199–200, 203, 206, 208–9, 211, 214–15, 220–22, 224, 230, 235, 238–240, 258,

283–85, 303–4, 307, 318, 325–26, 329, 333, 342, 352, 357, 360–62, 366–68
Spirit, 192, 195, 199, 204, 210, 214, 222, 233, 289, 291–92, 331, 353–54
Spiritual, 3, 5, 6, 10, 119, 168, 184, 189, 294–95
Status, rhetorical, 90, 109, 115–16, 118–19,
Stereotypical, 28, 63, 65–66, 68, 97, 100, 177, 211–12, 329
Story-telling, 58, 65, 70, 79, 97, 228, 277, 369, 372–73, 375
Streitgespräch (conflict story), 29, 80, 87, 220
Synoptic comparison, 5, 23, 150, 153, 169, 185, 244–46, 248, 375–76

Tactics, 115, 234
Tax Collectors, 33, 67, 80–81, 84, 86, 88, 94, 103–5, 133, 141, 151, 217, 284, 315, 323, 325–26, 335–38
Theo-logical, 239
Theology, 3–25, 29, 33–56, 60, 69, 72–88, 95–96, 100, 103, 105–6, 109, 123, 126–27, 129, 132, 137, 140, 143–45, 147, 159, 161, 165, 176, 181–82, 184, 212, 224, 240–43, 245, 252, 256, 259, 262, 264, 278, 282–86, 290, 300, 308–9, 313–15, 319–20, 324–27, 330, 336, 347–48, 353–54, 357–58, 360–67, 373–74
Theophilus, 23, 145
Topos, 152, 240
Torah, 57–58, 141–43, 145
Toulmin's analysis, general presentation, 30–33, 88, 170, 253–54, 256; Rebuttal, 31, 32, 88, 98–99, 105, 337; Counter-rebuttal, 105, 322, 338
Toulmin, other references, 16, 30, 33, 57, 59, 71, 88, 98–99, 104–105, 167, 240, 252, 255, 276, 337–38, 348, 364, 369, 370
Traditional interpretation, 5–6, 13, 18, 23, 29, 34, 36, 39, 45–46, 48–49, 54–55, 67, 73, 82, 84, 121, 157, 159, 175, 177, 186, 211, 311, 316, 329, 343, 347, 358, 362, 372
Travel narrative, Lukan, 245, 246
Tree-owner, 310

Unambiguity, 40
Universal, 15, 29, 31, 144, 253, 361

Unplugged reading, 10, 19, 22–36, 41, 44, 48–49, 53, 55, 77, 79, 108, 146, 157, 167, 177, 251, 279, 362, 367, 373–75

Vilification, 59, 75, 82, 143, 220
Villain, 63, 66, 70, 81, 97, 99, 151, 330

Vineyard, 138, 150, 152–53, 156, 158, 161, 165, 168, 309, 343, 374
Violence, 72, 138, 151, 155–56, 268

Warrant, *see* Toulmin's analysis

Zealots, 156

Index of Ancient Sources

Old Testament

Genesis
37:20…..150

Exodus
23:7…..142

Leviticus
11:44…..105

1 Samuel
28…..331

2 Samuel
12:1-4…..15, 22, 26
12:7–9…..22

1 Kings
21:1-29…..150

2 Chronicles

7:14…..336
24:17-21…..150
26:10…..150

Job
1:1…..60
1:8…..60

Psalms
1:1…..100
1:3…..150
118…..153
118:22…..162
118:22-23…..149

Proverbs
10:12…..104, 105, 326
17:15…..142
24:24…..142

Song of Songs
8:11-12…..150

Isaiah
3:14-15…..150
5:1-7…..149
5:22-23…..142
42:7…..331, 365
49:15…..93, 322
54:10…..322
61…..259
61:1-2…..130

Jeremiah
7:25-26…..162
12:7-17…..150
25:4…..162
29:19…..162

Daniel
2:44-45…..149
5…..357

New Testament
Page numbers including a
 thorough discussion of each
 parable appear in **bold text**.

Matthew
5:13…..322, 376
5:15…..376
5:22…..116
5:28…..116
5:32…..116
5:34…..116
5:39…..116
5:44…..116
5:45…..139
6:22-23…..376
7:16-20…..376
7:24-27…..273, 375
8:12…..100
12:33…..376
13:42…..100
13:44…..122
13:50…..100
15:14…..268
20:1-15…..138
20:1-16…..374
21:33-46…..150
21:39…..153
21.41…..169
22:1-6…..100
22:13…..100
22:15-22…..58
22:23-33…..58
24:51…..100
25:30…..100

Mark
12:1-12…..150
12:4…..160-61
12:8…..153
12:18…..45

Luke
1–2…..176
1–9…..54
1:1…..23, 153
1:5-80…..163
1:13…..161
1:36…..161
1:53…..122
1:57…..161
2:35…..155
3–4…..176
3:1-19…..163
3:2…..161
3:7…..189
3:17…..155
3:9…..155, 190
3:17…..155, 189
3:22…..161
4:18…..144
4:18-19…..130, 331, 365
4:18:21…..176, 366
4:23…..12, 185-86, 189, 192, 195, 198, 201, 203, 210, 214, 217, 222, 227, **255-57**, 268-69, 351
4:24…..189-90, 192, 195, 198, 203, 209, 216, 222, 230, **257-59**, 263, 275, 352,
4:25-27…..257
4:29…..155
5…..143
5:17-26…..142

5:21…..124, 142
5:27-32…..82
5:30…..33, 124
5:31…..12, 33, 192, 195, 199, 203, 210, 214, 222, 225, 227, **259-61**, 352
5:31-32…..143
5:32…..33, 260-61
5:34-35…..191, 192, 195, 198, 204, 208, 214, 222, 230, **261-63**, 352
5:36…..12, 191-92, 195, 198, 201, 203, 209, 216, 222, 228, 230, **263-265**, 330, 352
5:37-39…..12, 186, 192, 195, 198, 200-1, 203, 210, 214, 222, 230, 264, **265-266**, 352
5:39…..190
6:1-11…..82
6:2…..124
6:7…..124
6:20-49…..188, 220
6:24-25…..365
6:27…..266
6:27-36…..72, 139
6:31…..267
6:32-36…..131
6:35…..73, 139, 143
6:36…..74

6:38…..190, 192, 195, 198, 203, 209, 215, 222, 233, 253, **266-67**, 351, 354, 370
6:39…..186, 192, 195, 198, 201, 202-3, 210, 214, 222, 227, 267-69, 351
6:39-45…..267
6:40…..192, 195, 198, 203, 209, 216, 222, 227, 268, **269-70**, 351
6:41-42…..191, 195, 198, 203, 210, 214, 222, 227, 268-69, **270-71**, 351
6:41-45…..270
6:42…..270
6:43-44…..269
6:43-45…..190, 192, 195, 198, 203, 210, 214, 222, 230, 268, **271-73**, 351, 376
6:45…..190
6:48-49…..192, 195, 198, 206, 209, 215, 222, 233, **273-74**, 351, 375
7…..132
7:13…..73
7:20-23…..163
7:24…..189
7:24-27…..273, 375
7:24-35…..163
7:26…..163
7:28…..164

7:30…..162
7:32-34…..192, 195, 198, 204, 208, 214, 222, 233, **274-77**, 351
7:33-34…..163
7:37-38…..278
7:34…..133, 142,
7:41-42…..131
7:41-43…..12, 192, 195, 199, 206, 211–12, 214, 233, **277-78**, 301, 355
7:43…..278
7:44-46…..278
7:47…..278
7:47-48…..131, 278
7:49…..278
8:5…..201
8:5-8…..12, 13, 192, 194-95, 198, 206, 210, 214, 222, 233, **279-81**, 300, 349, 351, 368, 372
8:9-15…..372
8:10…..282
8:10-15…..368
8:11-15…..19
8:16…..192, 195, 198, 203, 208, 214, 222, 225, 227, **281-82**, 293, 351, 353, 376
8:17…..282
8:33…..155
8:42-44…..304

INDEX OF ANCIENT SOURCES

9:7-9…..163
9:19…..163
9:22…..153, 155, 158
9:50—19:27…..245
9:51-56…..66
9:51—19:27…..246
9:54…..129, 155
10…..68, 73
10:1…..283
10:2…..187, 190, 192, 210, 274, **282-83**
10:13…..289
10:15…..155
10:21…..284
10:22…..184, 188, 192, 199, 203, 208-9, 214, 217, 221, 224, 230, **283-85**, 352, 360, 362, 366
10:25…..57, 59, 62, 126
10:25-28…..71, 286
10:25-29…..57
10:25-30…..54, 56,
10:25-37…..**53-75**, 82, 110, 118,
10:27-28…..57, 286
10:28…..57, 126
10:29…..57-59, 62
10:30…..155
10:30-35…..54, 56, 61
10:30-37…..3, 6, 10, 43, **53-75**, 192, 195, 199, 206, 208, 214, 223, 235, **285-86**, 318, 325, 349, 351, 355, 357, 368

10:31…..64
10:32…..64
10:33…..64, 73, 141
10:35…..62
10:36…..12, 58, 62, 67
10:36-37…..54, 62
10:37…..56-58, 62, 67, 70-71, 126, 286,
11…..74, 132, 165
11:1…..163
11:1-13…..190
11:11-13…..67, 163, 192, 195
11:4…..74, 131
11:5…..61
11:5-8…..12, 67, 110, 185-86, 192, 195, 199, 206, 208, 214, 223, 232-33, **286-88**, 335, 354, 362
11:5-13…..86, 139, 140
11:8…..232
11:9…..232, 288
11:9-10…..73
11:11-13…..67, 93, 198, 204, 208, 214, 223, 230, 287, **288-89**, 335, 354, 362
11:13…..12, 67, 73, 287, 289
11:14-26…..143
11:15-16…..295
11:17…..192, 195, 198, 203, 209, 215, 222, 230, **289-90**, 352
11:21…..12

11:21-22.....192, 195, 198, 204, 208-9, 214, 222, 227, **290-91**, 353
11:22.....155
11:23.....292, 293
11:24-26.....192, 195, 199, 204, 210, 222, 233, **291-93**, 353
11:27.....290
11:28.....293
11:29-33..... 294
11:33.....192, 195, 199, 203, 208, 214, 222, 227, **293-94**, 352, 376
11:34-36.....192, 195, 198, 204, 210, 214, 222, 230, **294-95,** 356, 376
11:35.....295
11:47-51.....162
11:49-51.....155
11:50.....162
11:53-54.....124
12:10.....306
12:13.....296
12:13-21.....122
12:16-21.....13, 167, 193, 196, 198, 201, 206-7, 212, 215, 218, 223, 235, **295-97**, 336, 338, 351, 357, 361-62
12:21.....297
12:22.....298

12:24.....187, 191, 193, 196, 199, 203, 208, 212, 215, 222, 230, **297-99**, 354, 362
12:27-28.....187, 191, 193, 196, 199, 203, 208, 212, 215, 222, 230, **300**, 354, 362
12:36-38.....177, 193, 196, 199, 200, 204, 211, 215, 223, 235, **300-2**, 354, 356
12:36-48.....12
12:37.....138, 340
12:39.....186, 193, 196, 199, 201, 203, 211, 215, 223, 230, **303-4**, 356, 361
12:40.....303, 361
12:41.....303, 304
12:42-44.....305
12:42-48.....118, 138, 193, 199, 206, 211, 215, 223, 235, **304-7**, 349, 351, 357, 361
12:45.....135
12:45-46.....305-6
12:46.....155
12:46-48.....168, 171
12:47-48.....138, 155, 306
12:48.....306
12:50.....155
12:54-56.....12, 193, 196, 198, 203, 208, 215, 223, 230, **307-8**, 345, 356,
12:54-59.....129, 131, 132

12:58-59…..185-87, 193, 196, 199, 203-4, 211, 215, 223, 233, **308-9**, 334, 356, 357
12:59…..308
13…..132
13:1…..340
13:1-4…..184
13:3…..155
13:4…..131
13:5…..155
13:6-9…..193, 196, 199, 201, 206, 211, 215, 223, 233, **309-10**, 351, 357
13:17…..310
13:19…..193, 198, 206, 210, 214, 223, 228, 230, **310-11**, 353
13:21…..193, 196, 198, 205-6, 209, 214, 223, 228, 230, **311-12**, 353
13:23…..313, 373
13:24…..313
13:24-27…..313
13:24-29…..187, 193, 196, 199, 206, 211, 215, 223, 233, **312-14**, 351, 357, 373
13:28…..100
13:33…..158
14:1-24…..82
14:8-10…..315

14:8-14…..12, 185-86, 193, 196, 199, 201, 204, 211, 215, 223, **314-16**, 349, 351, 355
14:11…..315
14:12-14…..190, 315-16
14:15…..317, 319
14:15-23…..100
14:16-24…..193, 196, 200, 206, 211, 215, 223, 235, 313-314, **316-19**, 325, 355, 356, 368
14:18-21…..319
14:24…..319
14:25-35…..128
14:26-27…..320, 321
14:28-30…..12, 191, 193, 196, 199, 204, 209, 215, 218, 223, 225, 227, **320**, 351
14:29-30…..168
14:31-32…..12, 25, 191, 193, 196, 199, 204, 210, 215, 223, 227, **320-21**, 351
14:34-35…..193, 196, 198, 203, 209, 214, 223, 230, **321-22**, 337, 349, 351, 376
15…..18, 48, 62, 68, 74, 79-82, 85-86, 92, 102, 104, 106, 123, 125-26, 128-30, 133, 143, 169, 152, 176, 220, 238, 331
15:1-2…..125, 127-28, 130-31, 133, 142, 365
15:1-3…..56, 82

15:2 …..73, 123-24, 129, 133, 139, 140
15:3-7…..87
15:3-32…..133
15:4…..6, 61, 84, 90, 133
15:4-6…..67, 82, 88
15:4-7…..6, 12, **82-89**, 191, 193, 196, 199, 201, 206, 210, 216, 222, 228, 230, 238, **323-34**, 353, 355, 369
15:4-10…..77, 105
15:4-32…..128-29, 139-41, 217
15:6…..90
15:7…..12, 73, 86-88, 95, 98, 129, 133, 143, 194, 323, 365
15:8-9…..82-89, 90, 324-25
15:8-10…..186, 191, 193, 196, 199, 201, 206, 209, 214, 222, 229-230, 238, 324-325, 353, 355
15:9…..129
15:10…..12, 73, 83, 85-88, 92, 95, 98, 133, 194, 365
15:11…..62
15:11-32…..4, 13, 20, 73, 77-106, 141, 193, 196, 199, 206, 209, 211, 215, 220, 222, 235, 238, 240, 318, 325-26, 329, 353, 355, 362, 367-68
15:11-24…..91
15:17…..90

15:18…..92
15:20…..69, 73, 141
15:20-25…..70,
15:21…..92
15:25-32…..91, 98, 101
15:28-30…..71
15:28-32…..134
15:30…..99, 105
15:31…..96, 103, 141
15:32…..99
16…..109, 128, 176
16:1…..111, 124, 128-29, 133, 135
16:1-9…..107-47, 167, 169, 193, 196, 199, 205-6, 211, 215, 223, 235, 315, 326-27, 353, 355, 368
16:1-13…..129, 217
16:2…..118, 124, 129, 133, 156
16:2-3…..112
16:3…..111-12, 126
16:3-4…..124, 129
16:4…..118-19, 126, 132
16:4-8…..131
16:5…..111-12, 117
16:5-7…..112
16:8…..108-14, 117, 122, 126, 137, 138, 141
16:8-9…..113-14, 119
16:9…..108-110, 113-16, 119, 122, 125-26, 135
16:9-13…..123

16:10.....113
16:10-13.....107-8, 121, 135, 136, 139
16:11.....113
16:11-12.....104
16:12.....121
16:13.....190, 193, 196, 199, 203, 209, 211, 214, 223, 230, 328, 351
16:14.....128
16:16.....136
16:19-22.....329
16:19-31.....13, 132, 167, 193, 196, 199, 206, 212, 215, 223, 235, 328-31, 336, 339, 352, 365, 367
16:22-31.....168
16:23-31.....329
16:25.....365
17:7.....12
17:7-9.....186
17:7-10.....12, 103, 138, 156, 185, 193, 196, 199, 200, 204, 211, 215-16, 223, 231, 301, 332-33, 351
17:10.....132
17:20.....333
17:22.....333
17:29.....155
17:34-35.....188, 191
17:37.....190, 193, 196, 198, 203, 208, 215, 223, 227, 333, 345, 356
18.....134
18:1.....334
18:1-8.....67, 86, 110, 139, 144
18:2-6.....12, 21, 68, 72, 140, 193, 196, 199, 201, 206, 211, 215, 223, 231-33, 252, 287, 334-35, 351, 354, 362
18:6.....111, 194, 334
18:6-7.....12
18:7-8.....73, 334
18:9-14.....67
18:10.....194
18:10-14.....13, 193, 196, 206, 212, 215, 223, 235, 284, 315, 335-37, 338, 351, 355, 362
18:14.....23, 336
18:17.....188-89, 191
18:25.....187-91, 193, 196, 198, 203, 208, 215, 223, 227, 322, 337-39, 351
18:31-34.....153, 158, 177
19:1-10.....142
19:7.....133
19:9.....103
19:9-10.....90
19:11.....341
19:11-27.....118, 138

19:12-27…..13, 193, 196-97, 199, 201, 206, 210-12, 215, 223, 235, 273, 307, 340-43, 356, 357, 368
19:15-27…..171
19:24…..168
19:25…..340
19:27…..155, 340
19:41-44…..156, 158
19:47-20:8…..159
19:48…..168
20…..155, 169, 177
20:1…..343
20:1-8…..159, 169
20:2…..169, 331
20:3-4…..161
20:3-8…..164
20:4…..164
20:5…..172
20:5-6…..158, 161
20:6…..172
20:8…..161, 170, 173
20:9…..172
20:9-16…..13, 118, 194, 197, 200-1, 206, 211, 215, 220, 222, 234, 235, 307, 343-44, 352, 357, 366, 368
20:9-19…..149-77
20:10…..168
20:11…..168
20:12…..168
20:13…..366
20:14…..168
20:15…..153, 162
20:16…..138, 158-59, 168, 225, 343
20:17…..162
20:18…..159
20:19…..157, 158, 159, 173
20:20-26…..159
20:26…..170
20:27…..25, 46, 59
20:27-28…..44, 45, 59
20:28-32…..46
20:29-32…..14, 44-47, 59
20:29-33…..189
20:33…..46
20:33-38…..59
20:33-40…..44
20:34-36…..47
20:34-40…..45
21:5…..166
21:5-6…..156, 158
21:20-24…..156, 158, 166
21:29-31…..186, 190, 194, 197, 198, 201, 204, 210, 214, 224, 227, 344-45, 356
22:70…..157
23…..188
23:35…..256
23:28-30…..156, 158
23:66—24:49…..150

24:47…..159

John
1:18…..161
5:19-23…..209
5:19-21…..284
5:39…..331
8:3-11…..58
8:58…..116
10…..6, 85
10:7…..116

Acts
2:23…..163
4:11…..150
8:14-25…..72

Romans
2:5…..297
9-11…..319
11:29…..319

1 Corinthians
3:10-15…..145
4:1-4…..145
9:17…..145

Galatians
4:2…..145
5:2…..116

Ephesians

1:10…..146
3:2…..146
3:9…..146

Colossians
1:25…..146

1 Timothy
1:4…..146

Titus
1:2…..146

Hebrews
13:12…..153
13:12-13…..100

James
4:6…..336
5:20…..104, 326

1 Peter
2:4-8…..150
4:8…..104, 326
4:10…..146

Other ancient documents

Wisdom of Solomon
2:10…..161

Gospel of Thomas

22…..188
47:1-2…..328
65-66…..150

Josephus, Antiquities

xviii, 5…..25, 321

Jerome, Letters
121, 6…..145